"*Changing Theory* aims, with intelligence and energy, to engage in the remaking of our conceptual instrumentarium by recovering, through keyword analyses in sixteen languages, what capitalism, colonialism, and the rest sought to destroy. The contributors constitute a galaxy of today's most innovative and critical thinkers from the Global South and make this book an unprecedented—and never more needed—resource for theoretical renovation."

Sheldon Pollock, Arvind Raghunathan Professor Emeritus of Sanskrit and South Asian Studies, Columbia University

"...an impressive array of essays evidencing what today is indisputable: the irreversible shift of knowledge, understanding, and sensing away from 500 years of the consolidation of Western knowledge, regulations of knowing, and vocabulary. The book has stellar reconstitutions of hitherto marginalized praxes of living and knowing...a signal contribution to the explosion of the North Atlantic Universal and the rise of the Planetary Pluriversal."

Walter D. Mignolo, William Hane Wannamaker Distinguished Professor of Romance Studies, Duke University, and author of *The Politics of Decolonial Investigations* (2021)

"...takes aim at the unconcern for linguistic difference in critical vocabularies of the global public sphere, and introduces a rich selection ofkeywords...that critique colonial modes ofmeasurement, logical argument, and physical orientation in the world. The juxtaposition of terms, each examined from the perspective of the specific language in which its theory speaks, advances the project of constituting non-universalist epistemologies. A bold experiment in critical world-building from the Global South, this volume is an indispensable tool for reimagining concept-geography [and] cultural translation... *Changing Theory* changes 'theory' as we know it."

Emily Apter, Silver Professor of French and Comparative Literature, New York University

"*Changing Theory* forces us to think about the world differently by 'doing things with words.' This brilliant set of reflections by major contemporary theorists on key concepts from the languages of the Global South is a rich provocation to change the world by changing the tools we think with."

Supriya Chaudhuri, Professor Emeritus, Jadavpur University

"By focalizing the central problem of conceptualization through the prism of multilingualism, this book provides a many-sided looking glass to the vexed question of theory and its assumed universalism...once we think through languages beyond the Europhone, theory becomes more vital and closer to home."

Ato Quayson, Jean G. and Morris M. Doyle Professor of Interdisciplinary Studies, Stanford University

"This work is a milestone, marking the Global South both as a field and as an epistemological revolution that is happening around the world. It is not only limited to criticism and deconstruction of colonial knowledge, Eurocentrism, or the North as intellectual lens, as most post-colonial theory has done, but re-discovers the contemporary nature of Southern concepts, and in their singularities and mutually associated global context, reconstructs the world's picture and the universe of our knowledge...This book will be remembered as a classic."

Wang Hui, Professor, Department of Chinese Language and Literature, Tsinghua University

CHANGING THEORY

This book is an original, systematic, and radical attempt at decolonizing critical theory. Drawing on linguistic concepts from 16 languages from Asia, Africa, the Arab world, and South America, the essays in the volume explore the entailments of words while discussing their conceptual implications for the humanities and the social sciences everywhere. The essays engage in the work of thinking through words to generate a conceptual vocabulary that will allow for a global conversation on social theory which will be necessarily multilingual.

With essays by scholars, across generations, and from a variety of disciplines – history, anthropology, and philosophy to literature and political theory – this book will be essential reading for scholars, researchers, and students of critical theory and the social sciences.

Dilip M. Menon is the Mellon Chair in Indian Studies at the University of Witwatersrand, and Director, Centre for Indian Studies in Africa. He is a historian of South Asia and has recently been working with oceanic histories and questions of epistemology from the Global South. His recent publications include the co-edited volumes *Capitalisms: Towards a Global History* (2020) and the forthcoming *Ocean as Method: Thinking with the Maritime* (Routledge, 2022).

Professor Menon was recently awarded the 2021 Falling Walls Foundation Prize for Social Sciences and Humanities.

Transdisciplinary Souths

How might we theorize, think, articulate and critically/creatively inhabit the multiple and overlapping Souths of today's world? How do we enable these Souths to speak to each other, question each other, in ways that complement and expand the work upon which they are already embarked with each other? It is becoming increasingly clear that in order to better understand and contribute to the multiple processes and ways of becoming-Souths, a radically transdisciplinary approach to the study and analysis of, critical interventions in, and dialogues within and between Souths needs to be implemented. Intersectional thinking at the crossroads of race and ethnicity, class and labour, gender and corporeality, not to mention climate change and ecological destruction, demands a combination of perspectives and methodologies to deal adequately with complex planetary dilemmas. This series offers a hospitable forum for innovative intellectual inquiry that seeks to break out of extant disciplinary frameworks so as to address new questions emerging from contemporary Souths. Facilitating cross-border exchanges and polyglot negotiations between the most disparate fields of intellectual and scientific inquiry, thereby resisting the disciplining effect of enclave-thinking, the series aims to contribute to the transformation of knowledge production and associated practices across multiple Souths.

As a gesture of international solidarity, the editors of the series TRANSDISCIPLINARY SOUTHS donate the editors' royalties to the charitable organization PRO ASYL e.V. in Frankfurt am Main. PRO ASYL supports the cause of asylum seekers by providing public advocacy and legal advice.

Claiming the City in South African Literature
Meg Samuelson

Changing Theory
Concepts from the Global South
Edited by Dilip M. Menon

For more information about this series, please visit: https://www.routledge.com/Transdisciplinary-Souths/book-series/TRDS

CHANGING THEORY

Concepts from the Global South

Edited by Dilip M. Menon

LONDON AND NEW YORK

Cover Illustration & Design: Givan Lötz & Adéle Prins,
www.prinsdesign.co.za

First published 2022
by Routledge
4 Park Square, Milton Park, Abingdon, Oxon OX14 4RN

and by Routledge
605 Third Avenue, New York, NY 10158

Routledge is an imprint of the Taylor & Francis Group, an informa business

British Library Cataloguing-in-Publication Data
A catalogue record for this book is available from the British Library

Library of Congress Cataloging-in-Publication Data
Names: Menon, Dilip M., editor.
Title: Changing theory: concepts from the global south/edited by Dilip M Menon.
Description: Milton Park, Abingdon, Oxon; New York, NY: Routledge, 2022. | Includes bibliographical references and index.
Identifiers: LCCN 2022001317 (print) | LCCN 2022001318 (ebook) | ISBN 9781032187525 (hardback) | ISBN 9781032226477 (paperback) | ISBN 9781003273530 (ebook)
Subjects: LCSH: Critical theory–Developing countries. | Sociology–Developing countries.
Classification: LCC HM480 .C46 2022 (print) | LCC HM480 (ebook) | DDC 301.0109172/4–dc23/eng/20220119
LC record available at https://lccn.loc.gov/2022001317
LC ebook record available at https://lccn.loc.gov/2022001318

ISBN: 978-1-032-18752-5 (hbk)
ISBN: 978-1-032-22647-7 (pbk)
ISBN: 978-1-003-27353-0 (ebk)

DOI: 10.4324/9781003273530

Typeset in Bembo
by Deanta Global Publishing Services, Chennai, India

CONTENTS

ILLUSTRATIONS

CONTRIBUTORS

Amy Niang is Associate Professor of Political Science, Africa Institute of Sharjah and Research Associate, Department of International Relations, University of Witwatersrand. She is the author of *The Postcolonial African State in Transition: Stateness and Modes of Sovereignty* (2018); co-editor (with Baz Lecocq) of *Identités sahèliennes en temps de crise: histoirse, enjeux et perspectives* (2019) and (with Ismail Rashid) *Researching Peacebuilding in Africa: Reflections on Theory, Fieldwork and Context* (2020).

Arjun Appadurai is Goddard Professor of Media, Culture, and Communication at New York University and Max Weber Global Professor at the Bard Graduate Centre (BGC) in New York. He is a widely cited scholar who works on globalization, cities, design, and social violence. He is a member of the American Academy of Arts and Sciences and a Member of the UNESCO Commission on the Futures of Education. His most recent book (with Neta Alexander) is *Failure* (2019).

Caio Simões de Araújo is Postdoctoral Fellow at the Wits Institute for Social and Economic Research (WiSER), at the University of the Witwatersrand. Before joining WiSER, he held a research position at the Centre for Indian Studies in Africa (CISA). In collaboration with the *Gay and Lesbian Archives for Action (*GALA) of South Africa, he is currently heading an oral history project, *Archives of the Intimate: Queer Histories of Mozambique.* His research interests involve the history of Afro-Asian decolonization, transnational histories of race and anti-racism, and gender and sexuality in the Global South.

Cynthia Kros is a historian and heritage specialist who has published widely in the fields of heritage studies and the history of education. She is the author of a monograph, *The Seeds of Separate Development: Origins of Bantu Education* (2010), and the co-editor of *Archives of Times Past: Conversations about South Africa's Deep*

History (2022). She is currently an Honorary Research Associate with the History Workshop at Wits and an Honorary Research Associate affiliated to the Archive and Public Culture Research Initiative at the University of Cape Town.

David Szanton is a social Anthropologist based in Berkeley, California. He was Humanities and Social Science Program Officer with the Ford Foundation in Manila and Bangkok (1970–1975), staffed the interdisciplinary South Asia and Southeast Asia research committees at the Social Science Research Council (1975–1986), and edited *The Politics of Knowledge: Area Studies and the Disciplines* (1974). Working closely with the Mithila painters since 1977, he co-founded the Ethnic Arts Foundation in 1980, and the Mithila Art Institute in Madhubani, Bihar. He has published widely on Mithila painting, and curated numerous exhibitions in the US and India.

Dilip M. Menon is the Mellon Chair in Indian Studies at the University of Witwatersrand, and Director, Centre for Indian Studies in Africa. He is a historian of South Asia and has recently been working with oceanic histories and questions of epistemology from the Global South. His recent publications include the co-edited volumes *Capitalisms: Towards a Global History* (2020) and the forthcoming *Ocean as Method: Thinking with the Maritime* (Routledge, 2022).

Professor Menon was recently awarded the 2021 Falling Walls Foundation Prize for Social Sciences and Humanities.

Edgar C. Taylor is Lecturer in the Department of History, Archaeology and Heritage Studies at Makerere University and a Research Associate of the Centre for Indian Studies in Africa (CISA) at the University of the Witwatersrand. He is writing a book about racial populism and urban governance preceding the Ugandan Asian expulsion of 1972. His research interests are in youth politics and decolonization, legal contestations of racialized citizenship, public heritage, and the history of archival management in Uganda. He is also co-editing a collection about knowledge and decolonization in Uganda's public life to be published by James Currey in 2022.

Edwin Etieyibo is Professor of Philosophy at the University of the Witwatersrand. He specializes in ethics, social and political philosophy, and African philosophy, intercultural philosophy logic and critical thinking. His publications include *Disabilities in Nigeria: Attitudes, Reactions, and Remediation* (2017); *Decolonisation, Africanisation and the Philosophy Curriculum* (2018); *African Philosophy in an Intercultural Perspective* (2021); and *Africa's Radicalisms and Conservatisms I: Politics, Poverty, Marginalisation and Education* (2021). He is presently the Editor-in-Chief of the *South African Journal of Philosophy*.

Francesca Orsini is Professor Emerita of Hindi and South Asian Literature at SOAS, University of London, a Fellow of the British Academy, and the author of *The Hindi Public Sphere* (2002) and *Print and Pleasure* (2009). She is interested in literary multilingualism in the *longue durée* and has just finished a book on the multilingual literary history of North India. She co-edits with Debjani Ganguly the *Cambridge Studies in World Literatures and Cultures* and is an editor of the *Journal of World Literature.*

Hlonipha Mokoena is Associate Professor and Researcher at WiSER (Wits Institute for Social and Economic Research) at the University of the Witwatersrand, Johannesburg. Her book *Magema Fuze: The Making of a* Kholwa *Intellectual* (2011) is an intellectual biography both of a person and a class of native intellectuals. She is currently working on a book about African men in military and police service in South Africa. She has also written catalogue essays for the South African artists Zanele Muholi, Mohau Modisakeng, Sabelo Mlangeni, Sam Nhlengethwa, and Andrew Tshabangu.

Iracema Dulley is Fellow at the ICI Berlin - Institute for Cultural Inquiry, Germany, and Affiliated Professor at the Federal University of Sao Carlos, Brazil. Her research interests lie in the fields of sociocultural and philosophical anthropology, history, and social theory. Drawing on fifteen years of engagement with colonial and postcolonial Angola, her work has addressed interrogations of processes of differentiation, ethnographic writing, translation, naming, witchcraft, and missionization. She is the author of *On the Emic Gesture* (2019), *Os nomes dos outros* (2015), and *Deus é feiticeiro* (2010).

Jay Ke-Schutte is Assistant Professor at the Department of Sociology and Anthropology at Zhejiang University in the PRC. Trained as a linguistic anthropologist, their published work has been on the semiotic ideologies of non-Western encounters – with particular focus on the political economy of multilingualism, the (an)aesthetic affordances of semiotic technologies, and the intersectional dynamics of interaction in Afro-Asian interactions. Their current book project explores the tensions between contemporary cosmopolitan identity politics and the historical awareness of 'Third-World' socialism playing out in raciolinguistic encounters between African students and their Chinese interlocutors in university settings in China.

John Wright is Research Associate in the Archive and Public Culture Research Initiative at the University of Cape Town. He previously lectured in history at the University of Natal/University of KwaZulu-Natal in Pietermaritzburg. His main field of research is the history of southern Africa before colonial times, with a focus on the KwaZulu-Natal region. He has published widely in this field. He is one of the editors of the *James Stuart Archive of Recorded Oral Evidence Relating to the History of the Zulu and Neighbouring Peoples* (6 volumes, in progress), and also of *Archives of Times Past: Conversations about South Africa's Deep History* (2022). He lives in Johannesburg.

Kaveh Yazdani held a faculty position at the University of Bielefeld before accepting his current appointment as Assistant Professor at the University of Connecticut. He is the author of *India, Modernity, and the Great Divergence: Mysore and Gujarat, 17th to 19th c* (Brill, 2017) and a co-editor, with Dilip M. Menon, of *Capitalisms: Towards a Global History* (Oxford, 2020).

Magid Shihade is an independent scholar. His research and publications explore social, cultural, and political shifts among Palestinians, modernity and violence, settler colonialism, decolonization, and the work of Ibn Khaldun.

Mahmood Kooria holds research positions at Leiden University (the Netherlands) and University of Bergen (Norway) and is Visiting Faculty of History at Ashoka University (India). He authored *Islamic Law in Circulation: Shāfiʿī Texts Across the Indian Ocean and Mediterranean* (forthcoming) and co-edited with Sanne Ravensbergen, *Islamic Law in the Indian Ocean Worlds: Texts, Ideas and Practices* (2021) and with Michael N. Pearson, *Malabar in the Indian Ocean World: Cosmopolitanism in a Maritime Historical Region* (2018).

Mahvish Ahmad is Assistant Professor in Human Rights and Politics at the Department of Sociology, London School of Economics and Political Science. Her first project, *Sovereign Destruction*, studies shifting modalities of state violence, with a particular focus on Pakistan's southern province of Balochistan. Her second project, *Thought Under Siege*, centers the thought of grassroots movements in sites of violence, paying particular attention to anti-colonial and anti-authoritarian archives in the Global South. She has earlier been a journalist covering military and insurgent violence in Pakistan, and co-founded the bilingual English/Urdu magazine, Tanqeed.Org, with Madiha Tahir.

Noha Fikry is a PhD student in sociocultural anthropology at the University of Toronto. She is interested in human–animal relations and the anthropology of food, with a particular focus on Egypt. In her current doctoral research, she explores multispecies relations of food in rural and urban spaces in contemporary Egypt, to develop theory, concepts, lexicon, and ethnographic insights of various interactions and bonds with animals in the Global South.

Saarah Jappie is Program Officer for the Social Science Research Council's Transregional Collaboratory on the Indian Ocean and is an Associate Member of the Oceanic Humanities for the Global South Initiative and a research associate of the Visual Identities in Art and Design (VIAD) Center at University of Johannesburg. She is a scholar and a writer based in Brooklyn, New York. Trained formally in history, her interests lie in interdisciplinary approaches to histories of the Indian Ocean world with a focus on cultural mobilities across islands of Southeast Asia and Southern Africa in the aftermath of early modern slavery and exile.

Saul Thomas teaches modern Chinese History and Anthropology at the School of the Art Institute of Chicago. He is the Editor of *China's Twentieth Century: Revolution, Retreat and the Road to Equality* by Wang Hui (2016).

Shalinee Kumari is a contemporary artist drawing on the aesthetics and iconography of the ancient Mithila painting tradition to express personal struggles, women's liberation, and visions of a better world, as well as feminist critiques of capitalism, global warming, patriarchy, and dowry. She has exhibited widely in India, the U.S., and France. Initially trained at the Mithila Art Institute in Madhubani, Bihar, she has co-authored two essays with anthropologists about her paintings dealing with gender relations, marriage, and the social exploitation of women. She lives in Hyderabad with her daughter and teaches Mithila painting to engineering students at IIT Hyderabad and IIT Bhilai, Chhattisgarh.

Shonaleeka Kaul is Professor at the Centre for Historical Studies, Jawaharlal Nehru University, New Delhi, and an intellectual and cultural historian of early India, specializing in Sanskrit literature. She is the author of *The Making of Early Kashmir: Landscape and Identity in the Rajatarangini* (2018) and *Imagining the Urban: Sanskrit and the City in Early India* (2010). She has also edited four volumes on representations of space, time, and consciousness in early Indian literature and the arts.

William R. Pinch is Professor of History at Wesleyan University and a historian of the Indian subcontinent, particularly the Indo-Gangetic region over the past five centuries. His books include *Peasants and Monks in British India* (1996) based on caste and religious asceticism in the nineteenth and twentieth centuries and *Warrior Ascetics and Indian Empires* (2006), contextualizing the life and career of the eighteenth-century Saiva warlord Anupgiri Gosain ('Himmat Bahadur'). Pinch's current writing revisits the 'Mutiny' violence at Meerut in May of 1857. He is also finishing a joint translation of two eighteenth-century early Hindi ballads from Bundelkhand, with an eye on their historical and historiographical registers. Pinch is a consulting editor for *History and Theory*.

PREFACE AND ACKNOWLEDGMENTS

This volume is the result of over a decade of conversations, provocations, and collaborations. All thinking happens from a location, and I cannot imagine that this book could have been conceived in a place other than South Africa, given the ongoing principled political project of decolonizing education. The #Rhodesmustfall and #feesmustfall university wide agitations of 2015 not only raised questions of unequal access to higher education but also brought up fundamental questions of a postcolonial epistemology and pedagogy. Ngugi's call in the 1980s to decolonize the mind resonated with a new generation of receptive minds, as the universities resounded to the names of Freire, Fanon, bell hooks, Angela Davis, and political leaders like Lumumba and Sankara. What was clear was a disillusionment with postcolonial theory, deeply implicated as it was in a Euro-American episteme and the politics of the American academy. There was a call to address the amnesia regarding indigenous language and traditions of reflection as much as the dominance of the English language. This volume emerges out of the maelstrom of the politics of that period that sought to remake the University and its syllabi and reorient knowledge to the Global South.

The Centre for Indian Studies in Africa was set up in 2010 at the University of Witwatersrand with generous and substantial funding from the Andrew W Mellon Foundation. The intellectual thrust of the Centre, through its graduate and postdoctoral program as well as teaching, workshop, and conferences, is to engage with post national histories of the Indian Ocean and knowledge from the Global South. In 2017 and 2018, the Centre held Theory from Africa workshops drawing on participants from the continent and exposing them to intellectual traditions from Asia, Africa, the Caribbean, the Arab World, and Latin America. I would like to thank not only the young interlocutors but those who taught in these workshops with passion and commitment: Anthony Bogues, Gillian Hart,

Chakanetsa Mavhunga, Nivedita Menon, Magid Shihade, and Brian Meeks. In 2019, we collaborated with the American University in Beirut and the Arab Council for Social Sciences to hold a workshop on Afro-Asian theory. Thanks to Anaheed al-Hardan and Seteney Shami for making this possible, as also to Anaheed, Mjiba Frehiwot and Syed Farid Alatas for teaching the workshop. The Andrew W Mellon Foundation also made possible the visits of Walter Mignolo and Wang Hui to the Centre for short fellowships, allowing for an engagement with decolonial theory and new theorizing from China.

The National Institute for Humanities and Social Sciences, under the headship of Sarah Mosoetsa, gave a substantial grant for inviting scholars from the Global South to speak about traditions of thinking from Asia, Africa, and the Caribbean. This allowed for the visits of Francesca Orsini, V Geetha, Bryan van Norden, Peter Adamson, and David Shulman. Bryan with his deep knowledge of Chinese classical philosophy and his combative attitude to the provincialism of the discipline of philosophy and Peter with his amazing project of the History of Philosophy Without Gaps expanded both the space and time of our thinking of the Global South.

These intellectual exchanges were the background to two conferences on thinking concepts from the Global South. The first was held at the University of Witwatersrand in 2016, and the second at the University of Cape Town in 2018. I would like to thank Shahid Vawda, Archie Mafeje Chair in Critical and Decolonial Humanities, University of Cape Town, for partly funding the second conference as well as making superb arrangements for accommodation, transport, and infrastructure. Rhoda Isaacs was the backbone of the organization of the Cape Town conference, just as the Administrative Officers of CISA, Lerato Sekele and Kagiso Makoe, were for the two events. Of the original participants, Peter Park, Annu Jalais, Udaya Kumar, and Victoria Collis-Buthelezi were unable for several reasons to contribute to the volume. Rahul Ram and Neo Muyanga contributed to the conversation with thoughts on doing music from the Global South and Rahul collaborated with the saxophonist Sisonke Xonti to show us what a musical conversation would look like. Manuela Ciotti and Raimi Gbadamosi spoke about art practice and curation and widened our engagement. I would like to thank the others who did contribute for their patience over four years as the papers were being collated and shopped around for publication! Alongside these formal congregations have been deep conversations over the years with my distinguished colleagues and friends: Isabel Hofmeyr, the late Bhekizizwe Peterson, Sarah Nuttall, Achille Mbembe. Arjun Appadurai, Prasenjit Duara, Gyan Prakash, Thomas Blom Hansen, Faisal Devji, Akeel Bilgrami, Javed Majeed, Jon Soske, Kaveh Yazdani, Russell Pavlov-West, and Fernando Resende have been important interlocutors and robust, but appreciative, critics of the project of thinking from the Global South.

Apart from the peer reviewers of the manuscript who were both appreciative and acerbic about the project, there have been others who have read and commented on the formulation of the project. Here I would like to thank Ajay

Skaria, Rana Dasgupta, Aditya Nigam, Nivedita Menon, Francesca Orsini, Anne Garland Mahler, and Magalis Armillas-Tiseyra. There are many others who in conversation, emails, and Facebook exchanges have provoked more nuanced thinking on my part. The only reason why they are not mentioned here is that their names would constitute a chapter on their own.

If it takes a village to raise a child, it takes a world to launch a new intellectual project.

Dilip M. Menon
University of Witwatersrand
July 2021

1

CHANGING THEORY

Thinking Concepts from the Global South

Dilip M. Menon

Euro-American theory provides our existing academic interpretations of the world in various ways; the point, however, is to change them. The impulse toward theorizing anew has always arisen within the urgency of historical conjunctures. Historically, decolonization provided an impetus within the Global South to imagine new relations to the past, present, and future; free of the political and intellectual teleologies imposed by the civilizational hierarchies of a colonial epistemology. There arose the necessity to look back, neither with nostalgia, nor anger. Rather, it was imperative to recover from the paradigm imposed by colonial rule that had allowed for an engagement with native pasts only as irrelevant, outmoded, or mired in forms of imagination unsuited to the idea of the modern. Colonialism had inculcated an amnesia toward local forms of intellection with their own long histories. More important, it gave a determinate geographical location to the provenance and genealogy of thought (philosophy as originating in Greece, or in the European Enlightenment). This occluded the history of the circulation of conceptions and culminated in the lethargic as much as learned habit of making distinctions between 'western' and 'eastern' ideas. Finally, in now colonized spaces, it only allowed for the consolation of a distant golden age when there had been the efflorescence of thought; a body of thought that was now deemed irrelevant for the present condition of modernity. Sudipto Kaviraj theorizes the emergence of a *Euronormality*: an implicit reorienting of the social sciences everywhere toward European conceptualizations that were mere universalizations of its own parochial histories (Kaviraj 2017). The universalization of European particularism, needless to add, was the result of violence: wars, conquest, and the imposition of new structures of pedagogy.

The idea of modernity itself was not only a temporal concept. It was also a political one, based on the self-regard of the former colonizing powers that allowed them to hold themselves up as models for emulation. Addressing amnesia

DOI: 10.4324/9781003273530-1

in its various manifestations drove the exigent impulse to theorize; to recover from the loss of self and of an indigenous imagination under alien rule (Devy 1995). One could have used the metaphor of the compass oriented toward the North to characterize intellectual production in the former colonized world. However, this image itself is a normalized one, reflecting amnesia. The Chinese, as we know, created their compasses to point to the true South which was their cardinal direction: geographical as much as ethical (in the sense in which we use the phrase moral compass). The orientation to the 'South' was not only about physical direction but about metaphysical balance. The users of early Chinese compasses were as much concerned with orientation as an ethical and metaphysical imperative – in line with the compass's primary geomantic purpose – as they were about finding physical directions in the physical universe.

This chapter concerns itself programmatically and polemically with the politics of knowledge in the academic space and addresses primarily the question of an insularity that projects itself as universality i.e., the globalization of theoretical production arising from a limited geographical space and its particular trajectories of development. It asks that we broaden our archive of concepts not only through engaging in transdisciplinary conversations, but also through moving away from Euro-American formulations to a conversation across regions, that is also necessarily multilingual. The project of finding new ways of conceptualizing needs to be done not under the sign of a commensurability that establishes a meretricious and falsely transparent translation of ideas across spaces. It is not about rendering visible words and ways of thinking across the Global South through mere translation within a monolingual space, which entrenches the politics of English as a universal language of rendition (Mizumura 2014; Mufti 2018). A true conversation must engage with the nuances and hardness of multilingualism as much as the possible quiddity of concepts. All political locutions arise from a sense of place; existing, constructed, and imagined. This chapter imagines a speaking from the Global South, a space that bears the wound of former colonization, and therefore the loss of ways of thinking, imagining, and living. As de Sousa Santos puts it, this is an 'epistemological rather than a geographical south' from which an 'alternative thinking of alternatives' can be carried forward (Santos and Meneses 2019).

As I have argued elsewhere, I believe that thinking about the Global South (its traditions of intellection and its conceptual categories, as much as their imbrication with the miscegenated genealogies of Western ideas) is a project that we need to embark on (Menon 2018). We have been through the enterprise of thinking *from* the Global South, which has meant, as in the case of postcolonial theory, the reiteration of a European episteme, but merely from our location. This does not mean a nativist rejection of European theory or an insistence that we work only on our spaces. The 'space' that comprises Africa, Asia and Latin America, and the Caribbean cannot be thought without considering international relations of power and capital. We cannot also be unreflective of the interpellation of the Global South in the period of the Cold War and the fact that we live in the time of the continuing 'decomposition' of its political and intellectual structures (Prashad 2013; Kwon 2006; Whitfield 1998). As Ann Laura Stoler has recently argued, 'we live in a temporal and affective space in which colonial inequities endure' and there is the imperative to think of the (post)colonial skeptically and insist on 'imperial durabilities in our times' (Stoler 2016). This means too that we cannot think about the South as a *merely* theoretical space, leading us to verbal prestidigitation like North of the South, South of the North, and so on – Detroit as South in the United States, Johannesburg as North in Africa.

Theorizing from the South

If we are to frame the temporality of theorizing from the Global South, Partha Chatterjee's formulation of the moments of departure, maneuver, and arrival within Indian nationalist discourse is a compelling heuristic device to think with (Chatterjee 1986). Chatterjee characterizes the intellection of anticolonialists in India as moving through three moments: *departure*: the moment of a break from tradition and the consequent desire for Europe (in the works of the nineteenth-century Bengali litterateur Bankim Chandra Chatterjee); *maneuver*: a reconstitution and reimagining of indigenous thought as against an idea of Europe (Gandhi); and *arrival*: the confident assertion, with its compromises, of an independent nation (Jawaharlal Nehru). I adopt the triad of concepts but invest a different set of meanings to these moments.

The long conjuncture of decolonization, as countries in Asia and Africa achieved independence from the end of the Second World War to the 1980s, had already created an impulse to decolonize the mind. This *moment of departure* with its staggered temporality was accompanied by the making of nations, the creation of pedagogical and economic infrastructure, and the emergence of a new generation of intellectuals. The emergent new native elite may have been rooted in nationalism. However, they had been schooled in structures of pedagogy that were governed by knowledge in thrall to a Euro-American idea of the University and a replication of its disciplinary formations. The very idea of national being was governed by a split consciousness. The reality of the postcolonial nation was seen in empirical terms: thick descriptions of social and economic inequalities, as much as visions of science and technology-driven futures that were governed by the sign of self-reliance. However, when it came to theorizing, intellectuals drew upon inherited social science paradigms – what Tagore called histories from elsewhere – rather than on indigenous traditions of intellection about self, community, politics, and ethics.

Ashis Nandy and Ngugi wa Thiong'o were among the first to address the colonial wound of amnesia, as it were, dredging language as much as psychoanalytic frames to think about resources of thought that had not been hijacked by a conception of singular trajectories of development toward a Western state of being (Nandy 1983; wa Thiong'o 1981). Fanon was the penumbral presence in their thought, the idea of the psychic devastation inflicted by colonialism and the need to heal were the dominant themes. Nandy looked at the implicated selves of colonizer and colonized and in a characteristically innovative juxtaposition, studied the early works of Kipling and the oeuvre of the Hindu mystic Vivekananda as contending with the discourses of hypermasculinity generated by colonialism. He was clear that there were other psychic resources within Indic traditions that allowed for a recovery of self, particularly in Gandhi's invocation of the 'feminine', of passive resistance, and of the notion of care and love as central to politics. Ngugi, in a parallel move, asked for a decolonization of the mind against the biggest weapon unleashed against the native mind. He called this the 'cultural bomb' that annihilated a people's belief in their languages, their heritages of struggle, and 'ultimately in themselves', which made them see 'their past as one wasteland of non-achievement' (wa Thiong'o 1981, 3). Both Nandy and Ngugi departed from the idea of the postindependence moonshot to the modern by addressing the amnesia toward what lay at hand; the intellectual resources and categories that would allow for the restitution of damaged selves.

The theorizing of the next generation represented the *moment of maneuver.* It reflected the presence within Euro-American academe of a postcolonial elite that bristled against the condescending characterization of the spaces that they came from as being not-yet-modern (Dirlik 1997). Dipesh Chakrabarty in his broadside against existing descriptions of decolonized societies, spoke of a reckoning of lack, a dispiriting accounting of absences – of capitalism, modernity, or of real democracy (Chakrabarty 2000). However, he was also conscious of the 'conceptual gifts', as he called them, of historicism and of politics, from nineteenth century Europe which allowed for reflection on the way forward. Postcolonial theorists like Chakrabarty, Spivak, and Bhabha challenged the imposition of singular trajectories of the future, deploying European epistemology with verve and skill, and denying derivativeness through adroit categories like *hybridity, interstitiality, strategic essentialism,* and *provincialization* (Gandhi 1998; Loomba 1998). These categories are revealing of the strategy of maneuver; one had to position oneself within an already determined field. If one were being uncharitable, mimicry as theorized by Bhabha, was seen as the way forward; like-yet-not-like, the unreadability of imitation as repetition or difference. However, postcolonial theory was characterized by a distinct forgetfulness toward indigenous systems of intellection; the theorists have been schooled in a paradigm framed by Euromerican social theory and its internal dissensions and critiques.

We stand now at the threshold of a *moment of arrival,* with theorizations that start with the idea of intellection from the Global South as their premise. In one sense, it is a taking up of the standard again, a theorizing from where we are, continuing a resistance to what Ngugi had called the method of 'Europhone Theory' and 'African fact'. A slew of recent work that engages with forms of thinking in Africa, Asia, South America, and the Arab world has allowed us to question the Eurocentricity of postcolonial theory and to engage with indigenous landscapes, epistemologies, and temporalities (Chen 2010; Cusicanqui 2020; Eze 1998; Escobar 2018; Elshakry, M 2014; Elshakry, O 2020; Santos 2018). There are many distinct intellectual trajectories here pointing to different futures of interpretation. What is very clear in these works is an engagement with long histories of intellection and debate in the Global South. Euro-American epistemologies were transformed by their commensuration with already existing fields of interpretation. The act of reading Darwin or Freud in Egypt, for example, is not one of startled discovery but a negotiated and careful process of translation, situating within existing paradigms, and a questioning of the universalist assumptions of historical and psychological evolution. The South American thinkers rethink the temporality of the modern by displacing the Enlightenment as the *fons et origo*. They put the violent Spanish conquest and the genocide of native peoples by Europeans at the beginning of European engagement with the world at large. Modernity is inaugurated less by the cogitations of the *philosophes* than by the genocide perpetrated by the *conquistadores*.

Modernity and coloniality therefore are the dyad with which the world must be thought, which results in the idea of the pluriverse and of pluriversality rather than the emergence of any singular set of ideas that then are disseminated by Euro-America as the markers of civilization (Mignolo and Walsh 2018; Escobar 2020). These works engage at one level with the frictions encountered by intellectual paradigms and concepts from Europe as intellectuals in the Global South grapple with them or deploy them strategically. At another, they work with indigenous ideas that do not merely mirror European categories but have a purchase in local imaginations and ways of being which are distinctive and rooted. Most important, they restore, each in different ways, Euro-American violence – physical and epistemic – to its central place in the making of the world that we inhabit.

Word Making and World Making

In this moment of *arrival*, we need to think with questions of inheritance as much as a rejection of a colonial patrimony. The concepts we think with – from modernity to secularism and democracy – have embedded in them both an implicit ideal trajectory as much as a hierarchical politics of spaces (Kaviraj 2005). Words must arise from their worlds. For too long we have thought with the trajectories of a European history and its self-regarding nativist epistemology that was rendered universal largely through the violence of conquest and empire. As the aphorism goes, a language is a dialect backed by an army. Benedict Anderson has argued that colonialism generated a double consciousness of the world: the connection between colony and metropole – London and Delhi; Jakarta and Amsterdam; Hanoi and Paris (Anderson 1998). This seems to suggest that the geography generated by empire exhausted the possibility of other worlds and connections. However, existing networks before the onset of colonialism were never severed entirely as Engseng Ho shows in his magnificent study of the uninterrupted flow of people, ideas, and commerce over half a millennium from the Hadramawt to South East Asia (Ho 2006).

Moreover, empire created what I have called new 'geographies of affinity' which exceeded the incarcerative and schematic maps that reflected merely the imperial hubris of control (Menon 2012). Rebecca Karl, in her work on late nineteenth-century Chinese nationalists shows how they drew on the historical experiences of the resistance in the Philippines to American imperialism; the Boer resistance to the British; and going back in time, to the partition of Poland in the eighteenth century that sparked off nationalism (Karl 2002). Such alternative geographies of resistance generated their own vocabularies and concepts like that of *swadeshi* – of one's world – in the early twentieth century in India. Much of this new work has alerted us to the parallel and emergent maps of a 'colored cosmopolitanism', of 'entanglements' beside the map of empire, and of the world of oceanic movements that laughed to scorn the inscribing of imperial borders and shadow lines in the dust (Manjapra 2014, 2020; Mawani 2018; Slate 2017).

In this volume, there are 20 chapters by scholars, across generations, and from a variety of disciplines: from history, anthropology, and philosophy to literature and political theory. Each chapter is on a word in a particular language, and the chapters cover words in 16 languages from Asia, Africa, the Arab world, and South America. They explore the entailments of a word while suggesting that these have conceptual implications for the humanities and social sciences everywhere. A summary of the implications of these words is offered in this chapter, weaving these through some general considerations on what it may mean to think with a vocabulary from the Global South.

Guanxi/ubuntu Jay Schutte elaborates on the idea of cultural translations in everyday interactions through an engagement with the experience of African students in China, who are at the same time teachers of English as a foreign language. Their very presence in China is the outcome of deeper histories of visions of Third-World solidarity and the military and financial aid provided under Mao to African countries in their wars of liberation. In many senses, it reflects both the detritus of earlier imaginations of geographies of affinity, as well as those presently under construction as China sees a new role for itself on the African continent as an economic and political power. An emerging language of negotiation of power, identity, and intersubjectivity emerges from the presence of these sedimented and proleptic histories, and the key terms are *guanxi* and *ubuntu*. The Mandarin word refers to the cultivation of networks of social relationships and influence, built through affect as much as the vectors of power and wealth. The Nguni Bantu term speaks to the idea of dividuality, that humans become persons within networks of relations and obligations. It is in the translation of these terms into everyday interactions – veering between 'cosmopolitanism and cultural inscrutability' – that a kind of commensurability emerges with the always present possibility of misunderstandings as much as creative misrecognitions. Since the working out of *guanxi/ubuntu* happens within relationships rather than in the elaboration of an abstract principle, instrumentality poses a constant friction: the giving of gifts can grade into corruption, friendship can appear as an attempt to forge a relation of patronage. This requires a constant working at affinities and negotiation of cultural difference and what Schutte terms as 'intersubjective contingencies' may be seen as a 'transnationally portable resource', to understand a world characterized by movement, migration, and increasingly, people 'out of place' (Stonebridge 2018).

Tarbiyya Relations between humans and animals are seen within histories of violence, domestication, and companionate love. These appear to be distinct categories, for after all can one kill that which one loves? Noha Fikry, in her study of the rearing of animals on the rooftops of Cairo, looks at the inherent ambiguity of, and the segueing between these categories. Through a series of layered anecdotes involving the gendered labor of women rearing animals for family consumption, Fikry details the landscape of affective bonds between humans and animals that are deeply bound up with questions of nutrition in countries of the Global South. *Tarbiyya* encompasses a range of meanings from ownership, friendship, and control to improving the essence and 'thickening' of an object of nurture. While the trajectory of *tarbiyya* is toward consumption of the animal reared, eating is about an intimate knowledge of what one eats. The maternal care imparted to the animals – hens, rabbits, and goats – involves a balancing of many sentiments, discipline as much as love. It is opposed to industrial farming in which the animals are separated from the human as objects, and in ingesting them, one eats 'histories of violence'. Fikry stresses the need to engage with the landscapes of affect in the Global South, where the human and animal live in proximity and are implicated in economies of gentleness, passion, and blood shedding. This chapter explores the humanimal relation as it were in the Global South where the end result of eating an animal is implicated in prior histories of care and nurture.

There are clusters of ideas that we can think together when reflecting on words and worlds. The first is of the ineluctable relation between language and life worlds. This is usually overlooked when we engage with the act of theorizing as opposed to description. We could indeed ask of the elite postcolonial theorists from the decolonized world – who present themselves as the resistant underdogs of the academic hierarchies of knowledge production – can they, as subalterns, speak? Or does a theoretical production from Europe speak through them? To go back to Chakrabarty's idea of the gift of the Enlightenment, one is reminded of Derrida's reading of the idea of the *pharmakon* as both remedy and poison (Derrida 1981). If life worlds must provide the infrastructure for thinking, raising questions of acquiring, and working with the knowledge of languages other than English, French, etc., as much as situating oneself within existing traditions of intellection in Asia and Africa is important. Overcoming amnesia and developing a sense of thinking from a place is central to the work of theory. We need to move away from merely critiquing the shortcomings, prejudices, and occlusions of a theory that comes from elsewhere and move robustly toward recognizing its possible obsolescence or irrelevance for our concerns. A critique of Kant for his 'proto-racism', as the philosopher Bernasconi termed it, was necessary and timely when it was done. In the moment of arrival, we must ask ourselves, does

Kant have anything to contribute at all to the enterprise of theorizing from the Global South? (Park 2013; Vial 2016). *This is not about a retreat into nativism but of choosing our conversations after arriving at a true recognition of what we have to say.*

The second question is that of intelligibility and translation of ideas. We do need to converse across intellectual traditions even as we recover from what Maria Lugones has termed the 'colonial wound' (Lugones 2010) and begin to think with Confucianism, or Buddhist philosophy, or African ways of being in the world. This makes the question of language as much as conceptualizing important, while recognizing that the issue is not of producing one-to-one commensurability. We need not swing from asking misplaced questions of whether there are ideas of individualism or secularism in African and Indian languages to the equally ill-conceived venture of assuming that concepts in the languages of the Global South have exact and resonant equivalents in English and European languages. What we need is the beginning of a conversation in a space which has been dominated by a monologue, as much as monolingualism. In Werner Herzog's film *Where the Green Ants Dream* (1984), set in Australia in a landscape of contest between white settlers and Aboriginal people, there is a scene in which a white judge arbitrates claims for land. Aboriginals and their interpreters present demands based on existing indigenous occupation of territory as well as ancient claims to ancestral dreaming spaces. Decisions are made till a lone Aboriginal appears and speaks eloquently and for long about a claim. The judge asks for an interpreter and on enquiry is told that the man is dumb. Nonplussed, the judge asks what this means since the man is so obviously voluble. He is told that the man is the last speaker of his language so no one understands him; he may as well be 'dumb'. In the end, the act of theorizing is a speaking to the world and this anecdote serves as a parable of the limits of communication. While untranslatability may be an exigent issue, we must also see it as a conjunctural and temporal one. Given time and engagement, meaning may emerge. Or not.

Three chapters raise the questions of approximation, commensurability, and the anxieties raised by the imperative to translation in intercultural conversation.

Andāj Arjun Appadurai in his study of understandings of measurement in a village in Maharashtra, India, emphasizes the contextual nature of understandings, stressing both local variations and the ubiquity of approximation. The idea of *andāj* (Marathi, Urdu, Hindustani) or estimation is central to an idea of measurement mediated by social and ecological variability as much as context. 'All measurement is opinion, and all valuation is negotiable', and as Appadurai expresses it pithily, 'to be accurate is to be approximate'. This is not to suggest that there is a distinct peasant, or South Asian peasant mentality, in the manner of exploring the primitive mind, but rather that ideas such as measurement are socially and culturally located and are not always context-free universals. In the conduct of agricultural production, management, and considerations of the future within a zone of contingency, governed by nature, and the boundaries between technical, ritual, and everyday activity blur. Meanings are rooted in local, oral contexts and do not draw upon textual prescriptions of precision.

Within a cognitive landscape with its multiple registers of lunar and solar calendars, seasons, agricultural temporalities, and different measures for different crops, the idea of 'imprecision' becomes a symptom of the contingency of circumstance. Within this landscape of proliferation and circumstance, even in the resolution of disputes, compromise and negotiation become the standard rather than the mere abstraction of a 'just' decision. An idea such as *andāj* works along the fault lines of the relations between people and contexts in exploring a seeming abstraction such as the idea of measurement and is thus more open to the possibilities of a world of motion such as we live in.

Logic Edwin Etieyibo attempts to move away from a Eurocentric universalism and the presumption of prescriptive logic to suggest the relativity of logic in African societies (particularly among the Acholi people of Uganda). Within academic philosophy, logic, reasoning, and rationality segue into each other as concepts and are seen as the benchmarks of modernity as opposed to traditional societies. The presence of these modes of thinking then becomes the basis for distinctions between primitive and civilized mentalities. Etieyibo contests the idea of universal rules of logic – the binaries of true and false – and suggests that in African philosophies and ways of being we must reckon with trivalent or polyvalent logics. Since human beings are seen as belonging to two worlds, relating to visible and invisible beings, the imagination is not governed by binaries such as human/nonhuman, sacred/secular which are indeed being called into question of late within the social sciences. Etieyibo stresses the 'contextuality, rationality, and relativity of logic'. In contrast to a 'western' ontology,

> it is not the case that African ontology is idealism or realism; rather, one might say that it is idealism, realism and both. Also, it is not the case that African ontology is spiritualism or materialism; rather, one might say that it is spiritualism, materialism and both.

Here again, the stress is on the possibilities of multiplicities in the reckoning of the world, not governed by the separations introduced by a certain trajectory of post-Enlightenment thinking, that has been unsettled of late, for instance, by the perspectivism of philosophical anthropology (de Castro 2016).

Izithunguthu John Wright and Cynthia Kros consider James Stuart, an official in the Natal Colonial Civil Service and a Zulu linguist, who began to compile an English-Zulu dictionary in South Africa. Between 1897 and 1900 he engaged in discussion with over 50 individuals about ideas of self, community, history, and politics to arrive at equivalences between English and Zulu words. Word had got around of the enterprise and an elderly man, Gcabashe, associated with Zulu royalty, decided to take the newly introduced train service to the city to meet with Stuart. Given the immediate circumstance of a rebellion, and tensions in the area, Stuart had his own agenda in what became less a conversation, and more an enquiry of Gcabashe. At some point, Gcabashe tells Stuart, 'You can write and remember; for our part, we are merely *izithunguthu*'. As John Wright and Cynthia

Kros point out in their chapter, this one word encompasses many meanings, ranging from Gcabashe's sense of personal discomfiture to a more general sense of the disequilibrium in the conversation. That Stuart is asking questions that are not those of Gcabashe's and that the latter has no answers to give that accord with the paradigm of Stuart's enquiries is also encompassed by the word. The word gestures toward the incommensurability inherent in the colonial encounter. If colonialism is a process of establishing equivalences and absorbing histories and cultures into a singular and hierarchical narrative, *izithunguthu* represents the recalcitrance of the particular that exceeds the enterprise of empire. It is what surfaces as the unease that never goes away and creates a politics of incommensurability. Truly a word that creates an archipelago of similar experience through the colonized world, the encounter between power and the principled obdurateness of the colonized.

A third and related question is one of time. What is lost when one reflects with the social theory of modernity, and its abbreviated sense of time, that creates a timeline from the Enlightenment in Europe? The idea of time here is a judgment on societies that are present at the same time as Euro-America but inhabit their own temporality, rather than the putative common time of the modern (Fabian 1983). How far back then, does one have to go to write a history of the present? This is not merely an empirical question of deciding whether one wants to work with hundred-year stretches of time or go back a few hundred, perhaps thousand years, to establish the longue durèe of processes. One of the consequences of periodization (ancient, medieval, modern) is the establishment of a caesura between these periods at the same time as assuming a continuity within (Davis 2017). There is a further complication arising in colonized spaces that the time of the modern, which also is the time of the colonial, is seen as distinct and separate from the earlier periods which are not just temporal segments but also involve judgments of lack i.e. the lack of political stability, rationality, or traditions of thinking equality. While Confucius or the Buddha may have been sages, they are not seen as thinkers or philosophers in a modern sense, since 'philosophy' is seen as invoking a set of questions that trace their genealogy to Greece (van Norden 2017; Adamson 2016-20). As Derrida has observed,

> philosophy has never been the unfolding responsible for a unique, originary assignation linked to a unique language or to the place of a sole people. Philosophy does not have one sole memory. Under its Greek name and in its European memory, it has always been bastard, hybrid, grafted, multilinear and polyglot. We must adjust our practice of the history of philosophy, our practice of history and of philosophy, to this reality which was also a chance, and which more than ever remains a chance
>
> *(Derrida 1994).*

Derrida raises the significant questions of special origin that is always already corrupted by miscegenation and what he calls chance, or mere contingency.

From the Global South, we might perhaps prefer to term contingency as conquest and conscious erasure.

This introduces another set of problems. A page of contemporary Western philosophy may have references to Plato as much as Augustine, Spinoza, and Levinas, from different spaces and times. The invented genealogy with Greece (Bernal 1987, 2001) and years of commentary as much as political and intellectual consolidation in Western Europe (inflected by empire and the demand for a 'European canon') has made Plato a contemporary of Foucault, so to speak. On the other hand, in Indian philosophy, the idea of the hermetic spaces of 'ancient' and 'medieval' India has entailed that those who work on 'modern' India do not look back to engage with reflections on aesthetics, political economy, or jurisprudence. The colonial caesura has meant that to work with the abbreviated time of the modern, there is a resort to theorizing from Europe. Those who work on 'ancient' India are misperceived as Indologists, whose work is of little relevance for theorizing the present. The iniquitous imperial shadow of the division into Hindu, Muslim, and British (not Christian!) periods is reflected, for example, in seeing the texts and thinkers of the 'medieval' period as unavailable for thinking the modern. This reflects an inability to think with connected histories and the circulation of ideas. Moreover, it freezes the idea of provenance thus generating an inability to think about miscegenated genealogies. There is a general suspicion about the availability of ideas of freedom, equality, and emancipation within Asian and African traditions of thinking; resulting from centuries of condescending imperial rhetoric on the rescue of the native from the sleep of reason (Mahbubani 2009; Dabashi 2015). Just as the thought of Aristotle and Plato has had to be recuperated from their uncritical location in a slave society; or Kant from his anti-blackness and misogyny; (Eze 1997; Bernasconi and Cook 2003) there is much theoretical work to be done in recovering political philosophy and thinking about freedom from Asian, African, and South American traditions of thought.

Four chapters take up the questions of freedom, nation, history, and politics; concept words that are seen as signs of a unique Western tradition of conceiving the individual, collectivities, and the record of collective action over time. These constitute ways of thinking the political, but also raise questions on what, indeed, is the political. Prathama Banerjee raises the problem of 'what is it that becomes political and in modern times assumes a kind of constitutive priority' (Banerjee 2020), thus historicizing the very idea of the political. To this, we may add the further complication of the constitution of the political in different spaces each with their own particularities.

Eddembe Edgar Taylor's chapter takes up the idea of freedom in the decolonizing world and its appropriation and renditions by the populace as against the definitions offered by the colonial state as much as liberation movements in waiting. In the context of 'patriotism and a protean public', meanings proliferate and the anchoring of the idea of freedom in the nation-state gets unmoored. Even as an idea of freedom rooted in a particular trajectory of the emergence of ideas of the individual and nation circulates between Europe, Africa, and Asia, and within the emergent public spheres of Africa and Asia, words acquire layers of meaning in a field of indigenous ways of thinking the self. As the Luganda word eddembe becomes the rallying cry for freedom, as *uhuru* does in Kiswahili, it accretes to itself ideas such as *wiathi* – self-mastery, and *ekitiibwa* – honor, which are at one level ways of reconstituting self after the wound of colonialism. To this implication of freedom from a prior bonded self, is added a breaking away from traditional authority, in which the idea of reciprocity and community had been the way of containing the aspirations of individuals. For some freedom may have meant the overthrow of colonialism, for others it was the overthrow of traditional authorities, and yet others saw real freedom as a return to customary forms of rule as against bourgeois politicians. There is a strong understanding of the coercive elements and exclusions of freedom, and eddembe addresses the tension between power and consent. It is a word that does not imagine freedom as a breaking away from the bonds of mutuality and has a nuanced appreciation of power amidst the presence of necessary hierarchies. Taylor provides a nuanced social and historical approach that militates against a Hegelian idea of the diffusion of an idea of freedom from the West to spaces that lacked the concept.

Minzu Saul Thomas asks the question of whether the idea of the nation arises from an indigenous context or whether it is situated in emergent and ever-changing conceptual frameworks. The word enters Mandarin through a late nineteenth-century borrowing of the Japanese neologism for nation/volk and acquires meanings within two distinct domains: the idea of *minzuxing* or national character, and *minzu jiefang* or national liberation. The first carries connotations of blood and common ancestry, as much as a sense of hierarchy, with darker-skinned nations at the bottom. This, as Thomas argues, was not surprising since the emergence of the idea of minzu was consequent on and coeval with European imperialism. The European idea of nation was both hierarchical and racist (in the sense that Europe was presented as already having the idea of the nation; other parts of the world, less civilized, had yet to acquire the idea). As he puts it, 'this baggage was the inheritance of modernity and the embracing of it'. The idea of minzu jiefang emerges under Mao and imagined an affinity with the darker-skinned nations of the world, a truly decolonizing notion. The idea of minzuxing – a looking inwards – was submerged in Maoist China. Instead, there was an emphasis on a comity of nations that had an affinity because they faced the common predicament of imperialist domination. Post-Mao, with the reappraisal of China's relation to the West, there is a resurfacing of racism and a loss of the idea of a geography of emancipation that was associated with minzu jiefang. Moreover, China acquires a new role in the world as we have seen earlier in Schutte's chapter on the transformation of the idea of Third-World solidarity with the burgeoning interest of the Chinese state and capital in the continent of Africa. As Thomas points out, the Maoist idea of minzi jiefang represented an emergent concept from the Global South which saw the idea of nation as a relational one with an implicit idea of a common emancipatory project.

Kavi Some nations have a history, in others, there is the sleep of reason and therefore no awakening to historical consciousness. Hegel's philosophy of history has thrown a long shadow over the spaces of Asia and Africa, and even indigenous scholarship has labored under the sign of absence; history being another item in the long reckoning of lack. Shonaleeka Kaul explores the Sanskrit idea of kavya and the intimate relation between the poet (*kavi*) and the historian. The capacity of the poet for deep vision and description means that when one separates poetry from history questions of intuition and symbolism get lost. Objectivity, that obscure object of desire, and the product of the nineteenth-century romance with the state, engendered a distrust of what James Mill saw as the 'ungoverned imaginings' of the South Asian muddle of history and poetry. Kaul attempts to bring together language, emotion, and narration – the poet and the historian – and shows the inseparability of the didactic from the aesthetic in the writing of history in India in the ancient and early medieval period. History was an ethicized commentary that evaluated kingship and governance according to moral principles: good conduct, righteousness, and generating order from chaos. Monarchy, like all political forms, was seen as a contingent form, 'a fickle institution' subject to the whims of fate as much as the character of kings. Since the idea of history was about serving purposes and values, it had to stand above, or besides, the transience of humans and their institutions. Kaul argues that 'Sanskrit poetry's preference is not for linearity or synchronicity alone but for a recursivity and synchronicity of a fashion alongside', and a 'purposive cultivated transhistoricity' was cultivated. Here again, we see that to render the historical imagination of the Global South in terms of that of Western notions of linear historicity leads to an impoverished understanding of the nature of both times as much as history.

Raj In a continuity with Kaul, William Pinch tries to explore the idea that under colonialism, Indian intellectuals turned to literature rather than theory to understand modernity. The idea of raj in Sanskrit is related to sovereignty – of self, intellection, as much as territory. It collapses the inner–outer distinction by relating asceticism, or forms of self-control, to secular power, or the control over others. This chapter thinks through an unusual range of thinkers from eighteenth-century historical poetry on warrior ascetics and Bankimchandra Chatterjee the nineteenth-century litterateur, through to Kipling and Gandhi. In each of these the relation between self-cultivation, knowledge, detachment, and action is seen as undergirding the project of sovereignty as opposed to the mere devotion to power among the European colonizers. Whether in the dyadic relation in Kipling's novel between Kim and the lama, the historical novels of Bankimchandra exploring the eruption of an ascetic insurgency, or Gandhi's relation between satyagraha (truth force) and swaraj (self-rule) the fundamental question is of the conceptualization of sovereignty in a dispersed terrain where the boundaries of the interior and exterior are miscible. In the story of Anupgiri *gosain,* the warrior ascetic, his religious practice, and martial prowess are not seen as incompatible or at odds. It represents the attempt to harmonize different modes of existence and create a balance between the detached, the action-oriented, and inertia. The property of raj disposes one to restless and destabilizing action, and by itself, it compromises the quest to sovereignty. This chapter looks at the idea of the political through the idea of self-mastery as much as the mastery of the world and brings into a creative relation the tension between the binary of the inner and the outer.

How to Think with Words

How are we to think about generating concepts from the Global South? In one sense, this question is redundant since those studying Indian or African philosophy, or indeed forms of anthropology interested in the question of how 'natives' think, have always engaged with words and their entailments. The problem then would be merely one of transcending disciplines and bringing the work already done to bear on reflections on social theory from our parts of the world. This is a pragmatic answer and addresses the silos within which our academic work is done. There may be a more fundamental problem arising from the politics of academic publishing in the sense that establishing commensurability involves using already established disciplinary jargon. So, Ibn Khaldun's idea of *asabiyya* may translate well in political theory or sociology journals on West Asia but to bring it into the realm of historical writing on spaces in Europe, South Asia, or Africa, it requires glossing. Or the use of *rasa* theory from South Asia (Pollock 2018), if extended beyond the aesthetic realm or into another geographical space it demands explanation in a way that the use of words like *jouissance*, *différance*, or *oikumene* do not. There is assumed to be a hard particularity, quiddity even, associated with words from the Global South. They do not seem to travel well, just as academics from these spaces at times encounter checks at borders and are often denied entry into Euromerican spaces.

Asabiyya Magid Shihade considers the concept of group solidarity, central to the thinking of the fourteenth-century Arab thinker known as ibn Khaldun, in the light of the devastation in the Arab world because of neoliberalism as much as the rise of Islamism. Arguably, these are resolutely modern phenomena which represent the impoverishment of an idea of the political – trapped in the either/or of market or religion – which urgently necessitates the need for another vision. Shihade asks the poignant question, which has been raised earlier in this introduction, of 'why the knowledge of the global south is not available to the elites of the global south' to think with. Texts such as that of ibn Khaldun are seen as belonging to an ancient past or to the space of the theological, therefore not relevant for modern times. This dilemma must be thought through within the conjuncture of the end of the decolonizing ideal (and the occlusion of the poignant question 'is Palestine post-colonial as yet?') and the demise of a larger politics of solidarity. Shihade considers the framing of the transition of early societies in ibn Khaldun who suggests that rather than the idea of moving from the state of nature to social contract, there are instead the logics that emerge from the move from smaller groups to larger groups. What secures group solidarity is the secular spirit of guaranteeing a life of dignity, thought, and labor (the security of a fair wage so that people produce for the economy and do not migrate). The other entailments are the discouragement of monopolies, the light hand of the state, and the provision of education for all. Thinking afresh with the idea of asabiyya becomes part of the project of creating a political vocabulary of 'political being in the global South'. This chapter too revisits the ideas of Third World solidarity and the spirit of Bandung as fragments of hope amidst the ruin of our times.

Dādan One of the imagined trajectories of the world is toward capitalism and the Global South has been seen as the space in waiting (not yet capitalist) or the space that is merely the stage (acted upon by capitalism). One of the ways in which the Persian word dādan (advance and a promise to deliver) has been understood is through equating it with the putting-out system that preceded the emergence of industrial capitalism in Europe. Kaveh Yazdani surveys the standard tropes of the transition story of merchant capital penetration in rural areas, the emergence of factories and the supersession of weavers, and the growing disjunction between urban and rural. The narrative that he contests is that of the consigning of whole spaces of endeavor of small producers to the teleological narrative of proto-industrialization, industrialization having been achieved only in Europe. He traces a continuity of advance money payments for production in South Asia in which dādani produced control over the producer but to a lesser degree than in Europe. Merchant control over production in many cases did not lead to the transformation of production, again in contrast to Europe (India produced more commodities than Europe until the early 19th c.). Yazdani rethinks the conventional narratives of mercantile capital and commercial capitalism within the space of South Asia and its connections with the other great landed empires of the Ottoman and Safavids. Words and forms circulated through this vibrant economic space.

In their book *Words in Motion*, Anna Tsing and Carol Gluck conceptualize a 'global lexicon' of words that travel, acquiring layers of meaning as it does so (Gluck and Tsing 2009). As they put it, 'We have chosen words that do work in the world, whether organizing, mobilizing, inspiring, excluding, suppressing, or covering up … [we] track these words as they cross cultural borders and become embedded in social and political practices…' (Gluck and Tsing, 20). The chapters consider words like '*seguranza*/security', *komisyon*/commission, '*aqalliyya*/minority', *saburaimu*/sublime', and so on. It is a social, political, and ethnographic treatment that tends to follow the grain of academic politics. These are words with a history of theoretical exposition and practical governmentality from Europe that then come to be translated into thought and practice in the Global South. The direction of travel is predictable as it follows the trajectory of modernity eastwards into formerly colonized spaces that then engage in the task of what Pascale Casanova termed 'intranslation'. In her work on the dissemination of the novel within the 'world republic of letters', Casanova argues that initial engagements with the form of the novel involved translating European novels into indigenous languages allowing for the artifact to be domesticated as it were within an indigenous imaginary (Casanova 2007; Menon 2011). The direction is unilinear and the domestication of Western modernity and its concepts the desired outcome. There appears to be little 'friction' to use Tsing's own conceptualization in the movement of Western concepts rooted in a particular history into another domain (Tsing 2005). It is the story of a romance; two concepts come together, overcome all obstacles, and meld together.

Travel, whether of migrant bodies or of theory, is governed by protocols of movement and their restriction. In the case of the popular uprisings in the Middle East and North Africa of 2011, they were swiftly named the Arab Spring, absorbing them into a European history and vocabulary of political dissent: the 1848 revolutions and the 'springtime of the peoples'. The concept of *asabiyya* was too located in a dense history as also a contemporary perception of Islam as the space of unfreedom for it to travel well (Lacroix and Filiu 2018; Shihade 2020). The assiduous commentary that has allowed the fictive and continuous genealogy between ancient Greece and Europe has also rested on an occlusion of the Arab bridge. What allowed for the Renaissance in Europe and the turn to the ancient world was the remembering of figures like Ibn Rushd and Ibn Sina (Europeanized subsequently as Averroes and Avicenna) and their engagement with Greece in the age of classical Islam (Goody 2004). So, the question we must ask is what allowed the travel of European knowledge? There is the obvious answer of colonialism and power which allowed for the projection of European nativism as a universal. This becomes evident in the words that remain untranslated in the engagement with social theory around the world: *praxis*, *polis*, the Hegelian idea of *aufheben*; or the Lacanian idea of the *Imaginary*. If one were to think of words from the Global South that have acquired this status of untranslatedness/universality, it would be words like *fatwa*, *jihad*, *karma*, *dharma*, *yin*, *yang*, *ubuntu*, and so on. For instance, in Colin McCabe's updating of Williams's *Keywords*, *karma* finds mention as the only non-European word in the book! (McCabe 2018). These words become metonyms for the civilizations that they come from, seemingly encapsulating only the essence of their ways of being and thought. Other ideas do not travel well; they remain mired within their localism.

Marumakkattāyam Mahmood Kooria reflects on social formations that travel and words that do not in his chapter on matrilineal forms of kinship in South and South East Asia. Marumakkattāyam is a Malayalam word that connotes the idea of inheritance through the female children of an original female ancestor, but the word itself encompasses a range of meanings, indeed confusions. The word *marumakkal* may connote nieces and nephews as much as sons and daughters in law and the suffix *tāyam* means a line of descent. The geography of matrilineal forms extends across the Indian Ocean and is found among both Hindus and Muslims in South and South East Asia as well as in eastern and western coasts of Africa. Apart from the diversity of terminology, there is also the symbolic role that matriliny plays in anthropology as reflecting an earlier form prior to the emergence of patriliny/patriarchy. Engels's characterization of the end of matriliny as reflecting the world historical defeat of the female sex is picked up by the feminist movements of the late twentieth century, further adding to misperceptions of form and content. Ideas of historical transition, nostalgia, and a politics of emancipation come together around an extremely protean form and a cluster of meanings that are untranslatable across regions. Kooria looks at the rendering of meanings of the word within Malayalam dictionaries of the nineteenth century when colonial law was trying to come to terms with what it saw as an aberrant form. There is little clarity to be found amidst the profusion of contradictory meanings on offer. It is almost as if the need for consistency was overridden by a belief that this form of kinship too would pass. However, the form has remained resilient in South East Asia and this allows us to think about the phenomenon of forms that travel and words that do not.

A *locus classicus* for thinking with concepts is Raymond Williams's *Keywords*. It is presented neither as a dictionary (implying a completeness within a language) nor as a glossary (implying completeness within a specified field) but as an 'inquiry into a vocabulary' (Williams 1985). There is a suggestion of arbitrariness that is intellectually appealing; an insight into a personal choice of words that are a point of entry into a changing landscape. They are 'elements of problems' a phrase that implies connections and entanglements between words as they are deployed and extrapolated in different contexts and times. Fundamental to such an enterprise is the faith that certain words are not transparent and need working and worrying with; one must chart their itineraries within a landscape to comprehend them less as indicative of one meaning but rather as embodying potentialities. Questions must be asked of words, other than establishing a correspondence and equivalence with another word yielding merely a deceptive clarity. Williams says, 'in any major language, and especially in periods of change, a necessary confidence and concern for clarity can quickly become brittle, if the questions involved are not faced' (Williams 1985, xxviii). An enquiry into words demands both an economy of delineation as well as an openness to a proliferation of meanings. To step back from the timidity of a desire for precision would allow for an understanding that 'the variations and confusions of meaning are not just faults in a system, or errors of feedback, or deficiencies of education...they embody different experiences and readings of experience' (Williams 1985 xxxv). Williams opens the possibility of exploring words relationally as well as thinking about the problem of individual enunciations that are connected to experience. This is the work that needs to be done with the languages that we work with: of building words into concepts and establishing landscapes of meanings and connections. There is arguably a hermeticism in Williams's enterprise; that of a limited landscape of the space of the island and a forgetfulness of empire, that must be surmounted and critiqued.

Two chapters deal with the issue of travel and words of travel in largely stay-at-home societies. The experience of travel arises out of situations of exigency, economic opportunity, or political repression and leaves the traces of this movement to places elsewhere and occasional return. A third chapter looks at the travel of an idea within the space of a historical geography created by power, the experience of colonialism, and slavery across the Atlantic Ocean that connects Africa and the Americas.

Rantau Saarah Jappie's chapter explores the meanings of the Indonesian *bahasa* word rantau, meaning to wander. The language is embedded with the idea of migration and has borrowings from other languages like Sanskrit and Dutch, pointing to longue durèe histories of movement across 'a watery landscape'. The shoreline is both a noun and a process in this archipelagic geography; for an adult male, 'to shoreline' – to cross the horizon – is to grow. Jappie looks at groups like the Minangkabau of Western Sumatra and the Bugi-Makassar speakers whose lives are made in maritime movement as a rite of passage and whose experiences are sedimented in the language. The figure of the perantau, the person who has lived and learned elsewhere, reflects histories of movement and return, as also itineracy. Itineracy and tales of travel create for those who stay at home an 'imagined geography' and rantau creates a space of 'imagined familiarity' across the ocean, as for instance in the connection between Southern Sulawesi and Cape Town. The story of the sufi saint Shaikh Yusuf connects these two points in the ocean and generates a map of Islamic cosmopolitanism that creates its own spacetime. Between the shorter histories of empires and nations is this 'third space' that in many senses creates a para-time, a time that sits beside other times which also becomes the crucible of a vocabulary of restless travel.

Musafir Mahvish Ahmad thinks with a concept arising from exigent circumstances, where the idea of mobility is related to the very idea of life itself. The word musafir is found in Arabic, Swahili, Kurdish, Hindi, Urdu, and Balochi; the last named the language of Balochistan where the chapter is set. The presence of the word in so many languages also reflects a history of state formation, mercantile activity, labor migration, and political exile across a wide region. The ethnography is set in the immediate and ongoing context of the ongoing political conflict between Balochi young men and a repressive Pakistani state, a continuation of a longer attempt by states to control this region from the late nineteenth century onwards. The musafir or traveler becomes the metaphor of the region, rendering themselves illegible to the state through incessant movement through Iran, Afghanistan, and India, as also ideologically suffused landscapes like that of the USSR in earlier times. One travels not only for one's own safety, or carrying the message of dissension; one travels for others, so that they may be free. This movement – darbadar – from door to door, without a home – khanabadosh, happens within the space of the Global South; it is not a search for financial mobility or worldly possessions. It is horizontal travel within the space of dar ul Islam, the space of a righteous Islam; vertical travel toward enlightenment and dissolution of self, or *fana*; and travel inwards toward spiritual growth. The root of musafir from the word safar meaning travel has also the Quranic connotation of bringing light or unveiling; the musafirs as they travel expose themselves to revelation as much as they reveal the hidden workings of a transient secular power. As Ahmed points out, the word musafir, 'is already a concept', accreting meanings as it moves.

Feitiço/umbanda Iracema Dulley in her chapter studies a word that carries within itself a history of movement of people and ideas, as also the rendering of the world within a civilizational hierarchy during the age of colonialism. The word fetish (simply put, an object seen as having magical powers), which has a rich and varied life within Marxism and psychoanalysis is derived from the creole word *fetisso*, which in turn is derived from the Portuguese *feitiço* (from the Latin fictitious or false) and relates to the world of spells, charms, and incantations. The circulation of the word within the Lusophone Atlantic is related to the phenomenon of Portuguese colonialism in Africa and the creation of a linguistic and cultural space from Brazil to Angola. This is, as Dulley argues, 'a space of commensuration and of creating alterity', and the word surfaces as *feitiço* in Umbanda the Afro-Brazilian religion that is a mix of Catholicism, animism, spiritism, and indigenous American beliefs. This chain of dissemination across a wide spatial and temporal swathe and the 'translational displacements' resists the becoming fixed of meaning that is itself the fetish of language. Colonial Portuguese dictionaries and contemporary dictionaries of the Umbundu language in Angola refer back to each other in a recursive way, resisting the fetish of 'the promise of equivalence' and locating meaning in the space of undecidability. Dulley explores subtly the relation between the idea of translation and the fetish of commensurable meanings putting dissemination and 'contagion' at the heart of the permanent generation of meanings within movement.

The move from word to concept that we have yet to initiate comes with an attendant set of questions. Not all words are inherently open to conceptual exposition and if they are, they may relate to contexts of experience. Thus, one cannot move blithely from an Upanisadic, Buddhist, or Yoruba world of thinking to a universal one without doing violence to the potentialities of the word and its limits. We must engage with the idea of the untranslatable, that some words acquire conceptual entailments not only through the task of exposition, but perhaps only within distinct worlds. There might be something ineffable in cultural and historical terms about words from certain traditions that do not allow for an easy carrying over or *translatio*. Even as we think with the idea of conversation across traditions, this must be borne in mind. As Johannes Bronkhorst wrote recently, introducing the idea of *sabda* and reflecting on the relation between language and reality in classical Indian philosophy,

> The most serious mistake a modern reader can make is to assume that Indian philosophers were just like modern philosophers, the main difference being that they lived many centuries ago, in India, and expressed themselves in different languages, mainly Sanskrit. This would be overlooking the fact that most human activities, including philosophizing, are profoundly embedded in the beliefs, presuppositions, and expectations that characterize the culture and period in which they take place
>
> *(Bronkhorst 2019, 3–7).*

Two chapters consider this very problem of cultural embeddedness, words that do not travel, as they were. What are the larger conceptual implications for words rooted in specific contexts; do they still allow for their use as analogy, metaphor, or comparison?

Nongqayi Hlonipha Mokoena considers the phenomenon of the oddity of a black policeman within a racialized society where the black body is the subject of policing itself. Is the black policeman an anomaly, a race traitor, or just an aspiring body? Are they to be characterized as 'ragtag, inauthentic' as can be seen in one modern translation of the Zulu word nonqayi as 'tinpot cops'? Words don't, as Bakhtin observed, come to us out of dictionaries, they come from the mouths and minds of speakers from where we appropriate them. So, whether we approach this word through the missionary mediation of language, or the colonial official's engagement with Zulu, or more contemporary renditions by historians (tinged by a Manichaean view of an apartheid past), words are not necessarily transparent. We see the word, as if through a glass darkly, within perceptions of the language itself. Dictionaries that place Zulu in a global world with the promise of transparency and equivalence, as also accounts that see the distinctive 'eternal innovative possibilities' of Zulu by virtue of it being an onomatopoeic language, each engage with contrasting paradigms of viewing ineffability and the surmounting of it. The simple question of the difficulty of rendering a word becomes the more complex one of its meanings across historical time, both in itself, as much as in the minds of those who translate it. Between language, dialect, dictionaries, and ideologies the landscape of meaning is vast. Thus, from a simple question – how does one translate the word that means black policeman? – we are led into the realms of particularity as much as ambiguity. We are left with the irony that the word nongqayi was the word chosen by white policemen when they started an in-house magazine in 1907. Within a contested etymology it encompassed a range of meanings from the more general 'the moon watcher', to the specific 'night watchman', to the more fanciful reading in the magazine as an enforcer of laws under King Shaka Zulu.

Naam Amy Niang unpacks the rootedness and the history of this word in Mooré, and its valence in the precolonial Voltaic region (Burkina Fasso, Ghana, Niger, and Mali) between the sixteenth and nineteenth centuries. Naam relates to a principle of authority as also customs and heritage and was central to the process of state making in the region. In many senses the meaning of naam was tautological, in that it meant, 'that which allows someone to lead'. It arose within the history of migrations of people and the resulting distinction between powerful strangers and autochthons, with the need to create a balance of power as also a hegemonic ideology of rule. If naam was about state making and the rulers possessed it (leading to attempts to freeze the principles that underlay its possession and/or acquisition), opposed to it was tenga, 'the religious domain' of the first settlers. While naam was a political project of 'totalization', it could never aspire beyond mere authority, because tenga was related to a transcendental idea of cosmic balance. Moreover, naam was less about an intrinsic Weberian charisma, a capacity as it were, and more about the dynamics of influencing outcomes. While Niang posits naam as belonging to a self-referential world – the tautology of naam being that which those with naam have – there are filiations here to ideas of the compromised nature of power and its necessary subordination to a cosmic moral principle. There is an opacity here that does not allow us to quickly segue into notions of dharma or the principles of a world before disenchantment. At the same time, the resonances of the perennial conflict between secular power and a transcendental ideology allow us to think with cultural embeddedness and ineffability in more supple ways.

There could be two ways of thinking about this problem. The first is the insistence of Edouard Glissant on what he calls the 'right to opacity', a refusal of the reduction of difference to mere transparency. As he asserts, his stance does not premise itself on obscurity or inhospitality. It is not about generating impenetrability but rather, insisting on 'irreducible singularity' (Glissant 1997, 190). Resisting an easy commensurability is an act of responsibility, that recognizes the possible opacity of the other in a twin gesture. Another way of conceiving the question of untranslatability is, as Barbara Cassin suggests, of apprehending it as not one of addressing the generation of meaning alone. It is also a question of temporality; that a word or concept is untranslatable for the moment and may in the future travel better. It points not only to questions of inadequacies of interpretation, or an inherent quiddity, but to potentialities: that time generates new contexts and conjunctures of receptivity (Cassin 2014; Apter 2013). Moreover, there is the question of interminability: that the work of translation is never really done or finished. This question is central to Koselleck's method of seeing words in time, not only as prisoners of their temporal location, but that 'new time' creates concepts that arise to meet the challenge of history (Koselleck 2002). The birth of a new world generates the birth of new words to conceptually frame newness. Language remains fundamentally open and ambiguous rather than merely being the residue of all human experiences till then. Given the moment of arrival that we inhabit, and the search for a new conceptual vocabulary, we stand at the cusp of new historical redefinitions. Koselleck puts it thus:

> A word can be unambiguous in use...The concept, on the other hand, must retain multiple meanings to be a concept. *The concept is tied to a word, but it is at the same time more than the word.* According to our method, a word becomes a concept, when the full richness of a social and political context of meaning, in which, and for which, a word is used is taken up by the word. Concepts are thus concentrations of multiple meanings [emphasis added]
>
> *(quoted in Olsen 2014, 172).*

It is in the conversations between words, the insurrection of anecdotes, that a conceptual universe emerges.

When we speak about developing words into concepts and the work involved in doing so, there is always the drag of tradition. Intellection happens within a field of questions about provenance, genealogy, and exposition as much as hermetic ideas of African, Indian, or Chinese philosophy. There are certain protocols of thinking and regimes of concepts within which one deliberates, as we have seen with the work of Williams (an English glossary) or Koselleck (a European conceptual universe). Glissant brings to such ideas a bracing rejection of tradition in the name of a moment of thoughtful pause, of an extended, but not permanent impenetrability. Conceiving of thinking from the Global South (an imagined unity generated by political affinity) we are only too conscious of a layered and differentiated as much as a polyglot landscape of ideas and reflection (Menon 2018). Once one posits a plurality of traditions, there arises a plurality of ways of thinking and a more disparate set of objects. This can be alarming, in that we may be opening to the anarchy of diversity, and we become querulous of the object of our enquiry. However, if we imagine the departure we are making as the beginning of a set of conversations across traditions (which are themselves internally differentiated), then a more provisional approach becomes possible.

We can begin to think with the power of anecdotes in conversation as much as pedagogy through the introduction of analogy, disjuncture, and exemplarity. And above all to introduce the idea of a provisional thought rather than one informed by certitude. Walter Benjamin reflects on the idea of the anecdote thus:

> Uprising of the anecdotes…The constructions of history are comparable to instructions that commandeer the true life and confine it to barracks. On the other hand: the street insurgence of the anecdote. The anecdote brings things near to us spatially, lets them enter our life. It represents the strict antithesis to the sort of history which demands 'empathy' which makes everything abstract. '*Empathy': this is what newspaper reading terminates in.* The true method of making things present is: to represent them in our space (not to represent ourselves in their space). Only anecdotes can do this for us'
>
> *(Benjamin 2002, 846).*

Such an engagement works with the conversational mode and the 'insurgency' of the example offered in an anecdote. The anecdote is situated within a conversation but points beyond it to a field of possible connections and is based on indirection: a pointing to as much as a pointing away from. While anecdotes appear to be merely elements of a conversation, they gesture toward histories, practices, persons that are condensed in a story. Amlan Dasgupta in his study of musical practices and musical pedagogy within North Indian *gharanas* or lineage – schools of music – points to the centrality of anecdotes to instruction in musical evocations as much as carrying forward the distinctiveness of the style of a *gharana* (Dasgupta 2005, 2012).

If we think about the anecdote less through Schlegel's wonderful metaphor of the perfection and self-containment of the hedgehog, and more as rooted in conversation, reiteration, and contexts, we can see that words and concepts can be unmoored from the putative languages and worlds of meaning to which they 'belong'. They become part of conversations as people move across the globe, as states govern, and dictionaries and glossaries are compiled. The connectedness of territories and histories is both established and nurtured through these dialogic encounters. We encounter languages and therefore words and their subsequent transformation into anecdotes that are exchanged making for a porosity of the idea of language itself. Unmoored from the idea of nation and national and ethnic identities, we can imagine the travel of these words as they make connections – rantau and musafir; ubuntu and guanxi – resisting the fetish of monolingualism and of translation.

The idea of anecdotes that link different times and spaces and exceed the time present in a narration, can be thought through with Edouard Glissant's idea of archipelagic thinking. Non-contiguous and scattered islands are brought together through acts of imagination of affinity and thought itself is required to be flexible and limber to make the connections. As he puts it 'errant thought silently emerges from the destructuring of compact national entities…at the same time, from difficult, uncertain paths of identity that call to us' (Glissant 1997, 19). To exceed the idea of bounded space and internal connections to move to the idea of space as constructed and imagined by imagined connections, allows us to see anecdotes, fragments, and islands can be held together through the work of imagination, creating other narratives. The Caribbean itself becomes a narrative constructed of islands/anecdotes brought together through the ingenuity of imagining relation: 'the Caribbean is…a sea that explodes the scattered land into an arc. A sea that diffracts…the reality of archipelagos…a natural illustration of the thought of Relation' (Glissant 1997, 34).

Pajubã Caio Simões de Araújo's chapter looks at words emerging in conversations, secret and public, circulating through the Black Atlantic and bringing in African linguistic forms into a racialized Brazilian society. An exemplification of errant thought that explodes borders, to invoke Glissant. The word pajubã is of indeterminate linguistic origin, by itself referring to linguistic experimentation, and is believed to have Yoruba origins (derived from the word for secret or mystery). This etymology cannot be established with any certainty and Caio engages with the social history of the circulation of the word and its multiple locations in queer sociability, in Candomblé religion and gay spirituality, in street speak as an 'anti-language' of opposition, and through circulation in the media, making an appearance as a word to be parsed in the national high school examinations! The chapter explores the movement of the word in the world of dissident male masculinities, and the relation of marginal groups and argots within the larger queer space of the Global South. It contests the centering of Euro-American narratives as much as the representation of the Global South within the trope of homophobia alone. Pajuba also relates to the group of travesti and the diverse performance of gender identities, positing queerness in the Global South as a living archive that generates a profusion of words, connections, and performativities.

Ardhanariswara David Szanton and Shalinee Kumari take up visual art in eastern India, the genre styled as Mithila painting, within which the idea of Ardhanariswara (the god who is half female) resists gender binaries. The fourteenth-century art form is customarily traced back to the legend of Ram and Sita's marriage in the Hindu epic Ramayana and used to be traditionally painted on the walls of the room in which the newly married couple lay. A drought in the region in the 1960s and the intervention of the government commoditizes this form which makes its way from the inner sanctum of homes to paper and begins to circulate as 'folk art'. Over the years and with the inflections of the caste of the painters, and the change of generations there are constant changes in iconography. As the paintings move out from the hermetic space of the village home the themes of the world begin to enter it as anecdotes that sit beside the religious iconography. Shalinee Kumari, who is herself an artist and an art historian, brings in the concerns of her generation regarding gender equality. The ardhanariswara figure who represents the 'complementarity and interdependence of difference' becomes the ideal for the married couple, freeing them from the gendered performances imposed by patriarchy. In her paintings, Shalinee also shows how both men and women are affected by larger forces like capitalism, represented as the poison that the god Shiva must swallow to save the world. This dialogue between the religious and the secular, between the gendered expectations of different generations, and with the emergent ideologies of feminism and the environment make Mithila painting a living archive. No longer trapped in the trope of 'folk art', Shalinee's paintings deploy conventional iconography for unconventional ends and initiate a dialogue with the changing present.

Conclusion

Doing theory from the Global South stems from the exigent demand for decolonizing knowledge and developing a conceptual vocabulary from traditions of located intellection. We cannot go on as we are doing, Southern fact, Northern theory, as it were. The issue is not so much of producing concepts commensurable with those generated by Euromerican epistemology like the ideas of the sublime, or of reason, logic, etc. which we can see for example in the works of African thinkers within the tradition of analytical philosophy (Ikuenobe 2004). Questions like is there an idea of logic, mind, matter in Indian/Islamic/Chinese/African/Caribbean/American traditions of thinking are moot. How can we make our conceptual vocabulary without our effort being overdetermined by the anxiety of how it would translate or travel within a Euro-American conceptual world? The idea of translation lies at the heart of the social sciences, since it seeks to make visible worlds of thought, life, and material production. While we live in an interconnected world (through the histories of colonialism, migration, and telecommunications) language is the threshold on which we stumble, as we try and enter spaces of thought other than ours.

English has emerged for contingent historical reasons as the hegemonic language of international communication whether in politics, academics, or tourism (Mufti 2018). However, the question of a universal language raises several theoretical issues. Postcolonial theory while it sought to make visible intellection from spaces that were once seen as mere recipients of Enlightenment from Europe, resolved this problem by rendering visible colonized spaces through an existing library of categories. Categories derived from a Euromerican historical experience have been used to render transparent processes in Asia, Africa, and elsewhere. Democracy, modernity, capitalism, class, history, ethics, and politics have been some of the universal categories that have been the prisms through which the diversity of the world has been refracted back into a singularity of concepts.

The search for commensurability and the tyranny of monolingualism has characterized academic practice whether in Europe or the spaces that it colonized. Concepts from a European history, such as secularism, individualism, and rationality in all their singular brightness have traveled well. Social sciences in the postcolony have assiduously found these categories to be in existence, waiting to come into being, or culturally absent without dwelling on whether indigenous concepts have related to time, history, and self differently. Societies and individuals are not commensurable in some absolute way, it is merely a heuristic hubris that assumes this. And of course, the sheer relief of there being equivalence which allows comparisons between Mongolia and Munich, Rotterdam, and Rajasthan. However, given the ways of power in the world, travel is a privilege as also an act of power. Concepts from Asia and Africa are seen as mired in particularism; the fact that the idea of universals is merely a European self-regarding nativism that was backed by armies is often forgotten.

A final chapter brings together the question of status and of time, and of changing relations of power. It is a fine way to complete the volume to think with a word that evaluates paradigms as transient, always allowing for the insurrection of subordinated knowledges and peoples.

Awqāt/aukāt A word that is used in Urdu in India to denote status, but which has a presence in Arabic, Hindi, and Persian with similar connotations. Francesca Orsini explores the genealogy of the word in dictionaries from colonial times and shows that the word *awqāt* has roots in the word *waqt* meaning time. Thus, the question of status comes to be connected at the hip to time; that status is changeable is inherent in the very word itself. In a hierarchical society such as India, governed by caste and multiple ineffable distinctions, the word *awqat* is located in a landscape of inequality and right. The idea that everyone has a right to be someone or do something is not generally recognized. Thus, if persons aspire above their station to do or say something, the rebuke is, what is your *awqāt* that you dare to say/do this? What Orsini shows is that in the postindependence landscape of northern India, inequality has been challenged not only by policies of affirmative action, but also by the emergence of movements among the dalits or the former untouchable castes, and a lower caste politics leading to the ascension of a dalit leader as Chief Minister of the state of Uttar Pradesh. *Awqat* has changed with *waqt* and the hierarchies have been unsettled. Now it is possible for a dalit to say, when challenged by an upper caste, 'what is your *awqat* that you can speak like this to me?' A word for our times of the questioning of hierarchies when lives considered dispensable are beginning to matter. A word that compresses the intimate connection of status and time and speaks across borders to spaces not only in the Global South but across the world. A word that embodies a conceptual possibility through its 'concentration of multiple meanings'.

Within intellectual traditions in the Global South, there have been reflections on notions of self, community, and governance for several hundred years preceding the growth of a Euro-American conceptual vocabulary forged in the crucible of empire and Europe's self-appointed role in the world. Recovering these categories of thought is not merely an act of sentimentality, it is rather, a stepping out beyond the glare of an ignorance created by Euro-American categories. It is an attempt to think of societies and polities on their own terms and from within their concepts. Some of these may be translatable into categories familiar to existing social science theory; some may sit beside known concepts as markers of alterity, and yet others may be distinctive to a locale of life and thought. Not all conceptions are translatable across cultures and this gives us occasion to think about the hubris of the universal assumptions of our academic practices.

References

Adamson, Peter (2016–20) *A History of Philosophy without Gaps*, 5 volumes. Oxford: Oxford University Press.

Anderson, Benedict (1998) *The Spectre of Comparisons: Nationalism, Southeast Asia, and the World*. London: Verso.

Apter, Emily (2013) *Against World Literature: On the Politics of Untranslatability*. London: Verso.

Banerjee, Prathama (2020) *Elementary Aspects of the Political: Histories from the Global.* South Durham: Duke University Press.

Benjamin, Walter (2002) "First Sketches Paris Arcades I", *The Arcades Project*, translated by Howard Eiland and Kevin Mc Laughlin. Cambridge, Mass.: Harvard University Press.

Bernal, Martin (1987) *Black Athena: The Afro-Asiatic Roots of Classical Civilization (The Fabrication of Ancient Greece, 1785–1985)*, volume 1. Rutland: Rutland Local History and Record Society, 1987.

Bernal, Martin (2001) *Black Athena Writes Back: Martin Bernal Responds to his Critics.* Durham: Duke University Press.

Bernasconi, Robert and Sybol Cook ed. (2003) *Race and Racism in Continental Philosophy.* Bloomington: Indiana University Press.

Bronkhorst, Johannes (2019) *A Śabda Reader: Language in Indian Classical Thought.* New York: Columbia University Press.

Casanova, Pascale (2007) *The World Republic of Letters*, translated by M.B. Debevoise. Cambridge, Mass.: Harvard University Press.

Cassin, Barbara ed. (2014) *Dictionary of Untranslatables: A Philosophical Lexicon*, translation edited by Emily Apter, Jacques Lezra, and Michael Wood. Princeton, NJ: Princeton University Press.

Chakrabarty, Dipesh (2000) *Provincializing Europe: Postcolonial Thought and Historical Difference*. New Jersey: Princeton University Press.

Chatterjee, Partha (1986) *Nationalist Thought and the Colonial World*. London: Zed Books.

Chen, Kuang-Hsin (2010) *Asia as Method: Towards Deimperialization*. Durham: Duke University Press.

Cusicanqui, Sylvia (2020) *Ch'ixinikax Utxiwa: On Decolonizing Practices and Discourses*, translated by Molly Geidel. London: Polity Press.

Dabashi, Hamid (2015) *Can Non-Europeans Think?* London: Zed Press.

Dasgupta, Amlan (2005) "Women and Music: The Case of North India", in Bharati Ray ed. *Women of India: Colonial and Post-Colonial Periods (History of Science, Philosophy and Culture in Indian Civilizations, Volume IX)*. Delhi: Sage Publications.

Dasgupta, Amlan (2012) *My Life: Sangeet Samrat Khan Sahab Alladiya Khan*. Kolkata: Thema Publishers.

Davis, Kathleen (2017) *Periodization and Sovereignty: How Ideas of Feudalism and Secularization Govern the Politics of Time*. Philadelphia: University of Pennsylvania Press.

De Castro, Eduardo Viveiro (2016) *The Relative Native: Essays on Indigenous Conceptual Worlds*. Chicago: HAU Books.

Derrida, Jacques (1981) "Plato's Pharmacy", in *Dissemination*, trans. Barbara Johnson. Chicago: University of Chicago Press.

Derrida, Jacques (1994) "Of the Humanities and the Philosophical Discipline: The Right to Philosophy from the Cosmopolitical Point of View (The Example of an International Institution)",Translated Thomas Dutoit, *Surfaces*, IV, 310 Folio 1. https://id.erudit.org/iderudit/1064974ar (accessed 15 October 2020)

Devy, Ganesh (1995) *After Amnesia: Tradition and Change in Indian Literary Criticism*. Hyderabad: Orient Longman.

Dirlik, Arif (1997) *The Postcolonial Aura: Third World Criticism in the Age of Global Capitalism*. Boulder, Col.: Westview Press.

Elshakry, Marwa (2014) *Reading Darwin in Arabic, 1860–1950*. Chicago: University of Chicago Press.

Elshakry, Omnia (2020) *The Arabic Freud: Psychoanalysis and Islam in the Middle East* Princeton, NJ: Princeton University Press.

Escobar, Arturo (2018) *Designs for the Pluriverse: Radical Interdependence, Autonomy, and the Making of Worlds*. Durham: Duke University Press, 2018.

Escobar, Arturo (2020) *Pluriversal Politics: The Real and the Possible*. Durham: Duke University Press.

Eze, Emmanuel Chukwudi (1997) "The Color of Reason: The Idea of "Race" in Kant's Anthropology", in Emmanuel Chukwudi Eze ed. *Postcolonial African Philosophy: A Critical Reader*. Oxford: Blackwell Publishers.

Eze, Emmanuel Chukwudi (1998) *African Philosophy: An Anthology*. Oxford: Blackwell Publishers.

Fabian, Johannes (1983) *Time and the Other: How Anthropology Makes its Object*. New York: Columbia University Press.

Gandhi, Leela (1998) *Postcolonial Theory: An Introduction*. New York: Columbia University Press.

Glissant, Edouard (1997) *Poetics of Relation*, translated by Betsy Wing. Ann Arbor: University of Michigan Press.

Gluck, Carol and Anna Lowenhaupt Tsing (2009) *Words in Motion: Toward a Global Lexicon* Durham: Duke University Press.

Goody, Jack (2004) *Islam in Europe*. Cambridge: Polity Press.

Ho, Engseng (2006) *The Graves of Tarim: Genealogy and Mobility Across the Indian Ocean*. Berkeley: University of California Press.

Ikuenobe, Polycarp (2004) "Logical Positivism, Analytic Method, and Criticisms of Ethnophilosophy", *Metaphilosophy*, 35, no. 04: 479–503.

Karl, Rebecca E. (2002) *Staging the World: Chinese Nationalism at the turn of the Twentieth Century*. Durham: Duke University Press.

Kaviraj, Sudipta (2005) "An Outline of a Revisionist Theory of Modernity", *Archives Europèennes de Sociologie* 46 no. 04: 497–526.

Kaviraj, Sudipta (2017) "Marxism in Translation: Critical Reflections on Indian Political Thought", in Raymond Geuss and Richard Bourke ed. *Political Judgement: Essays for John Dunn*. Cambridge: Cambridge University Press.

Koselleck, Reinhart (2002) *The Practice of Conceptual History: Timing History, Spacing Concepts*, translated by Todd Samuel Presner. Stanford: Stanford University Press.

Kwon, Heonik (2006) *After the Massacre: Commemoration and Consolation in Ha My and My Lai*. Berkeley: University of California Press, 2006.

Lacroix, Stephane and Jean-Pierre Filiu (2018) *Revisiting the Arab Uprisings: The Politics of a Revolutionary Moment*. New York: Oxford University Press.

Loomba, Ania (1998) *Colonialism/Postcolonialism*. London: Routledge.

Lugones, Maria (2010) "Toward a Decolonial Feminism", *Hypatia* 25, no.4: 742–759.

MacCabe, Colin and Holly Yanacek (2018) *Keywords for Today: A 21st Century Vocabulary*. New York: Oxford University Press.

Mahbubani, Kishore (2009) *Can Asians Think*? Singapore: Marshall Cavendish International.

Manjapra, Kris (2014) *Age of Entanglement: German and Indian Intellectuals Across Empire*. Cambridge, Mass.: Harvard University Press.

Manjapra, Kris (2020) *Colonialism in Global Perspective*. Cambridge, Mass.: Harvard University Press.

Mawani, Renisa (2018) *Across Oceans of Law: Komagata Maru and Jurisdiction in the Time of Empire*. Durham: Duke University Press.

Menon, Dilip M. (2011) "Un Cosmopolitisme Local", in Pascale Casanova ed. *Des litteratures combatives: L'internationale des nationalisms litteraires*. Paris: Raisons d'Agir.

Menon, Dilip M. (2012) "The Many Spaces and Times of Swadeshi", *Economic and Political Weekly* 47, no.42: 44–52.

Menon, Dilip M. (2018) "Thinking About the Global South: Affinity and Knowledge", in Russell West-Pavlov ed. *The Global South and Literature*. Cambridge: Cambridge University Press.

Mignolo, Walter and Catherine Walsh (2018) *On Decoloniality: Concepts, Analytics, Praxis*. Durham: Duke University Press.

Mizumura, Minae (2014) *Fall of Language in the Age of English*. New York: Columbia University Press.

Mufti, Aamir (2018) *Forget English: Orientalisms and World Literatures*. Cambridge, Mass.: Harvard University Press.

Nandy, Ashish (1983) *The Intimate Enemy: Loss and Recovery of Self Under Colonialism*. Delhi: Oxford University Press.

Norden, Bryan van (2017) *Taking Back Philosophy: A Multicultural Manifesto*. New York: Columbia University Press.

Olsen, Niklaus (2014) *History in the Plural: An Introduction to the Work of Reinhart Koselleck*. London: Berghahn.

Park, Peter K.J. (2013) *Africa, Asia, and the History of Philosophy*. New York: SUNY Press.

Pollock, Sheldon (2018) *A Rasa Reader: Classical Indian Aesthetics*. New York: Columbia University Press.

Prashad, Vijay (2013) *The Poorer Nations: A Possible History of the Global South*. New Delhi: Leftword Books.

Santos, Boaventura de Sousa and Maria Paula Meneses (2020) "Epistemologies of the South – Giving Voice to the Diversity of the South", in Bonaventura de Sousa Santos and Maria Paula Meneses ed. *Knowledges Born in the Struggle: Constructing the Epistemologies of the Global South*. London: Routledge, 2020.

Santos, Bonaventura de Sousa (2018) *The End of the Cognitive Empire: The Coming of Age of Epistemologies of the South*. Durham: Duke University Press.

Shihade, Magid (2020) "Asabiyya-Solidarity in the Age of Barbarism: An Afro-Arab-Asian Alternative", *Current Sociology*, 68, no. 02: 263–278.

Slate, Nico (2017) *Coloured Cosmopolitanism: The Shared Struggle for Freedom in the United States and India*. Cambridge, Mass.: Harvard University Press.

Stoler, Ann Laura (2016) *Duress: Imperial Durabilities in Our Times*. Durham: Duke University Press.

Stonebridge, Lyndsey (2018) *Placeless People: Writing, Rights and Refugees*. Cambridge, Mass.: Harvard University Press.

Tsing, Anna Lowenhaupt (2005) *Friction: An Ethnography of Global Connection*. Princeton, NJ: Princeton University Press.

Vial, Theodore (2016) *Modern Religion, Modern Race*. Oxford: Oxford University Press.

Wa Thiong'o, Ngugi (1981) *Decolonizing the Mind: The Politics of Language in African Literature*. London: J Currey.

Whitfield, Stephen (1998) *The Culture of the Cold War*. Baltimore: Johns Hopkins University Press.

Williams, Raymond (1985) *Keywords: A Vocabulary of Culture and Society*. Oxford: Oxford University Press.

PART I
Relation

2

UBUNTU/GUANXI

Jay Ke-Schutte

Thinking from the South, the intervention this collection undertakes is necessarily one of translation – between scales of representation and materiality, between ontology and epistemology, and crucially between chronotopes of encounter. As such, thinking from the South – in its very proposition – is compelled to shift the interzone of encounter from 'the West' and a world full of its aspirationally cosmopolitan 'Others' to a more horizontal, thus ultimately more multilingual conception of intersubjective *interactions* and collaboratively *translated* personhoods. These interactions and translations unfold in a world of mutually negotiated alterities that resist the flat, commensurative relativisms of Anglo-multiculturalism in a still-decolonizing world. For a generation of postmodernists, exploring such fraught social interzones of endlessly becoming alterity seemed to induce a representational delirium, leading to an initially ecstatic rejection of so-called 'structure' and 'translation,' eventually culminating in the awkward, privileged avoidance of society and the human altogether. This remains the intellectual equivalent of retreating into a gated community – away from the unsettling discomfort of an increasingly stratified world. Destabilizing this logic, among other steps, entails the embrace of translation as an intersubjective imperative and social fact, without the expectation of universal commensurability that remains appropriately impossible in a multilingual world.

In this chapter, I thus explore the indispensability of translation as a social practice not only in the particular instance of Afro-Chinese interactions, but in the broader context of non-Western encounters beyond the settler–colonial encounter. This is a step that I hope will be of benefit to many projects of intellectual decolonization that take *thinking from the South* as their starting point. Demonstrating a pragmatics of postcolonial translation, I analyze the reflexive, intersubjective mediation of Southern African and Chinese 'culture' concepts – those of *Ubuntu* and *guanxi* (关系) – as my primary example for discussion.

DOI: 10.4324/9781003273530-3

I begin with a discussion of affinities between these concepts as they have been written about, or publicly contextualized in some of their respective genealogies; I then move to a discussion of their reflexive translation in contemporary Afro-Chinese encounters. Following this, I conclude with a discussion about how a pragmatics of translation intervenes in a number of popular nonrepresentational or anti-translational literatures in the Western humanistic social sciences.

In their independent and synthesized contextualizations, *Ubuntu* and *guanxi* share a general feature of 'intersubjective interdependency' – a convergence of interpretations that has allowed many Africans in China to treat not only the respective cultural ideologies of *Ubuntu* and *guanxi* as malleable enough to permit a translation of one into the other, but also the capacity to reflexively repurpose the pragmatic deployment of these concepts for limited gains within a still-inequivalent context of encounter and exchange. In line with these observations and drawing on the shared intersubjective sensibilities of *guanxi* and *Ubuntu*, I will define translation – always simultaneously interpersonal and intertextual – as a pragmatics of mediating incommensurability. Thus, translation as a process that not only acknowledges difference can additionally be understood as a vital and inevitable social process that is both reflexively referred to and relied upon to permit transformations of social and material worlds without reducing cultural concepts – like *Ubuntu* or *guanxi* – to arbitrary propositions under the banner of cultural relativism.

Here, I would like to add a brief word concerning methodology and research ethics in this chapter. The important insight from a pragmatics of translation, and particularly my use of it, is that an encounter and interaction is never a single event, but ultimately encompasses a wider social context as well as a socio-spatiotemporal trajectory that is evidenced through the interaction. What the reader may initially discern as a series of 'individual encounters' in the context of an interaction-based ethnography is a misleading understanding of what happens between the ethnographic context and the subsequent representational act of ethnographic writing – historical or anthropological.

'Single' interactions are meant to diagram, with depth, positionalities, contexts, and dispositions that are occupied by a broad range of subjects over time in the ethnographic context. It would be profoundly monolingual – in the Lockean sense – to believe that an ethnographic interaction represents (a) a singular event, and (b) 'real' people, since textual representations are extensions of social realities as opposed to the realities themselves. Just as no large-scale quantitative survey will ever capture why subjects, collectively, behave the way they do, an interactional analysis is by its very nature incomplete. This is because no interaction is ever a social isolate – given that they encompass a distillation of language, performances, and ideas that are never, and have never been, the sole authorial objects of interlocutors. Understanding that there is no one-to-one correspondence between the number of interview subjects and the possibilities of their alignments, perspectives, opinions, and indeed personae, it is inevitably the ethnographer who – through mediating between ethnographic context, research institutions, writing, and critical reception – is undertaking the burden of qualitative exploration and evidence-based argumentation. Here, I can only claim that my informants and their social milieu were observed in depth, in a context full of informants, longitudinally, and that I conducted over 200 interviews over a period of four years. However, should the reading audience really be persuaded by me or any ethnographer simply saying so in a methodology or a footnote, especially when the 8000 words of a chapter can only accommodate a fragmentary representative sample from years of observation and interviews? These are disciplinary and conceptual biases that my work is directly aiming to write against and, thus, the interactions explored in this chapter and in my work, generally, are precisely a reaction to default ethnographic textures (as they are commensurated in much contemporary American anthropology) that attempt to perform ethnographic multiplicity which ultimately reduces the depth of ethnographic insight.

Beyond Synchronic Guanxi

In Western anthropologies of Chinese *guanxi* (Yang 1994, Bian 1994, Kipnis 1997, Bell 2000) the concept has often been understood through two of its more obvious iterations. Firstly, it might manifest in many Chinese social settings in a variety of modalities, including the exchange of gifts like luxury goods or 'red pockets' (that contain money); patronage and patrimony networks (particularly in government institutions); as well as an array of functional and dysfunctional techniques, tactics, and economies of corruption. This latter kind of *guanxi* has been the central theme and focus of a number of MBA-style courses and guidebooks providing financial guru-like advice on 'how to do networking in China', although this MBA-style *guanxi* caters to a more Western- and instrumentally inclined understanding of the short-term and transactional appearances of *guanxi*. Critiquing such token essentialisms of *guanxi* – both their self-help appropriations and orientalisms within Euro-American corporate literature and education – a number of anthropologists of (but mostly not *from*) China have pointed out how such approaches run the risk of reducing *guanxi* to a purely instrumental social practice, lacking specificity in its hyper-local 'Chinese' context. Here, *guanxi*'s more 'ethical' or 'practice'-based dimensions appear to be 'rescued' by scholars like Andrew Kipnis (1997). For Kipnis, in particular, *guanxi* has a mutually constitutive affinity with another Chinese concept of intersubjectivity, one that is inseparable from *guanxi's* contextual and co-textual meanings: *renqing* (人情). Building on French sociologist Pierre Bourdieu's (1977) work, Kipnis suggests that *renqing* emerges within a simultaneously 'embodied' and 'compassionate' habitus that *guanxi* sustains and is sustained by – intersubjectively – persons mutually committed to maintaining habitus in a mainly nonreflexive, 'beneath conscious' manner. Following Kipnis, *guanxi* exists in a dis-articulable equilibrium with *renqing*. Following his former teacher, anthropologist Judith Farquhar (2002), it can additionally be argued that *guanxi* might do so in ways that are simultaneously particular to, and reiterated through, embodied practices that both constitute and are constituted within an intersocial space-time: that of an anthropologically delineable community, society, or polity (Munn 1986, Bourdieu 1977).

However, at the heart of this rescue attempt by Western anthropologists of China, there is a persistent tension between 'cultural' determinism and emergence of the 'everyday'. In much of this West-to-Other anthropology, *guanxi* and *renqing* – *still* read through an orientalist gaze – are unproblematically maintained through the work of the everyday. In much of this writing, which negates the dialectical in favor of the linear-descriptive, it is as though *guanxi* were hermetically sealed from the continuous re-making and re-defining of its meanings through interactions among those for whom *guanxi* matters. There is still a presupposition that the definer and reader of 'cultural' terms and concepts is able to observe a synchronic durability of *guanxi*, which somehow overshadows, and yet escapes, the notice of those undertaking the labor of *guanxi*'s diachronic maintenance. A way past this contradiction may be attendance to interactional and intercultural contextualizations of *guanxi* that take seriously the reflexive, diachronic mediation of such ideas not only among subjects who believe they own such concepts but also for their interlocutors who believe they have cultural analogues for the same ideas. Such an approach, to be sure, would be more dialogical and dialectical by its very nature. In this vein, it will be argued that 'culture concepts' like *guanxi* have a vibrant cultural and historical life in Sino-Other encounters that entail Third Worldist histories and genealogies.

From Guanxi to Ubuntu

Diverging from the inalienable romance of cultural synchrony, what I argue and demonstrate aligns with a few important (if somewhat marginalized) critical theoretical analyses that have attended to the ways 'China' continues to make itself through making its others – particularly in relation to the play of external and internal forces that are necessarily ideological and political in the making of 'culture' (Yang 2015, Rofel 2007, Liu 2015, Liu 2004, Vukovich 2012). Importantly, such approaches do not provincialize the 'cultural' but understand culture as very much at stake in the vibrant making and contestation of social life under the predatory as well as contradictory conditions of cultural alienation and appropriation that typify the experience of modernity in postcolonial and postsocialist settings. *Guanxi* is both a cultural and (self-)orientalized 'culture' term that has had a vibrant life in pre- and postsocialist China, and that has seen its fair share of colonial translations and reductions. *Guanxi*'s reflexive referability – manifested in a vast range of '*guanxi* talk' across time, space, and languages – makes it both a contested and ideal lens through which to explicate the tension between intercultural awareness and cultural fetishism that haunts even the most mundane interaction between mutually constituted others, particularly in the context of Afro-Chinese cultural translations.

Guanxi, for many Chinese, thus imbricates a meta-awareness of intersubjectivity as social practice which is made apparent through *guanxi* talk. *Guanxi*, in this sense shares affinities with the trans-Southern African intelligibility of *Ubuntu* as not only a similar moral and ethical contingency that animates intersubjective relations, mediations, or supernatural efficacies but once again as an idea that is reflexively accessible through *Ubuntu*-talk. My emphasis in this chapter is on *Ubuntu*-talk as a living, intersubjective object of cultural reference, and as a translational analogue for *guanxi* in Afro-Chinese encounters. Here, I am *not* engaging Ubuntu as an analytical proposition in contemporary African and Africa-engaged analytical philosophy, as demonstrated in the debate between Matolino and Kwindingwi (2013) and Metz (2014), as well as the subsequent commentary by Chimakonam (2016). My response to this issue is that – regardless of the logical propositions of the 'life', 'death', or 'afterlives' of Ubuntu as analytical object – *Ubuntu* remains rehearsed and discursively under continuous maintenance in the 'language games' of those for whom the existence of *Ubuntu* remains indispensable. Following Michael Silverstein's (2004: 621–622) elaborate discussion of the discursive maintenance of 'cultural concepts', it might be analytically expedient to grant *Ubuntu*'s pragmatic and public materiality, as a portable and transmissible discourse object, beyond its suffocating reduction to existential binarism.

In this more public and pragmatic realm, *Ubuntu*'s ethical and co-textual dependency – that is its reliance on reception as much as representation – has been articulately captured by African language and literary scholar, James Ogude:

> In the Nguni saying popularized by [Desmond] Tutu, 'Umuntu ngumuntu ngabantu' (a person is only a person in relation to other persons), the idea is that no individual can become a person without the role played by other individuals and by society more wholly and generally. In other words, humans are made to be interdependent with each other. Humans realize and fulfill their selfhood only in interplay with others as a moral and metaphysical destiny.
>
> *(Ogude 2019: 4)*

It is important, however, that the moral and ethical contingencies of *Ubuntu* might also include witchcraft. As with *guanxi*, *Ubuntu* is as much the condition of possibility for mutually beneficial social relations, as it affords propensities for mutual destruction. Such transcendental ethical propensities have been partially – though not fully – explored in the innovative work of Adam Ashforth, where he frames witchcraft's contingent relationship with *Ubuntu* – witchcraft as a kind of 'dark matter' of *Ubuntu* (2005). In his excellent *Madumo: A Man Bewitched* (2000), Ashforth demonstrates this principle at work in the life of his friend and informant, Madumo, who must counter the effects of witchcraft directed toward him through his close kin ties. In Madumo's bewitching, *Ubuntu* – as the mutually constitutive force that engenders one's personhood through others – is the metaphysical infrastructure that permits both the efficacy of witchcraft and commonality of personhood between subjects.

In this vein, anthropologists John and Jean Comaroff (2012: 102) have described *Ubuntu* as 'a common African humanity' that has profound consequences for how we understand the nature of reflexive personhood maintenance as a feature of Southern African social life across cultural communities. In popular culture, *Ubuntu* is often explained in English through the phrase 'I exist because you exist', by a number of commentators including notable public figures like South Africa's Desmond Tutu and Nelson Mandela. This double-edged public life of *Ubuntu* permits insights into exploring the dark side of *guanxi* – *fubai* (腐败) or 'corruption' – a relation that anthropologist Cheryl Schmitz's recent exploration of witchcraft 'translation' in the context of Sino-Angolan encounters evocatively suggests but does not quite articulate (Schmitz 2020). With the exception of this excellent work, Chinese and Western sinologists have been somewhat loath to explore the relationship between *guanxi* and its dialectically negating shadow: witchcraft.

In contrast, attention to the everyday governance of China reveals a fairly explicit public awareness of *guanxi*'s corrupting or *fubai* affordances. In both rural and urban settings in the People's Republic of China (PRC), this public awareness is manifested officially, not only in the form of large-scale anti-corruption campaigns but also at the marginal scale of everyday policing where public messaging ubiquitously warns passers-by of the inveigling influence of 'dark forces' (or *heishili* 黑势力) – referring to criminal, political, or religious fundamentalist underworlds. China observers attuned to the discursive transformations of public anti-corruption advocacy in the PRC would not fail to have noticed a recent historical sequence of anti-corruption political campaigns: starting from 'fighting the tiger' (*dalaohu* 打老虎) campaign in 2013 – metaphorically meaning to persecute corrupted government leaders – and then followed by the 'squashing the flies altogether' (*dahu paiying* 打虎拍蝇) campaign, referring to the purging of mid-level corrupted officials; one sees a steady propaganda build-up to the '[eliminating] the dark and evil forces' (*hei e shili*黑恶势力) which began around 2018, targeting kinship-based organized crime. In this discursive shift it would be difficult to miss the escalating degree of insidiousness of these campaigns: from tigers to flies, to dark and evil forces – a shift that mirrors the shrinking distance between public criminality and the 'intimate' realm of the 'common person' (*putong ren* 普通人).

It would be both anachronistic and overly simplistic to view Chinese corruption's witchcraft-like manifestation in relation to *guanxi* as a by-product of the spectral machinations of neoliberalism operating in the shadows of Sino-governmentality – particularly given that there is nothing spectral, cabalistic, or 'hidden in the shadows' about the PRC's relationship to capital. Rather, outside of Western sinology, there is a much older genealogy of thought exploring the dualistic – both loving and corrupting – dimensions of *guanxi*. This genealogy is associated with (arguably) China's most famous anthropologist, Fei Xiaotong.

Contrasting the intersubjective ethical pluralism of Chinese social relations with Western social organizational principles based on monotheistic moral centrism, Fei Xiaotong famously outlined what he calls societies with a 'differential mode of association'. By way of Mencius, he analyzes the interactional basis of intersubjective ethics while also demonstrating his own pragmatics of translation in analyzing cultural concepts like *guanxi*:

> Mencius replied, 'A benevolent man neither harbors anger nor nurses resentment against a brother. All he does is to love him. Because he loves him, he wishes him to have rank. Because he loves him, he wishes him to be rich. [For the emperor to love his brother] was to enrich
>
> [his kin] and let him have rank. If as emperor he had allowed his brother to remain a common man, could that be described as loving him?'
>
> A society with a differential mode of association is composed of webs woven out of countless personal relationships. To each knot in these webs is attached a specific ethical principle. For this reason, the traditional moral system was incapable of producing a comprehensive moral concept. Therefore, all the standards of value in this system were incapable of transcending the differential personal relationships of the Chinese social structure. The degree to which Chinese ethics and laws expand and contract depend on a particular context and how one fits into that context.
>
> *(Fei [1947] 1992: 78)*

For Mencius and Fei Xiaotong, interaction and ethics are fundamentally intertwined – there are no ethics without interactions to recruit them and no interactions without ethical maintenance. Here, Fei Xiaotong also demonstrates the translational implications of web-like contingencies of intersubjective relations decades before Geertz. Elaborating on the ethical capaciousness of *guanxi*, he continues:

> I have heard quite a few friends denounce corruption, but when their own fathers stole from the public, they not only did not denounce them but even covered up the theft. Moreover,
>
> some went so far as to ask their fathers for some of the money made off the graft, even while denouncing corruption in others. When they themselves become corrupt, they can still find comfort in their 'capabilities'. In a society characterized by a differential mode of association, this kind of thinking is not contradictory. In such a society, general standards have no utility. The first thing to do is to understand the specific context: Who is the important figure, and what kind of relationship is appropriate with that figure?
>
> *(ibid.)*

As with *Ubuntu*, persons are maintained through their mutual contingencies – both through their ethical recruitment and through their seemingly contradictory, yet ultimately dialectical, ethical propensities. There is no ethics of *guanxi* without its contingent propensities for corruption, just as there is no *Ubuntu* without its propensity for witchcraft. Conversely, a consideration of Fei Xiaotong and China's contemporary public anti-corruption discourses should prompt us to ask why such similar social insights and intersubjective contingencies have (with a few exceptions) not been taken seriously in the context of Southern African governance. Particularly in the context of South African corruption discourse, the consideration of Fei Xiaotong's ethical pragmatics would quickly demonstrate the limits of referring to government corruption as antithetical to *Ubuntu* as a naïvely incorruptible intersubjective ethics.

Pragmatics of Translation

Having highlighted a few grounds for contiguity in discussing *guanxi–Ubuntu* translations, and having speculated about certain grounds for their comparison or shared affinities, a question must be addressed: how do contemporary Chinese and African actors pragmatically bring *guanxi* and *Ubuntu* and their intersubjective underpinnings into a shared field of recognition and reflection? Answering this question necessarily entails identifying and 'siting' translation as pragmatic imperative between African and Chinese subjects (Niranjana 1992).

As Tejaswini Niranjana has suggested, the act of translation – considered capaciously – is a political act (ibid.). As such, political acts are by their nature pragmatic and performative acts in that *doing* and *defining* become inextricable semiotic events. Building on this approach to translation, what follows will draw on a long genealogy of pragmatist thought including the ideas of several anti-imperialist and Third Worldist thinkers, from Du Bois (1903) to Mills and Gerth (1953). At the same time, I must qualify that I understand pragmatist thought as something that is not merely reducible to William James, Charles Peirce, and the Johns: Dewey and Austin, but rather part of a shared humanistic heritage of thought – one in which ideas are understood as constituted through, as well as constitutive of, reflexive processes of mediation. An example of this heritage is demonstrated in the pragmatic sensibility through which Fei Xiaotong interprets the ethical and pragmatic imbrications as well as genealogies of Chinese (and indeed other) intersubjective modalities of social organization – ideas that have been around at least since the early versions of the *Dao De Jing* (道德经), *The Analects* (論語), and *The Mencius* (孟子), and have been transformed, maintained, and syncretized via Neo-Confucians and a broad range of East Asian literary and historical scholars down to the present.

At the same time, a pragmatics of translation opposes the understanding that 'culture' is the exclusive analytical object of anthropologists who are uniquely situated to identify, 'translate', and study it. Rather, it prompts us to embrace the fact that cultural translation is an almost mundane reality in most societies that must confront diverse human interactions as their simultaneously ethical and pragmatic foundations – culture *does*, life is *lived*, and translation is *done*, regardless of 'loss' or anyone's semiotic nihilism. Actual inter-cultural, -linguistic, and -subjective translations – those happening between persons reflexively invested in receptional and representational labor – are pragmatic translations. Their pragmatic effects and reflexive meta-semantics – that is their definability as translational events – constitute perhaps the closest thing to a 'bounded' or 'defined' semiotic subject, object, process, or 'event'. Understood in this vein, a pragmatics of translation opposes the conventional semantic or metaphysical concern with cultural translation as cause for existential dread and liberal horror in much of the Anglocentric Western academy. This position necessarily proposes that we can in fact have pragmatic translatability and intersectional incommensurability at the same time. As the Americans might say: 'We can walk and chew gum at the same time'. The subsequent discussion provides a unique opportunity to demonstrate an example of what this might look like.

From Ubuntu to Guanxi

Drawing on a key series of interactions that emerged during my dissertation work (Schutte 2018, and Ke-Schutte 2019), I will now discuss a situation where mediation between *guanxi* and *Ubuntu* becomes a key site for excavating a pragmatics of translation. In a research period between 2012 and 2016 in Beijing's Haidian district, I frequently observed one informant, Patrice Moji,[1] making statements about his shared cosmopolitanism with various interlocutors: Chinese, African, and white 'Internationals'. Patrice Moji was a senior MA student who had been living in Beijing for a few years. He was one of my informants and regarded himself as a cultural translator between Chinese and African students in Beijing. From these interactions, I gathered that Patrice believed there to be a privileged position of mobility that permitted one to be situated as a translator, that cosmopolitan aspiration was a condition of possibility for translation: 'You cannot be a translator unless you have gone from one place to another', he once noted. Elaborating on his claims of cosmopolitanism, he compared Beijing's obvious mass urbanism to the contrasting spaces of both his childhood background in Southern Zimbabwe and his experiences as an undergraduate student in South Africa – the place where we first met a few years prior while Patrice was an undergraduate.

On one occasion, I learned that Patrice's teacher Prof. Li (力) was holding a banquet for a group of his students. Prof. Li, who I also knew as an informant, was a Chinese language and literature professor at Da Hua University – a pseudonym for one of the most elite educational institutions in Beijing. In addition to Patrice, Professor Li had reached out to me with an invitation. During the elaborate dinner – which included Peking duck, double-cooked pork, fried string beans, and a number of other delicacies (with rice only served on request) – Patrice told a story about his grandfather's travels to China and the Soviet Union as a Zimbabwean diplomat. He explained that many in his clan had middle names indicative of his grandfather and family's political alignments. 'Marx', 'Mao', 'Lenin', 'Fidel', and 'Trotski' abound in family birth records.

As I have indicated elsewhere, Patrice's overly elaborate set-up was very much intentional and directed toward establishing a Third-World socialist rapport with Prof. Li, given that he desperately needed Professor Li's letter of recommendation to maintain his scholarship at Da Hua University (Ke-Schutte 2019). Before and after the banquet, Patrice reflexively noted that he was building rapport as an instrumentalization of *guanxi* – a conceptual vocabulary he acquired after arriving in China. Patrice's labor was explicated during a climactic moment during the banquet ritual, where participants are meant to toast the professor in brief, laudatory speeches – a common practice during relatively frequent teacher–graduate student gatherings in the Chinese Academy. Patrice raised a glass of liquor (or *baijiu* 白酒) and proclaimed: '*disan shijie da tuanjie*' (第三世界大团结) ['to Third-World solidarity!']. Acknowledging Patrice, Prof. Li responded in deliberate English while obviously noting my presence as the white anthropologist at the table of whose alignments he could not be certain. Looking at me, Prof. Li seemed to make up his mind and stated (by way of translation): 'Third-World solidarity!' as though Patrice's toast not only required translation, but that I needed to be appraised of who it included (and perhaps who it did not).

I learned from both parties later that Prof. Li had in fact written the elicited letter of recommendation. Whether engineered or coincidental, this was taken by Patrice as evidence of both his prowess in managing social relations and the ritual efficacy of historical invocation – that he had pragmatically deployed *guanxi* through his own translation of it.

A few days following the banquet, I met with Prof. Li to discuss what had transpired. Since *guanxi* was a regular topic of conversation between us and having benefited on multiple occasions from Prof. Li's *guanxi*, I couldn't resist the opportunity to gauge his reflexive awareness of Patrice's engineered hailing. The position he held at his university was officially that of an academic professor; however, due to his social connections and skills in acquiring them, he became more known as a highly talented broker between educational, political, and private-sector interactional spaces. In a Chinese bureaucratic setting, he would easily be understood as the *guanxi* artist or manager of an institution – an unofficial, but indispensable, position in most Chinese organizations. As I have noted, beyond just being 'someone who networks well', a *guanxi* artist is someone who is particularly skilled at recognizing, building, and maintaining *guanxi* relationships (Ke-Schutte 2019). For Prof. Li, the emphasis on an aptitude for recognition and reception as imbricated translational processes – rather than on performance and production of instrumentalized rapport – was an important nuance in distinguishing the effective management of *guanxi* from competent networking.

By the accounts of Prof. Li's own peers, he was such an excellent manager of *guanxi* 'that he was able to send his children to [an Ivy League] university in America'.

Perhaps as part of this skill set, Prof. Li also mastered a genre of self-exoticism which I had seen him perform with predominantly white visiting scholars and officials from US institutions, with whom his institution had formed beneficial ties. In these interactions with his US visitors, he had to manage two performances. On the one hand, he had to advertise China's emerging 'cosmopolitan' educational status, while on the other, he needed to advertise himself as an expert on 'socialist' political or administrative protocol in China: a translator of otherwise 'inscrutable' signs to his American colleagues. This dual performance allowed him to motivate his own indispensability. Beyond his obvious skill at managing *guanxi*, Prof. Li was also uncharacteristically keen to engage in a genre of *guanxi* talk, in which he was willing to reflexively discuss making *guanxi* in detail and at length (ibid.).

He noted that it wasn't merely about giving people money or 'things', emphasizing that this was the 'the lowest *guanxi*'. Instead, he noted the centrality of contextual self-awareness: 'who you are' and 'what you have' and that, in turn, this awareness should be extended to 'who others are to you'. This contextually shifting relationship between you-to-others, and others-to-you underpins the central question in the *guanxi* interaction: 'Why would I spend my time on *guanxi* with others?' Here, he emphasized that – in the cultivation of *guanxi* relationships – we needed *to want to spend time on others* – a degree of sincerity, however instrumental it may obviously be, is an essential part of making *guanxi*. 'Take you, for instance', he noted to my slight alarm:

> You have a good attitude, but as someone from Africa, you are not as useful to me as an American graduate student or Professor. [However], you are easier to build a relationship with, and if there is mutual benefit, that is a good thing for both of us…You and I both have to understand and meet our mutual obligations to each other…otherwise we sabotage one another.
> *(Ke-Schutte 2019: 328)*

The importance of sincerity is demonstrated in Prof. Li's invocation of attitude. Both seem to matter in calculating whether to commit to a *guanxi* relationship or not, since 'attitude' would be a strong indicator of an interlocutor's willingness to reciprocate and maintain the relationship – one that precariously might leave both interlocutors vulnerable to sabotage, or possibly witchcraft.

Seeing an opportunity to shed light on his earlier interaction with Patrice, I asked whether he and Patrice Moji had a *guanxi* relationship? He responded emphatically that they did not, adding: 'I don't mean to sound like a bad person, but he can't offer me anything since he is only a student' (Ke-Schutte 2019: 328). Given that Prof. Li wrote many recommendations for his student and also aligned himself – at least performatively – with Patrice's recruitment to 'Third-World solidarity', a question emerges: is 'conscious' or, perhaps more accurately, 'reflexive' knowledge about being in a *guanxi* relationship a necessary and sufficient condition to deny its emergence in an interaction?

This question certainly proved to be at stake in Patrice Moji's interpretation of the exchange at the banquet as well as its aftermath. When I asked him about it, Patrice provided a translation of his own. He understood *guanxi* to be fundamentally translatable and in fact substitutable with another intersocial category drawn from social settings that were mutually intelligible to us, *Ubuntu*: 'Look, it [guanxi] is *the same as* Ubuntu' (Ke-Schutte 2019). Patrice's own translation attempts an iconizing equivocation of *Ubuntu* as being 'the same as' *guanxi*.

This iconizing modality of interactions where the motivation of sameness is at stake has been evocatively captured in the work of anthropologist Summerson Carr. Interpreting the pragmatist philosopher Charles Sanders Peirce, she notes the ways in which iconic signs 'gain their meaning in a contiguous relation to their object (as in the case of smoke and fire) and also from symbols, which have an arbitrary (that is, conventional) relationship with that which they represent', that – following Peirce – 'iconic signs are necessarily "motivated"'. In this sense, icons are

> 'the product of the analogic practices of language users as they selectively establish relationships of likeness…[gaining] their meaning not because they naturally resemble some unmediated thing in the world but instead because a community of speakers collectively designates that one kind of thing is like and therefore can come to stand for another.
>
> *(Carr 2011: 26)*

Beyond drawing equivalences between words – since Carr's work is focused on interactional settings where interlocutors have an overlapping language community – Patrice's translation of *Ubuntu* into *guanxi* brings entire notions of intersubjective space-time in relation to one another. The resulting effect is not only the augmentation of the social-semiotic range of *guanxi* but also that of *Ubuntu*. Furthermore, rather than essentializing both *Ubuntu* and *guanxi*, Patrice's pragmatic translation via iconization of these concepts should perhaps be understood as an attempt to bridge very different theories of social relations that nonetheless allow for intersubjective contingencies and their personhoods: a cultural translation as a transnationally portable resource.

In my own attempt to provoke Patrice's meta-talk of translation – perhaps mirroring what Peter Mwepikeni (2018) has depicted as an abuse of the *Ubuntu* concept to further neoliberal extraction in the guise of Rainbow Nationalism – I responded to his transfiguration with a well-known quip among fellow South- and Southern African students: 'I thought *Ubuntu* was dead?' (Ke-Schutte 2019: 329). For many postapartheid and 'postcolonial' subjects, this more cynical take on *Ubuntu* is often suggestive of alienations or anomic disillusionments of various forms (Durkheim [1893] 2013): from the ties of kinship and basic human compassion to a corrosion of cultural forms of belonging and emplacement typified by increasing and destructive commitments to self-interest. These conditions are furthermore understood as eradicating the underlying ethical space-time of *Ubuntu* through which one might be or become a person through other persons (Makgoba 1999: 153). Responding to my pessimism, Patrice noted: 'maybe *Ubuntu* is dead for us, but *guanxi* is alive for them' (Ke-Schutte 2019: 329). Pragmatically, Prof. Li's letter-writing constituted sufficient evidence – for Patrice – that a translatability between *guanx*i and *Ubuntu* did exist.

Importantly, neither *guanxi* nor *Ubuntu* are terms that can fully represent an inalienable cultural romance for Prof. Li and Patrice. On one occasion Prof. Li lamented, having had a failed meeting with an associate:

> You know, *guanxi* has really changed. When I was young, giving a person a ride in a truck or feeding them some dumplings was enough [to secure loyalty for life]. Now [this is] not the case…You know, under Mao, *guanxi* was a lot more real…look, I'm not saying [the cultural revolution] was a good time, but *guanxi* meant more because it was all [we] had.
>
> *(Ke-Schutte 2019: 330)*

Conclusion: From a Semantics to a Pragmatics of Translation

The preceding interactions with and between Prof. Li and Patrice Moji demonstrate a pragmatics of translation – one drawn from an actual 'micro-interaction' (as opposed to those announced, yet seldom demonstrated by a number of American Foucauldian devotees). This approach contrasts with much current China–Africa-related scholarship, particularly research situated in China, which has concerned itself mainly with macro-scale phenomena often providing compelling insights concerning political and economic dimensions of Sino-African interactions (Bodomo 2012, King 2013, Chang et al. 2013, Brautigam 2009, Li 2012, Snow 1989). These studies rigorously attempt to delineate and summarize the various strategic interests of China, African nation states, and a conspicuously silent Western audience, often marshaling vast swathes of data to depict very large social formations on a continental scale. As Kenneth King (2013) has noted, however, our picture of the actual people involved in this interaction remains incomplete. This is troubling since, at least from my preliminary research, it appears that what constitutes the capacities for intersubjective personhood is very much at issue in measuring the 'success' or 'value' of an educational development initiative, the scale of which is unprecedented on the African continent. 'Who Africans are' and 'who Africans are capable of being' – to themselves, their sponsors, their communities, as well as other aspirational or elite audiences – depends largely on acquiring and performing capacities to speak, network, and move without cultural constraints in a Chinese world. It is the recruitment of translation in the service of such goals that is at issue in actual face-to-face interactions between Africans and Chinese as non-Western interlocutors that must cultivate their own trans-languages (Hanks 2010). But how does a pragmatics of translation – in the still-decolonizing South – unsettle the post-translational lament of the Northern academic anglosphere? By way of extended conclusion, I hope to meditate on how a pragmatics of translation might productively engage a number of 'settled' assumptions around what Gayatri Spivak once termed 'the politics of translation' (1993).

Translation, in the explicitly linguistic sense, has been a central concern for literary theory (Sakai 1997, Spivak 1993) in ways that it has not been for anthropologists who in the past have borrowed or recruited terms like *mana* or *hau* as disciplinary analytics (Durkheim [1912] 1995, Mauss [1925] 1967), and yet more recently have come to disavow or lament the nihilistic impossibility of translation (Asad 1986). There have been notable critical exceptions, in linguistic anthropology, to both this polemical legacy of translational 'borrowing' and post-translational 'nihilism' (cf. Michael Silverstein 2017 & 2004). In their work, Michael Silverstein (2003) and Greg Urban (1996) have elaborated some of the imbricated problems with both 'translation' and its 'impossibility', demonstrating the limits of actualizing either, in the strictly literary sense. The understanding here is perhaps that translation – in so far as it is understood to be a practice of 'commensurating meaning' between languages – has analytical limitations when applied to a spoken language and its inextricable context of signification. This is because language, when understood to be inseparable from the life world of its community of users, is always a mutually constituting process rather than an object. Thus, it is more akin to a process, dialogically and semiotically unfolding in the moment-to-moment of real-time speech (Silverstein 2003 and 1976, Irvine and Gal 2000, Keane 1997 and 2007, Agha 2007, Urban 1996, Bakhtin 1981, Austin 1975). Thus, the 'target' and 'matrix' languages in the context of a translation might be seen to be constantly under construction, rendering translation as a stabilization of meaning, a somewhat remote goal. Yet, outside of the Andersonian language ideologies of the 'West', this precariously maintained state of translation and translatability has never been about the stabilization of meaning but rather the commitment to translational maintenance – both entextualized and interactional. For those committed to the endeavor of translation – like African students and their Chinese teachers in Beijing – the achievement of a translation, however imperfect or fleeting, exists as an unquestionable horizon of possibility even if a durable permanence or stabilization never emerges.

Of course, in its more metaphorical uses, translation has been a classical concern for scholars of 'culture' more-or-less up until the *Writing Culture* (Clifford and Marcus 1986) 'crisis'. Given the obvious, if somewhat problematized, resilience of this analytic (Sakai 1997, Spivak 1993, Derrida 1974, Sakai 1997, Chakrabarty 2000, Silverstein 2003, Urban 1996) and its contestations (Asad 1986, Abu-Lughod 1998, Clifford and Marcus 1986), particularly in the domain of 'cultural translation', a key question emerges: how is it that a concept so closely associated with the formal uses of 'language' seems to have such broad a purchase for an immensely divergent group of disciplinary concerns?

This question, however, presupposes language as a stable category to begin with – as though we know where language or multilingualism begins and ends. Rather, we should ask instead how 'purely linguistically' a concept like translation glosses once the analyst unsettles the very category we call 'language' to begin with? However, in the monolingual seminar rooms of Global North, such extensions of translation as metaphor don't even seem worthy of consideration in the work of scholars like Bruno Latour (1996), Adrian MacKenzie (2002), and Stefan Helmreich (2007). In their discussions, particularly in the case of Latour, translation bypasses its linguistic and semantic associations in favor of generating the emergent nature of ontological legibility as both the object and outcome of 'translational' or 'transductional' processes that are left bracketed in their analyses. Here, the Southern scholar is compelled to ask: how does Latourian translation understand the relationship between emerging formations of subjectivity that are not in engagement with the translation or translation-defining Global North? In my case, the translational labor of Afro-Chinese interactants on Beijing's university scene would easily disappear in the network of social relations and cultural mediations enveloping subject formation in the definitions of nonrepresentational or post representational translation. Additionally, how would we do so without considering the fact that these subjects both speak and reflect on translation as reflexive process? Here, the preceding discussion provided a unique opportunity to engage these questions by way of demonstrating how cultural translation cannot be disarticulated from the culturally situated social relations practices, institutions, and infrastructures that translating subjects both performatively constitute and depend on.

However, such primitivist and orientalist circulations differ drastically from the attempt at cultural translation unfolding between Prof. Li and Patrice, and indeed within a great many other Afro-Chinese encounters unfolding at present. Rather, we can understand their respective recourse to *guanxi* and an *Ubuntu* translation of *guanxi*, as standing-in for a humanistic attempt to disrupt often alienating, machine-like, automatic, and bureaucratic social institutions that surround most other aspects of their interaction: the global inequalities and inevitable racisms that haunt Patrice's educational endeavor and Prof. Li's mostly under-appreciated and 'hidden' affective labor in managing it. In the face of their respective, but fundamentally unequal, alienations of labor and personhood, both *guanxi* and *Ubuntu* can be seen as a refuge – a 'cultural' space-time of reintegration representing transcendent cultural justifications for enduring forms of solidarity. Cultural translation, as a condition of possibility for generating such a 'cultural' space-time, might only then be understood as a way of resisting a contemporary corruption of expectations of mutual obligation – perhaps suggestive of the spectral residue of 'organic divisions of labor' within 'mechanical divisions of labor' (Durkheim 2013, Benjamin 2007). In this way, we might understand *guanxi* and *Ubuntu* as coming to ground 'Third-World solidarity' as the romantic promise of a social bondage that mutually excludes the immediate, utilitarian purchase of the 'First World' either by China or Africa. However, such speculative possibilities were less easy to discern, since both interactants were careful to hedge – despite frequent recourse to utopic imaginaries of culture and history – that these terms are not immune to historical forces and re-appropriation, and certainly could not unfold in an ideological vacuum. Regardless of apparent obstacles, their attempts at cultural translation persist.

For subjects like Prof. Li and Patrice, misrepresentations, misunderstandings, and mistranslations will and certainly do abound, but the attempt at translation – despite the violence of its failures – remains unmitigated between non-Western others. These must be accounted for rather than denied, preferably by researchers from the Global South, and building analytical approaches to cultural translation that are drawn from contexts that disrupt, complicate, diversify, and provincialize encounters between 'the West and its Others'. From this standpoint, cultivating a pragmatics of translation will be an important empirical starting point to decolonizing the study and framing of various scales of 'cultural encounter'.

Note

1 All names of the subjects represented in this document have been anonymized. Given that naming practices for African subjects are an important aspect of the analysis, I chose names that served a similar function – diagramming historical socialist alignments. Fortunately, such alignments are so prominent in Afro-Chinese histories of Non-Alignment that finding similarly glossing alternatives did not prove difficult.

Bibliography

Agha, A. 2007. "Recombinant Selves in Mass Mediated Spacetime." *Language and Communication* 27: 320–335.

Asad, T. 1986. "The Concept of Cultural Translation in British Social Anthropology." In *Writing Culture: Poetics and Politics of Ethnography*, eds. Clifford, J. and Marcus, G.E. Berkeley: University of California Press.

Ashforth, A. 2000. *Madumo, A Man Bewitched*. Chicago: University of Chicago Press.

Ashforth, A. 2005. *Witchcraft, Violence, and Democracy in South Africa*. Chicago: University of Chicago Press.

Austin, J.L. 1975. *How to do things with Words*. Cambridge: Harvard University Press.

Bakhtin, M.M. 1981. *The Dialogic Imagination: Four Essays*. Austin: University of Texas Press.

Bell, D. 2000. "Guanxi: A Nesting of Groups." *Current Anthropology* 41 (1): 132–138.

Benjamin, W. 2007. "The Work of Art in the Age of Mechanical Reproduction." In *Illuminations: Essays and Reflections*, ed. Hannah Arendt, 217–253. New York: Random House.

Bian, Y. 1994. "Guanxi and the Allocation of Urban Jobs in China." *China Quarterly* 140: 971–999.

Bhabha, H.K. 1994. *The Location of Culture*. New York: Routledge.

Bodomo, A. 2012. *Africans in China: A Socio-Cultural Study and its Implications on China-African Relations*. New York: Cambria Press.

Bourdieu, P. 1977. *Outline of a Theory of Practice* (trans. Richard Nice). London: Cambridge.

Carr, S.E. 2011. *Scripting Addiction: The Politics of Therapeutic Talk and American Sobriety*. Princeton: Princeton University Press.
Chakrabarty, D. 2000. *Provincializing Europe: Postcolonial Thought and Historical Difference*. Princeton: Princeton University Press.
Chimakonam, J.O. 2016. "The End of Ubuntu or Its Beginning in Matolino-Kwindingwi-Metz debate: An Exercise in Conversational Philosophy." *South African Journal of Philosophy* 35 (2): 224–234.
Clifford, J. and G.E. Marcus. 1986. *Writing Culture: Poetics and Politics of Ethnography*. Berkeley: University of California Press.
Comaroff, J and J.L. Comaroff. 2012. *Theory from the South or, How Euro-America is Evolving Towards Africa*. London: Paradigm Publishers.
Derrida, J. 1974. *Of Grammatology*. Baltimore: Johns Hopkins University Press.
Du Bois, W.E.B. 1903. *The Souls of Black Folk*. Chicago: A. C. McClurg & Co.
Durkheim, E. [1893] 2013. *The Division of Labour in Society*. London: Palgrave Macmillan.
Durkheim, E [1912] 1995. *The Elementary Forms of Religious Life* (trans. K.E. Fields). New York: The Free Press.
Farquhar, J. 2002. *Appetites: Food and Sex in Post-Socialist China*. Durham: Duke University Press.
Fei, X. [1947] 1992. *From the Soil: The Foundations of Chinese Society*. Berkeley: University of California Press.
Hanks, W.F. 2010. *Converting Words: Maya in the Age of the Cross*. Berkeley: University of California Press.
Helmreich, S. 2007. "An Anthropologist Underwater: Immersive Soundscapes, Submarine Cyborgs and Transductive Ethnography." *American Ethnologist* 34 (4): 621–641.
Irvine, J.T. and S. Gal. 2000. "Language Ideology and Linguistic Differentiation." In *Linguistic Anthropology: A Reader*, ed. Duranti, A. Malden: Blackwell.
Ke-Schutte, J. 2019. "Aspirational Histories of Third World Cosmopolitanism: Dialectical Interactions in Afro-Chinese Beijing" *Signs and Society* 7 (3): 314–341.
Keane, W. 1997. *Signs of Recognition: Powers and Hazards of Representation in an Indonesian Society*. Berkeley: University of California Press.
Keane, W. 2007. *Christian Moderns: Freedom and Fetish in the Mission Encounter*. Berkeley: University of California Press.
King, A.Y. 1991. "Kuan-hsi and Network Building: A Sociological Interpretation." *Daedalus*, 120(2), 63–84.
King, K. 2013. *China's Aid and Soft Power in Africa: The Case of Education and Training*. Woodbridge Suffolk and Rochester, NY: Boydell and Brewer.
Kipnis, A. 1997. *Producing Guanxi: Sentiment, Self and Subculture in a North China Village*. Durham: Duke University Press.
Latour, B. 1996. "On Actor-Network Theory: A Few Clarifications." *Soziale Welt* 47: 369–381
Liu, L. H. 2004. *Clash of Empires: The Invention of China in Modern World Making*. Cambridge: Harvard University Press.
Liu, P. 2015. *Queer Marxism in Two Chinas*. Durham: Duke University Press.
Mackenzie, A. 2002. *Transductions: Bodies and Machines at Speed* London; New York: Continuum.
Makgoba, M.W. 1999. *African Renaissance: The New Struggle*. Cape Town: Tafelberg and Mafube.
Matolino, B. and W. Kwindingwi. 2013. "The End of Ubuntu." *South African Journal of Philosophy* 32 (2): 197–205

Mauss, M. 1967. *The Gift: Forms and Functions of Exchange in Archaic Societies*. New York: W.W. Norton.

Metz, T. 2014. "Just the Beginning for Ubuntu: Reply to Matolino and Kwindingwi. *South African Journal of Philosophy* 33 (1): 65–72.

Mills, C.W. and H.H. Gerth. 1953. *Character and Social Structure: The Psychology of Social Institutions*. New York: Harcourt, Brace.

Munn, N. 1986. *Fame of Gawa: A Symbolic Study of Value Transformation in a Massim (Papua New Guinea) Society*. Cambridge and New York: Cambridge University Press.

Mwipikeni, P. 2018. "Ubuntu and the Modern Society." *South African Journal of Philosophy* 37 (3): 322–334.

Niranjana, T. 1992. *Siting Translation: History, Poststructuralism, and the Postcolonial Context*. Oakland: University of California Press.

Ogude, J. 2019. "Introduction." In *Ubuntu and the Reconstitution of Community*, ed. Ogude. Bloomington: Indiana University Press.

Rofel, L. 2007. *Desiring China: Experiments in Neoliberalism, Sexuality, and Public Culture*. Duke University Press.

Sakai, N. 1997. *Translation and Subjectivity: On "Japan" and Cultural Nationalism*. Minneapolis: University of Minnesota Press.

Schmitz, C.M. 2020. "Kufala! Translating Witchcraft in an Angolan–Chinese Labor Dispute." *HAU: Journal of Ethnographic Theory* 10 (2): 473–486.

Schutte, J.H. "Third-World Cosmopolitanism in White Spacetime: Intersectionality and Mobility in Sino-African Encounters." PhD diss. University of Chicago, 2018.

Silverstein, M. 1976. "Shifters, Linguistic Categories, and Cultural Description." In *Meaning in Anthropology*, eds. Basso, K.H. and Selby, H.A. New York: Harper and Row.

Silverstein, M. 1998. "Improvisational Performance of Culture in Realtime Discursive Practice." In *Creativity in Performance*, ed. Keith Sawyer, R. London: Ablex.

Silverstein, M. 2003. "Translation, Transduction and Transformation: Skating Glossando on Thin Semiotic Ice." In *Translating Cultures: Perspectives on Translation and Anthropology*, eds. Rubel, P.G. and Rosman. Oxford & New York: Berg Publishers.

Silverstein, M. 2004. "'Cultural' Concepts and the Language-Culture Nexus." *Current Anthropology* 45 (5): 621–652.

Silverstein, M. 2017. "The Fieldwork Encounter and the Colonized Voice of Indigeneity" *Representations* 137 (1): 23–43.

Spivak, G.C. 1993. "The Politics of Translation." In *Outside in the Teaching Machine*, ed. Gayatri Spivak. London and New York: Routledge.

Urban, G. 1996. "Entextualization, Replication and Power." In *Natural Histories of Discourse*, eds. Silverstein, M. and Urban, G. Chicago: University of Chicago Press.

Vukovich, D. 2012. *China and Orientalism: Western Knowledge Production and the P.R.C.* Oxon: Routledge Press.

Yang, M. 1994. *Gifts, Favors and Banquets: The Art of Social Relationships in China*. Ithaca: Cornell University Press.

Yang, F. 2015. *Faked in China: Nation Branding, Counterfeit Culture, and Globalization*. Bloomington: Indiana University Press.

3

TARBIYYA

Noha Fikry

On a rooftop in Egypt, overlooking a four-story family home in a lower-middle-class neighborhood in coastal Alexandria, 24-year-old Malak sat with a protruding belly nurturing her awaited son. Tall, with an oval face, and piercingly sharp wide eyes, Malak is a housewife married to the love of her life. As we sipped coffee on a hot day in June, she narrated her unforgettable memory of delivering her first child, Salma. This was two years ago, when Malak was only 22 years old. After rushing to the hospital, Malak spent the following 14 hours in pain, more pain, and an impatience to see her first child come to life. As we spoke, Malak began frowning with disgust over the memory of the tasteless 30-day mandatory course of boiled chicken for lunch that followed the delivery. I confessed that chicken is the only meat protein that I eat, as she dared me to survive this strict and unpleasant postpartum diet. After a few minutes, we were joined by Malak's mother-in-law, Wafaa, a cheerful housewife in her early 50s with a round face and equally round and plump cheeks. I asked her about this strict dietary plan of boiled chicken, and her eyes lit up in surprise: had I not seen the film *Al-ḥafyd* (in English, the grandson)?

In one particular scene of this Egyptian film produced in 1974, a woman whose daughter has just delivered her first child discusses with her husband the necessity of having chicken in their extended family celebratory banquet. The husband shrugs it off in anger, why add chicken to the ever-expanding list of items he has to buy, including turkeys and pigeons? His wife sharply responds that these chickens are specifically for their newborn daughter, '*da il- 'ayiyyl yinzil min hina nuḥut maṭruḥu farkha min hina tisnid qalbaha*' (Farag and Salem 1974). The verbatim translation of this last phrase to English is interesting, as the mother indicates that the chickens replace the child that just left the body of the woman: 'The chicken supports the mother's heart in place of the child who just came out of her body'. While I went through the scene in my head, Wafaa stated

DOI: 10.4324/9781003273530-4

that a postpartum woman must be fed boiled chicken for one month after delivery. These chickens, however, are preferably raised and nurtured on one's rooftop to guarantee a specific quality and add known entities to these postpartum meals. Malak, since she first knew of her pregnancy, has been raising chickens on Wafaa's rooftop. While Malak has been nurturing the awaited first grandson, Wafaa has likewise been nurturing Malak's postpartum chickens. I rushed to ask Wafaa if it would have been so different to just buy a few chickens once Malak had delivered the child. Looking up in surprise, Wafaa assured me that nothing is ever like *tarbiyya*: the value of a rooftop/home-reared chicken inevitably outweighs that of a store-bought one.

Roughly translated as nurturing, teaching, or educating, *tarbiyya* in this rooftop rendition refers to rearing animals on one's rooftop or inside one's home. These rooftops are usually located on three- or four-story extended family homes in lower-middle- and working-class neighborhoods in Egypt, where many families raise some or most of their meat proteins. These animals include chickens, ducks, geese, rabbits, goats, sheep, and pigeons. Based on a year of ethnographic fieldwork in a number of these different neighborhoods, my research explores multispecies and human–animal relations on rooftops in Egypt. I rely on anecdotes and encounters from fieldwork to illustrate what the notion of *tarbiyya* adds to burgeoning multispecies research in the Global South. My interlocutors always used *tarbiyya* to refer to the practice of rearing rooftop animals, whom they often call 'rooftop children'. By the same token, my interlocutors also used *tarbiyya* to assert and take pride in a particular knowledge and trajectory of their own food. I thus ask: what does it mean to eat a 'rooftop child'? What happens when we invoke *tarbiyya* not only as an invocation of human–animal relations in the Global South but also as a cultural descriptor of one's food? Guided by these questions and rooftop meals and reflections, I argue that *tarbiyya* refers to a particular value/understanding of food, one that is rooted in an intimate human–animal relation of nurturance, feeding, and discipline. *Tarbiyya*, invoked in different rooftop instances, weaves together these sentiments in a nuanced multispecies canvas, one that cannot be reduced solely to nurturance, love, discipline, or teaching. What follows is a brief attempt to explore multispecies engagements with disciplining rabbits, dealing with suicidal turkeys, and other rooftop animals and meals.

From (Multi)Species to *Tarbiyya*: Concepts from the Global South

In the first few days of fieldwork, I found it hard to explain my research interests to my interlocutors. In Arabic, the word species or *faṣila* – and, worse yet, multispecies – is hardly used in common parlance.[1] I found it easier to introduce myself as a researcher interested in human–animal relations, since the Arabic word for animals, *ḥayawānāt*, is more familiar and less intimidating. It only took a few minutes for my interlocutors to mistake me for a veterinarian – who is indeed interested in animals too – and to bombard me with endless questions on falling feathers and rooftop flu seasons (see Fikry 2018). I shifted gears and explained to each of the families that I am interested in anecdotes, especially those that involve themselves and their rooftop animals. After a few visits, I became known as Noha who is interested in *tarbiyya*. Before I began fieldwork, while reading existing literature, or in writing up my research proposal, I never expected *tarbiyya* to be the main conceptual building block of my research and my hopeful intervention in a multispecies toolkit from the Global South.

In his introduction to this volume, Dilip Menon reminds us that we cannot continue our research through the [obsolete] formula 'southern fact, northern theory'. Fieldwork engagements and anecdotes are not mere 'data' or facts that we would then explain and translate using northern theory for a predominantly northern audience. Menon argues that this is not merely about resentment or critiquing shortcomings in northern theory, as the opening anecdote of this section illustrates. It is rather that it is our role as critical scholars from the Global South to recognize northern theory's 'possible obsolescence or irrelevance for our concerns' (p. 8). In a short article titled 'diversifying affect', Yael Navaro raises similar questions on the heritage and genealogies of our conceptual 'toolboxes' (2017, p. 209). Navaro argues that in the particular case of conceptualizing affect, scholars are usually bombarded by Western genealogies and philosophies of what affect means and what it invokes. Building on her fieldwork in Antakya, Turkey, she explores the different resonances that affect might have in different geographies, particularly non-Western ones. She eloquently asks, 'How can we trace and compose putatively non-Western inspirations for affect, ones that do not regurgitate by now well-established comprehensions of it' (p. 210)?

In an intriguing ethnography of dogfighting, cockfighting, and pigeon flying as three modes of 'more-than-human sociality' in rural Pakistan, Muhammad Kavesh uses the Urdu word *shauq* to describe the layers of these multispecies relations (2021, p. 7). Translated as passion, delight, yearning, and desire, *shauq* has a different genealogy when compared to the English translation 'hobby'. Kavesh theorizes *shauq* as a form of passionate labor, a mode of being with animals, a source of personal joy, and a meaningful activity. Flowing organically from fieldwork, *shauq* is the word that Kavesh's interlocutors used most often to conceptualize 'this more-than-human sociality that binds human and animal lives through care and neglect, love and violence, and affection and indifference' (p. 8). Taking my cue from these different scholars, I use *tarbiyya* as my guiding concept in these multispecies rooftop relations and hopefully other multispecies pockets in the Global South. As I argue elsewhere (Fikry, 2019), my point of departure was always: what vocabulary do my interlocutors use in telling me about their rooftop engagements, how do they describe their everyday tasks, how do they refer to the different animals, and what language do they use to refer to their multispecies bonds with goats, ducks, and chickens? *Tarbiyya* was always mentioned alongside other words and meanings, contouring a porous 'conceptual universe' in which *tarbiyya* unfolds[2] (Menon, 2021, p. 22). These conceptual universes are rooted in the geographical and sociological universes where fieldwork engagements took place, and these universes always delineate the conceptual work that a concept offers.

Rooftops are a zone of existence in Egypt, a country of the Global South ranking 54th of 107 countries in the 2020 Global Hunger Index, struggling with malnutrition, food affordability, and food quality, especially among underprivileged groups (Global Hunger Index, 2020). The practice of *tarbiyya* therefore narrates not only human–animal bonds of nurturance but also an everyday struggle of the majority of working- and lower-middle-class families to make ends meet and keep their bellies full. In the absence of affordable access to meat proteins, and where most cheap meat and poultry are either imported or frozen or lack a known source, families opt for *tarbiyya*, which ensures food of a particular quality to the family. The cost of *tarbiyya* is significantly lower than buying a chicken or other meat proteins from a butcher: for example, while a store-bought turkey costs around $32–$45, it would cost less than a quarter of that amount to rear it at home. It is not just cost that matters, however, as it takes a lot of [gendered] physical and emotional labor for *tarbiyya* to work. Departing from multiple [Western] trajectories in multispecies research centered on apolitical companionship and love (Schuetze, Newman, Astacio, 2010), *tarbiyya* is centered on an economy of nutritional need, social-class injustices, and a trajectory of multispecies relations that include nurturance and love but also meals and bellies. Building on Menon's eloquent remark on 'the universalization of European particularism', I take *tarbiyya* as an essential contribution to extending multispecies engagements and theorizing beyond a predominantly European toolkit[3] (Menon, 2021, p. 1).

Thicker, Higher, Better: An Etymological Exploration

On concepts and their worlds, Menon emphasizes the importance of anecdotes in delineating a conceptual landscape. As he puts it, 'it is in the conversations between words, the insurrection of anecdotes, that a conceptual universe emerges' (p. 21). In the opening anecdote of this chapter, *tarbiyya* evokes a world of multispecies nurturance, one in which a maternal figure cares for, labors, and invests much time and resources in rearing rooftop animals. But the conversation does not stop at care and nurturance, and perhaps a brief exploration of the linguistic roots of *tarbiyya* can guide us further. I sought the help of *Lisan al-Arab,* a nine-volume classical Arabic dictionary written by North-African lexicographer ibn-Manzur. In *Lisan al-Arab*, the etymological root of *tarbiyya* is r b y. Stemming from this root are a number of interesting words, including *rabb*, which is commonly used to refer to not only God but also any person owning, claiming power over, reforming, befriending, taking care of, or handling someone or something else (ibn-Manzur, 1998, p. 1546). For example, a father is commonly referred to as *rabb al-usra*, which would translate to the owner/handler of the family. This form of relationship, though evidently implying a power dynamic or authority, transcends or complicates a simplistic translation to ownership. Ownership, friendship, and care are all encompassed within the same conceptual landscape of *rabb*, and thus, *tarbiyya*. As such, it is hard to leave it at an assumed human superiority to animals in the case of rooftop *tarbiyya*. This is clearer when we ask what a particular relationship does. Another word sharing the same etymological root provides a potential answer. *Yarbu* in Arabic describes something as growing, increasing, or becoming higher (p. 1572). This is used upon describing growing plants and when referring to any interest added to money (specifically known as *riba*, which is prohibited in the Quran). The word *rabā'ib*, again sharing the same etymological root, refers to any animals raised at home, particularly those that are consumed as food such as cattle (p. 1574). As one final insight from *tarbiyya*'s etymological neighbors, *rubb* refers to molasses or the essence of a fruit reached when using certain cooking techniques (p. 1550). Through simmering and thickening certain fruits, *rubb* is the reward left in the pot. Beyond the dictionary, chefs commonly use *tarbiyya* to refer to the act of thickening a sauce or a soup through adding flour. It is the very thick and heavy consistency of the sauce/soup which gives it the *tarbiyya* label.

In this brief etymological exploration, we thus have an act of owning, caring for, handling, or befriending, combined with an implied intervention that increases, thickens, or improves the status of that which is the object of *tarbiyya*. Thinking with rooftop *tarbiyya*, it is humans – more specifically women – who handle, befriend, and nurture rooftop animals. *Tarbiyya* can be regarded as an act of 'increasing' or 'improving' through providing a proper shelter in a shaded and spacious rooftop. *Tarbiyya* can also be regarded as an act of thickening the flesh of the animals, through a nurtured and carefully prepared feed. The question here becomes: what happens when owning, befriending, improving, and thickening are referring to a chicken or a goat? What does it mean for a served meal of chicken or turkey to be befriended, thickened, and nurtured? While *tarbiyya* shares conceptual space with these different etymological neighbors, there are particularities to rooftop multispecies *tarbiyya* that further stretch its conceptual space. On rooftops, *tarbiyya* refers not only to a human–animal relation but also to delicious meals. *Tarbiyya* is a human–animal relation that translates into a particular trajectory of food. An insurrection of anecdotes, walking us through the basic ingredients of multispecies *tarbiyya*, illustrates these relations and meals further.

Rooftop Children & Duties: An Everyday Guide to *Tarbiyya*

On one fieldwork visit on a hot summer day, Malak decided to tease Wafaa while illustrating to me the weight and burden that *tarbiyya* can often be. As we sipped our Turkish coffee, Wafaa told me that I should consider rearing a few chickens where I live, not just because I am interested in *tarbiyya* for my research, but because it provides excellent training for my prospective maternal life and its required skills. Implicitly, this was a subtle critique to Malak who refuses to participate in any rooftop *tarbiyya* duties, on the premise that she was never interested in it and that her family never reared any animals on their rooftop. Malak then decided to respond, as subtly as Wafaa. She told me that her husband Mostafa, who is Wafaa's oldest son, always complains about how Wafaa loves her 'rooftop children' more than she loves them. He complains of how much time Wafaa spends on the rooftop: preparing their feed, serving it, cleaning, and refilling food and water. Wafaa smiled in pride and with an approving nod: rooftop animals are *wiladha* (in Arabic, her children), and they demand more nurturance and love than her now-adult biological children. She assured me that *tarbiyya* is a lot of work, exactly like tending to a child or a toddler who has to be fed, cleaned, nurtured, and disciplined. As the previously discussed itinerary of meanings illustrate, *tarbiyya* usually includes love, nurturance, and the presence of an intimate bond. On rooftops, this translates into the time spent caring for, nurturing, and knowing each of the rooftop animals and their dispositions. On a typical day, Wafaa wakes up at around six in the morning, prepares breakfast for her rooftop children, and goes up to serve each of the animals in their separate rooms. She opens each of the rooms' doors for the animals to roam around freely before or after breakfast. She then goes up again in a few hours with a snack of vegetables and some household leftovers, while getting all the animals back in their rooms when the sun hits its peak. Close to sunset, Wafaa goes up for a final check, serving the last meal, making sure there is enough water for the night, and then goes down to have dinner with the family.

Things do not always go as planned, however. One day, Wafaa woke up a few hours late, only to discover that she forgot about an important appointment that Mostafa had. She rushed to the kitchen, fixed him breakfast, woke him up, and stayed with him till he left. With a sigh of relief, Wafaa poured herself some coffee and began cleaning the house. Because it was almost noon, Wafaa falsely thought that she must have served breakfast to her rooftop children first thing in the morning as she does every day. When it became noon, Wafaa felt her heartbeat racing, exactly as she would feel if one of her children was suffering. She immediately realized that her accelerated heartbeat meant that her rooftop children were suffering, and that she had forgotten to serve them breakfast. She dropped everything she was doing, rushed to the kitchen to fix their breakfast, poured some water, and ran up to the rooftop. It was a hot July day, so she found all the animals booking dehydrated and emaciated. The rabbits were almost asleep, and the ducks looked up at her with much sorrow. After serving them all the food she prepared, Wafaa spent a full hour next to the animals while crying with much guilt. She came down in tears, for how could she have forgotten about these rooftop animals who could not feed themselves while only caring about Mostafa, a grown-up who could indeed fix himself anything to eat before his appointment?

In this encounter, *tarbiyya* takes the form of an intimate maternal multispecies bond – a racing of one's heartbeat when things go wrong. The kinship label that Wafaa uses to describe this bond is about her role and sentiment as a maternal caregiver and the rooftop animals' role as creatures that require care, love, and continuous attention. Like any kinship relation, however, it takes a lot of work to be cultivated and sustained. *Tarbiyya* here is an all-day busy schedule of preparing food, serving feed, and taking up the responsibility of rooftop children seriously. It is also an affective labor of balancing sentiments, ingredients, and boundaries, as Wafaa goes on to illustrate.

Discipline and Punish: Holding Your Grounds in *Tarbiyya*

'Those cute little eyes can be difficult to handle', Wafaa pointed to one small grey rabbit as we sipped our customary Turkish coffee on the rooftop one day. I smiled and told her that the rabbit seemed cute and lovely, as she shook her head in absolute disagreement. She calls him 'the naughty rabbit': upon coming up to serve breakfast to her rooftop children one day, this rabbit looked at Wafaa, looked at the food with indifference, then walked away. She observed him for a while as he refused to approach the food. On the following day, the rabbit did the same. Wafaa decided to teach him a lesson: when food is served, you have to eat and be grateful. She took the rabbit to stay in a different room all by himself, offering only water and no food for two days. On the first day, he still looked at her with the same indifference. On the second day, however, his eyes were full of guilt and fatigue, as he looked at her as if begging her to feed him and take him back to the shared room. On the third day, Wafaa took him back to the shared room with all the other rabbits. When she offered their following meal, he was the first one to rush and eat as much as he could. And this problematic attitude never showed up again.

For Wafaa, it was very difficult not to give in to those little cute eyes when the rabbit realized his mistake after two days. She could have easily taken him back to the shared room, patted him on his furry back, and served him food and water quickly. But she refused, insistent on teaching the lesson in full. I asked her how she could be so strict, as she responded that it all comes with time and practice. *Tarbiyya* is about balancing sentiments carefully: show love but establish boundaries. Give food but create schedules. Cuddle and spoil, but only to an extent. She referred to raising human children again: can you ever raise children solely with endless love and pampering? My answer was a definite no, but I still had my doubts. These doubts were stoked further on Safaa's rooftop. Located in the southern part of Cairo, in a lower-middle-class neighborhood, Safaa's rooftop hums with the lives of a couple of goats, one sheep, and around a dozen chickens. Safaa lives in this four-story extended family home with her husband and her four children. Before he passed away a few years ago, Safaa's father-in-law used to live in this house until Safaa married his son and came over to live in a smaller apartment on one of the top floors of the house. When he passed away, Safaa relocated to the ground-floor apartment, which is the most spacious and inviting one in the building. Safaa is a welcoming housewife in her mid-40s, always relying on the help of her three daughters Toto (14 years old), Noor (11 years old), and Jana (8 years old) in rooftop duties and everything else. In spite of her relatively young age compared to my other female interlocutors, Safaa always insisted that her daughters do everything with her: they cook, serve food, fix tea and drinks, clean up on the rooftop, feed animals, attend to pregnant goats, and aid or observe deliveries. For her, this is all about disciplining them at a young age to take up household responsibilities seriously, and to follow her lead in *tarbiyya*.

As we went up on the rooftop one day, I noticed the frequent sound of little bells, which I never heard before. Unlike the cooing, clucking, and bleating registers, the jingle of bells was a new addition to the sensorial landscape of rooftops. I followed the sounds carefully till I noticed four goats with bells dangling from short ropes around their necks. 'It is all to protect this little sick one,' Safaa told me as she pointed to one pregnant and seemingly sick female goat sitting in a corner. The female goat looked sick, fatigued, and barely able to move. Safaa had to serve her food and water in a separate bowl from all the other goats and animals because she would not have been able to fight and race with them for food. This was the fourth pregnancy for the goat, and the most exhausting one so far. To protect the goat and the pregnancy, Safaa decided to place all of these small bells around the necks of the male goats. Whenever any male goat approached the pregnant female in an attempt to tease, annoy, or impregnate her, the bell around his neck would sound loud. Safaa would race up to resolve the fight and discipline the delinquent male goats.[4]

All throughout my visits, Safaa emphasized how discipline is essential to *tarbiyya*. Early on, she made sure to involve Toto, Noor, and Jana in all rooftop affairs. They exchange the everyday tasks of cleaning, preparing food, serving food, and observing animals on the rooftop. Safaa has installed a strict schedule for everything that relates to the rooftop: there are specific times for each meal to be served every day, for each of the animals to be allowed to roam around the rooftop freely, for them to go back into their separate rooms and get to sleep, and for cleaning the rooftop twice in a day. The order of serving food on the rooftop begins at 7 am every day and goes as follows: goats, chickens, and ducks, then finally rabbits. Proudly, Safaa told me that each of the rooftop animal species has a sense of when it is getting its food: when she goes up to serve the chickens, the goats would never dare rush at the food, at her, or cause any disturbance – they know that it is not time for their meal yet. Safaa takes equal pride in her biological children who can take up rooftop and household duties perfectly *and* in her rooftop children who listen, obey, and follow all her instructions and schedules.

For Safaa and Wafaa, *tarbiyya* here is about the skill of keeping a rooftop intact with discipline. It is about being in control, with echoes of *rabb* and its claims to authority evident through the anecdotes in this section. Both Safaa and Wafaa pointed to an untamed and undisciplined nature, one that transforms through the careful and decisive intervention of humans. Through acts of disciplining, confining, punishing, instilling schedules, and creating rooftop routines, humans narrate *tarbiyya* as an act of arguably 'improving' the lives of the animals.

Tarbiyya makes sure that animals were raised in a disciplined, nurturing, and consistent environment, one in which menus and selves are kept in check. The question remains as to whether eating a disciplined animal makes any difference in its taste. What does *tarbiyya*, here translated into discipline, do to the taste and quality of this animal as it becomes food? A quick juxtaposition of variations of chicken [breasts] makes this clearer.

'Nothing Beats *Tarbiyya*': Of Bellies & Feed

In thinking about *tarbiyya* and its labor of nurturance and discipline, we cannot lose sight of the ultimate goal of rooftop rearing: feeding families. Rooftop *tarbiyya* is strictly gendered: it is women who take up all rooftop cleaning, feeding, and in most cases slaughtering animals, and this is primarily to fulfill an expectation falling upon women to feed their families. It is women who ultimately cook, buy groceries, and choose recipes and ingredients. The social expectation falling upon women is thus not one of feeding families but rather feeding families *well*. The definition of well here encompasses all the different ingredients of *tarbiyya* discussed throughout this chapter. 'Well' is about taste, quality, and thriftiness, but it is also about a particular intimate knowledge of the food, here translated into a maternal multispecies nurturance that gives the food its particular value. Rooftop or home-nurtured meat proteins attest to a successful housewife who cares to feed her family well.

Nahed does a better job delineating this conceptual universe of *tarbiyya* as centered on food and its quality, as the following anecdote illustrates. On a rooftop located in another lower-middle-class neighborhood in southern Cairo, cheerful 60-year-old Nahed lives with her husband, her daughter Eman, and her daughter-in-law Sahar in a four-story extended family home. This is where Nahed moved when she got married to her husband when she was 16 years old and where she began sustaining a rooftop thriving with goats, chickens, rabbits, and ducks. After plenty of discussions – or better yet, arguments – on my poor food choices and my refusal to eat any red meat, Nahed finally settled on a delicious fieldwork meal for all my visits: *macaruna béchamel* and *firakh pané*, a dish of pasta in a thick and rich white sauce along with freshly breaded and fried chicken breasts. While I devoured my staple fieldwork meal one afternoon, Nahed asked me if I had ever tasted chicken breasts as delicious as hers. Fieldwork compliments aside, I nodded in absolute certainty: I had never tasted chicken breasts as tender and delicious as Nahed's. I began asking her about her brand of breadcrumbs, oil, or whether she adds any spices to the breading, as she affirmed that none of these would ever make a big difference. In a tone of unparalleled confidence, Nahed asserted: '*Mafish zayy il-tarbiyya*', or nothing beats *tarbiyya*. She went on to challenge me as to whether any butcher or industrial farm would go as far in nurturing and caring for their poultry or meat, as I again nodded agreement.

Nahed took me to her tiny kitchen, in which a huge basket full of leftovers stood in a corner. This 'rooftop basket' is where Nahed and Sahar keep everyday household [non-meat] leftovers, vegetable peels, and stale bread. They have also agreed with a fava beans store owner downstairs to send them all his vegetable leftovers and peels before he goes home. With every meal, Nahed or Sahar mix a share of fodder or corn with these generous leftovers to nourish rooftop animals with a varied and 'clean' diet.[5] In winter, Nahed wakes up slightly earlier than usual to peel around half a kilo of onions, cut them down into very little pieces, and serve them with breakfast as an immunity booster. To provide an extra share of calcium especially to younger animals, Nahed also grinds quicklime finely and adds it to the rooftop ground in each of the rooms. Between meals, rooftop animals – especially chickens, ducks, and geese – usually root around on the rooftop's muddy and foddered ground to sharpen their beaks and look for remains of food. This is how finely ground quicklime makes its way to rooftop animals' bellies. Through these everyday choices and preparations, Nahed proudly ensures that she knows and decides upon everything that enters the bellies of the animals, thus ensuring the quality and taste of the food she serves to her family. Nahed then jumped to the juxtaposition quickly, asking me whether I know what industrial farm chickens and animals eat?

Upon replying that I indeed do not, Nahed went on with the comprehensive description of the feed of industrial and commercially grown farm animals: these animals are fed with an appalling combination of protein concentrates, the most important ingredient of which is fishmeal, or the discarded leftovers of butchers and fish stores. The discarded fat, feathers, and bones are usually burnt, dried, and powdered to be served as feed for these animals to swell up quickly and generate the highest profit in the shortest amount of time. In purchasing an industrial farm or a commercially grown animal, you are therefore eating these violent histories of dubious feed and swelling bodies. In contrast to this feed is a rooftop carefully chosen menu of varied household leftovers of bread, rice, vegetables, pasta, along with finely ground quicklime, diced onions in winter, and other immunity boosters. The nurturance, care, orderly schedules of feed, and overall discipline that Safaa and Wafaa instill are other ingredients of rooftop animals' feed. In these routines and everyday food choices, *tarbiyya* refers to a particular value/understanding of food, one in which knowledge and control of an animal's gastronomic history – through an intimate multispecies relation – is what defines the quality of a rooftop animal. By knowing and choosing what goes into the belly of an animal, females fill the bellies of their families with trusted, nurtured, and delicious food.

This takes us back to thickening as one of the components of *tarbiyya*'s conceptual universe: while both rooftop and industrial farm animals are eventually 'thickened' through various acts of feeding and rearing, each of these modes of thickening exposes different relations. A body fattened with fishmeal and protein concentrates is different from one fed on household leftovers and onions. *Tarbiyya* denotes a rooftop body nurtured with quality feed, handled by a loving maternal human female in an overall nonindustrial context where profit is never part of the equation. Rooftop animals are never sold or traded; they are reared for the sole purpose of feeding families well. *Tarbiyya* thus narrates a thickened rooftop body with an intimate multispecies relation of nurturance, discipline, and carefully controlled gastronomic biographies. While I mentioned the disparity in the prices of a rooftop reared and a store-bought animal in the beginning of this essay, Nahed's anecdotes invite us to push these initial reflections further. Cost is essential, economies and class inequalities are central, but *tarbiyya* and its stretching conceptual universe allow us to extend to notions of taste, multispecies relations of food, and the importance of nurturing one's own food in challenging situations. *Tarbiyya* pushes us to refine the questions we ask, especially pertaining to food access. For example, instead of asking whether lower-middle-class families eat chicken or meat every day, we would ask what kind of chicken or meat do lower-middle-class families eat and how often? What are the multispecies relations that inform or affect the taste and quality of these meat proteins?

Conclusion

In this essay, I explore *tarbiyya* as an essential building block in a human–animal relations conceptual toolkit from the Global South. Loosely standing for nurturing, rearing, and disciplining, *tarbiyya* is the word most frequently used to describe human–animal relations on Egypt's rooftops. In the absence of affordable and trusted meat proteins, many lower-middle- and working-class families rear a number of animals on their rooftops for nutritional sustenance. These animals include goats, chickens, rabbits, ducks, and geese. I rely on a series of anecdotes based on one year of ethnographic fieldwork on different rooftops in Egypt to sketch the initial components of *tarbiyya*. Through engagements with etymologies, naughty rabbits, pregnant goats, and postpartum chicken-based diets, I argue that *tarbiyya* refers to a particular value/understanding of food, one that is rooted in an intimate human–animal relation of nurturance, feeding, and discipline. Through knowing, nurturing, and controlling a rooftop animal's feed, women rely on *tarbiyya* to provide food of a particular quality and trajectory to household members.

To contribute to a conceptual toolkit from the Global South, I suggest we begin with the socioeconomic and geopolitical realities of our contexts. *Tarbiyya*, for example, describes a multispecies relation of food thriving in a country suffering hunger and malnutrition. *Tarbiyya* thus narrates not only multispecies nurturance and care but also gastronomic biographies of well-fed families in a context of dire nutritional and economic necessity. Stretched beyond rooftops, *tarbiyya* opens up space for interdisciplinary research on the centrality of human–animal relations in understanding food values in Egypt and hopefully elsewhere in the Global South. It offers valuable insight into the boundaries, limitations, and context-specific renditions of human–animal relations in the Global South. Rooted in our sociopolitical, historical, cosmological, and cultural realities, a conceptual toolkit on multispecies relations from the Global South carves out space for pockets of relations that are otherwise deemed unworthy of attention or unfitting by gatekeeping clichés.

Notes

1 For a useful critique of the Euroamerican origin of species as a concept, see Reinert 2016.
2 It is important to note another word that used to be common in describing animal-rearing practices prior to *tarbiyya*. *Qany*, according to *the Dictionary of Egyptian Arabic*, refers to the act of rearing animals (1986, p. 720). In Egypt, *qany* was also commonly used to refer to a man's relationship to his wife, with a connotation of property and protection. I only heard of *qany* through Egyptian films in the 1980s and 1990s, and it was mentioned only once or twice during my fieldwork. Though I believe *qany* significantly overlaps with *tarbiyya*, I choose to focus on *tarbiyya* as the main concept guiding these rooftop engagements and mostly commonly used among my interlocutors.
3 On a similar note to Menon, Kim Tallbear notes the limitations of Western multispecies/interspecies thought and the need for indigenous standpoints and theorizing in the field of human–animal studies (Tallbear 2011).
4 After a few weeks from this conversation with Safaa, I received the sad news that the goat had delivered her kids but that she passed away right after delivery.
5 Clean here refers to vegetarian food items, since using nonvegetarian items as feed gives a rancid-like taste to poultry and cattle. On another level, and this will become clearer later in the essay, clean here refers to the knowledge of what goes into the animals' bellies.

References

Al-Ḥafyd. (1974). [Film]. Atef Salem. dir. Egypt: Dollar Films.

Fikry, N. (2018). *Challenges of fieldwork in Egypt: Changing/challenging theoretical leanings*. Available from: https://www.opendemocracy.net/en/north-africa-west-asia/challenges-of-fieldwork-in-egypt-changingchallenging-th/ [Accessed 8th July 2021].

Fikry, N. (2019). Rooftop recipes for relating: Ecologies of humans, animals, and life. *Anthropology of the Middle East*. 14(2), 42–54. Available from: https://www.berghahnjournals.com/view/journals/ame/14/2/ame140204.xml [Accessed 8th July 2021].

Global Hunger Index. (2020). *2020: Global Hunger Index by severity*. Available from: https://www.globalhungerindex.org/ranking.html [Accessed 8th July 2021].

Hinds, M., Badawi, E. (1986). *A dictionary of Egyptian Arabic*. Beirut: Librarie du Liban.

Ibn-Manzur. (1998 [1882]). *Lisan al-Arab*. Cairo: Dar al-Ma'arif.

Kavesh, M. (2021). *Animal enthusiasms: Life beyond cage and leash in rural Pakistan*. London: Routledge.

Menon, D. (2021). Changing theory: Thinking concepts from the global South. Unublished ms.

Navaro, Y. (2017). Diversifying affect. *Cultural Anthropology*. 32(2), 209–214. Available from: https://journal.culanth.org/index.php/ca/article/view/ca32.2.05/152 [Accessed 8th July 2021].

Reinert, H. (2016). About a stone: Some notes on geologic conviviality. *Environmental Humanities*. 8(1), 95–117. Available from: https://read.dukeupress.edu/environmental-humanities/article/8/1/95/61708/About-a-StoneSome-Notes-on-Geologic-Conviviality [Accessed 8th July 2021].

Schuetze, C., Newman, C., Astacio, P. A. (2010). *Gleanings from a para-site: The multispecies salon II.* Available from: https://culanth.org/fieldsights/gleanings-from-a-para-site-the-multispecies-salon-ii [Accessed 8th July 2021].

Tallbear, K. (2011). *Why interspecies thinking needs indigenous standpoints.* Available from: https://culanth.org/fieldsights/why-interspecies-thinking-needs-indigenous-standpoints [Accessed 8th July 2021].

PART II
Commensuration

4

LOGIC

Edwin Etieyibo

Introduction

In philosophy and within the domain of rationality and logic there is a tendency toward universalism, a universalism that is Eurocentric. This chapter challenges this tendency and orientation by making a case for what one might call the 'relativity' of logic. The relativity of logic or the case of logic relativity is one that speaks to the discourse around concepts from the Global South. This is so insofar as the idea of the relativity of logic is a recognition, on the one hand, that there's no universalism to logic, and on the other hand, that there are substantive contributions to logic from the Global South. While the focus of this chapter is on logic, in particular the sense in which one can talk about logic relativity in African philosophy, it piggybacks on debates around rationality in African philosophy.

Whereas a few scholars in African philosophy have had quite a bit to say about rationality and African philosophy, not much has been discussed in relation to logic and African philosophy. [For some of the literature on logic and African philosophy broadly and discussions about logic and rationality see Biakolo, 2003: 9–21; Martin, 1970: 231–239; Lévi-Strauss, 1966; Lévy-Bruhl, 1923 & (1985) (1910); Lukes, 1970:208–213 & 1982:261–305; Senghor, 1956; Sogolo, 2003:244–258; Omoregbe, 1998:3–8; Winch, 1958 & 1964:307–324; Oruka, 1983: 383–396; Ocaya, 2004:285–294; Momoh, 2000; Fayemi, 2010; Etieyibo, 2016; Chimakonam, 2019; Hebga, 2020; Mabalane and Etieyibo, 2020).] In saying this, that is in placing rationality side by side with logic in African philosophy, I must hasten to point out that I am not thereby suggesting that rationality and logic are the same, or that any discussion of rationality must necessarily implicate or exhaust or lead to a discussion of logic. In other words, one can

DOI: 10.4324/9781003273530-6

discuss rationality without discussing logic, although one may by discussing logic be discussing one form of rationality.

Having said this and although rationality is neither synonymous with logic nor a discussion of rationality necessarily implicates a discussion of logic, one might point out that there are connections between rationality and logic. The connection exists insofar as both, at some level, concern reasoning and insofar as logic can be taken to be a manifestation or one form of rationality. Rather, what I am suggesting by placing them together is that given that one of the core issues at the heart of the debate decades ago (in the 1970s and 1980s in particular) in relation to whether or not African philosophy existed concerns rationality one would have expected that much work would have been done in logic roughly in tandem with discussions on rationality.

In some of the discussions on rationality in the literature, one of the most contested issues concerns whether rationality is relative and contextual or not (and as it implicates logic one can think of it in terms of universalism vs particularism) (see Mabalane and Etieyibo, 2020). If we suppose that it is the case that rationality is relative and contextual, then the question that I am interested in exploring in this chapter is whether logic, which is about rationality and which concerns reasoning and the principles or rules or processes used in good and sound thinking and reasoning, is relative. My broad goal is to highlight the place of contexts in logic, namely the relativity of logic. And by relativity of logic, I mean that taking contexts into account seems relevant in our discussion of logic. That is, the idea of the relativity of logic is an idea that takes logic to be contextual or context sensitive to a particular place and culture and to particular views of reality. In pursuing this idea, I will broadly be investigating the question as to whether there are some logical principles of reasoning by which any given thought system can be judged to be logical or illogical. In other words, I will be looking at whether some logical principles or rules are universal, if yes, in what sense they are universal, and whether their instantiations and content are context sensitive.

In broaching and examining these issues I should be taken to be indirectly gesturing to one way that one might think of logic in the African (philosophical) tradition and worldview, and as different from logic in the Western (philosophical) tradition and worldview. As a way of giving sense to my gesturing to the idea of the relativity of logic, I will discuss logic and the Acholi language and *Ezumezu* logic with specific reference to the disjunction rule and the law of excluded middle. The central idea that I hope will come out from these examples and discussion is that certain language may take a less restrictive view of some logical principle or rule (as in the case of the Acholi language and disjunction), and that logic in African philosophy is trivalent or polyvalent and not bivalent (particularly, in reference to the law of excluded middle).

What Is Logic?

The general tendency in the literature is to flamboyantly associate logic with terms like rationality and reasoning. However, in specific, descriptive and more technical terms, logic is taken to be: (a) the principles/rules/processes used in good sound thinking and reasoning, (b) the structure of propositions as distinguished from their content, and (c) the method and validity in deductive reasoning. This description of logic in terms of its specific and technical sense is consistent with the four different senses of logic that Thomas Hofweber has identified, namely, logic as the study of (i) artificial formal languages, (ii) formally valid inferences and logical consequence, (iii) logical truths, and (iv) the general features, or form, of judgments (Hofweber, 2011). And for how we might think of the relationship between the different senses of logic see Hofweber (2011).

If we take the above to give us some general idea of logic, then one important question is: 'Are there some logical principles of reasoning by which any given thought system can be judged to be logical or illogical?' Or simply, 'Are there universal principles of logic'? Broadly, in the literature we can group responses to this question into three camps (the yes camp, the no camp, and the yes/no camp).

In the no camp one might take Peter Winch, Claude Lévi-Strauss, Godwin Sogolo, and Meinrad Hebga to be its representatives. In 'Understanding a Primitive Society' (1964), Winch argues that what we have is the incommensurability of different forms of life, where different forms of life call for different paradigms of discourse. Here he follows Ludwig Wittgenstein's claim that the logic of our reasoning resides in the language that we speak. In *The Idea of a Social Science and Its Relation to Philosophy*, Winch reiterates the point that logic is context sensitive:

> Criteria of logic are not a direct gift of God, but arise out of, and are only intelligible in the context of, ways of living or modes of social life. It follows that one cannot apply criteria of logic to modes of social life as such. For instance, science is one such mode and religion is another; and each has criteria of intelligibility peculiar to itself. So, within science or religion actions can be logical or illogical: in science, for example, it would be illogical to refuse to be bound by the results of a properly carried out experiment; in religion it would be illogical to suppose that one could pit one's own strength against God's; and so on. But we cannot sensibly say that either the practice of science itself or that of religion is either illogical or logical; both are non-logical.
>
> *(1958:100–101)*

As for Claude Lévi-Strauss, he argues that although the modes of knowledge acquisition are not necessarily the preserve of any one culture, there are fundamental differences between what might be called modes of knowledge acquisition in traditional societies and nontraditional societies. It is important to note that traditional societies and nontraditional societies are what Lévi-Strauss and Lévy-Bruhl call primitive societies and nonprimitive or scientific societies, respectively. The target of Lévi-Strauss' attack is Lévy-Bruhl's claim that primitive societies are prelogical. In his seminal work, *The Savage Mind* (1966), which was a response to the arguments of Lévy-Bruhl about the prelogical nature of primitive societies, Lévi-Strauss argued that the primitive mind is logical, and this can be seen from the structural orderliness of their conceptual schemes, namely, their nominal and classificatory systems and myths. In other words, primitive people have not only a genuine scientific spirit, they also have logical-categorial abilities (Lévi-Strauss, 1966:17; see also Biakolo, 2003: 9–21).

In the same vein as Winch and Lévi-Strauss, Sogolo argues that the idea of the 'universals of logic and reason are not, *of necessity* acceptable' and binding on everyone (2003:248). Although he acknowledges that 'logic presents us with a systematic framework, a pattern of reasoning that is accepted as intelligible' logical rules; however, 'like other conventional rules, are drawn up for those who wish to play the logician's game to learn and apply' (Sogolo, 248). His point is that logical rules cannot have a compelling force on all people since they govern a large part of our experimental world. He notes, 'There can be nothing universal about any drawn-up rules intended for reasoning in a given pattern; such rules cannot be compelling on all people' (Sogolo, 2003:248). This sentiment has equally been expressed by Barry Barnes and David Bloor as follows:

> In fact, logical concepts and terms have assigned meanings and roles different from their usage in ordinary discourse. Logical connectives such as 'and', 'or', and terms such as 'if, 'then', 'entailment', 'implication', etc., are assigned technical meanings which deviate from their ordinary usage. To that extent, it is right to define logic as 'a learned body of scholarly lores… a mass of conventional routines, decisions, expedient restrictions, dicta, maxims, and ad hoc rules' (Barnes and Bloor 1982:41). There can be nothing universal about any drawn-up rules intended for reasoning in a given pattern; such rules cannot be compelling on all people.
>
> *(Barnes and Bloor 1982:41)*

And as part of the yes camp and in support of the view that if there are some logical principles of reasoning by which any given thought system can be judged to be logical or illogical such principles must be internal, Meinrad Hebga (2020) notes:

> What, you may ask, is the criterion of judgment for the internal coherence of a logical system. Evidently it cannot be another logical system accepted as the norm and measure of human thought. The thesis of contradictory logics is precisely a denial of such intellectual imperialism. Each system will be self-sustaining and will accept nothing as its criterion but first truths and common sense. If it can be reduced to these by successive stages, it is coherent and intrinsically true.
>
> *(Hebga, 2020:7)*

In the yes camp we have Steven Lukes (1970, 208–213; 1982:261–305) and Martin Hollis (1970:231–239). The general disposition of this camp is the claim that there is the universality of certain logical rules and methods of drawing inferences like the law of identity and non-contradiction (which all rational people should follow; or all reasoning processes ought to heed). Not only this, but there is also the additional claim that every rational person should follow the classical laws of thought (which were formulated by Aristotle), fundamental axiomatic principles or rules that ground rational discourse in the sense that they guide one's thought (consciously or unconsciously) or lie behind human thought.

Although the question: 'Are there some logical principles of reasoning by which any given thought system can be judged to be logical or illogical? Or 'Are there universal principles of logic?' may be said to have divided scholars into the no and yes camp there is sense that one can point to the existence of a third camp, what one might call the yes and no camp. In this camp the position is that although there are some criteria for appraising a thought system (logic, belief claims, etc.) that are context-dependent (the evaluation is done from within the culture itself) there are some that are universal criteria for appraising a thought system (the universality of certain logical rules or criteria – the evaluation is done from outside the culture itself). It appears that one representative of this camp is Levy-Bruhl, and to an extent, one may add Léopold Sédar Senghor.

As for Lévy-Bruhl, his central claim is that societies with 'primitive mentality' are different from societies with 'civilized mentality' in that the former exhibits a pre-logical mode of thought (unscientific, uncritical, contains evident contradictions) and governed by the 'logic of sentiments' (Lévy-Bruhl, 1923 & 1985 (1910); see also Biakolo, 2003: 9–21). Although there seems to be some ambiguity as to what Lévy-Bruhl means by 'pre-logical' he is clear that 'Prelogical does not mean alogical or antilogical. Prelogical, applied to primitive mentality, means simply that it does not go out of its way, as we do, to avoid contradiction. It does not always present the same logical requirements' (Lévy-Bruhl, 1923:21). The fact that Levy-Bruhl claims that the pre-logical mind does not always present the same logical requirements he seems to grant that the thoughts implicated in primitive mentality have their own logical principles, although of a different sort. These logical principles are what he calls the laws of 'mystical participation' (1923:21). It is these logical principles, i.e., the laws of mystical participation that grant thoughts of primitive mentality that status of some *form of logic* (Lévy-Bruhl 1985 (1910)).

Lévy-Bruhl's idea of the law of mystical participation has been echoed in a different form by Senghor, who argues that traditional people do not make a distinction between a number of categories or concepts, namely, between the subject and the object, the organic and the inorganic, themselves and the land they inhabit. That is not to say that Senghor is claiming that traditional people do not exhibit some form of reason. Like Lévy-Bruhl, he takes traditional people to exercise some form of reason. However, his point is that the reasoning traditional people exhibit is of a different kind because it is determined by mystical representations. So, whereas for Lévy-Bruhl 'the logic of sentiments' governs the reasoning of traditional people, for Senghor such reasoning is governed by 'intuitive reason' (Senghor, 1956; See also Sogolo, 2003:246).

The discussion so far about the universality or lack thereof of principles of logic leads me to the central issue that I wish to address and explore further in this essay, which is that concerning contextuality, rationality and relativity of logic. One of those that have reminded us about the context-sensitive nature of logic discourse in general and logic in African thought, in particular is Henry Odera Oruka. In 'Sagacity in African Philosophy' (1983), he notes that 'One does not need to understand the rules, nature and scope of formal logic in order to think critically. In any African thought system, there exists valid principles of inference like modus ponens along with other logical principles and the three fundamental laws of thought' (383–396). The same point has been more recently reiterated by Joseph Omoregbe when he said, 'The 'power of logic is identical with the power of rationality' and the 'ability to reason logically and coherently is an integral part of man's rationality…it is therefore false to say that African people cannot think logically…unless they employ Aristotle's or Russell's forms of logic or even the Western type of argumentation' (Omoregbe, 1998:4).

Some Rules in or Principles of Logic: The Disjunction and the Law of Excluded Middle

The Disjunction

The way the disjunction rule is understood in traditional formal logic is that the disjunction is true when either or both disjuncts are true (see Etieyibo, 2016). The idea that the disjunction is true when either or both disjuncts are true highlights two senses of disjunction. The first is *exclusive disjunction* and the second is *inclusive disjunction*. Both *exclusive disjunction* and *inclusive disjunction* signal the two ways that the disjunction might be true.

In the *exclusive disjunction* sense, a disjunctive statement is true if *one* (and not both) of the disjuncts is true. The following is an example: 'The word ant has 3 letters or 5 + 2 =10.' Since the first fact or proposition or disjunct is true, the entire sentence is true. If we put this in the language of truth table this disjunctive statement can be marked as T or F = T. And in the *inclusive disjunction* sense a disjunctive statement is true if *both* disjuncts are true. An example is 'the University of the Witwatersrand is in Cape Town or Blue is a color.' Since only one of the facts or propositions or disjunct is true, the entire sentence is false. This disjunctive statement can be marked in the truth table as F or T = F.

The Law of Excluded Middle

According to the law of excluded middle, every proposition is either true or false. That is, a proposition cannot both be true and false or not be true or false. Stated differently, a thing or something either exists or does not exist; it cannot both exist and not exist or not exist at all. As Aristotle expresses it thus, 'there cannot be an intermediate between contradictories, but of one subject we must either affirm or deny any one predicate' (Aristotle, 350 BCE/2018: Book IV, Part 7). This understanding of the law of excluded middle can be represented symbolically in terms of *exclusive disjunction*: 'P is true, or P is false,' where only one of these propositions or disjuncts holds or is true.

The Acholi Language and Logic

In 'Logic in the Acholi Language,' Victor Ocaya claims that 'The Acholi language has all the elements sufficient for the business of logic' (2004:285). I want to test this claim, in the next sections, in respect of the disjunctive rule and the law of excluded middle.

Disjunction in Acholi Language

According to Ocaya (2004), there is no *inclusive disjunction* in Acholi; the language only makes provision for *exclusive disjunction*. The disjunctive connectives in the Acholi language are: (a) *nyo* and (b) *onyo*. Both refer to *or*. An example, which Ocaya gives is *Okello ka pe paco, ci tye I poto*, which translates to 'Okello is either at home or in the fields.' As Ocaya notes, disjunction or a disjunctive statement in the Acholi language 'is always 'either...or...and not both.' That is, according to the Acholi language, 'a situation such as that envisaged by the inclusive disjunction does not make sense.' (Ocaya 2004: 289)

What We Learn from Disjunction in Acholi Language

There are several things that we can take from or may be said about disjunction in the Acholi language. One thing is that the definition of the disjunctive rule is not challenged by disjunction in the Acholi language. However, we might say that it is defined slightly differently. The fact that disjunction can be defined slightly differently opens up the space for the relativity of logic. Undoubtedly, given that the Acholi language does not recognize *inclusive disjunction* the Acholi language would not define disjunction as true when *both* disjuncts are true. Rather, it will take the disjunction to be true when *either* proposition or disjunct is true. One implication of this is that the Acholi language takes a less restrictive view of disjunction.

Of course, this has consequences in terms of performing derivations or trying to establish the validity of arguments or argument forms in the sense that if one were to employ disjunction in the Acholi language one might be unable to take advantage of the resources offered by *exclusive disjunction*. The other thing that may be said about disjunction in Acholi language is that the advocation of *exclusive disjunction* and jettisoning of *inclusive disjunction* is simply a question of the limits of a language. Well, certainly given that the Acholi language only recognizes *exclusive disjunction* we might say that the limit imposed on the disjunction is simply a consequence of the limit of the Acholi language. I will say more about this more generally later when I talk about the possible grounds for trivalent or polyvalent logic.

The Law of Excluded Middle in Acholi Language

In the Acholi language, Ocaya suggests that the law of excluded middle is challenged (2004:289). It is challenged in the sense that it doesn't take the view that every proposition is either true or false or that something either exists or does not exist. The example Ocaya gives to illustrate this claim is that of a substance and its being hot. One thing we may say about a substance, say water or some other liquid in the Acholi language is this: (1) *Piny Iyet*, which means 'It is hot,' which we can take as P. Another thing we can say about it is: (2) *Piny pe Iyet*, which translates to 'It is not hot' (~P). These two things, according to Ocaya, are not the only things that we can say about water. We can also say (3) *Piny Iyet-Iyet* (P & ~P), which means 'It is hot and not hot,' and which in the English language is typically taken to be 'It is rather hot.' Ocaya claims that *Piny Iyet-Iyet* is a distinct category of beingness or a state of *being* of a substance or some thing or stuff that lies somewhere between the two other categories of *Piny Iyet* and *Piny pe Iyet*. This idea suggests that the English word 'rather' is not captured by the Acholi idea of *Iyet-Iyet*. Additionally, the third category of *Piny Iyet-Iyet* as a distinct category of beingness is different from the idea of being lukewarm, which is more or less used to signify something that could or should be hot but is only moderately warm or being tepid or indifferent. If this is right, then we have in the Acholi language a good example of logical thinking going against the classical law of excluded middle.

Ezumezu Logic and the Law of Excluded Middle

The possibility of *Piny Iyet-Iyet*, as a distinct and third category of beingness, may be taken to be supported by the idea of *Ezumezu*, as defended by Jonathan Chimakonam, in a draft manuscript 'Ezumezu as a Methodological Reconstruction in African Philosophy: Toward Anarchistic (Conversational) Orderliness' and in his book *Ezumezu: A System of Logic for African Philosophy and Studies* (2019). In both places, Chimakonam notes that *Ezumezu* gives us an alternative logic or logical system and that it is a logic that is dynamic or flexible and three-valued. Chimakonam's formulation of *Ezumezu* logic in the context of the classical laws of thought, specifically the law of excluded middle can be expressed as follows: 'Onona-etiti: (T) A ∧ (T) ~ A or (T) A ∧ (F) A {which reads A is both true and false (both and)} (Chimakonam, draft manuscript: 16). For Chimakonam's discussion of this principle and other principles in the context of a broad African logic see Chapters 5 to 7 of Chimakonam (2019).

On this reading, what *Ezumezu* gives us are some three distinct categories of beingness: *truth*, *false* and *unity* (where *unity* can be taken to be a complement of *truth* and *false* or *true* and *false*). That is, the Onona-etiti law in *Ezumezu* logic 'accounts for the intermediary values (not altogether true and not altogether false) and includes what was excluded by the classical law of excluded middle' (Chimakonam, draft manuscript: 16).

What We Learn from the Law of Excluded Middle, Acholi Language and *Ezumezu* Logic

What is obvious from the discussion on the law of excluded middle, Acholi language and *Ezumezu* logic is that the law of excluded middle might be problematic from the point of view of certain contexts. Or simply, that the law of excluded middle might be defensible in some contexts or cultural space but not in others. Or that trivalent or polyvalent logic is as viable and plausible as trivalent logic. Whereas a bivalent logic is a two-valued logic, a polyvalent logic and a trivalent logic are respectively many-valued logic and three-valued logic. The classical law of excluded middle is a bivalent logic because it excludes a third category of beingness – something either exists or does not exist; it cannot both exist and not exist or not exist at all. By contrast, trivalent logic allows for the possibility of a third category of beingness – something can (a) exist, (b) not exist, and (c) both exist and not exist. This idea of taking contexts into account in defining logic or whether something exists or not as envisaged in (a)-(c) is what I am referring to as the relativity of logic.

Possible Ground of Trivalent and Polyvalent Logic

What is the possible ground or grounds for thinking that trivalent or polyvalent logic is plausible? One ground is suggested by Ocaya when he says: 'Natural language may be open to the influence of psychological and social factors that are too complex to be reduced to the all-inclusive dichotomy of true or false. So, perhaps a polyvalent logic may be needed to provide for more than two values' (Ocaya, 2004:289). Chimakonam suggests another possible ground. In his discussion of *Ezumezu* Logic and the law of excluded middle, Chimakonam takes *Ezumezu* to give us an alternative logic or logical system and as referring to logic that is dynamic or flexible and three-valued (Chimakonam, draft manuscript; Chimakonam, 2019). However, unlike Ocaya who takes the possibility of trivalent logic to be grounded on language influenced by psychological and social factors, Chimakonam takes reality or ontology to ground it. According to Chimakonam, the additional law that is suggested by *Ezumezu* logic captures the general way reality is reflected in the Igbo language (Chimakonam, draft manuscript; Chimakonam, 2019).

I do think that both Ocaya and Chimakonam are right. And indeed, they both do not disagree. For if one thinks that language shaped by or influenced by psychological and social factors is only but a reflection of what there is, namely reality, then insofar as logic or any logical system reflects language such logic or logical system is grounded in reality. We can represent this as follows:

Language (La) reflects Reality (R)	La = R
Logic or any Logical System (LS) reflects Language (La)	LS = La
Therefore, Logic or Logical System (LS) reflects Reality (R).	/:.LS = R

If we put this in the form of a conditional argument, we will have an argument that looks like this:

If there is any La, then it reflects R	$La \supset R$
If there is LS, then it reflects La	$LS \supset La$
There is La	La
There is LS	LS
Therefore, if there is La, then it reflects R and if there is LS it reflects R	/:.$La \supset R$. $LS \supset R$

If this is right, then what one should investigate as the possible ground for thinking that trivalent or polyvalent logic is plausible is reality (captured by what might be called ontology). But how would such reality look like, in particular, how would an African reality or ontology look like? I now briefly turn my attention to this.

African Reality or Ontology

Various scholars have described the African ontology as holistic and communitarian or communalistic. This ontology can be taken to be non-reductionist and to reject simple binaries (see Bujo, 1998; Sindima, 1990; Tangwa, 2004; Opoku, 1993; Etieyibo, 2014 and 2017; Onyewuenyi, 1991; Murove, 2004; Ijiomah, 2006; Teffo and Roux, 1998). The African ontology does not subscribe to binaries because it does not take reality to be simply a contestation between two *beings* or substances or stuffs. And it is non-reductionist in the sense that it does not reduce reality or the things that are or exist to one single *being* or substance or stuff or thing. So for example, it is not the case that African ontology is idealism or realism and realism; rather, one might say that it is idealism, realism, and both. Also, it is not the case that African ontology is spiritualism or materialism; rather, one might say that it is spiritualism, materialism, and both. This of course contrasts with Western ontology, which thrives in binaries and is reductionist, according to which reality is either idealism or realism (and certainly not both) or spiritualism or materialism (and certainly not both).

Let us illustrate how this sort of communitarian or communalistic and holistic ontology will play out if we are to describe the way one, say humans exist or their *beingness*. If for the sake of getting the reasoning going, we take the worlds of the visible and invisible to be fundamental and given and if we accept that the African communalistic ontology takes the visible and invisible worlds as not disparate, then humans can be said to belong to both worlds. Humans belong to both worlds or between two worlds (the invisible world of invisible beings and the visible world of visible beings). As beings or members of the visible and invisible worlds, humans relate freely with the beings in the two worlds. They relate to the visible world in their daily or regular commute with other beings (humans) of this world. And they relate to the invisible world in their daily or regular commute with spirits (ancestors, living dead and nameless dead). It is this way of describing existence or *beingness* that warrants the claim that the African worldview is communitarian or communalistic and holistic.

If the African ontology, which captures the African worldview/reality, is communalistic and holistic my claim is that logic insofar as it reflects this ontology would also be holistic. By this I mean that the ontology and logic neither takes values to be disparate and bivalent but trivalent where all the values are united in some complementary sense. The idea that African logic does reflect or ought to be thought of as reflecting African ontology should not really be surprising given that there has been growing suggestion that there is a close relationship between African ontology and other areas of African philosophy and that African ontology which captures African reality colors or shapes or influences the other aspects of African philosophy and worldviews (see Ogbonnaya, 2017; Etieyibo, 2017). The point to be taken from all of this is that the claim that in African philosophy what we have is trivalent or polyvalent logic is advanced if it is the case that African ontology is communalistic and holistic just in case it can be argued that African logic reflects African reality or ontology.

Conclusion

If the answer or answers to the question: Are there some logical principles of reasoning by which any given thought system can be judged to be logical or illogical? suggest that logic is in some sense contextual and relativistic, then it is the case that such relativism in the context of African philosophy has further been highlighted by my discussion of logic and the Acholi language and *Ezumezu* logic with specific reference to the disjunction rule and the law of excluded middle. For example, the idea of the relativity of logic – which is a different way of saying that logic is contextual or context sensitive to particular place and culture and to particular views of reality – is the idea that what we have in African philosophy is trivalent or polyvalent logic and not bivalent logic (as we have in Western philosophy).

To conclude let me just highlight one issue that arises from my claim that African logic is trivalent or polyvalent insofar as African ontology is holistic and just in case it can be argued that African logic reflects African reality or ontology. The implication is that if one takes philosophers to be separated by, say, their commitment to ontology and logic, that is some philosophers take what is primordial or what grounds other areas of the philosophical enterprise to be logic and others ontology, then I seem to be siding with the latter. Let us call philosophers that are committed to ontology (i.e. those that take ontology to be primordial) as primordial 'ontologists' and those that take logic to be primordial 'logicians'. The logicians, I will claim, argue that one needs to first establish some logical system, what sort of things are to be admitted into one's rational framework before determining what *stuff* or *beings* or substances there are. By contrast, the ontologists say that the logicians have put the cart before the horse;

and that one first needs to determine what the framework of reality is, what sorts of things exist or can exist before we can determine whether there can only be certain logical categories that capture such stance and understanding of reality. In my taking side with the ontologists in this discussion I can be taken to be saying that ontology is primordial. In which case my claim is that given the argument that African ontology is trivalent, then we should expect that African logic as well as other areas of African philosophy will mirror or reflect this, namely, be trivalent.

References

Aristotle (350 BCE/2018). *Metaphysics*, Translated by W. D. Ross with an Introduction by Edith Johnson. Digireads.com.

Barnes, Barry and Bloor, David (1982). 'Relativism, Rationalism and the Sociology of Knowledge,' in M. Hollis and S. Lukes (eds.), *Rationality and Relativism*, pp21–47, Oxford: Blackwell.

Biakolo, Emevwo (2003). 'Categories of Cross-cultural Cognition and the African Condition,' 2nd edition, in P. H. Coetzee and A. P. J. Roux (eds.), *The African Philosophy Reader*, pp9–21, New York: Routledge.

Bujo, Benezet (1998). *The Ethical Dimension of Community*, Nairobi: Paulines Publications.

Chimakonam, Jonathan (2019). *Ezumezu: A System of Logic for African Philosophy and Studies*, New York: Springer.

Chimakonam, Jonathan (draft manuscript). 'Ezumezu as a Methodological Reconstruction in African Philosophy: Toward Anarchistic (Conversational) Orderliness,'

Etieyibo, Edwin (2014). Psychophysical Harmony in an African Context,' Symposium on the *Metabolism of the Social Brain*, Akademie der Künste, Berlin, Germany, October 25–26, 2014.

Etieyibo, Edwin (2016). 'African Philosophy and Proverbs: The Case of Logic in Urhobo Proverbs,' *Philosophia Africana*, Summer/Fall 2016 18(1): 21–39.

Etieyibo, Edwin (2017). 'Ubuntu and the Environment,' in Adeshina Afolayan and Toyin Falola (eds.), *The Palgrave Handbook of African Philosophy*, pp633–657, New York: Palgrave Macmillan.

Fayemi, Ademola Kazeem (2010). 'The Logic in Yoruba Proverbs,' *Itupale Online Journal of African Studies* 2: 1–14. Also reprinted in Fayemi, Ademola Kazeem (2010). 'The Logic in Yoruba Proverbs,' in Jonathan O. Chimakonam (ed.), *Logic and African Philosophy: Seminal Essays on African Systems of Thought*, pp123–139, Wilmington, Delaware and Malaga: Vernon Press.

Hebga, Meinrad (2020). 'Logic in Africa,' in Jonathan O. Chimakonam (ed.), *Logic and African Philosophy: Seminal Essays on African Systems of Thought*, pp5–14, Wilmington, Delaware and Malaga: Vernon Press.

Hofweber, Thomas (2011). 'Logic and Ontology,' *The Stanford Encyclopedia of Philosophy* (Spring 2021 Edition), Edward N. Zalta (ed.), https://plato.stanford.edu/archives/spr2021/entries/logic-ontology/.

Hollis, Martin (1970). 'Reason and Rituals,' in B. R. Wilson (ed.), *Rationality*, pp231–239, Oxford, Blackwell.

Ijiomah, Chris O. (2006). 'An Excavation of Logic in African Worldview,' *African Journal of Religion, Culture and Society* 1(1): 29–35.

Lévi-Strauss, Claude (1966). *The Savage Mind*, London: Weidenfeld & Nicolson.

Lévy-Bruhl, Lucien (1923). *Primitive Mentality*, London: Allen & Unwin.

——— (1985) (1910). *How Natives Think*, Princeton: Princeton University Press.

Lukes, Steven (1970). 'Some Problems about Rationality,' in B. R. Wilson (ed.), *Rationality*, 208–213, Oxford: Blackwell.

——— (1982). 'Relativism in its Place,' in M. Hollis and S. Lukes (eds.), pp261–305, *Rationality and Relativism*, Oxford: Blackwell.

Mabalane, Keanu Koketso and Etieyibo, Edwin (2020). 'Universal or Particular Logic and the Question of Logic in Setswana Proverbs,' in Jonathan O. Chimakonam (ed.), *Logic and African Philosophy: Seminal Essays on African Systems of Thought*, pp141–172, Wilmington, Delaware and Malaga: Vernon Press.

Momoh, Campbell Shittu (2000). 'The 'Logic' Question in African Philosophy,' 2nd edition, in Campbell S. Momoh (ed.), pp175–192, *The Substance of African Philosophy*, Auchi: African Philosophy Project. Also reprinted in Momoh, Campbell Shittu (2020). The 'Logic' Question in African Philosophy,' in Jonathan O. Chimakonam (ed.), *Logic and African Philosophy: Seminal Essays on African Systems of Thought*, pp189–206, Wilmington, Delaware and Malaga: Vernon Press.

Murove, Munyaradzi Felix (2004). 'An African Commitment to Ecological Conservation: The Shona Concepts of Ukama and Ubuntu,' *Mankind Quarterly* 45: 195–215.

Ocaya, Victor (2004). 'Logic in the Acholi Language,' in Kwasi Wiredu (ed.), *A Companion to African Philosophy*, pp285–294, Oxford, Blackwell.

Ogbonnaya, Lucky (2017). *Between Ontology and Logic: An Interrogation of Chimakonam's Criterion of African Philosophy*, New York: Palgrave Macmillan.

Omoregbe, Joseph (1998). 'African Philosophy: Yesterday and Today,' in Emmanuel Chukwidi Eze (ed.), *African Philosophy: An Anthology*, pp3–8, Oxford: Blackwell Publishing Limited.

Onyewuenyi, Innocent (1991). 'Is There an African Philosophy?,' in Tsenay Serequeberhan (ed.), *African Philosophy: The Essential Readings*, pp29–46, New York: Paragon.

Opoku, Kofi Asare (1993). 'African Traditional Religion: An Enduring Heritage,' in J. Olupona and S. Nyang (eds.), *Religious Plurality in Africa: Essays in Honour of John S. Mbiti*, pp67–82, Berlin and New York: Mouton de Gruyter.

Oruka, Henry Odera (1983). 'Sagacity in African Philosophy,' *International Philosophical Quarterly*, 23(4): 383–396.

Senghor, Léopold Sédar (1956). 'The Spirit of Civilization, or the Laws of African Negro Writers and Artists,' *Presence Africaine, Special Issue*, June–November.

Sindima, Harvey (1990). 'Community of Life,' in Charles Birch, William Eakin, and Jay B. McDaniel (eds.), *Liberating Life*, Maryknoll: Orbis.

Sogolo, Godwin (2003). 'Logic and Rationality,' 2nd edition, in P. H. Coetzee and A. P. J. Roux (eds.), *The African Philosophy Reader*, pp244–258, New York: Routledge.

Teffo, Lesiba J. and Roux, A. P. J. (1998). 'Metaphysical Thinking in Africa,' in P. H. Coetzee and A. P. J. Roux (eds.), *Philosophy from Africa: A Text with Readings*, pp134–148, Johannesburg: International Thomson Publishing Southern Africa.

Tangwa, Godfrey B. (2004). 'Some African Reflections on Biomedical and Environmental Ethics,' in Kwasi Wiredu (ed.), *A Companion to African Philosophy*, Oxford: Blackwell.

Winch, Peter (1958). *The Idea of a Social Science and its Relation to Philosophy*, New York: Routledge & Kegan Paul.

——— (1964). 'Understanding a Primitive Society,' *The American Philosophical Quarterly* 1: 307–324.

5

ANDĀJ

Arjun Appadurai

The Problem[1]

Rural terminologies for measurement, and the ideas and epistemological strategies they embody, present several problems that make them worth investigating. First, they differ radically from contemporary Western, scientific systems in their assumptions and in their popular expressions. Contemporary Western systems regard measurement as a distinct technical activity, subject to rigid and relatively abstract standards; in turn, these standards (as concepts) are sharply distinguished from the instruments of measurement; further, such instruments are clearly separated from the objects or phenomena they are intended to measure. Measurement in the contemporary West, therefore, is regarded as a precise technical activity, theoretically free of social, moral, or cultural coloration, a value-free descriptive activity. This state of affairs, of course, reflects a long and complex historical process, whereby scientific conceptions come to dominate more practical and cosmological ones, and technical progress both encourages and expresses this tendency. It is, of course, outside the scope of this chapter to explore this Western story, but its implications are reasonably clear.[2]

In rural India, by contrast (as in many agricultural communities in the world), the terminology of measurement reflects a radically different universe of meanings and practices. The activity of measurement is interwoven with other modes of evaluation and description. Its terminology does not recognize the boundary between technical, ritual, and everyday activity. The standards embodied in the terminology are frequently simply labels for the instruments of measurement. The instruments are often themselves standardized descriptions of the phenomena or objects themselves. By extension, measurement in such contexts is neither precise nor value-free, but is shot through with the signs of local variation, cosmological symbolism, and the vagueness and approximateness which

DOI: 10.4324/9781003273530-7

characterizes ordinary life. The language of measurement is, therefore, not the 'cool' language of technical description and comparison but the 'hot' language of judgement and evaluation, embedded in particular social contexts and signifying larger cultural and cosmological understandings.

These contrasts, which constitute a significant problem of cross-cultural analysis in their own right, lead to the second problem posed by rural Indian terminologies of measurement, and this is a problem of method for those social scientists concerned with understanding rural life in general, and its agricultural framework in particular. Economists and sociologists (both Indian and Western) come to rural communities armed with just those assumptions, instruments and techniques of measurement which are most alien to the indigenous ethos of measurement. This is, of course, especially true of large, quantitatively oriented, survey-based studies concerned with 'aggregate' patterns of behavior. It is equally true of agronomic and economic studies which, even when they are small-scale, contain the same assumptions. The terminological, cultural, and rhetorical clash this encounter must provoke is rarely acknowledged, much less diagnosed or interpreted. Anthropologists, who might be expected to be more forthright in addressing the problem, given their more holistic, 'humanistic', local and cultural orientation, have also largely avoided the problem, possibly because they have often ignored or underplayed the practical/agricultural aspects of rural life altogether. Historians of rural India have generally done not better, but in their case, they are coping with the double refraction of records that frequently themselves are the product of external and extra-local processes of translation, distortion, and political standardization. There is, therefore, some methodological urgency in trying to describe and interpret rural and local systems of measurement, as far as possible, in their own terms, before leaping in with clocks and censuses, surveys and tape-measures, rain-gauges, and aerial photographs, all of which are a cultural world apart from the human beings they seek to 'measure'. The implications of such caution for research oriented toward agricultural development should need no elaboration. Neither the purposes of scholarship nor those of directed social change are served by ignoring this particular terminological chasm.

The third problem posed by rural terminologies of measurement concerns the contrast between regional and civilizational modes of discourse, within India. As in other kinds of terminology, the language of measurement remains highly localized, idiosyncratic, historically conservative, and relatively intractable to external efforts at standardization. Until the period of colonial rule, rural systems of measurement (whether of land, money, or taxation) remained highly fragmented. Colonial rule, and its post-independence successor, can be read in part as being involved in an uphill battle to subordinate such variation to national (and international) standards. This process continues today and is dealt with toward the end of this chapter. Of course, long before colonial rule, certain Hindu civilizational standards had clearly penetrated rural terminologies. An excellent case is that of the Hindu calendar which today, in some form, affects the rural perception and organization of time. But, as we shall see, this pan-Indian terminology plays a very uneven and sometimes secondary role in rural discourse involving measurement.

To the extent that the indigenous textual tradition contains information relevant to rural modes of measurement, this might be worthy of more systematic investigation, but, in general, these texts are likely to contain a variety of culturally and historically generated standards (how many days should a Brahmana observe death pollution? What is the duration of a nakshatra? What portion of the yield of the land is the king's share? Etc.), rather than revealing the nature of rural systems of measurement, seen as examples of language in use.[3] For, as I hope to show, measurement in rural India is above all a practical activity, rooted in a complex cosmology, but oriented to solving the myriad problems of daily rural life. In this sense, it is likely that all these local systems in India share a good many features (as perhaps do all premodern agricultural systems) but what they share is unlikely to be, except in a superficial sense, a common Hindu terminology. It is also possible to make the case that rural Indian systems of measurement, rooted as they are in agricultural activity, constitute an especially interesting topic of study, because of the relative paucity of premodern texts dealing directly with agriculture. In any case, they constitute an excellent entry into the mentality and ways of knowing of rural folk in India, and a crucial point of contact between peasant discourse and agricultural practice.

If the data contained in this chapter are even reasonably persuasive, they should also make a strong methodological argument: namely, that rural concepts of measurement require not simply to be glossed with their nearest Western equivalents but, like other cultural phenomena, to be interpreted in context. This is what, at least in a preliminary way, I expect to achieve in the remainder of this chapter.

The Ethnographic Context

The descriptive examples in this chapter are the product of a research project conducted in 1981–82 on culture and consumption in a rural community in Maharashtra, here referred to by the pseudonym Vadi (Appadurai, 1984, 1989, 1990, 1991). Vadi is a village in Western Maharashtra in the Purandhar taluka of Poona District. It lies in the mixed ecological zone where the eastern slopes of the Sahyadri mountains (the Western Ghats) give way to the semi-arid drought-prone area of the Deccan Plateau. It is approximately 40 Km southeast of Pune (Poona) and about 6 Km from the market town and taluq headquarters of Saswad. The village consists of approximately 200 hearths,[4] distributed socially and spatially in a bewildering combination of family types and dwellings. About 75% of these families reside in the village proper, while the rest live in about seven clusters of dwellings in the surrounding fields.

Agriculture is virtually the sole means of livelihood in the village, although many households have at least one person working in Poona or Bombay. Land is scarce, and the large majority of farmers own less than 5 acres of land. Irrigated land is less than 25% of the total, and comes mostly from wells powered by electric pumps. Dependence on rainfall is very high, and the average annual precipitation is no greater than 625 mm (25″). Jowar (sorghum) and bajri (pearl millet) are the main crops, and also form the staples of the local diet. Also grown, however, are modest amounts of sugarcane, rice, wheat, pulses, onions, coriander, and a large number of other vegetables. Of the large number of vegetables grown, onions and coriander are grown principally for sale and the remainder are intended primarily for home consumption. Many adult men and women work as agricultural laborers in the villages surrounding Vadi and in Vadi itself, in addition to working their own minuscule plots. The large number of villagers engaged in salaried jobs in Poona and Bombay is regarded as the product of land-scarcity and labor-surplus in Vadi, and as a device to smooth out the unpredictable, and often inadequate yields of local holdings.

The village is dominated by the ideology of subsistence, which may be defined as characterized by a constant fear that income from agriculture will fall short of household consumption needs. Even the big farmers (i.e., those with more than 10 acres of land) share this ideology, although they are in transparently better economic shape than their poorer neighbors. Almost 95% of the families in Vadi belong to the Maratha caste and these are largely divided into five out-marrying patrilineages. There are no more than 15 households belonging to other castes, the bulk of these belonging to what were traditionally regarded as 'untouchable' categories. This gives the village a considerable feeling of social homogeneity which is deepened by the shared subsistence predicament of the majority of families. In an environment characterized by low capital, low and uncertain rainfall, largely unirrigated land, relatively poor soil, tiny holdings, and uncertain cash income from urban employment and local agricultural labor, it is no surprise that men and women in Vadi are deeply preoccupied with the struggle to make ends meet. These struggles result in constant, though perhaps often unspoken, calculation. Such calculation, however, rarely conforms to formal models of planning, choice, estimation of probabilities, scanning of alternatives, or entrepreneurial risk-taking. In what then does it consist? The beginning of an answer to this gigantic question lies in close inspection of local models of measurement, which both underline and symbolize key aspects of this very particular brand of calculation.

The Practical Ethos of Peasant Measurement

The general ethos of peasant measurement can best be grasped by noticing its intimate relationship to a host of practical considerations. Far from representing a technical system externally applied to specific situations, its conceptions and terms are frequently simply historically formed and culturally derived metaphors for these situations. Thus, there are a few abstract and general standards but rather a host of specific terminologies appropriate to different classes of phenomena.

Take the terminology of time, for example: major agricultural moments and key seasonal transitions are referred to in the idiom of the Hindu calendar, and oriented by the complex system of lunar months, nakshatras, and tithis contained in a regional panchānga (almanac). But the key activities of agricultural production (sowing, harvesting, ploughing, etc.) are temporarily demarcated by the gross binary contrast between the kharif- and rabi-growing seasons (roughly June–September and October–February). Yet other issues related to the erratic supply of water, the variable pressure on farmers' time, and the climatic context of agriculture are discussed in terms of the tripartite division of the year into a wet (Pāvsālā), cold (hivālā), and hot (unhālā) season. The term hangām (season) is applied to both the dual and tripartite classifications. Very complex events are often discussed in terms that conflate each of these systems: thus, a marriage may be recollected as having taken place in a certain nakshatra, in the hot season, just before the kharif sowing of sorghum. The same high degree of specificity applies to the measurement of different crop-yields: while the yield of basic grains is measured in poti (a large fiber bag), the yield of onions is measured in bags of different sizes and with another name (pishvī), the yield of coriander (kothimbīr) is measured in khurāda (a small basket) and of sugarcane in truck-loads. Traditional wells are often measured by the number of oxen required to raise the steel containers containing their water, by the number of months during which they yield water, or by the number of farmers who share their water.

It follows from this practical proliferation of terminologies that the standards of measurement are frequently themselves labels for the instruments of measurement. Thus, as in the previous example, the yields of grain and vegetables are frequently measured by standards (bags, bunches, truck-loads, cart-loads, etc.) which are identical with the instruments of measurement themselves. Perhaps the best examples of this conflation of standards and instruments can be seen in the use of the human body for measurement. For agricultural activities that involve the measurement of small lengths, a measure called the pānd is used which refers to an adult's normal pace-length: thus, the width of one farmer's plot which is otherwise undivided from his neighbor's plot is frequently measured in pānd; similarly, a farmer may speak of planting 13 pānd of coriander (although he will measure the yield in the baskets used for collecting the coriander harvest). In a situation where plot-sizes are frequently extremely small, (less than half acre) and where cropping-patterns are extremely involute, the practical function of this measure is obvious.

In domestic or ritual contexts, especially involving informal and small-scale transactions in grain, salt, sugar, flour, or other dry food-items, villagers speak of fist-full (mūth-bhar) or of a vanjala (a measure referring to the full capacity of the two open palms held contiguously). In the planting of onions for the growing of onion-seeds the distance between the plants is measured in hand-spans (vīt) and in the planting of garlic the cloves are spaced three finger-lengths (bota: tin botāche antarane). In a looser and more metaphoric way, meals are often judged as being stomach-filling (pot-bhar) or not, and in estimating the labor requirements of key agricultural tasks (such as ploughing or sowing), complex multivariate standards are referred to which include the variables of number of men ('bodies'), bullocks, and working days.

Just as the standards of measurement are not abstractions distinct from the instruments used in their application (as a mile is distinct from the milestones that embody its extent, and the hour from the hands and the face of the clock that measure its passage), so also the instruments of measurement are often simply standardized forms or metonyms of the objects or phenomena they are used to measure. Thus, distances are frequently measured by reference to the shared practical knowledge of fixed points in the natural or manmade landscape and the duration is frequently measured by reference to collectively recalled events in the past or expected events in the future. This can frequently be frustrating for the investigator who seeks an independent (i.e., abstract) measure of time or space and who in the absence of the shared and tacit experience and knowledge which makes such measures meaningful, responds to them as tautologies which in a certain logical sense they are. (e.g., Question: How far is your family's well from the village? Answer: Just on the other side of the river – nadīchyā palīkade or Question: When did you buy your bullocks? Answer: Just before I planted my kharif bajri last year [kharīf bājrī pernīchā agodar]). Examples of the metonymic relationship between instrument of measurement and object to be measured also abound: garlic-yields are often measured in bunches (pend), rainfall by the degree of run-off in fields, tasks by the amount of men and bullocks and days required to complete them (rather than by such abstractions as man-hours). The extreme examples of such tautological propositions are when, for example, a farmer is asked what his sorghum yield was last season, he replied that it was just enough for his family's consumption needs (gharchyā khānyāsāthi parvadla); or when asked for how many days he has to rent bullocks for the kharif sowing of jowar, he replies that he rents them for as long as it takes to complete the job. Such tautological statements are entirely uninformative to the outside investigator precisely because their experiential and tacit context is not well understood by villagers. The give and take between villagers on matters of measurement, frequently, has this tautological and uninformative quality. In a negative sense, these features of the rural mode of measurement (i.e., the thin line between the standards and the instruments of measurement and the equally thin line between the instruments and the objects/phenomena to be measured) are the product of the lack of precise technologies. But in a positive sense, they result from the fact that the language of measurement is a part and parcel of the practical contexts that have generated it. This context-sensitivity of measurement does not imply that the bewildering array of standards and measures is an atomized and incoherent aggregate. Indeed, the opposite is the case, and in a later section of this chapter, I will address with the relationship between standards and measures.

The observation that rural terminologies of measurement refer to standards, instruments, and measures that are intimately, indissolubly, and intricately rooted in practical contexts immediately directs our attention to the culturally and historically shaped environment in which such terminologies function. The practical wisdom of farmers (of which terminologies of measurement are an essential part) is geared to coping with certain attributes of their environment. This is not, however, to suggest that rural modes of measurement are in any simple way determined by ecological or technological factors. Rather the accumulated cultural and historical experience of a certain set of ecological, technological, and social factors is expressed in the terminology of measurement. The environment of Vadi is characterized by high degrees of variability, uncertainty, and fluctuation in regard to the key phenomena.

Variability characterizes every key feature of the human and natural environment of Vadi. The types of land (both in external agronomic categories as well as in local categories) belonging to the farmers of Vadi vary considerably in terms of depth, moisture-retentiveness, stoniness, slope, and other factors of which local farmers are aware. A few farmers possess contiguous plots with uniform soil properties, and further, these small and fragmented holdings vary in terms of their access to water, their distance from the farmer's home, their exposure to the dangers of grazing animals, and their vulnerability to crop-theft. This social and ecological variability both causes and complicates the extremely convoluted cropping patterns of individual farmers. These cropping-patterns are, in part, efforts to compensate for the variability of their plots, and what they imply is another level of variability in terms of what farmers feel they have to do from day to day, from week to week, from month to month, from season to season, and from year to year. The temporal dimension of variability is uncertainty and this is above all perceived as the central problem regarding rainfall, in Vadi, as in other villages in arid and semi-arid regions. Indeed, coping with the uncertainty of rainfall, in villages such as Vadi, may be regarded as the most continuous and conspicuous preoccupation of farmers: predicting the rainfall, organizing agricultural activities around the fact or expectation of rain, husbanding and allocating rainwater, etc. But rainfall is not the only source of uncertainty: plant disease, labor availability (both for buyers and sellers of labor), and crop-yields are equally perceived as uncertain.

The most frequent quantitative consequence of the variability and uncertainty of the rural world of Vadi, is fluctuation: in crop-yields, in prices for commodities (both bought and sold, both agricultural and household), in supplies of essential goods (like fertilizers, diesel-fuel, and even electricity), in supplies of essential services (like those of laborers or of other specialists). These kinds of variability, uncertainty, and fluctuation permeate the lives of farmers in Vadi. Terminologies of measurement in an environment of this sort, are rooted in practice in a double sense. On the one hand, their extreme specificity and context-rootedness reflect the material conditions of this environment. On the other hand, such terminologies reflect the culturally organized struggle to live tolerable lives, and eke out tolerable livelihoods against the rhythms of such variability, fluctuation, and uncertainty. From this predicament flows a language of measurement, which is intimately linked to the tasks of ordinary life. But ordinary life, in a village like

Vadi, is hardly smooth, regular, or free of surprise. Rural terminologies of measurement, therefore, take on a number of other interrelated properties which are explored in each of the following sections of this chapter.

Measurement as Approximation

Contemporary, scientific modes of measurement may be said to be predicated on the assumption that to be accurate is to be precise. In such rural worlds as that of Vadi, it may well be argued that to be accurate is to be approximate. This feature of peasant discourse involving measurement is in fact, once properly understood, less paradoxical than it seems. At any rate, approximation is the most obvious, ubiquitous, and inescapable feature of peasant discourse about their livelihoods. Its concealment is the single largest methodological weakness of those disciplines that seek to analyze rural life in general and agriculture in particular.

Once recognized, it appears in the form of the following contradiction, which ought to be familiar to anyone who has attempted to study rural life at first hand. On the one hand, most farmers in rural areas impress outside investigators as knowledgeable, thoughtful, and reflective about their own lives and about their agricultural problems. They appear to be constantly weighing their needs, scrutinizing their resources, marshalling their capabilities, and evaluating their prospects. In relation to each of these activities, they strike the observer as being shrewd, calculative, and practical in very specific ways. On the other hand, these very farmers are frequently irritatingly vague in their answers to questions about yields, costs, dates, numbers, and virtually anything else that the investigator wishes to measure precisely. Their replies are often reluctant, their estimates shift even in the course of a single conversation; frequently, they simply do not seem to possess the answers to questions that appear very salient to their lives.

Most agricultural researchers bulldoze their way through this embarrassing contradiction in a variety of ways. The ambiguity, vagueness, and elasticity of a farmer's responses are frequently put down to a variety of factors such as their lack of literacy, their suspiciousness of the motives of the investigators, their lack of precise recording and measuring devices, and the like. These explanations may have something to do with the frustrating imprecision of farmers' discourse about the measurable aspects of their lives, but what I would like to suggest is that such imprecision is indeed part of the calculative wisdom of such farmers, and is part of a terminology of measurement that reflects the conditions in which they function and the kind of flexibility that is most appropriate to the analysis of these conditions.

In my own experience in Vadi, both in conversations with me and in conversations at which I was present, I have almost never witnessed a specific quantitative question which has been answered with a single number or figure. Whether the issue involves time, distance, prices, costs, yields, human or cattle, or electric-pump counts, the reply is almost always given in terms of what may be described as the hyphenated measure i.e. a response which involves two numbers or quantities as if they were a single quantitative evaluation. Examples of such hyphenation are limitless, and exceptions are few and striking. Ask a farmer how many acres of land he owns and he is likely to reply: 7–8 (sat-āth) acres; ask him when he is going to harvest his onions and the reply may well be that he will do so in 6–7 (sahā-sāt) days. Ask him how often his onions have to be watered and he might say 12–15 times. When one farmer asks another when next he is going to Poona, he is likely to reply that he will do so in 2–4 weeks, or when one villager tells another when they will meet to discuss a matter of mutual interest, he might suggest 3–4 p.m. (tīn-chār vājtā). Ask a villager about the cost of fertilizer for his coriander crop and he is likely to report that it was 50–60 rupees. Ask him how many women he employed last year to harvest his onions and a typical reply would be 8–10.

It would be easy to attribute such hyphenated terminology to various disabilities of farmers like illiteracy, poor memory, bad records, poor instruments, and downright mental laziness. In some cases, these charges may well have some basis. What I would like to suggest, however, is that this hyphenated terminology, especially for numerical measurement, is directly related to the variability, uncertainty, and fluctuation that characterized their condition, and which I discussed in the previous section on the ethos of measurement. For every hyphenated measure cited in the previous paragraph, it is possible to make the case that the underlying problem is one of these three features of their situation. However, much a farmer may wish to be sure when in the coming week he is going to harvest his onions, the coordination of labor, with his own other commitments, and with weather conditions, makes it ridiculous to be committed to a specific day, even within a short foreseeable future. How often he waters his onions depends on the precise frequency of rainfall during the growing season (which is uncertain), the plot on which he is obliged to grow them, the functioning of the electric pump of the well in which he has a time-share (pālī), and so on. His plans to go to Poona are constrained by such a large variety of contingent circumstances which constrain him that only a loose plan makes sense. As for prices, whether of fertilizer, labor, or other goods, these fluctuate sufficiently (from season to season and sometimes from week to week, from job to job, from village to village) that only hyphenated responses are reasonably adequate. Even in the seemingly straightforward case of the amount of land he owns, the farmer has to consider his fallow lands (some of which are permanent, fallows and therefore are countable in one sense and discountable in another) and those portions which are taken up by wells, channels, hedges, cattle or human paths, threshing-grounds, storage areas for the piles (buchchād) of harvested, but unthreshed grain, and so forth. In this last case, of course, some farmers do give precise responses based on the amounts to which they hold legal title in the land-records, while others give the more accurate hyphenated response.

This phenomenon of hyphenation in indigenous rural terminologies of measurement, then, can be succinctly characterized as a perfectly reasonable, and accurate, tendency to respond to a certain class of quantitative enquiries with ranges rather than absolute unilateral measures. Replies framed in terms of ranges reflect the ongoing effort of farmers to typify experiences of quantity which are frequently characterized by uncertainty and fluctuation and only rarely by certainty and fixity. It must be added that this is not only characteristic of farmers' responses to the quantitative enquiries of the outside observer but is entirely characteristic of their verbal transactions with each other. Needless to say, this aspect of the terminology of measurement causes considerably more frustration to the investigator seeking single and unambiguous responses, than to the actors themselves who share the knowledge and experience of the host of variables that encourage the language of ranges and discourage the language of discrete measures.

Yet even this is a very rough and excessively functionalist account of the role of approximation in the terminology of measurement in Vadi, and the hyphenated measure is only one aspect of the rhetoric of approximation. The statements in which such hyphenated measures occur, when closely examined, reveal that farmers, in making estimates of quantity, do not typically distinguish what, from the external point of view, appear to be facts from possibilities and these in turn from norms or standards. Thus, a question about the yield of a particular crop may be answered with a hyphenated measure referring to the occurrence of such a yield (don poti jhālī), or to the regular (i.e., typical) occurrence of such a yield (don poti hotāt/miltāt), or to the predictable amount of the yield (don poti milel). These locutions are frequently used interchangeably without any systematic effort to distinguish them conceptually. Of course, this terminological ambiguity varies somewhat in regard to issues involving the past as opposed to the future, but this is more a grammatical than a conceptual qualification. Of course, under heavy prodding by the investigator, farmers are willing to specify which of these they actually mean in any given context (fact; possibility; regularity), and further can be coaxed to substitute single measures for hyphenated ranges, as they doubtless are frequently made to do. The point is that in their everyday discourse with each other they neither feel nor exert pressure for such elimination of ambiguity.

This property of peasant discourse involving measurement might be briefly characterized by its preponderance of subjunctives (may be, might be, could be, might have been, could have been, etc.). This role of the subjunctive mood in the language of measurement has implications for the relationship between measures and standards in such a system, which are explored in a later section. For the moment, it is simply worth remarking that the frequent use of hyphenated measures is not a direct function of uncertainty, variability, and fluctuation in the measurable environment but of these factors culturally mediated through a terminology that tends to conflate specific events, their ranges of possibility, the regularities which typify them, and the standards to which they ought to conform.

In a world dominated by measurement as approximation, farmers are frequently self-conscious and aware of this dimension of their everyday discourse.

As a result, a kind of meta-language of approximation has evolved, which is employed in much discourse regarding measurement. Thus, farmers frequently use the word andāj (meaning rough or approximate) to qualify this or that proposition. Thus, it may be said that last year's yield of sorghum was roughly (andāje) 2–3 poti or that the almanac gives them a rough idea of when to expect rainfall (panchāngātun pāvsāchā andāj milte). Related terms in this meta-language of approximation are javal-javal (near-about), kamī-jāsta (more or less), and, in the case of more sophisticated villages, sarāsarī (average). Used in combination with the grammar of the subjunctive, discussed previously, these terms punctuate the language of measurement and draw even the most precise assertions into the world of the approximate. Measurement as approximation implies a certain kind of social and cultural world which is discussed in the following section.

Measurement as Negotiation

Given the intimate link of local modes of measurement to practical contexts and their frequent expression in the language of the approximate, it further follows that the activity of measurement is, in a very important sense, a social activity. Given the paucity of abstract standards and the dearth of instruments distinct from the objects they are meant to measure, individuals are not perceived to have direct or independent access to the measures of their environment. Measurement, therefore, is always seen as a matter of opinion, and rarely as a matter of firm, or final, or indisputable knowledge. This is simply a different perspective on the terminology of the subjunctive discussed in the previous section. This terminology, by its very nature, is the language of uncertainty and of estimation. By extension, either explicitly or implicitly, it belongs to the idiom of give and take, of debate, of negotiation. This is always implicit in discussions of measurement. But it is frequently explicit.

The contrast between measurement as opinion and measurement as knowledge not simply is a surface characteristic of rural discourse, but I think characterizes an important set of implicit epistemological assumptions about the limits on the knowability of certain phenomena. Given the various characteristics of the ethos of rural measurement discussed earlier, it makes sense that measurement can never be certain, and the capacity to measure is rarely subject to the kind of technical and abstract methods which make it equally, and impersonally, available to each person. Whether by consensus, or by conflict, measurement is always a social activity, in which persons pool their respective estimates to arrive at some final, socially sanctioned estimate. In their culturally and experimentally ossified forms such estimates become standards, quantitative products of a particular social, cultural, and historical experience of a given environment.

The exchange of estimates almost always characterizes discussions about measure. But even when there is no explicit discussion of measures, negotiation, and a potential plurality of estimates is always acknowledged. This does not mean that the tone of such opinions, for example when farmers are discussing the yields of hybrid grains on a particular piece of land, is always hesitant or tentative. Opinions can be held deeply and voiced dogmatically. But it is recognized that other opinions are always possible in most matters of measurement. So also, the opinion of some (believed to be wiser, shrewder, older, better informed, etc.) may affect the final consensus more than that of others, but it is precisely the social role of the various opinion-holders and the social framework of the particular context which determines the consensus measure, rather than reference to any abstract, context-free, value-neutral standard, or instrument of measure. This is as true of discussion about yields, prices and crop-mixtures, as it is of debate about land-holdings, village population figures, or frequency of rainfall.

It is, of course, true that the more public, collective, and aggregate the phenomenon, the more its measurement consists of opinions, and the more private, individual, and singular the phenomenon the more its measures are likely to be spoken of as matters of 'fact' and not of opinion. But this is only tendency, and it is very rarely that the matters of measurement are regarded entirely as matters of fact. Thus, it is not at all rare, for a question regarding the age of a particular individual, to lead to a lively discussion, in which the respondent himself is accorded no special epistemic privilege and is viewed as expressing one legitimate opinion among many. Thus, when the investigator encounters a particular measure (say of the population of the village) invariably in his discussions, it is not so much because this measure is a product of some context-free tool of enumeration, but rather because there is such complete agreement on it that opinions on it have become standardized, and the fact has become, in Pierre Bourdieu's sense, 'official'.

If this analysis of the socially negotiated nature of measurement is reasonable, then it follows that the frequently noted 'bargaining' or 'haggling' characteristic of premodern bazaar behavior is not simply a function of imperfect markets and socially embedded economic transactions but is rooted in the idea that all measurement is opinion and all valuation is negotiable. Similarly, it has frequently been noted that in dispute-settlement in peasant contexts, the effort is frequently to arrive at a socially acceptable compromise rather than an abstract 'just' decision. What has not been so clearly seen is that measurement itself is a socially negotiated activity, no more subject to abstract measures than other matters of dispute or debate.

Conclusion

It would have been natural to conclude this chapter with some discussion of the relationship between measurement and social change in Vadi, but any detailed discussion of this topic would be out of place, since almost four decades have lapsed since I conducted the fieldwork on which this chapter is based, and I have not had a chance to go back to Vadi. In any case, the short duration of fieldwork is hardly the best lens into this kind of change, which involves small and subtle shifts over large spans of time. But a few comments may not be inappropriate. Vadi, like rural communities all over the world, is now subject to stronger and more rapid external forces than ever before. Banks and markets, clocks and calendars, surveys and salaries, census-forms and ration-cards, electric-pumps and electricity-bills, fertilizer factories, and radios: each of these, over the last decades, represents new symbols of precision in a world of approximation. Common to many of these agents of precision is the phenomenon of cash, the rapid process of monetization of a subsistence economy. On the whole, however, it seems as if growing precision in the standards and instruments of measurement had not in the early 1980s significantly affected the mentality of calculation and the ethos of measurement.

This ethos remains rooted in agricultural practices and conceptions which are of considerable antiquity. The language of measurement continues to blur the line between standards and instruments as well as between instruments and the object to be measured. The grammar of this language continues to be dominated by approximation, and the activity of measurement is still regarded as subject to social negotiation, rather than to abstract, independent, or context-free standards. Such shifts as have occurred are largely shifts in vocabulary: kilos have replaced seers and maunds, hectares sometimes replace acres and gunthas, Western names for months occasionally replace their indigenous counterparts. But the larger ethos of measurement, as it has been described in this chapter, changes slowly and imperceptibly. For those of us who practice a social science based on quite other ideas of measurement, some rethinking of method appears to be indicated.

Notes

1 Since this chapter is not elaborately footnoted, let me note some prior work that has been extremely influential in the formulation of the ideas contained here. In regard to the general approach to the analysis of cultural systems, I owe a great deal to the many writings of Clifford Geertz, in particular an essay called 'Common Sense as a Cultural System' (1975). Equally influential, especially in regard to the cultural ethos of peasantry, has been *Outline of a Theory of Practice* by Pierre Bourdieu (1977) and, by the same author, 'The Attitude of the Algerian Peasant Toward Time' (1963). I have also benefitted by a great deal of work by agro-economists working in India. In particular, I have derived much benefit from the prolific writings of N.S. Jodha on the agricultural economics of the semi-arid tropics (for one example see, Jodha 1992).

2 This essay is based on fieldwork done in 1981–82 in rural Maharashtra. For a variety of reasons, it was never published. I have changed as little as possible of the tone and tense, since it is my view that the terms and concepts of agricultural measurement do not change much in short periods of time. Still, this essay should be read as an effort to capture a rural epistemology at a specific moment in time in order to open a discussion about the durability of such an epistemology and how it might change over time.

3 Although a detailed discussion of the ancient roots of current rural systems of measurement is outside the scope of this paper, mention should be made of a first-class book by Saradha Srinivasan, *Mensuration in Ancient India* (1979). This study provides a superb overview of the textual as well as the inscriptional material relevant to ancient Indian measurement, and, amongst other things, indicates the rural and practical origin of many classical terms of measure.

4 The facts and figures in the following paragraph are tentative, since the results of a survey conducted by the author are still not fully analyzed.

References

Appadurai, A. (1984) 'Wells in Western India: Irrigation and Cooperation in an Agricultural Society', *Expedition* 26 (3), pp. 3–14.

———. (1989) 'Small-Scale Techniques and Large-Scale Objectives', in Bardhan, P. (ed.) *Conversations Between Economists and Anthropologists*. New Delhi: Oxford University Press, pp. 250–282.

———. (1990) 'Technology and the Reproduction of Values in Western India', in Marglin, S.A. and Marglin, F.A. (eds.) *Dominating Knowledge: Development, Culture and Resistance*. Oxford: Clarendon Press, pp. 185–216.

———. (1991) 'Dietary Improvisation in an Agricultural Economy', in Sharman, A., Theophano, J., Curtis, K., and Messer, E. (eds.) *Diet and Domestic Life in Society*. Philadelphia: Temple University Press, pp. 207–232.

Bourdieu, P. (1963) 'The Attitude of the Algerian Peasant Toward Time', in Pitt-Rivers, J.A. (ed.) *Mediterranean Countrymen: Essays in the Social Anthropology of the Mediterranean*. Paris: Mouton, pp. 55–72.

———. (1977) *Outline of a Theory of Practice*. Cambridge (UK): Cambridge University Press.

Geertz, C. (1975) 'Common Sense as a Cultural System', *The Antioch Review*, 33 (1), pp. 5–26.

Jodha, N.S. (1980) 'Intercropping in Traditional Farming Systems', *The Journal of Development Studies*, 16 (4), pp. 427–442

Srinivasan, S. (1979) *Mensuration in Ancient India*. Delhi: Ajanta Publications.

6

IZITHUNGUTHU

John Wright and Cynthia Kros

The Journey of a Word

In the period May–June 1903, in the course of research that he was privately doing on the histories and cultural practices of Africans in the colony of Natal, magistrate James Stuart held intensive discussions on the past at his home in Durban with 89-year-old Thununu kaNonjiya Gcabashe. As they spoke, Stuart made notes of his interlocutor's statements. On 10 June, in the margin of one of his notebooks, he scribbled a record of a comment apparently made to him by Gcabashe: 'You can write and remember but *tina* [*si*] *izitungutu nje*' – for our part we are simply *izitungutu*.[1]

Stuart's notes of his conversations with Gcabashe today form part of the James Stuart Collection, which since the late 1940s has been lodged in the Killie Campbell Africana Library in Durban. The core of the collection consists of records that he made in the period from the late 1890s to the early 1920s of discussion with some 200 individuals on the history of what is now the KwaZulu-Natal region. It forms the single most important archive of evidence on the history of African societies in the region from the mid-eighteenth century onward. The chapter that we present here is part of ongoing work that we and others are doing on Stuart's working methods and on the lives of his discussants, Thununu Gcabashe among them.

In making notes of his conversations with isiZulu-speaking discussants, it was Stuart's common practice to jot down words and phrases that were new to him. In this particular case, he did not indicate what the word *izitungutu* meant, though his underlining of it suggests that he wanted to investigate the issue further. We wonder where any enquiries he made would have taken him. There is no entry for *isitungutu*, the singular form of the word, in A.T. Bryant's major *Zulu-English Dictionary* of 1905 (Bryant, 1905). The only place where we have

DOI: 10.4324/9781003273530-8

been able to find it is in the fourth edition of Bishop John Colenso's *Zulu-English Dictionary*, also published in 1905. Here *isitungutu* is given as 'One flustered or put out, made to forget by being scolded or cross-questioned, though well-informed' (Colenso, 1905, p. 627).

These are the only written mentions of the word *isithunguthu* (to give it in modern orthography) that we have so far come across. The word does not appear in modern isiZulu dictionaries, and was not known to isiZulu-speaking academics whom we consulted in 2014 and 2015. Today it appears to be unknown outside the small circle of scholars to whom it has been introduced since 2014. If it has ever had much of a public life, we have not yet seen the evidence for it.

What did Gcabashe actually mean in uttering the word in the way he did to Stuart? In using the word *izitungutu*, to whom was he referring? Why did he describe himself to a colonial official as one of them? Did he have in mind a distinct category of people, or merely a loose plural number? Who were the 'you' that he sets against the 'we'? And what did Stuart's writing down of oral accounts of the past signify to him? These are some of the basic questions that engaged us as we began thinking about the conversation between the two men, and that have shaped the discussion in this chapter.

As we describe in more detail below, John Wright first came across Stuart's note on *izitungutu*, and started thinking about the meaning of the word, in 2013. It was another two years or so, in the course of research that we were doing together into the nature of the archive of the times before European colonialism in Southern Africa, before we began to think jointly about the possible significance not only of the word *izitungutu* as used by Gcabashe but also of the sentence in which it was embedded. What Gcabashe was in effect saying, it seemed to us, was, 'In the face of written history, we are becoming put out about the standing of our own knowledges of the past', with the 'we' referring to African narrators of oral history.

If this was indeed the meaning that he intended, he was making a powerful comment on the changing nature of knowledge-making in colonial Natal in the early twentieth century. From his position as an elder deeply invested in shaping oral accounts of the past, he was referring to a moment in his experience of developments which had seen African oral discourses about the past becoming progressively marginalized, and in many ways effaced and supplanted, by the written discourses of the European colonizers who had governed much of the region since the 1840s. Before his own eyes, the old man was witnessing the setting-down and fixing of his statements about the past in a form that ultimately he had no control over.

Gcabashe's statement about *izithunguthu* is a rare comment from a knowledgeable oral narrator of the past. In this chapter, we make a preliminary exploration of the contexts in which it was made. We first recount how Stuart's note was rediscovered and taken up by academic historians. We briefly explore the possible circumstances in which it found its way into Colenso's *Dictionary*. We then go on to discuss Stuart's notes of his conversations with Gcabashe, as rendered in volume 6 of the published *James Stuart Archive* (Gcabashe, 2014), in a way that combines historical contextualizing with a close textual reading. We focus closely on the nature of the exchanges between the two men, with the aim of bringing out how Gcabashe was working to articulate his relationship with the magistrate who had invited him to talk about the past. We seek to hear both Stuart's and Gcabashe's voices more clearly, and hence hear something of the wider resonances of the word *isithunguthu*.

Our approach to the meaning of *isithunguthu* has shifted slightly since we wrote the version of the paper that we presented to the conference held by the Centre for Indian Studies in Africa in Johannesburg in October 2016. Our original title, '*Isithunguthu* – one who knows but is made to forget', highlighted the notion of 'forgetting' in the gloss given in the Colenso *Dictionary*. A commentator at a workshop of the Archive and Public Culture Research Initiative at the University of Cape Town in November 2016 made the point that it might be more productive to think about Gcabashe's statement as coming from a person who had been 'flustered or put out' rather than 'made to forget'. We have taken up this perspective, as it makes for a less categorical and more open-ended reading of his statement. Our chapter is in part about the journey of a word, in part about the intellectual journeys of Gcabashe and Stuart at specific points in their lives, and in part about our own journey in thinking about *izithunguthu*.

Rediscovering '*Isithunguthu*'

Sometime after it had appeared in Stuart's notes and in Colenso's *Dictionary*, the word *isithunguthu* seems to have fallen out of the vocabulary of isiZulu-speaking intellectuals. As we note above, it does not appear in any of the isiZulu dictionaries published since that time. In effect, the word did not begin to resurface until 2013 when, in the process of editing Stuart's notes of his conversations with Gcabashe for publication in volume 6 of the *James Stuart Archive*, Wright came across the marginal note quoted above. He found it an intriguing enough statement for him to make his own note of it, which he put away in a file, marked 'Sense of History among Stuart's Informants', that he had been keeping for much of the long period he had spent in working on Stuart's papers.

In editing Gcabashe's statement, Wright was unable to establish a clear meaning for *isithunguthu*. Influenced by the tenor of earlier conversations about the nature of 'civilization' between Stuart and certain of his *amakholwa* (Christian) interlocutors,[2] he saw the word as possibly derived from the verb *ukuthungulula*, to open the eyes, discover, untie, undo. In the event, this was the gloss that was published in volume 6 of the *James Stuart Archive* the following year (Gcabashe, 2014, pp. 289, 312). The implication was that Gcabashe was having his eyes opened by what he was learning in his conversations with Stuart – which is something radically different from the meaning of *isitungutu* given in the Colenso *Dictionary*.

Wright's discovery of the entry in Colenso came soon after volume 6 of the *James Stuart Archive* had gone to press. In the second quarter of 2014, Carolyn Hamilton, National Research Foundation Chair in Archive and Public Culture at the University of Cape Town, and a leading figure in the study of Southern Africa's past before the colonial period, was drawing up a call for papers for a conference that she was planning on the making of the different forms of archive pertinent to this past. At the end of July, she wrote to Wright, with whom she had worked on research papers over a long period, to express her view that the title of the conference should come out of the *James Stuart Archive*. This gave Wright the incentive to go back to his files, from which he picked out the note on Gcabashe's comment. In once again puzzling over the meaning of '*izitungutu*', he turned to Colenso's previously neglected *Dictionary*, and discovered that Gcabashe had meant something quite different from what he had originally thought. It seemed that the old man was commenting on what recording of the past in writing was doing to the oral histories known by *izithunguthu* like himself. Wright indicated this in a letter to Hamilton in August 2014, and went on:

> If this is the case, then Thununu is speaking directly to the issue that you raise in the proposal [for the conference] about the historical erasure of the oral archive. It seems to me a statement that deserves to be brought in somehow, about an extraordinarily important historiographical moment.

Hamilton at once picked up the word *isithunguthu* as saying something significant about the nature of discussion among intellectuals in rural African societies of the time. Her response was to headline the word in the title of the proposed conference: '*Izithunguthu*: Southern African Pasts before the Colonial Era, Their Archives and Their Ongoing Present/Presence'. In her call for papers, she featured Gcabashe's comment, together with the entry for *isitungutu* in the Colenso *Dictionary*, as epigrams. And so, the word was launched into the wider academic world.

The conference, held at the University of Cape Town in July 2015, was attended by some fifty people. How far the word has lodged in their historical consciousness, and how far it has since circulated beyond members of this group, are things we cannot know. By the same token, we cannot know how far the word was taken up by the audience of several dozen who heard Wright speak at the launch of volume 6 of the *James Stuart Archive* at the conference of the Southern African Historical Society held at the University of Stellenbosch two weeks before the APC conference.

For her part, Kros was excited by the possibilities that the word *izithunguthu* seemed to open up when she first heard Wright speak about it at the Stellenbosch conference. She had been working on more contemporary narratives articulated by the widows of the striking miners killed at Marikana by the police in 2012 (Kros, 2017). The women were determined to overturn the dominant images disseminated by the mining industry and its allies of their dead husbands as barbarians. The women well understood how much harm a particular narrative could do to their search for justice and compensation. For Kros, there was a link with the idea that more than a hundred years previously an isiZulu-speaking man had commented to a British colonial official on the advantage that written narrative had over those who tried to retain their remembered history against its onslaught. In 2016, when this chapter was written for a conference on concepts from the Global South, widespread student protests were taking place in South Africa, and calls for the decolonization of knowledge in the country's educational institutions were being loudly voiced. The proposed conference seemed to be an ideal forum for bringing the notion of *isithunguthu* to the attention of a wider academic audience, and further opening up discussion of its significance.

Finding a Focus

Our first idea was to argue for the usefulness of the notion of *izithunguthu* as a label for protagonists of a particular, and today little known, set of discourses about the past in late-colonial Natal, that is, of oral discourses current among Africans living in the rural areas. We aimed to set our discussion against consideration of two other sets of discourses about the past that were then being articulated in the colony and elsewhere in Southern Africa. One was developing among the British settlers who were in the final stages of making themselves politically dominant in the subcontinent. The other was developing among the small but growing group of *amakholwa*, or Christian Africans, who were seeking a place in colonial society on a par with that of Europeans.

In the event, we quickly moved on from this idea. We realized that, historically, the supposedly distinct discourses that we were in the process of identifying had drawn on one another in ways that the literature had hardly begun to examine.[3] Our ideas on how to focus the paper began firming up after Kros had done a first-pass reading of Stuart's lengthy notes of his conversations, extending over the years 1897–1922, with Socwatsha kaPhaphu Ngcobo. In contrast to the contextualizing approach to Stuart's notes that Wright had developed over years of editorial work on them, Kros was interested in probing what a close textual reading could reveal about the nature of the conversations between Stuart and his discussants. It seemed logical that we should combine the two approaches in an examination of the record of Stuart's conversations with Gcabashe to see if it could help us establish more clearly where his comment on *izithunguthu* had come from.

Putting '*Isithunguthu*' into Writing

We do not know what the roots of the meaning of *isithunguthu* are, nor how far back in time they go. What resonances did the word carry in the era before the coming of writing to the KwaZulu-Natal region in the second quarter of the nineteenth century? They could not have been about writing and remembering:

were they about being knowledgeable but thrown off balance by questioning on the part of authorities in African societies? Or did the word have other meanings, now lost, and did it begin to resonate in the particular way that we discuss in this chapter only as colonial rule bore down more heavily on the African inhabitants of the colonies of Natal and, subsequently, Zululand in the later nineteenth century? These questions remain open as we discuss the biography of the word *isithunguthu* in the early twentieth and early twenty-first centuries.

For numbers of Africans who experienced the questioning and breaking down of their knowledge of particular matters by magistrates and lawyers in the unfamiliar and often hostile environment of the colony's law courts, the meaning of *isitungutu* as given in the Colenso *Dictionary* of 1905 would have made much sense. It is significant that the word does not appear in the first edition of the *Dictionary*, published in 1861 (Colenso, 1861), when colonial rule in Natal did not yet lie heavily on most of the African population. Nor does it appear in the third edition, published in 1884 (Colenso, 1884), and probably seen through the press by the Bishop's daughter Harriette after his death the previous year. But by 1905, the word was widely enough in circulation among isiZulu-speaking people for it to have come to the notice of Harriette Colenso (and perhaps other persons who may have helped her to revise the *Dictionary*), and for her to have included it in the edition published that year. Colenso was herself a fluent speaker and writer of isiZulu (Guy, 2003, p. 347) and, as Jeff Guy has shown, had had long experience of discussions with Africans who had suffered at the hands of colonial authority in Zululand and Natal (Guy, 2001). She had also had prolonged experience of the workings of the colonial law courts through her involvement in the defense of Dinuzulu kaCetshwayo and others accused of treason after the Zululand rebellion of 1888 (Guy, 2001).

For the contemporary meaning of *isithunguthu* to become clearer, we need to know much more than we do about intellectual currents of the time in Natal and Zululand. We need to know particularly how ideas about the past and present were being made and circulated among African people in the rapidly changing societies of the rural areas, such as the society that Gcabashe lived in. Recently this subject has become the focus of a number of probing academic studies (Hamilton, 1998; Mokoena, 2011; Hamilton and Leibhammer, 2016; Hamilton, 2021), but as a field of research, it is still in a comparatively early stage of development.

Thanks to James Stuart's practice of assiduously making notes of his conversations on the past with his interlocutors, we have some idea of the circumstances in which the word *izithunguthu* was brought to written life in the interchange between him and Gcabashe. From the 1970s, annotated renditions of his notes of the conversations he held with his discussants, with passages originally recorded in isiZulu translated into English, have been published by the University of Natal Press (from 2002, the University of KwaZulu-Natal Press) in the successive volumes of the *James Stuart Archive* (Webb and Wright 1976-2014). In this chapter, we base our discussion on the materials in the published volumes for ease of access on the part of the reader. At the same time, we would like to highlight a point made elsewhere by Carolyn Hamilton (2011, pp. 335–8) and by Wright (2015, pp. 144–6) that the reorganized, edited, and translated texts in the *James Stuart Archive* cannot be seen as identical to the original notes in the Stuart Papers. Nor, to draw in brief on a perspective developed by Hamilton (2015) over years of research, can either the original notes or the edited renderings be seen in any simple way as records of what are commonly called 'oral traditions'. Rather, they are notes of conversations about the past which were shaped by views of history held by both Stuart and his discussants, and by their particular interests at the time of their conversations.

The Context of a Conversation

From Stuart's notes of his conversations with Thununu kaNonjiya, we learn that the latter was of the Gcabashe offshoot of the Qwabe clan. According to Stuart's reckoning, he was born in about 1814 (Gcabashe, 2014, pp. 280, 309), in other words, a little before the rise of the Zulu chief Shaka to political prominence in the KwaZulu-Natal region. He grew up in the South-East of the emerging Zulu kingdom in a region previously ruled by a succession of Qwabe chiefs. As a young man, he served as an *inceku*, or personal attendant, in the household of Dingane, who succeeded Shaka as Zulu king after being party to his assassination in 1828. Much of what Gcabashe told Stuart about his own life consisted of anecdotes about his experiences in this role. Sometime after the overthrow of Dingane in 1840 by his brother Mpande, supported by parties of Boer settlers from the Cape, Gcabashe left the Zulu kingdom to go and live in the region south of the Thukela River, which was annexed by the British as the colony of Natal in 1843. Here he lived and worked for many years, and then at some stage moved back north of the Thukela to an area near the country of his Qwabe ancestors. During his long life, he seems to have acquired a reputation as a person with deep knowledge of the past. It was this that brought him to the attention of James Stuart, then a magistrate in Durban, who in 1903 invited Gcabashe to visit him to discuss Qwabe history and custom (Wright, 2019, pp. 1-4).

For his part, Stuart had been born in Natal in 1868, and had been brought up in the colony and educated in England. He grew up speaking isiZulu in addition to his native English, and from 1888 held posts in the administration of native affairs in Zululand, which had been annexed as a British colony in 1887, and in Natal. From the late 1890s, he devoted much of his spare time to researching both published works and oral accounts on the history and customs of local African societies, and within a few years was aspiring to make himself the leading authority in this field. Though he shared many of the racial prejudices of the British settlers who dominated the politics of Natal, his prime motive was to establish as clear and detailed a picture as possible of the 'traditional Zulu' system of government in order to try to inform the making of native policy in Natal. As he saw it, British settler governments in the colony were heading in a dangerous direction by working to undermine the powers exercised by African chiefs over their adherents. In his experience, settlers in Natal more generally held ignorant and deeply prejudiced views of African ways of life (Wright, 1996; Hamilton, 1998; Hamilton, 2011; Wright, 2015).

Stuart was beginning his historical researches at a time when, historians generally agree, many African homesteads in Natal were facing conditions of crisis. Since at least the late 1870s, African communities in the colony had been experiencing increasingly severe shortages of land. In the later 1890s, many homesteads had been brought to the point of collapse by a series of droughts, locust invasions, and epidemics of cattle disease. On top of this, unsympathetic colonial governments dominated by white settlers were tightening up pass laws and increasing taxes on Africans in order to force them to become laborers in the towns and on white-owned farms (Marks, 1970; Lambert, 1995; Carton, 2000). Racially discriminatory laws, compounded by racist treatment at the hands of white officials and settlers, were keenly felt by Africans throughout the colony, as Stuart himself recorded in conversations with numbers of discussants.

Stuart's commitment to his ongoing project for developing as informed a knowledge as he could of African history and custom was very unusual for an official in a settler colony like Natal. Like most of his fellow colonists, he believed firmly that for the foreseeable future Africans should be governed by Europeans along 'traditional' lines, but in his case, this belief was combined with a strong respect for traditional cultural practices and a concern to understand them in depth in order to try to arrive at a more just system of governance. We learn from his notes of other conversations that, from very early in his career as a researcher, he engaged with his discussants in a way that often allowed for a relatively free exchange of ideas with them.[4] He saw these conversations not simply as a source of 'factual' information, but as a means of producing through argumentation the kind of knowledge that could inform better policy-making (Kumalo, 1976, p. 241). Knowledge, like light, he felt, was produced through friction, in this case, the friction of different ideas (Kumalo, 1976, p. 244).

Sometimes, as in a contentious debate with Lazarus Mxaba in Ladysmith, Stuart could resort to a certain amount of provocation to stimulate discussion (Kumalo, 1976, pp. 254–65). But in this particular case, Stuart afterward wrote that their arguments had led him to accept that 'that single mind with which I conversed was fully equal to my own, and therefore the owner (and all his race) must be worthy of belonging to that communion to which I belong' (Kumalo, 1976, p. 264). He saw dissent as productive of ideas, which may explain why later, in his conversations with Gcabashe, Stuart was prepared to let him follow his own train of thought.

Gcabashe as a Discussant of the Past

Early in his career as a magistrate, Stuart was posted to a number of different centers in Zululand, Swaziland, and Natal. His appointment as assistant magistrate in

Durban in March 1901 enabled him to establish a more settled existence, and to conduct his researches along the lines he had developed in Ladysmith. Gcabashe's name as a potential discussant of the past came up in the course of a conversation in Durban on 9 May 1903 between Stuart and Ndlovu kaThimuni (Zulu, 1986, p. 218), a leading figure in one of the houses of the Zulu clan who was a government-recognized chief in the Mapumulo district. At the time, Gcabashe was living at eNdulinde west of Gingindlovu on the outskirts of the old Qwabe country in southeastern Zululand. Stuart's approach to him was through Chief Magidi kaNgomane of the Mdletsheni clan in the Lower Tugela division, who sent one of his sons to fetch Gcabashe and accompany him to Durban (Gcabashe, 2014, p. 252). The journey would have involved walking perhaps ten kilometers (fortunately in the cool season of an often sweltering climate) from his home to the nearest station on the line of rail that was then being pushed north through coastal Zululand, and catching a train to Durban. He and his companion then made their way (by tram?) to Stuart's home in Musgrave Road on the Berea ridge overlooking the town. Gcabashe seems previously to have lived and worked in Natal for many years and had five children living in Durban, so was probably no stranger to the town (Gcabashe, 2014, pp. 258, 298).

This brings us to the question of why Gcabashe felt impelled to undertake what for him must have been quite an arduous journey and to talk about the past for nearly three weeks with a colonial official whom, as far as we know, he had never met. At one level he may have felt attracted by the prospect of narrating his own life experiences to a figure of standing in public life. He seems to have had a strong sense of himself as one of the few surviving custodians of the past with personal knowledge of the times of Shaka and Dingane. As he put it to Stuart, 'I know of no one who knows of Tshaka's days, or of Dingane's. I never meet anyone. They have all been killed off' (Gcabashe, 2014, p. 267).

Another factor in his decision, we suggest, may have been a desire to raise the status of his own house in official eyes by drawing attention to the closeness of the relations that had once existed between his family and the Zulu royal house under Dingane. He recounted to Stuart how, as a young man, Dingane had taken refuge from his father with Chief Phakathwayo kaKhondlo of the Qwabe clan. Phakathwayo had placed him under the guardianship of Nonjiya, Gcabashe's father, who was one of the chief's close advisers. Gcabashe had been born during Dingane's stay with his family, and it was Dingane, Gcabashe told Stuart, who had actually given him the name Thununu at the time of his birth. Years later, after Dingane had become king, he sent for the young Gcabashe to come and serve as one of his attendants at uMgungundlovu. He remained in the king's favor until he joined the secession of Mpande, the king's brother, from the Zulu kingdom in 1839 (Gcabashe, 2014, pp. 252, 253, 256).

We know nothing of what Gcabashe's experiences were during the increasingly difficult times of the 1890s and early 1900s, but it is unlikely that he and his family remained unaffected. In deciding to make a visit to Stuart, he may have been seeking to establish the importance of his house in the eyes of an individual whom he would have seen as an influential official. Highlighting the close relations that he and his father had had with Dingane would, he presumably calculated, not do any harm and might even bring some benefit.

In these years, disaffection with colonial rule was growing rapidly among Africans in Natal and Zululand (which had been annexed to Natal in 1897). Many people who, for a range of reasons, had been hostile to the Zulu royal house were recasting their attitudes to it. Numbers of them were beginning to look to it for leadership in resistance to white domination. Among them were influential figures in the Qwabe clan (Mahoney, 1998, pp. 227-9, 232; Mahoney, 2012, pp. 178-80). Gcabashe himself lived in a magisterial district where two senior members of the Zulu royal house, Mthonga kaMpande and Mkhungo kaMpande, ruled large chiefdoms (Colony of Natal, 1903, p. C25). We do not know what sort of relationships he had with them and with other chiefs in the district, but his move to establish a publicly known connection with a senior colonial official in the person of Stuart may also have had implications for his standing in local politics.

It may appear strange at first reading that Gcabashe seems to have had no qualms about describing to Stuart in some detail his services to a ruler who, in the eyes of Afrikaner nationalists at least, had for years been established as a 'bad native' for his killing of the Trekker leader Piet Retief and his party in 1838 (Ndlovu, 2017). But, just a year after the defeat of the Afrikaner-ruled South African Republic and Orange Free State by Britain in the war of 1899–1902, it does not seem to have been an issue that was of much concern to Natal colonial official James Stuart. If anything, one of his interests at this time was to establish a detailed picture of life under Dingane at uMgungundlovu, a place which, after discussion with another elder, Lunguza kaMpukane Mthembu, Stuart could describe as 'this great historic capital' (Mthembu, 1976, p. 345).

A Discourse of Knowledge-Making

A close reading of Stuart's notes of his conversations with Gcabashe strongly suggests that the latter wanted to do more than talk about the past, and that he invested great importance in wanting his account to be preserved in writing. In pursuing their social and political interests in the present, African elders had very probably always sought to mobilize what they saw as significant features of the past through the medium of oral discourses. When it became clear in the colonial era that it was the written word that really counted with the authorities, then it was important to go to the new centers of power for the spoken word about the past to be put into writing. As Hamilton (2015, p. 104) puts it in a general statement: 'We … find calculated attempts by the subjects of colonialism … to enter their experiences and their views into the formal archival record.'

Hlonipha Mokoena has highlighted the awareness among *amakholwa* in Natal of the longevity of the written word (Mokoena, 2011, p. 192), and it is highly likely that many non-*kholwa* elders like Gcabashe were just as cognizant of its power. But there is an ambivalence in his attitude to the making of the written record that emerges in his comment on *izithunguthu*. On the one hand, it is an observation on the power of writing to preserve memory. On the other, it suggests that Gcabashe felt that this power put *izithunguthu* like himself at a considerable disadvantage. While wanting to see his words preserved, he may also have seen the capturing of 'his' history by Stuart, the colonial official, as threatening to deprive him of a platform for speaking of his own knowledge of the past, knowledge which, apart from anything else, served to maintain crucially important links through time between his ancestors, himself, and his children. In another context, Isabel Hofmeyr has written cogently about the sense of failure experienced by elders who felt that their social roles as communicators of cultural skills between generations was being undermined by the intrusion of the written word (Hofmeyr, 1993). It may be that, in his particular interactions with Stuart, Gcabashe felt something of the same thing happening.

It is important to remember that we are able to hear Gcabashe's voice only through the notes that Stuart made, and that the transcription was by no means always verbatim. In keeping with his open-ended – and sometimes confrontational – method of engaging in discussion, however, Stuart was prepared to record Gcabashe's responses even when he seems to have judged them to be unproductive in terms of what he wanted to find out, or when they amounted to an admission of ignorance of the subject at hand. This practice, as well as the fact that Stuart documented some of his own musings on the apparent deficiencies in his interlocutor's knowledge, makes it possible to get quite a textured sense of their conversations, including the sticking points. Being able to identify the moments when Gcabashe was becoming irritated, or resisted Stuart's line of questioning, as well as the moments when Stuart himself was becoming frustrated, points up the particular nature of their conversations as a discourse of knowledge-making, one that we are only just beginning to unpack.

For his own part, Gcabashe seems to have a strong self-confidence in his own status as an authority in the past. He presented himself as an informed commentator on events he stressed he had witnessed first-hand. Where he did not know the answer to the questions put to him, he was prepared to say so. On several occasions when Stuart directly challenged him about his version of events, he refused to back down. In the face of skepticism or signs from Stuart that his answers to questions had not been very satisfactory, Gcabashe persevered with his own versions. He remained prepared to do so in the face of occasional contradictory statements from Ndukwana kaMbengwana Mthethwa and Jantshi kaNongila Mabaso, others of Stuart's discussants who were present through some or all of his conversations with Gcabashe. The latter's determination to assert his own views was made particularly clear in a heated – and probably high-stakes – exchange that Stuart recorded between him and Mabaso over the question of whether the Zulu king Shaka had been born in or out of wedlock (Gcabashe, 2014, p. 293).

The Quasi-Legal Environment

Gcabashe would already have had a long experience of living in an environment in which elders like him offered competing historical narratives in public and private gatherings. In their conversations, Stuart seems to have confronted him with different versions of the past as given by previous interlocutors (for example, stories of Shaka's birth as related by Ndlovu kaThimuni Zulu, Mhuyi kaThimuni Zulu, and Jantshi kaNongila Mabaso). This would have been in keeping with Stuart's notion, discussed above, that knowledge was generated from friction between differing viewpoints. Stuart also brought up accounts of the past which he derived from published sources, such as references to the Boers' visit to Dingane in 1837–1838. Gcabashe was not only aware of the challenges to his own account posed by competing histories, but was also sensitive to the need to defend his own version of the past in a quasi-legal setting. This was framed by Stuart's proclivities as a magistrate habituated to procedures of cross-examination and weighing up evidence (Hamilton, 1998, pp. 142–3, 152).

In the course of the discussions, Gcabashe was meticulous about presenting his qualifications as a credible witness. They resided mostly in his claims to have been present at central historical events, including the killing of Retief and his party in 1838, and the battle of Maqongqo at which Dingane was defeated by Mpande and his Boer allies in 1840, and in claims to have had Dingane himself as a source of information (Gcabashe, 2014, p. 253). His qualifications, in his view, also resided in his great age. As one who 'knew' the past, he was determined not to back down, especially not in front of Stuart. Though the latter was only in his mid-thirties, unmarried to boot, and therefore a 'boy', he had the authority of the government behind him, and was a figure who wielded the power of writing.

Points of Friction

Stuart began his conversations with Gcabashe on May 28, 1903. Over the next three days, he sought to elicit information on the early history of the Zulu and Qwabe, but soon found that Gcabashe had little to say on the subject and much preferred to talk about his own experiences in Dingane's time (Gcabashe, 2014, pp. 252–64). Stuart kept coming back to his own line of questioning, which suggests that he felt that Gcabashe was withholding information on the subject, but by the evening of 31 May he had been forced to conclude that 'Tununu knows nothing of the origin of the Zulu and Qwabe peoples, much less of such tribes as Mtetwa, Ndwandwe, aba se Langeni, and less still of the whole Native races' (Gcabashe, 2014, p. 264). He went on: 'Tununu cannot connect the Qwabe with the Zulu people. He *will not allow* (our emphasis) the Qwabes ever lived but in the neighbourhood of the Mhlatuze, Matigulu and Mlalazi, and yet he says both Qwabe and Zulu were the sons of Malandela and Zulu came from the north.... He *admits* (our emphasis) it is possible the Qwabe came from the north' (Gcabashe, 2014, pp. 264–5).

Stuart's use of the words 'not allow' and 'admits' suggests that he applied cross-examination in an attempt to cajole or goad Gcabashe into making statements, a procedure which was very probably beginning to cause Gcabashe the vexation that became apparent in his later remark about the *izithunguthu*. Despite his own dissatisfaction with the quality of Gcabashe's information, that same evening Stuart drew up a long list of 'queries' to put to him (Gcabashe, 2014, p. 265). Over the next few days, he once again found that Gcabashe either could not or would not tell him much about early history, while being happy to speak about his knowledge of Dingane's reign. One can sense the mounting frustration behind the note that Stuart made on the afternoon of 6 June to the effect that, 'Tununu is very disappointing as to where the inhabitants of Zululand originally came from' (Gcabashe, 2014, p. 283). Still he did not give up on Gcabashe, but once again made a note to ask him more questions.

On 10 June, Stuart had yet another series of questions ready for his interlocutor about early Qwabe history. It is here, on the same page as he listed these questions, that Stuart records Gcabashe as having remarked, 'You can write and remember but "*tina* [*si*] *izitungutu nje*"' (Gcabashe, 2014, p. 289). In this context, one cannot help but read it as an expression of irritation and fatigue that came in the wake of concentrated interrogation, and perhaps as a consequence of a perceived neglect on Stuart's part of the events and characters that Gcabashe believed were significant to the history he was telling. In spite of his own possible irritations, Stuart was motivated enough by his engagement with Gcabashe, and with Ndukwana Mthethwa, who was also present, to record the note that provides the central text of this chapter.

In this chapter, we have described something of the surfacing made by the word *isithunguthu* at two widely separated points in its journey through time – the first years of the twentieth century, and the second decade of the twenty-first. As spoken by Gcabashe, it seems to have signified a knowledgeable person whose knowledge was being undermined in processes of cross-examination by authority figures. More specifically, he was making a strong – and poignant – statement about what was happening to oral discourses about the past in African societies in Natal as colonial forms of knowledge-making and knowledge-archiving became firmly established. Now that the word has been rediscovered, more than a century later, by scholars concerned to open up the field of intellectual history in the era before colonialism, we can ask: how will it continue its journey, and in what direction?

Notes

1 The original of Stuart's note of Thununu's comment referred to is to be found in the James Stuart Collection (Killie Campbell Africana Library, Durban), File 60, nbk. 27, p. 12. In the haste of making the note, Stuart originally wrote '*tina zi izitungutu*' instead of the grammatically correct '*tina si izitungutu*'. For the published version, see Gcabashe, 2014, p. 289.

2 See in particular Stuart's notes of his discussions in Ladysmith in 1900 with John Kumalo and others (Kumalo, 1976).
3 Hamilton (1998) is a major exception.
4 See Stuart's record of his discussions with John Kumalo and others (Kumalo, 1976).

References

Bryant, A.T. (1905) *A Zulu-English dictionary.* Pinetown: Mariannhill Mission Press.

Carton, B. (2000) *Blood from your children: The colonial origins of generational conflict in South Africa.* Pietermaritzburg: University of Natal Press.

Colenso, J.W. (1861) *Zulu-English dictionary.* 1st edn. Pietermaritzburg: P. Davis.

Colenso, J.W. (1884) *Zulu-English dictionary.* 3rd edn. Pietermaritzburg: P. Davis.

Colenso, J.W. (1905) *Zulu-English dictionary.* 4th edn. Pietermaritzburg: Vause, Slatter and Co.

Colony of Natal (1903) *Blue Book on native affairs, 1902.* Pietermaritzburg: Department of Native Affairs.

Gcabashe, T. (2014) Statements of Thununu kaNonjiya Gcabashe in Webb, C. de B. and Wright, J.B. (eds.) *The James Stuart archive of recorded oral evidence relating to the history of the Zulu and neighbouring peoples*, vol. 6. Pietermaritzburg: University of KwaZulu-Natal Press, pp. 252–315.

Guy, J. (2001) *The view across the river: Harriette Colenso and the Zulu struggle against imperialism.* Charlottesville: University Press of Virginia.

Guy, J. (2003) 'The Colenso daughters: three women confront imperialism', in Draper, J. (ed.) *The eye of the storm: Bishop John Colenso and the crisis of biblical inspiration.* Pietermaritzburg: Cluster Publications, pp. 345–363.

Hamilton, C.A. (1998) *Terrific majesty: The powers of Shaka Zulu and the limits of historical invention.* Cambridge, MA: Harvard University Press.

Hamilton, C.A. (2011) 'Backstory, biography, and the life of the *James Stuart Archive*', *History in Africa*, 38, pp. 319–41.

Hamilton, C.A. (2015) 'Archives, ancestors and the contingencies of time' in Lüdtke, A. and Nanz, T. (eds.) *Laute, Bilde, Texte: Register des Archivs.* Göttingen: V&R Unipress, pp. 103–18.

Hamilton, C.A. (2021) 'Recalibrating the deep history of intellectual thought in the Kwazulu-Natal region' in Broodryk, C. (ed.) *Public intellectuals in South Africa: critical voices from the past.* Johannesburg: Wits University Press, pp. 21–43.

Hamilton, C.A. and Leibhammer, N. (eds.). (2016) *Tribing and untribing the archive: identity and the material record in southern KwaZulu-Natal in the late independent and colonial periods.* 2 vols. Pietermaritzburg: University of KwaZulu-Natal Press.

Hofmeyr, I. (1993) *'We spend our years as a tale that is told': oral historical narrative in a South African chiefdom.* Johannesburg: Witwatersrand University Press.

Kros, C. (2017) '"We do not want the Commission to allow the families to disappear into thin air": a consideration of widows' testimonies at the Truth and Reconciliation Commission and the Farlam (Marikana) Commission of Inquiry', *Psychology in Society*, 55, pp. 38–60.

Kumalo, J. (1976) Statements of John Kumalo and others in Webb, C. de B. and Wright, J.B. (eds.) *The James Stuart archive of recorded oral evidence relating to the history of the Zulu and neighbouring peoples*, vol. 1. Pietermaritzburg: University of Natal Press, pp. 215–272.

Lambert, J. (1995) *Betrayed trust: Africans and the state in colonial Natal.* Pietermaritzburg: University of Natal Press.

Mahoney, M.R. (1998) *Between the Zulu king and the great white chief: political culture in a Natal chiefdom, 1879–1906*. PhD dissertation, University of California, Los Angeles. Ann Arbor: UMI Dissertation Services.

Mahoney, M.R. (2012) *The other Zulus: The spread of Zulu ethnicity in colonial South Africa*. Durham: Duke University Press.

Marks, S. (1970) *Reluctant rebellion: The 1906–8 disturbances in Natal*. Oxford: Clarendon Press.

Mokoena, H. (2011) *Magema Fuze: The making of a* kholwa *intellectual*. Pietermaritzburg: University of KwaZulu-Natal Press.

Mthembu, L. (1976) Statements of Lunguza kaMpukane Mthembu in Webb, C. de B. and Wright, J.B. (eds.) *The James Stuart archive of recorded oral evidence relating to the history of the Zulu and neighbouring peoples*, vol. 1. Pietermaritzburg: University of Natal Press, pp. 297–353.

Ndlovu, S.M. (2017) *African perspectives of King Dingane kaSenzangakhona, the second monarch of the Zulu kingdom*. Cham, Switzerland: Palgrave Macmillan.

Webb, C. de B. and Wright, J.B. (eds.) (1976–2014) *The James Stuart archive of recorded oral evidence relating to the history of the Zulu and neighbouring peoples*. 6 vols. Pietermaritzburg: University of Natal Press/University of KwaZulu-Natal Press.

Wright, J. (1996) 'Making the *James Stuart Archive*', *History in Africa*, 23, pp. 333–50.

Wright, J. (2015) 'Socwatsha kaPhaphu, James Stuart, and their conversations on the past, 1897–1922', *Kronos*, 41, pp. 142–65.

Wright, J. (2019) 'Thununu kaNonjiya Gcabashe visits James Stuart in the big smoke to talk about history', *Natalia*, 49, pp. 1–12.

Zulu, N. (1986) Statements of Ndlovu kaThimuni Zulu in Webb, C. de B. and Wright, J.B. (eds.) *The James Stuart Archive of Recorded Oral Evidence Relating to the History of the Zulu and Neighbouring Peoples*, vol. 4. Pietermaritzburg: University of Natal Press, pp. 198–238.

PART III
The Political

7

EDDEMBE

Edgar C. Taylor

Freedom was a partially shared conceptual and political terrain of struggle in the late colonial world. African nationalist politicians framed freedom as a unitary concept that transcended regional and ethnic loyalties that formed part of the architecture of indirect rule (Nkrumah 1961). Some, such as Julius Nyerere and Jomo Kenyatta, celebrated the Kiswahili term *uhuru* as an ideal uniting East Africans not only against colonial rule but also in collective projects of post-colonial nation-building (Nyerere 1968; Kenyatta 1971). Their hope was that shared experiences of colonial subjugation would nourish a common vocabulary of emancipation, whose meanings could be controlled by a new ruling class. However, neither freedom nor *uhuru* nor numerous other terms that colonial subjects invoked to challenge their oppression were ever so easily contained. Nationalists had to contend with and often directly combat others' formulations of freedom. Those who found themselves outside of the nascent ruling elite swiftly rejected new rulers' claims to control the meaning of these words (Odinga 1967). A shared vocabulary did not inherently reflect commonly understood and stable meanings.

Freedom offered discontented colonial subjects a means of connecting their struggles across time and space. The ideal is central to Western civic and religious thought, deriving particular meaning in relation to slavery. As Orlando Patterson has argued, Freedom 'became a value, was constructed as a value, as an important, cherished, shared ideal, as a result of [Black] people's experience of slavery on a large scale' (Patterson 1992, 1991). In the Bible and Christian religious instruction, the word offered a way of representing emancipation from bondage and deliverance from sin. If missionary teachers regarded abolitionist teaching as a means of claiming European superiority over the imagined barbarism of African societies, their African students often incorporated their vocabulary into wider political struggles and conceptual projects (Glassman 2010). Colonial

DOI: 10.4324/9781003273530-10

subjects often presented themselves as slaves either of the colonial power or its local intermediaries and demanded emancipation from bondage (Peterson 2010). A common vocabulary offered activists a means of conceptually linking their struggles with those across time and space while forging an ideal of common purpose.

Language is not a static infrastructure. It shapes our conceptual worlds and facilitates the movement of ideas even as it travels and changes, often unpredictably. Nearly a century ago, the linguist Edward Sapir noted, 'Language is a guide to social reality' that 'powerfully conditions all our thinking about social problems and processes' (Sapir 1949 [1929]: 162). For structuralists like Ferdinand de Saussure, a language 'exists in the brain of each member of a community, almost like a dictionary of which identical copies have been distributed to each individual' (Saussure 1966 [1915]: 19). However, as subsequent generations of linguistic anthropologists and historians have shown, written dictionaries and codified word lists often serve as instruments of power that flatten linguistic diversity and paper over contested concepts. Moreover, boundaries of language, culture, and communication do not neatly overlap or endure evenly over time (Hymes 1968). A common vocabulary does not automatically produce a common set of understandings or conceptual hegemony.

The architecture of colonial administration fostered political imaginaries premised on the static alignment of shared language, culture, territory, and heritage. Africans who positioned themselves as chiefs and royals within a colonial symbolic economy often claimed that their authority rested on an inherited set of knowledge and rules. Ethnic patriots embarked on activist research itineraries as historians, linguists, and cartographers (MacArthur 2016). On paper, they frequently assembled communities united by patriarchal respect for self-appointed elder men (Peterson and Macolo 2009). In practice, their efforts animated struggles over the nature of political authority and social morality, in which women, outsiders, and youth rarely acted as the submissive subjects that their would-be rulers imagined them to be (Spear 2003). Nationalists attempted to transcend this framework with an alternative patriotism. Freedom from foreign domination, the justifying principle of nationalism, inverted colonial Manichaeism, imbuing the colonized with agency and locating the seeds of modernity in a national culture that was projected into an indigenous past, which was itself understood under an atemporal rubric of culture (Chatterjee 1986; Guha 1997).

Popular politics consistently frustrated and exceeded both nationalist and ethnic patriots' ideals of freedom (Hunter 2015). The social movements that undergirded nationalist parties drew on intellectual traditions and conceptual universes that both predated and emerged from the specific conditions of colonial rule. In their 'Documenting Freedom in Africa' project, Phyllis Taou and Jean-Marie Teno have archived dozens of interviews on conceptual formations from societies across the continent that, in their words, show 'evidence of the profound importance of freedom in contemporary Africa from different perspectives' (Taoua and Teno). In democratizing how freedom is defined and who defines it, their interviews show what intellectual histories of a partially shared global concept can look like from multiple positions in the Global South. Social historians have demonstrated the significance of such conceptual work to understanding class formation and popular activism. For example, in central Kenya in the 1950s, young men and women attempted to reshape the moral bonds that regulated the fruits of land and wage labor by invoking *wiathi*, an ideal of self-mastery that colonial capitalism had denied to them. Many former *Ikatha na Wiathi* fighters, otherwise known as Mau Mau, spoke of *wiathi* synonymously with freedom (Lonsdale 1992). Although their struggle was often refracted through the lens of British propagandists and foreign journalists, Mau Mau combatants' fight for *wiathi* intersected with struggles for freedom across the world, from Kampala to Harlem (Horne 2009).

This chapter examines how Luganda speakers used the English word 'freedom' in contestations over what a postcolonial social and political order should look like in Buganda Kingdom of central Uganda. Nationalist politicians, ethnic patriots, and ordinary subjects all employed a similar vocabulary of freedom, which was often translated with the Luganda word *eddembe*. However, each offered different, sometimes partially overlapping meanings informed by wider conceptual resources grounded in colonial and precolonial histories. As nationalists promised to lead a negotiated transfer of power to an elected government, elite patriots of Buganda Kingdom worried about their fate in a unitary state. In the late 1950s and early 1960s, charismatic activists with the backing of Kingdom Ministers pursued a populist campaign to redefine what freedom from colonial rule could mean in Buganda. They convened the largest political rallies in Uganda's history to that point, where they proclaimed the formation of a new anti-colonial organization, the Uganda National Movement, or UNM, which redefined anti-colonialism around traditional authorities rather than bourgeois politicians. Using the English word 'freedom' as its rallying cry, the UNM rejected elections unless the future of the kingdom and the power of its ruling elites were first guaranteed. The vehicle for their demands was the promise of economic emancipation through a social and economic boycott against Indian merchants, who dominated retail and wholesale trade.

However, royalist activists, like their nationalist adversaries, failed to enforce a hegemonic meaning of freedom as they attempted to subvert Kiganda ideals of democracy and legitimate authority to fit their aspirations for individual capitalist accumulation. Activists hoped to marshal a combination of new media and disciplinary violence in order to direct how Ugandans would imagine freedom at a moment when British colonialism appeared to be in crisis. As the UNM's boycott campaign grew and Kingdom officials prepared a unilateral declaration of independence, their followers subtly unsettled elites' and populist activists' claims to a monopoly on political authority. In so doing, they exposed Buganda's multilingual conceptual landscape as one of contestation rather than fixed meanings. They pursued this work all while proclaiming their allegiance to the Kingdom, to its king the Kabaka, and to the ideal of 'freedom'. To Protectorate officials and subsequent generations of royalist Baganda patriots, these mostly anonymous individuals were a united group of devotees to the Kabaka's government who carried forward a royalist ideology that aimed to elevate Buganda's ruling elite among other royal sovereigns. In this reading, Buganda's populist publics aimed to claim freedom and royal sovereignty within a European conceptual world. However, a careful reading of ordinary people's actions points to the diversity of conceptual resources that Luganda speakers used to shape ideas of freedom. Concepts such as *eddembe* and *ekitiibwa* (often translated as 'honour') offered multiple ways of understanding and challenging the rigid social and political hierarchies that characterized Buganda under British indirect rule. These concepts were not limited to elite politics but rather opened a terrain for contesting the obligations of rulers and subjects as well as the nature of legitimate authority.

**

In Buganda, crises in the structures of instrumental power have frequently precipitated social and intellectual innovations in how ordinary people attempt to build popular consensus and regulate their consent to be governed. Holly Hanson has argued that between 1200 and 1700, social institutions developed around ideas of 'reciprocal obligation' between figures of authority and their followers in order to facilitate access to land for banana cultivation (Hanson 2003; Schoenbrun 1998). Kings, clan heads, chiefs, and healers came into being through, and subsequently depended on, the consent of their followers, who could opt out of an exploitative relationship by moving around the fertile belt north of Lake Nyanja (Victoria). Over the following two centuries, traffic in slaves facilitated by expansionist wars made the consent of free individuals less important to aspiring rulers. As relations between leaders and their followers became increasingly coercive, people invoked earlier social ideals and invested in *Lubaale* deities as a check on unidirectional power. The Kabaka ruled through accommodation and negotiation with other forces, including clans, *Lubaale* priests, and chiefs. By the 1880s, Islam, Catholicism, and Protestantism offered another means of organizing allegiances at a time when legitimate authority was in crisis and Buganda's neighbors, such as Bunyoro, were militarily ascendant (Hanson 2003; Reid 2002).

Ideals about legitimate social and political relationships had emerged in Buganda over centuries of struggle and negotiation. The intervention of British colonizers in the late nineteenth century provided elites surrounding the Kabaka with an opportunity to assert order following two centuries of violent social disruption. They worked with British officials to enshrine a new order premised on the authority of a Protestant oligarchy within a constitutional monarchy. The resulting 1900 Agreement codified British Protectorate enforcement of this arrangement. Land, once allocated through intricate webs of negotiation, was privatized in the hands of the Kabaka, his appointed chiefs, and the British crown. Labor, once offered in carefully managed reciprocal relationships, became commercialized in a manner that promoted transactional relationships between landowners and migrant laborers. Once powerful figures, such as *bataka*, or 'clan' heads, and royal women, were largely excluded from the agreement between the British and Buganda's royal establishment (Kodesh 2010; Musisi 1993).

From 1900 into the 1950s, Buganda's political order under indirect colonial rule never achieved broad consent. Activists who claimed the mantle of clan leaders repeatedly challenged the Kabaka's legitimacy by invoking the authority of the *bataka*. In the 1940s, farmers revolted against the alliance of despotic chiefs and Indian cotton buyers. In 1945, the Kabaka's *Katikiro*, or Prime Minister, was assassinated. However, even expressions of support for reified custom could undercut the Kabaka's authority. When the *Namasole*, or Queen Mother, got remarried to a commoner in 1941, the Kabaka and his *Katikiro* offered their approval despite its divergence from historical precedent. Baganda outside the royal hierarchy denounced the move and offered it as evidence of the Kabaka's habitual breaching of Christian morality and 'customary' practice (Musisi 1991; Karlström 1999). Kabaka Mutesa's unpopularity only deepened in subsequent years. Mutesa, like his father Daudi Chwa, was perceived to be aloof from his subjects and consumed by immoral pursuits. Both men had considered abdicating their thrones and both apparently died of alcohol poisoning. Baganda recalled pasts defined by more equitable social relations, which offered bases on which to reject the Kabaka's claim to absolute authority (Summers 2006; Hanson 2003). Among the persistent demands of the *bataka* movement was for the popular election of chiefs as a means of reconstituting popular consent within a bureaucratic form. Indirect rule produced despotic institutions, but it did not yield consensus over the terms of authority.

Buganda's ruling elite feared the Protectorate government's centralizing impulses in the 1950s, and they worked to convince and coerce ordinary Baganda to subordinate their grievances within an outward performance of unity and devotion to the Kabaka. The Colonial Secretary Oliver Lyttleton suggested that Buganda, and indeed all of Uganda, would be subsumed in an East African Federation. When the Kabaka insisted that he could unilaterally withdraw Buganda from British protection and declare the kingdom's independence, Governor Andrew Cohen assumed that deporting the unpopular Mutesa to Britain would provoke tepid criticism if not outright support from his subjects. Instead, Mutesa's forced exile in 1953 sparked a crisis of both instrumental and creative power in Buganda. Although many Baganda resented the Kabaka's authoritarian pretensions, the Kabakaship still represented ties of patronage, loyalty, love, and reciprocal obligation that bound grandparents and grandchildren in a network directed around the royal family. The crisis provided an opportunity for elites in the Kabaka's cabinet and inner circle to marshal a widely and deeply felt sense of social crisis into an ideology of royal absolutism, in which loyalty to the Kabaka overshadowed ideals of mutual accommodation (Summers 2017, 2005b; Hanson 2022). Overt criticism of the centralized kingship and of the Kabaka all but disappeared from public debate in Buganda following his deportation. The new order that the kingdom's elite set out to build had a place neither for imperial citizenship nor for egalitarian postcolonial citizenship. They ensured that would-be citizens instead felt obliged to position themselves first and foremost as subjects of the Kabaka.

The political crises of 1950s Buganda were also crises of economic accumulation and consumption. The concentration of resources in towns during and after World War II, coupled with the tripartite racial language in which the colonial state invited East Africans to frame their claims to entitlements such as food, housing, and trading licenses, transformed how wealth could be assembled (Brennan 2012; Thompson 2003). The new situation enabled forms of economic entrepreneurship that were independent of predominantly rural practices of accountability. Chiefs' wealth in land and taxes depended on their capacity to balance coercion with the assertion of legitimately achieved consent. By contrast, the wealth generated by urban commerce depended on a different set of relationships, most of which led to wholesalers and creditors with access to networks of exchange and debt linking East African towns with the Indian Ocean, and ultimately to British banks (Bishara 2017). Indian traders composed wealth through networks of debt that often overlapped with family and community relationships. Those networks of economic and familial obligation facilitated conversations about personal and collective character through which Indian traders understood and evaluated their economic chances (Oonk 2013). These were conversations that were largely not shared by their African customers. For African ex-servicemen seeking to break into trade, for young men with a colonial education who sought recognition of their achievements in an urban milieu independent of chiefly authority, and for the women and immigrants who found a limited degree of economic autonomy in informal urban markets, the concentration of wealth in Indian commercial centers could appear to be detached from popular accountability and thus immoral. At the same time, their own prospects for economic, and thus social, autonomy often depended on those same networks through employment, lines of credit, and as sources of consumer goods. As urban centers expanded rapidly in the 1950s, the partial anonymity of urban commercial and social life only enhanced the moral anxieties of elites and commoners alike.

The political and economic crises of the 1950s provided an opportunity for Buganda's royal establishment to merge their political and economic aspirations into a populist movement. The Kabaka and his ministers had profited from their relationships with large Indian lenders, importers, and wholesalers. Many had leveraged their positions in order to enter Indian commercial networks and establish their own businesses. Although these enterprises brought them significant personal wealth, they also eroded their popular legitimacy, increasing the perception of the Kabaka's men as aloof and hostile to the norms of popular accountability. Meanwhile, large landowners feared demands that chiefs be elected, which would have threatened their transferable wealth. In a polarized climate, moderate reform threatened their economic, political, and social position. Populist mobilization that situated Luganda concepts in a racialized logic of urban entitlement helped to insulate them from – and to co-opt – decades of activism for the restoration of democracy. The new dynamics of urban life including novel forms of public address at mass rallies, combined with older practices of popular surveillance, slander, and violence, allowed self-interested entrepreneurs to manipulate popular expressions of collective accountability. Freedom offered a particularly compelling framing, even as it opened a conceptual universe that was far more democratic than colonial Buganda's political and economic structures.

★★

When the activist Augustine Kamya stepped in front of a microphone before 15,000 people in central Kampala in March 1959, Buganda seemed to be in the midst of upheaval. The growth of exploitative urban commercial relationships, the threats to Buganda's quasi-sovereignty, and the consolidation of royal power all conspired to push aspirations for horizontal citizenship based on historical ideals of mutual love and respect out of Buganda's late colonial public sphere. As nationalists framed freedom from colonialism as the narrow transfer of the Protectorate administration to African politicians, royalist patriots attempted to convince their followers that freedom was synonymous with the interests of the kingdom's hierarchy. Kamya channeled both conceptions of nationalism around a populist campaign to boycott Indian-owned shops and foreign consumer goods. He introduced a new political coalition of nationalists and royalists, who punctuated their speeches with calls of 'freedom!' At an earlier rally, he had proclaimed that the goal of the new Uganda National Movement (UNM) was 'to unite the people of Uganda and to liberate the country from foreign rule' (*Uganda Argus* 16 Feb 1959). Its members included the elite politicians Eridadi Mulira and Ignatius Musazi as well as so-called traditionalists, such as Yosia Sekabanja and Hajji Busungu. United by their calls for self-government, they strove to undermine colonial order by means of a boycott. Mulira and Musazi said that it was designed to force the Protectorate government to make concessions over citizenship and education policies. Kamya was more direct and garnered a much more fervent following. The goal, he stated, was 'to bring trade into the hands of Africans' (*Uganda Argus* 5 March 1959).

Kamya and his allies offered an alternative conception of 'freedom' from their nationalist critics, such as Milton Obote and Benedicto Kiwanuka. Obote and Kiwanuka each claimed authority as office holders in recently established political parties, the Uganda National Congress (later the Uganda Peoples Congress) and the Democratic Party, respectively. Obote's UNC drew support from three constituencies, each of which was suspicious of Buganda's royal elite: young antifeudal radicals, civil servants in the colonial bureaucracy, and conservative aristocrats from outside Buganda (Taylor 2019). Kiwanuka's largely Catholic base was equally wary of Buganda's Protestant elite. Both men offered nationalist visions defined by the subordination of individuals to the cause of national unity. After becoming independent Uganda's first Prime Minister, Obote declared, 'The sovereign people of this land have … been appointed by destiny to manipulate the decisive wheels and turning points in the history … of freedom' (quoted in Obote 1970: 7). For nationalists, freedom was to be found in the narrow exercise of voting by popular franchise and the legislative achievements that elected representatives could offer. Some within the UNM, such as Godfrey Binaisa, shared this ideal. He declared that the UNM would peacefully seek a transfer of constitutional power and provide all Ugandans with free education (*Uganda Argus* March 2, 1959).

Populists like Kamya rejected this narrow view of freedom and instead attempted to link the aspirations of Buganda's urban underclass with the interests of Buganda's royal elite. The Kabaka later referred to Kamya as 'a demagogue', while Protectorate intelligence officials considered him 'a master of mob oratory' (Kabaka 1967: 154).[1] Before forming the UNM, Kamya led a small pressure group, the Third Party to the Agreement. The name of the latter group referred to agreements that the Kabaka and his representatives signed with the British governor in 1900 and again in 1955. According to one of their pamphlets, the 'third party' referred to 'we, the people of the Buganda Agreement' who would protect the Kingdom's sovereignty and the Kabaka's 'peace and happiness'.[2] Royalist pressure groups such as the Third Party to the Agreement did not take direct orders from the Kabaka. Rather, their members saw themselves as defenders of a royalist order who could operate free from manipulative influences that exploited the polite norms of elite politics. For young insurgents like Kamya, the defining feature of this order was neither the absolutist authority desired by the Kabaka's ministers nor the popular accountability pursued by the *bataka*. Instead, the language of democracy was replaced by a language of freedom to pursue personal enrichment. Kamya's emphasis on economic capital allowed the Kabaka's men to form an economic alliance with like-minded young social entrepreneurs that was cemented by deeply felt understandings of royal authority. Ministers in the Kabaka's government funneled money to the movement, and neither the Kabaka nor his *Katikiro* offered public criticism of the UNM itself, despite sustained pressure from British authorities.[3]

The UNM needed compelling conceptual and coercive resources in order to mobilize people around its controversial appeal to royal authority and its call to sever economic and social ties along racial lines. If most Baganda vehemently defended royal institutions after 1953, an enduring suspicion of self-enriching elites surrounding the Kabaka remained. Likewise, even as the inequality and competitiveness of urban commerce fuelled racial populism, consumer products were inseparable from moral economies of urban life and therefore difficult to extricate from people's social lives. The UNM did not offer written manifestos, outlining a single ideology. Instead, it relied on public rallies as a means of bringing together diverse constituencies into a single movement, bonded through performative gestures of solidarity and mutual coercion. Kamya and his colleagues were renowned for their charismatic public speaking, and public rallies offered a means of appealing to people directly and of promoting forms of mutual surveillance.

UNM leaders punctuated each rally with two actions that appealed to Kiganda conceptions of justice, which proved wildly popular among attendees. First, speakers concluded each rally by leading their audience in the singing of Buganda's anthem *Ekitiibwa kya Buganda*. The anthem was composed in the 1930s to commemorate the victory of Protestant forces in Uganda's religious wars decades earlier. Despite its celebration of the kingdom's age-old honor (*ekitiibwa kya Buganda kyava dda*) rooted in the rule of a Christian elite, the concept *ekitiibwa* offered a potentially more egalitarian meaning. *Ekitiibwa*, or 'that which is feared', may connote 'honor, glory, prestige, dignity and respect', but as the linguist John Murphy observed, 'None of the preceding equivalents expresses the full meaning of kitiibwa which is perhaps the greatest ideal and the most sought after attribute of the Baganda' (Murphy 1972: 210). John Iliffe has described the ostensibly democratic connotations of the concept, which would have appealed to Buganda's urban underclass who were cut off from chiefly patronage and from economic advancement in urban commerce dominated by Indian traders. 'Buganda's politics centred on competition for office and its associated *ekitiibwa*, a competition open in principle to any man of talent and courage' (Iliffe 2005: 168). Much as royalist elites hoped to enshrine hierarchical authority, the energizing of Kiganda patriotism meant that core concepts such as *ekitiibwa* were not easily controlled.

The second ubiquitous feature of UNM rallies was the rallying cry of *eddembe*, in English, 'Freedom!', often accompanied by a 'V' finger sign. The first recorded uses of the word in Buganda were in Bible translations. Early converts to Christianity used *eddembe* to translate Biblical passages concerning the emancipation of servants into freedom. Nineteenth-century protestant missionaries imbued their work with the ideals of abolitionism, often using these same passages of the Bible to denounce practices of extreme dependency in Buganda. In the early twentieth century, with forced labor and the commercialization of land, many Baganda were also cut off from patronage relationships and burials that bound them to ancestors, descendants, and to kingdom authorities. They often complained of enslavement by chiefs and landowners who deprived them of their control over clan burial grounds and thus to their spiritual connections across generations (Hanson 2003; Summers 2005a). Freedom thus implied the ability to show love for patrons, dependents, and ancestors through reciprocal obligation without coercion.

In Luganda translation, 'freedom' was most often associated with *eddembe*, which may connote 'freedom' as well as 'opportunity', 'lack of worry', and 'peace' (Murphy 1972: 65). The Luganda version of Uganda's national anthem transforms 'Oh Uganda, land of freedom' into '*O Yuganda, ensi y'eddembe*'. It is also used today in phrases such as '*ddembe ly'obuntu*' (*ddembe* of humanity, implying democracy or civil liberties) or '*ddembe ly'okwogera*' (freedom of talking or speech).[4] On its own, *ddembe* may also imply 'peace', particularly when brought by proper leadership. For example, a folk song celebrates the resolution of successful wars against the neighboring Bunyoro Kingdom by proclaiming '*Obuganda nebufuna eddembe*' (Buganda got peace), which has earned the Kabaka the right to rest with his Queen (Kizza 2010: 199). The song shows that the peace of the kingdom should be reflected in the Kabaka. The term suggests, as Mikael Karlström puts it, 'liberty to carry out some particular activity without constraints imposed from above'. However, it also implies the restoration of just social order. It is often used interchangeably with *emirembe*, implying both 'calm' and 'royal reign' or 'epoch' (Karlström 1996: 486).

Luganda speakers who repeated the UNM's call of 'freedom' were invoking a wider set of ideals than the mere transfer of executive authority. They wanted the freedom to accumulate economic and social wealth in a competitive, morally compromised urban colonial situation by equating the Kabaka's formal supremacy with bonds of love and social order. The contentious history of political authority in Buganda under indirect rule meant that ideas about 'freedom' were inseparable from understandings of legitimate authority and elites' demands on their follower's labor. As a result, the UNM mobilized a popular understanding of freedom as a condition that could not be delivered unilaterally by a political elite. Lydia Boyd has argued that Kiganda notions of 'rights' are unifying and relational rather than absolute expressions of sovereignty (Boyd 2013). The phrase '*eddembe ly'obuntu*', for example, incorporates notions of people's liberty and collective peace. As Luganda speakers invoke notions of freedom, they also open up wider questions about the social relations that make peace and liberty possible.

Words such as 'freedom' and '*eddembe*' provided terrains of struggle over power relations at a moment when Buganda and the world seemed to be on the cusp of a new political and moral order. Meanings were not easily contained in the linguistic equivalencies offered in dictionaries. The UNM's rallying cry of 'freedom' positioned it within a wider field of anti-colonial struggle even as it opened struggles over authority that could challenge aspects of royal power. Ministers hoped to delegitimize criticism of the Kabaka and legitimate their own wealth through trade and industry, which bypassed popular social sanction. Others associated the freedom of the Kabaka with peace and democracy, recalling deeper histories of political harmony and consensus. For conservative royalists embedded in the new urban economy, the translation of these concepts into the English word freedom usefully obscured the democratizing ideals that informed them and justified their own personal financial pursuits.[5]

The UNM began as a centralized organization of activists, who rejected the ideals of liberal citizenship in favor of a campaign of disciplinary surveillance and violence. From the outset, Kamya declared that the boycott of non-African shops and foreign consumer goods would not be a choice but a precondition of social life. Those who failed to comply, by consuming banned products or consorting with Indians, would be subjected to social boycott. Anonymous leaflets warned, 'Every person should act as a detective on his friend'.[6] Individuals who were seen patronizing Indian-owned shops, drinking bottled beer, or even interacting with Indians were labeled '*babaliga*', literally those who walk with splayed feet, connoting infidelity. Boycott enforcers were known to slash their crops, burn their houses, and sometimes physically attack alleged *babaliga*, while market vendors refused to sell them food. One contributor to the Luganda language newspaper *Uganda Empya* compared *babaliga* with bats, which only wake up at night and fail to find anything to eat (*Uganda Empya* April 3, 1959). With urbanization and the expansion of British and Indian capital, individual consumers and vendors occupied a primary site of social power.

The formal institutions of the UNM barely lasted four months before being destroyed or driven underground. Protectorate authorities arrested, imprisoned, or deported its leadership to the north of the country. The Governor forbade all large gatherings. Newspapers that supported the boycott found themselves in trouble. *Munaansi*, for example, a new publication owned by two kingdom ministers, was shuttered and its editor arrested after printing a doctored photograph showing a woman bleeding from a police bullet at a pro-UNM rally.[7] The UNM and a series of successor organizations, such as the Uganda Freedom Movement and Uganda Freedom Convention, were also banned.[8] Despite British authorities' attack on the infrastructure that had supported the UNM's emergence, the boycott campaign continued well into 1960. Scholars' focus on print culture and elite intellectual history has missed how the UNM's conceptual and coercive strategies propelled contentious struggles over just authority in Buganda long after UNM leaders were removed from the scene and kingdom authorities had shifted objectives (Taylor 2016).

The UNM's call for mutual surveillance within communities relied on loyal activists, but the anonymity of enforcement also hypothetically allowed anyone to exert authority in ways that worried both Protectorate and Kingdom leaders. Anonymous letters, threats, and disciplinary violence provided a different register for boycott supporters to work in. Unlike the public theatre of political rallies, this register sustained a politics with an amorphous constituency, which challenged the authority of Kingdom elites even as it was used to promote conservative ethnic patriotism. As the Protectorate government began to crack down on the UNM's leaders, anonymous letters began to appear in public spaces urging people to continue the boycott while threatening those who did not comply. Rifts soon emerged between the ideals of centralized royal authority promoted by the Kabaka's ministers and the anonymous messages appearing in public. It soon became clear that enforcers of the boycott did not all operate with a shared understanding of what the achievement of freedom entailed.

Anonymous letters often adopted identities that positioned them outside of normative relations of authority. In July 1959, letters began to appear signed by '*Muzinge*' or 'Son of *Muzinge*' that claimed an authority to direct boycott activity and dispense punishment independently of the UNM or Kingdom officials.

This mysterious figure could appear anywhere and at any time to issue new instructions and to threaten wayward consumers. One *Muzinge* letter warned, 'If I inspect the shops again and find Brook Bond Tea, I will sentence the offender to death as I did to the "beer drinker"'.[9] *Muzinge* was a messenger and a commander, not a reporter. In Luganda, the name refers to a peacock, or 'king of the birds'. A popular folktale tells the story of a young girl who released a peacock from its cage against her parents' instructions, which caused her family to die of hunger without its eggs. The story tells how the girl's doomed parents drove her from home to be haunted in an endless search for the missing bird (Mubiru 2004; Mugambi 1994). The folktale, like *Muzinge* letters, warns of social boycott against those who neglect its importance and whose disobedience causes collective disaster.

Such letters enabled experimentation with command and surveillance that challenged centralized authority. In September 1959, *Muzinge* letters appeared urging farmers to stop selling Buganda's staple food matooke for shipment to Kampala as punishment for Kampalans' continued consumption of bottled beer. One handwritten letter found on a Kampala street announced, 'Anybody found selling or bringing [matooke] to Kampala ... will be heavily punished as one who has no respect for one's country'. The message ended with, 'BE CAREFUL!! FREEDOM-FREEDOM-FREEDOM'. Kingdom authorities who had tacitly supported the boycott now worried that food shortages would undermine their authority. When they sent lorries under armed escort to transport matooke to Kampala, *Muzinge* letters continued to appear condemning their action (*Uganda Argus* 19, 21, 23, 25, 26 September 1959).[10]

Activists professed their devotion to the Kabaka, but even the Kabaka became alarmed by the general hostility to central authority that the boycott provoked. He noted that areas of Kampala ostensibly under his jurisdiction, known as the *Kibuga*, were becoming increasingly threatening to authority in general – both from the Protectorate and the Buganda Kingdom. He informed the British Governor 'that he himself had "freedom" shouted at him, but often with a laugh. He did agree, however, that there was a hostile feeling toward Government and authority in Kampala, and that something should be done to "clear up" the Kibuga'. As violence connected with the boycott continued to spread in 1960, the Kabaka's government cooperated with Protectorate authorities to tackle crime in Kampala.[11] Disorder through the boycott had given the Kingdom momentary political leverage with Protectorate authorities, but it also threatened to foster unruly conceptions of freedom, order, and authority.

The most radical activists in Buganda's politics at this time did not leave a written archive, aside from transcriptions of their threatening letters. However, there is evidence that *eddembe* was an important organizing concept for their work. For example, Yakobo Sengendo was arrested in Kampala telling a crowd, 'they should try to start a "movement" all over Buganda, away from Kampala'. In contrast with UNM leaders, he is alleged to have advocated seizing weapons and police vehicles and overturning the authority of both Protectorate and Buganda Kingdom police. Police informants reported that Sengendo told people that, with this break in tactics from those of the UNM leadership, 'they were not going to shout "freedom", which was not a Luganda word, but "dembe"' (*Uganda Argus* 5 August 1959). Sengendo's declaration implied that the freedom offered by nationalists as well as UNM leaders was insufficient and justified violent measures.

Sengendo's invocation of *eddembe* suggests not only an act of rebranding from the UNM but also an effort to ground political action in a Luganda conceptual world surrounding the relationship between coercive power and consent. The English 'freedom' and the Luganda '*eddembe*' offered Luganda speakers a field of struggle over what Buganda's new political and social order would look like. However, their efforts – both politically and conceptually – were largely unsuccessful. The British and Buganda governments cracked down severely on the boycott's enforcers. Individuals received years-long prison sentences in some cases for merely uttering the word 'freedom' or '*abaliga*'. Buganda's royal elite understood that independent boycott activists could insulate the kingdom's hierarchy from culpability, but they could also unleash competing conceptions of the freedom entailed in loyalty to the Kabaka. As a result, Buganda's elite attempted to channel calls for freedom into a new political party *Kabaka Yekka* or 'King Alone' with a centralized platform. The new party enshrined loyalty to the Kabaka and his ministers into a new notion of simultaneous citizenship in a new Ugandan state *and* in subjecthood under the Kabaka, which required electoral conformity rather than popular mobilization. Many former UNM activists rejected the new party, which they believed undermined the collective ideals of their earlier struggle.[12]

The consolidation of nationalism and ethnic patriotism in the late 1950s masked struggles to shape meanings of freedom in Buganda and across the colonial world. Party politicians invoked freedom in a far more limited manner, as the transfer of sovereignty from Britain to a popularly elected government. Populist UNM leaders and royal elites wanted freedom to entail the protection of neotraditional authority and their private accumulation of capital beyond the sanction of popular consent. Despite their commitment to the same cause, boycott supporters had disrupted the channels of political patronage and control through which the Buganda Kingdom government operated. Attention to the ways that different actors used words such as freedom, *eddembe*, *babaliga*, *ekitiibwa*, and *muzinge* points to a conceptual world in which freedom and power were not fixed goals but an opening for struggle over the terms of political authority and the legitimacy of capitalist accumulation.

Notes

1 UK National Archives Colonial Office (hereafter UKNACO) 822/2064, Intelligence Report August 1960: E10.

2 Uganda National Archives Confidential (hereafter UNAC) 15 S9436/5, 'A Brief Doctrine to Enlighten All People', n.d. [October 1959?]: 54/1A. In 1961, Kamya

would inaugurate another group with a similar mission known as 'Amabega gwa Namulondo' or 'People Behind the Throne'. See Hancock 1970: 427.

3 The latter eventually issued public statements expressing the Kabaka's displeasure at the violence used to enforce the boycott. UNAC 15 S9436/5, 'Buganda Crisis 1959: Boycott Propaganda Against: White Paper'.

4 Wyrod further distinguishes between *eddembe ly'obubtu* as 'rights of humanity' and *eddembe ly'obwebange* as 'personal rights' (Wyrod 2016: 130).

5 Kamya maintained a list of businesses that were exempted from the boycott, which included those of several Buganda government ministers. Kamya also attempted to exempt Coca-Cola, after which he was appointed as a distributor for the company (Campbell 1975: 243; *Uganda Eyogera* 5 September 1960).

6 UNAC 78 S. 9436/12, Inf Dept, 16 September 1959: 85.

7 UNAC 15 S. 9436/5, Governor to Secretary of State, 10 October 1959: 43; UK National Archives Foreign and Commonwealth Office (hereafter UKNAFCO) 141/6640, Cartland, 23 May 1959: 7; UKNACO 822/1845, Governor to Secretary of State, 5 May 1959: 27.

8 UKNACO 822/1845, Governor to Secretary of State, 27 May 1959: 50.

9 UNAC 78/S9436.12, LegCo Proceedings, 26 February 1960.

10 UNAC 15 S9436/2, Anonymous Notice Muzinge, n.d. [before 14 September 1959]: 85; UNAC 15 S9436/2, Deputy Resident meeting with Ag Katikkiro Musoke, 16 September 16, 1959: 84A.

11 UNAC 15 S9436/2, Governor to Resident, 11 August 1959: 9A. On cooperation over crime, see UNAC 26 S8348 vol. 1, 'Meeting Regarding Law and Order', n.d. [March 1960]: 123A; UNAC 26 S8348 vol. 1, 'What I said at a meeting...', 23 March 1960: 127; UNAC 26 S8348 vol. 1, Resident Buganda, 11 April 1960: 137.

12 Interview with Christine Nkata, London, 12 May 2013.

References

Bishara, F.A. 2017. *A Sea of Debt: Law and Economic Life in the Western Indian Ocean, 1780–1950.* Cambridge: Cambridge University Press.

Boyd, L. 2013. 'The Problem with Freedom: Homosexuality and Human Rights in Uganda'. *Anthropological Quarterly* 86 (3): 697–724.

Brennan, J. 2012. *Taifa: Making Nation and Race in Urban Tanzania.* Athens, OH: Ohio University Press.

Campbell, H. 1975. 'The Political Struggles of Africans to Enter the Market Place in Uganda 1900–1970'. PhD dissertation, Makerere University.

Chatterjee, P. 1986. *Nationalist Thought and the Colonial World: A Derivative Discourse.* London: Zed Books.

Glassman, J. 2010. 'Racial Violence, Universal History, and Echoes of Abolition in Twentieth-Century Zanzibar'. In *Abolitionism and Imperialism in Britain, Africa, and the Atlantic,* edited by D. Peterson, 175–206. Athens, OH: Ohio University Press.

Guha, R. 1997. *Dominance Without Hegemony: History and Power in Colonial India.* Cambridge, MA: Harvard University Press.

Hancock, I. 1970. 'Patriotism and Neo-Traditionalism in Buganda: The Kabaka Yekka ('The King Alone') Movement, 1961–1962'. *Journal of African History* 11 (3): 419–34.

Hanson, H. 2003. *Landed Obligation: The Practice of Power in Buganda.* Portsmouth, NH: Heinemann.

Hanson, H. 2022. *To Speak and Be Heard: Seeking Good Government in Uganda, ca 1500–2015.* Athens: Ohio University Press.

Horne, G. 2009. *Mau Mau in Harlem? The U.S. and the Liberation of Kenya*. New York: Palgrave Macmillan.

Hunter, E. 2015. *Political Thought and the Public Sphere in Tanzania: Freedom, Democracy and Citizenship in the Era of Decolonization*. New York: Cambridge University Press.

Hymes, D. 1968. 'Linguistic Problems in Defining the Concept of "tribe"'. In *Essays on the Problem of Tribe*, edited by June Helm, 23–48. Seattle: University of Washington Press.

Iliffe, J. 2005. *Honour in African History*. Cambridge: Cambridge University Press.

Kabaka of Buganda. 1967. *The Desecration of My Kingdom*. London: Constable and Co.

Karlström, M. 1996. 'Imagining Democracy: Political Culture and Democratisation in Buganda'. *Africa* 66 (4): 485–505.

Karlström, M 1999. 'The Cultural Kingdom in Uganda: Popular Royalism and the Restoration of the Buganda Kingship'. Ph.D. Thesis, University of Chicago.

Kenyatta, J. 1971. *The Challenge of Uhuru: The Progress of Kenya, 1968–1970*. Nairobi: East African Publishing House.

Kizza, I. 2010. *The Oral Tradition of the Baganda of Uganda: A Study and Anthology of Legends, Myths, Epigrams and Folktales*. Jefferson, NC: McFarland & Co.

Kodesh, N. 2010. *Beyond the Royal Gaze: Clanship and Public Healing in Buganda*. Charlottesville: University of Virginia Press.

Lonsdale, J. 1992. 'The Moral Economy of Mau Mau: Wealth, Poverty, and Civic Virtue in Kikuyu Political Thought'. In *Unhappy Valley: Conflict in Kenya and Africa Book Two: Violence and Ethnicity*, edited by B. Berman and J. Lonsdale. Oxford: James Currey.

MacArthur, J. 2016. *Cartography and the Political Imagination: Mapping Community in Colonial Kenya*. Athens, OH: Ohio University Press.

Mubiru, B. 2004. *Muzinge the Bird*. Kampala: Fountain Publishers.

Mugambi, H. 1994. 'From Radio to Video: Migratory Texts in Contemporary Luganda Song Narratives and Performances'. *Passages* 8.

Murphy, J. 1972. *Luganda-English Dictionary*. Washington, D.C.: Catholic University of America Press.

Musisi, N. 1991. 'Women, "Elite Polygyny," and Buganda State Formation'. *Signs* 16 (4): 757–786.

Musisi, N. 1993. 'The Environment, Gender, and the Development of Unequal Relations in Buganda: A Historical Perspective'. *Canadian Woman Studies* 13 (3): 54–59.

Nkrumah, K. 1961. *I Speak of Freedom: A Statement of African Ideology*. New York: Frederick A. Praeger.

Nyerere, J. 1968. *Ujamaa: Essays on Socialism*. Dar es Salaam: Oxford University Press.

Obote, M. 1970. *Thoughts of an African Leader*. Kampala: Longman.

Odinga, A. 1967. *Not Yet Uhuru: The Autobiography of Oginga Odinga*. London: Heinemann.

Oonk, G. 2013. *Settled Strangers: Asian Business Elites in East Africa (1800–2000)*. New Delhi: SAGE Publications.

Patterson, O. 1991. *Freedom in the Making of Western Culture*. Basic Books.

Patterson, O. 1992. 'Orlando Patterson: Freedom in the Making of Western Culture'. C-SPAN Booknotes, 12 April 1992, http://www.booknotes.org/FullPage.aspx?SID=25534-1.

Peterson, D. 2010. 'Abolitionism and Political Thought in Britain and East Africa'. In *Abolitionism and Imperialism in Britain, Africa, and the Atlantic*, edited by D. Peterson, 1–37. Athens, OH: Ohio University Press.

Peterson, D. and G. Macolo. Eds. 2009. *Recasting the Past: History Writing and Political Work in Modern Africa*. Athens, OH: Ohio University Press.

Reid, R. 2002. *Political Power in Pre-Colonial Buganda: Economy, Society & Warfare in the Nineteenth Century.* Oxford: James Currey.

Sapir, E. 1949. 'The Status of Linguistics as a Science (1929)'. In David Mandelbaum ed. *Selected Writings of Edward Sapir in Language, Culture, and Personality*, 160–66. Berkeley: University of California Press.

Saussure, F. 1966. *Course in General Linguistics* (1915). Translated by Wade Baskin. New York: McGraw-Hill Book Company.

Schoenbrun, D. 1998. *A Green Place, A Good Place: Agrarian Change, Gender, and Social Identity in the Great Lakes Region to the 15th Century.* Portsmouth, NH: Heinemann.

Summers, C. 2005a. 'Grandfathers, Grandsons, Morality, and Radical Politics in Late Colonial Buganda'. *International Journal of African Historical Studies* 38 (3): 427–447.

Summers, C. 2005b. 'Young Buganda and Old Boys: Youth, Generational Transition, and Ideas of Leadership in Buganda, 1920–1949'. *Africa Today* 51 (3): 109–28.

Summers, C. 2006. 'Radical Rudeness: Ugandan Social Critiques in the 1940s'. *Journal of Social History* 39 (3): 741–70.

Summers, C. 2017. 'All The Kabaka's Wives: Marital Claims In Buganda's 1953–5 Kabaka Crisis'. *Journal of African History* 58 (1): 107–27.

Taoua, P. and J. Teno. 'African Freedom'. The University of Arizona College of Humanities. https://africanfreedom.arizona.edu

Taylor, E. 2016. 'Asians and Africans in Ugandan Urban Life, 1959–1972'. PhD thesis, University of Michigan.

Taylor, E. 2019. 'Affective Registers of Postcolonial Crisis: The Kampala Tank Hill Party'. *Africa* 89 (3): 541–561.

Thompson, G. 2003. *Governing Uganda: British Colonial Rule and its Legacy.* Kampala: Fountain Publishers.

Wyrod, R. 2016. *AIDS and Masculinity in the African City: Privilege, Inequality, and Modern Manhood.* Berkeley: University of California Press.

8

MINZU

Saul Thomas

In this chapter, I consider the Chinese term *minzu* 民族, a term commonly translated as 'nation' in English, as a 'concept from the global south'. I first address the status of *minzu* as an *indigenous* Chinese concept embedded within a traditional symbolic system, as some scholars contend, and counter that it was rather the new concept produced by China's encounter with Western imperialism. Yet I also argue that the concept of *minzu* cannot merely be considered a 'copy' of the Western concept of 'nation', for it was rather always conceived in relation to the West – *minzu* was embedded in an emergent conceptual framework which always explicitly or implicitly situated a Chinese *minzu* as well as the rest of the world in relation to the West. Furthermore, as China and the world as a whole both experienced revolutionary changes over the course of the twentieth century, the meaning of *minzu* was itself transformed. To illustrate these changes, I discuss two compounds prominent during different parts of the century which pointed to widely divergent formulations of *minzu* – *minzuxing* 民族性 ('national character') and *minzu jiefang* 民族解放 ('national liberation'). It is in the later formulation that I argue that *minzu* should be considered as a concept from the Global South. Finally, I argue that the respective rise and fall of these terms and the concepts behind them can be linked to the changing fortunes of a particular social location and intellectual framework – that of the urban, Western-oriented liberal intellectual – over the course of China's revolutionary twentieth century.

While the precise date of the first use of the term *minzu* is a matter of some controversy among scholars, there is near-universal acknowledgment that it appeared no earlier than the late nineteenth century, with most scholars agreeing that its first usage came just before or during the year 1900 (Harrison 2001, p. 104). Most scholars agree that *minzu* was a neologism borrowed from the Japanese, who had invented the term *minzoku* in the late nineteenth century by joining in a new compound the *Kanji*, or Chinese characters, for 'the common

DOI: 10.4324/9781003273530-11

people' (民) and 'clan' or 'lineage' (族) to translate *nationale*, *volk*, and similar analogues in various European languages (Doak 2007). The term quickly came to be adopted as the translation for the English term 'nation'. During this period, many urban educated Chinese avidly read Western works in Japanese translation, as well as essays by Japanese and Chinese thinkers grappling with and commenting on those works, and by the first few years of the twentieth century, this new compound, read in Mandarin as *minzu*, was rapidly taken up and embraced by increasing numbers of intellectuals. The most prominent thinkers and activists of the early twentieth century, including Liang Qichao, Zhang Taiyan, and Sun Yat-sen, prominently featured the concept of *minzu* in their core works and thus became enthusiastic promoters of the term (Duara 1995).

But the adequacy of treating *minzu* simply as a new term to translate 'nation' has been called into question. Frank Dikotter in *The Discourse of Race in Modern China* has argued the strong lexical 'overlap' between *minzu* and the concept of *zhongzu* (a word commonly translated as 'race') in that both terms often 'appear to stress the physical rather than the sociocultural aspects of different peoples', meant that both terms could be translated as 'race' (Dikotter 2015, p. xiv, 152 n.41). Western scholars had before this rarely dwelt upon the fact that many early twentieth century Chinese thinkers – including such influential figures as Sun Yat-sen – made race-based assessments of the inferiority of different peoples. Dikotter argued that previous scholarship had greatly underestimated the significance of the *minzu*–race connection and demonstrated with quotation after quotation from both major and minor intellectual figures, mostly from the nineteenth and early twentieth centuries, that this racialized use of *minzu* was widespread. Dikotter marshaled evidence to demonstrate that Chinese intellectuals believed that different *minzu* could be arrayed on a hierarchy of the most excellent to the most deficient, with darker-skinned peoples of the world figured as congenitally inferior, cementing the idea that *minzu* carried with it unambiguously racist connotations.

Secondly, Dikotter made the further and perhaps more provocative claim that the racialized worldview he suggested underlay the relatively new term *minzu* was in fact not new at all, but it was rather an instantiation of a deeply rooted 'indigenous mode of representation' or 'symbolic universe' denigrating 'barbarians' which could be traced back to some of the earliest written records. With this claim, Dikotter took aim at what he called the 'myth' perpetuated by some China scholars that traditional Chinese civilization was relatively inclusive, and that it always prized learning, cultivation, and educational achievement over the social background or ethnic origin, a disposition, termed 'culturalism' by the influential intellectual historian Joseph Levenson (Dikotter 2015, p. 3; Levenson 1965).

Though Dikotter's evidence for a persistent and prevalent racialized worldview during the imperial period has been called into question by many scholars (for example, Jenner 2001; Zarrow 2006; Müller 2008; Sun 2012), his claims about modern Chinese racialism seemed to ring true among many Western scholars. After the 30-year hiatus of the Mao era (1949–1976) during which travel between China and Western countries had almost ground to a halt, some Western scholars visiting China in the 1980s had reported the somewhat shocking experience of witnessing educated Chinese privately express unambiguously racist attitudes toward darker-skinned peoples (Feigon 1990, p. 108; Jenner 2001, p. 56). Furthermore, throughout the 1980s, there were several well-publicized clashes erupted between Chinese and African students studying in China, the most serious ending in a major riot in Nanjing in late 1988 (Sautman 1994; Lufrano 1994). These facts, combined with the copious evidence of explicit Chinese racism from late-nineteenth and early twentieth century sources, seemed to confirm the racialized nature of the Chinese worldview, particularly when racialized comments are made in terms of superiority and inferiority of different *minzu*.

In this light what, then, could *minzu* contribute as a concept from the Global South? The keys to this question, I argue, lie first in correctly assessing the origins and nature of the racialized sense of *minzu* prevalent in the earlier twentieth century and the post-Mao reform era, and apprehending the global significance of *minzu* during the Mao era, particularly how it related to Maoist China's efforts to affirm solidarity and ally with darker-skinned peoples against Western imperialism (Fennell 2013). We will first turn to the racialized sense of *minzu*.

At the time when *minzu* entered into Chinese intellectual discourse as a translation of European terms for 'nation' and their cognates around the year 1900, the European concept of nation was already thoroughly racialized. The Chinese lexical 'overlap' noted by Dikotter between *minzu* and *zhongzu* ('race') is hardly coincidental considering the fact that many Europeans in the nineteenth and even early twentieth centuries used 'nation' and 'race' almost interchangeably (Stocking 1987, p. 235). Nor was this overlap simply some accidental linguistic indeterminacy inadvertently transferred from the European to the Chinese context. The system of global relations China had been forcibly brought into by the year 1900 was utterly pervaded and regulated by the discourse and practice of racial hierarchy. Social thought, legal institutions, literature and the arts, natural science, and even the global regime of capitalist production and accumulation were deeply implicated in, shaped by, and in turn shaped the global racial hierarchy which had accompanied the emergence and expansion of modern European imperialism.

It is hardly necessary to appeal to a supposed 'predisposition', Chinese thinkers 'must' have had in the form of a traditional racialized framework in order to explain the widespread acceptance of the racialized worldview presented by the world European imperialist system. As many native institutions and categories were becoming marginalized, racial categorization and practices were becoming institutionalized as a part of the project and process of a new system of colonial governmentality and control in China as elsewhere in the world (Goldberg 2009, p. 1275), particularly in those districts of Shanghai and other cities subject to direct European colonial control. Not surprisingly, these areas became the heartlands for the new Western-oriented Chinese intellectual elite. Not a small portion of the Chinese intellectuals who were most famous for their propagation of the notion of a global racial hierarchy (including such figures as the first Chinese translator and propagator of social Darwinism, Yan Fu, and the famous eugenicist Pan Guangdan, among many others) studied abroad themselves.

But this is not to argue that the notion of a racial hierarchy was simply 'copied' by Chinese intellectuals from the West. To home in further on the meanings of *minzu* during this period and the processes which undergirded it, we can turn to the popular discussion among Chinese intellectuals in the early twentieth century of China's *minzuxing* (or its equivalent *guominxing*)[1] or 'national character' – that is, the specific qualities which supposedly distinguish the Chinese *minzu* from the other *minzu* of the world. Quite contrary to what one might expect from a racialized discourse describing one's own people, the consensus among the majority of Chinese intellectuals who participated in this discussion was that the Chinese *minzu* was deeply, if not fatally, flawed. This discussion was popularized by and frequently took form through discussion of the most popular work of fiction by modern China's acclaimed and influential author, Lu Xun, called 'The True Story of Ah Q' (Lu 1977). The 1921 story discusses the vicissitudes and tragic end of a landless peasant. The oddly named peasant Ah Q (his true name is unknown, Lu Xun tells us) is portrayed as ignorant, clownish, exceedingly provincial, at times ridiculously arrogant (given his lack of capabilities), and occasionally pathetically servile. Other than persistence at whatever task he is given, nothing is admirable about Ah Q. He is dirty, weak, and illiterate, his head is marked with ringworm scars, and he is completely oblivious to his debased condition. A set of events brought on by a combination of his own flaws and other misfortunes leads to Ah Q's arrest and eventual execution at the end of the story.

After its publication, the story was immediately understood by its readers as a metaphor, with Ah Q's flaws representing the flawed nature of the Chinese *minzu* as a whole. The impact on China's educated public was electric, and Lu Xun was catapulted to a national literary stardom which continues to this day. This story became a central reference in an entire discussion of China's flawed *minzuxing* or *guominxing* (Foster 2006).

While Lu Xun is widely recognized by scholars as expressing the anxiety of China's educated public over the problems facing their nation and the nation's need for critical self-evaluation, the question of what Lu Xun's work reveals about the concept of *minzu* prevalent among intellectuals at this time has gone largely unexplored. Several critical aspects of this concept of *minzu* are revealed by this phenomenon. The first is the belief that *minzu* could have particular characters, and that these characters could be expressed in terms of 'flaws'. Related to this is the implicit notion that China's (and presumably any other *minzu's*) flaws are in the end responsible for its "condition" as a whole with respect to other *minzu*.

If the Chinese *minzu* was conceived of as flawed, what was the standard to which it was being compared? The answer to this question was obvious to the participants in this discussion: it was flawed compared to a particular vision of the successful (wealthy, powerful, and scientifically advanced) *minzu* of Western Europe and the United States. The fact of China's weakness in comparison to European (and Japanese who had learned from them) power became an increasingly salient and burning issue toward the end of the nineteenth century, as the traditional political, social, and cultural orders were being rapidly undermined by various aspects of the continuing incursions. Numerous explanations for this weakness had been offered by different Chinese thinkers wrestling with this question – from inferior technology to political corruption and incompetence to an oppressive social structure to an outmoded traditional philosophical system. But beginning in the early twentieth century, some came to believe that the root of the problem lay, somehow, in the Chinese *minzu* itself. Liang Qichao and Sun Yat-sen were among those who promoted this idea, and focused in different ways on strengthening or reviving the Chinese *minzu* (conceived of somewhat differently by each of them). Lu Xun sought at this time to 'expose' what he saw as its most debilitating flaws, implicitly understood with respect to an idealized Western norm.

Lydia Liu showed in her pioneering study *Translingual Practice* that not only did the particular qualities, Lu Xun assigned to Ah Q, draw heavily from the American missionary Arthur Smith's patronizing assessment of 'Chinese characteristics' in his book of the same name, but that it was not a coincidence that the figure chosen by Lu Xun to embody the flaws of the *minzu* (including 'disregard for accuracy', 'talent for indirection', 'intellectual turbidity', etc.) was a peasant (Liu 1995; Smith 1900). Peasants made up the vast majority of China's population – it would seem reasonable that the character of the *minzu* would be displayed through the representation of a 'typical' member. But it is important to note the social position of the author and readers with respect to this 'typical' member of the *minzu* – an educated urban Chinese intellectual ascribing a set of flaws to that social position which they believed to be distant from and by many measures inferior to themselves: the backward, narrow-minded, dirty, and uneducated peasant (Liu 1995; Han 2005). Urban readers were unnerved by being confronted with the fact that as Chinese, they were inextricably bound to the backward figure of the Chinese peasantry.

Tani Barlow argues that the social category of 'intellectuals' (*zhishifenzi*), which characterized the new educated urban elite was a social position defined by its location between internal (their backward countrymen) and external (the modern, Enlightened West) others (Barlow 1991). This imagined relationship between the intellectual and the peasant was figured by urban Chinese in the same way as they saw the relationship between the modern West and the backward Chinese nation. It is in this way that the peasant Ah Q could represent the entire *minzu*'s condition – again, vis-à-vis the West. That is to say, the concept of the Chinese *minzu* – and by analogy other *minzu* as well – was tightly bound to the framework of backwardness and modernity, a basic structure in which the 'normal' Western nations reside at the top of a hierarchy, and other nations, with their various non-modern flaws, follow at succeeding stages below. To be sure, the Chinese intellectuals holding this view may have hoped that the Chinese *minzu* could rid itself of its flaws – perhaps by way of uplifting and educating the peasants to approach the 'normalcy' of the urban educated class. Lu Xun certainly hoped this, yet he wrote to a friend that 'I think right now there is no choice but to have the intellectual class [*zhishi jieji*]...find a solution, and talk about the masses later in the future' (Lu 1981, p. 26), and went on to discuss German and French educators whose methods they might follow. Yet his overall assessment of the ability of the masses of Chinese people to be improved was not entirely enthusiastic: 'no one can say with absolute certainty that the *guominxing* will definitely not change' (Lu 1981, p. 18).

This nature of this hierarchical *minzu* worldview posited in Westernized intellectuals' discussion of China's *minzuxing* brings to mind the analysis of the relationship between 'liberal' or 'Enlightenment' thought, hierarchy, and racism raised by such theorists as Prasenjit Duara, David Theo Goldberg, and Michel-Rolph Trouillot. Contrary to the common assumption that liberal Enlightenment thought was and is naturally opposed to racism (as today liberal intellectuals commonly describe racism as 'irrational', 'illiberal,' or even 'tribal'), both Duara and Goldberg argue that the model of objective rationality posited in Enlightenment thought – in which rationality, scientific thinking, and modernity is possessed by some (not coincidentally first and mostly in the West) and not others – can lend itself to a conception of racialized hierarchy, as in the implicit or explicit hierarchies devised by Kant and Hegel (Goldberg 1993; Duara 1995). The anthropologist Michel-Rolph Trouillot suggested that liberal Enlightenment thought obscures – even from itself – its own historical conditions of possibility or particular historical situatedness, presenting itself as objective knowledge consisting of or capable of achieving 'universal' truth untainted and unburdened by the social practices and institutions which purvey it. On the contrary, he argued that enlightened knowledge was marked and enabled by, and carried outside of Europe through, a particular set of unequal local and global social relations – the processes of imperialism and colonization (Trouillot 2003). That many non-Europeans resisted or seemed to have difficulty grasping and embodying the 'universal' truths brought from the West (what Trouillot wryly referred to as 'North Atlantic Universals' (Trouillot 2002) was seen as a sign of their inadequacy – either a lack of proper education, a stubborn clinging to irrational traditions, or natural incapacity. It was this liberal Enlightenment model of knowledge that was embraced by the modern, Western-educated Chinese as they pursued their discussion of China's *minzuxing* and developed its associated worldview.[2]

This connection between intellectuals grounding themselves in liberal or Enlightenment thought and a tendency toward categorizing Western nations as rational/normal vs. their own as deficient/flawed is not unique to Chinese intellectuals. Scholars of Western-oriented intellectuals in other non-Western or 'backward' regions have also noted such a concern with the deficiencies of the local national character (sometimes figured as the 'national culture') – posited as being expressed most purely in the local rural people. Timothy Mitchell notes that Western-educated Egyptian intellectuals identified 'defects in the Egyptian character' as the cause of contemporary political troubles, and the anthropologist Michael Herzfeld has noted a similar anxiety about national character – accompanied by particular anxiety and even 'shame' at the backwardness of the peasants – among urban liberals in Greece (Mitchell 1991, p. 109–111; Herzfeld 2005). This trend is not uncommon among urban Western-educated liberals throughout the non-West. Partha Chatterjee argues that the division of the world into a 'modern' West and essentially backward and traditional East constitutes the central 'thematic' of nationalist thought (generally the province of Western-educated liberals) throughout the colonial world (Chatterjee 1986). All of this suggests that it is a kind of Western-oriented liberal subject position that gave rise to the nation-view prevalent among intellectuals in China during the early twentieth century.

However, for all of the power of the social, institutional, and ideological supports which produced these meanings, including even the global imperialist formation of capitalism, the system was neither in stasis nor immune to internal or newly emergent countervailing tendencies. When we investigate the associated terms *minzuxing* and *guominxing* ('national character') over the course of the twentieth century, a striking fact comes into focus: the terms vanish almost completely from printed materials after 1949. The term *minzu* itself did not disappear – in fact, the term was as prominent as ever after the victory of the Chinese Communist Party (CCP). But the notion that a *minzu* could have a *xing* or 'character' either implicitly or explicitly carrying positive or negative characteristics was absent. During the Mao period, a substantially different concept of *minzu* had gained purchase.

Some light can be shed on the Mao-era concept of *minzu* by assessing another compound which gained increasing popularity from the late 1920s on: *minzu jiefang* or 'national liberation'. This term, promoted particularly by CCP activists and thinkers, contains within it an explicit reference to and condemnation of imperialism. While the concept of 'liberation' suggests that there is an inequality in the world of *minzu*, it is not presented as a natural phenomenon determined by inherent superiority and inferiority. Rather, the hierarchy of *minzu* implied by the concept of *minzu jiefang* is posited as an artificially imposed and illegitimate one. Contrary to an implicit or explicit assertion associating supposed 'flaws' of a *minzu* with its overall condition compared to other *minzu* in the world, the concept of *minzu jiefang* took as its focus the plight of *minzu* which had been conquered and were unjustly dominated by others, and implied that all *minzu* were deserving of sovereignty and dignity. Interestingly, the forces dominating those *minzu* who were struggling for liberation were not typically figured as 'oppressor *minzu*', but rather as a political force – imperialism. There should be, this concept implies, some measure of equality among *minzu* such that no *minzu* should be oppressed or exploited by these outside forces.

This alternative concept of *minzu*, cultivated within the CCP from the 1920s on, was shaped in part by Lenin's explicitly egalitarian, anti-imperialist theorization of what came to be called 'the national question' during and after the Russian Revolution.[3] But China's revolution of 1949, much more so than the Russian Revolution 30 years earlier, came to fruition during and as a major component and representative of a global anti-colonial upsurge, and revolutionary China's position as an Asian country having liberated itself from colonialism and imperialism gave it a credibility that the Soviet Union could not obtain, allowing China, for example, to participate and play an important role in the Bandung Afro-Asian Conference in 1955. China's support for anti-imperialist national liberation movements in Algeria, Vietnam, and elsewhere in Asia, Latin America, and Africa, even intensified after China's break with the Soviet Union in 1961.[4] Images, documents, and films depicting the rural peoples of Africa, Asia, and Latin America (as well, of course, as China) not as backward emblems of their nations' non-modernity, but as rational, normal, dignified people capable of fighting for their and winning their own liberation. China's role and anti-imperialist stance not only won broad support within the Global South, but instigated the National Security apparatus of the United States to identify China as an even greater threat than the Soviet Union to its ability to 'influence' and manage the non-European world in the interests of the global capitalist order it sought to reconstruct and 'lead' in the wake of the crumbling of the European empires (Peck 2006). Within the United States, too, activists such as W.E.B. DuBois and organizations such as the Black Panther Party upheld China as a key ally in the global struggle against racism and imperialism (Fennel 2013; Kelley and Esch 1999).

It was largely with the help of newly liberated African nations that China was admitted into the United Nations in October 1971, having previously been blocked from entry since the Communists' victory in 1949. China's ambassador to the United Nations, Qiao Guanhua, embraced this alliance and used the platform of the United Nations to castigate the continued political and economic domination and exploitation of peoples of Asia, Latin America, and Africa by the 'superpowers', declaring that 'states want independence, nations want liberation, and peoples want revolution', and that this was 'the irresistible trend of history' (Friedman 2015, p. 197). Deng Xiaoping addressed similar themes at a speech at the United Nations in 1974, encouraging Third World peoples to develop their own resources rather than relying on foreign capital, and cultivate cooperation among developing countries in order to change 'the present extremely unequal international economic relations' (Teng 1974).

It is also worthwhile here to undertake a closer examination of the relation between this *minzu*-view and the subject position and the Western-oriented educated urban intellectuals who had propagated the *minzuxing/guominxing* discourse of China's flawed national character. I have noted above that the peasant was figured by Western-oriented intellectuals as their own irrational unenlightened opposite. During the process of the revolution – and throughout the Mao period – the portrayal of peasants as backward, conservative, and ignorant was not only repudiated in content, but the epistemology underlying it was repudiated as well. Much of the knowledge of the social world possessed by the educated urban elite was not seen by the Chinese Communists as 'objectively' valuable and correct, but rather, to a large extent, as rooted in an elite class position that denigrated and justified the oppression of the rural poor. As opposed to conceiving the rural poor as 'deficient' and inferior, the Communists evaluated them from the standpoint of their status as the oppressed direct producers of social wealth – as morally worthy and as constituting the foundation of society.

It is well known that during the Mao period that intellectuals (by whom it is meant non-Communist, chiefly Western-oriented liberal intellectuals) were targeted and subjected to persecution (though often what was figured as persecution amounted to loss of former privileges and being made to live in the same conditions as the majority of the peasants). In truth, the social position of the Western-oriented educated urban Chinese came under siege and was struggled against. The institutional support which maintained it – most importantly the higher education system, concentrated in a handful of cities and accessible to a very small minority of the population – was, from the very beginning of the Mao era, identified as expanding the social distance between the educated urban and rural people, and was marked for complete transformation. In its place, the Communists instituted a system of participation in labor for students and teachers in both factories and rural agricultural areas in cooperation with local workers and peasants. The explicit goal of these policies was to decrease the social distance between mental and manual laborers and foster a sense of community and respect for rural laborers rather than derision. At the height of this trend, during the Cultural Revolution, the university entrance examination system was abolished, and the rural and urban poor were given priority for university slots – where they were now figured as 'worker-peasant-soldier' students – at the expense of the families of the previous educated elite who had monopolized those positions up to that point (Andreas 2009).

As the urban Western-oriented liberal intellectual subject position was sidelined, so was public denigration of the peasant, to the extent that such denigration was implicitly prohibited in the Mao period. While Lu Xun (who had before his death in 1936 come to praise the Communists and castigate their opponents) was promoted as an outstanding intellectual and moral exemplar, during this period, his 'True Story of Ah Q', which had done so much to establish his own fame, and shape the discussion of the flawed Chinese 'national character', was not promoted at all. As the ideological legitimacy and social basis for the Western-oriented liberal intellectual were undermined, so, too, was the ideological basis for imagining the *minzu* of the world as divided between the normal/rational and deficient/irrational also undermined.

With the death of Mao in 1976 and the initiation of the 'market reforms' soon after, a near-complete ideological economic and social reversal soon ensued. Externally, China's anti-imperialist agitation and support for national liberation movements rapidly declined as the government reoriented itself toward the West first to learn scientific and economic techniques in the name of modernization, and then promoted itself to the west as a stable and secure location for investment and commodity production. Internally, within a year of Mao's death, the Mao-era attacks on elitism in education and the deprivileging of the social position of the urban educated class were utterly repudiated by the new Party leadership (headed by a reoriented Deng Xiaoping) as having brought disaster to the Chinese *minzu* and delayed its modernization. As the post-Mao party elite vociferously promoted efficiency and technological acumen over equality, no more were students or teachers required or asked to participate with workers and peasants in factory or especially rural labor. A now even more highly competitive university entrance examination was restored, and state funding of education was increasingly channeled upward to the most elite schools. These schools again began to favor the already urban and privileged families, who again came to equate academic success with a general level of superiority. Previously harshly suppressed and undermined, now the social position of the intellectual was vindicated (Yan 2008; Andreas 2009).

With these changes, along with the gradual re-exposure of ever-larger portions of society to market capitalism, came the rapid decline of the status of the peasant in intellectual discourse (Yan 2008; Day 2015). Maoism as a whole – from its egalitarian ethos to the process of policy implementation – came to be blamed by intellectuals on the ignorance and backwardness of the peasants, and Mao was identified by some intellectuals as the 'emperor' who the traditional peasants had elevated to power. Artistic and film portrayals of peasants began to portray the peasants as dirty, old, and backward. Not coincidentally, Lu Xun's 'The True Story of Ah Q' enjoyed something of a renaissance and was adapted to film for the first time in 1981. And accompanying these developments was the revival of the discourse of China's inherently flawed *minzuxing*. In the immediate post-Mao decade, hundreds of articles, many books, and even academic conferences were devoted to determining the nature of China's flawed *minzuxing*. Some such works are still produced by Chinese intellectuals today.

The revival of discourse on China's flawed *minzuxing* is a clue that a hierarchical *minzu*-view had reappeared in the post-Mao period. This is born out in the emergence of an idealized vision of the West, and especially the United States, which proliferated among intellectuals in the 1980s (Chen 2003), against which some intellectuals again linked political and other social problems with an allegedly inferior *minzu* 'character' (Liu 1986). Nor was the reemergence of a hierarchical *minzu*-view confined to China-West comparisons. It was in the 1980's that 'an anti-African racism developed in university campuses', leading in a few cases to the clashes between Chinese and African students mentioned earlier in this essay. Barry Sautman noted and demonstrated through a survey the convergence of Chinese students' low estimation of Chinese peasants and Africans (Sautman 1994; Lufrano 1994; Cheng 2019).

A search of the related terms *minzuxing* and *guominxing* in the National Index to Chinese Newspapers (*Quanguo baokan suoyin* 全国报刊索引) shows the shifting fortunes of the terms over the course of the twentieth century, from their advent in the first years of the century, to their virtual disappearance during the Mao period from the 1950s through the 1970s, to their quick revival in the Reform Era beginning in the 1980s (see Figure 8.1).

Compared with the term *minzu jiefang* over the same period, we see what appears to be a mostly inverse relationship: the concept of *minzu jiefang* flourished while *minzuxing* and *guominxing* were nearly entirely absent from the newspapers during the Mao period, and then declined during the reform era while *minzuxing* and *guominxing* enjoyed revivals (Figure 8.2).

The account given above is neither meant to give an entirely uncritical defense of China during the Mao era, nor argue its Third World or African policy was beyond reproach. Whether born out of realpolitik or opportunism arising from competition with the Soviet Union, or some internal Cultural Revolution factional battles the nature of which is still unknown, Maoist China's missteps with regard to particular struggles in the Third World have been justly criticized (Prashad 2007). But these failures cannot erase the overall cultural and political significance of revolutionary

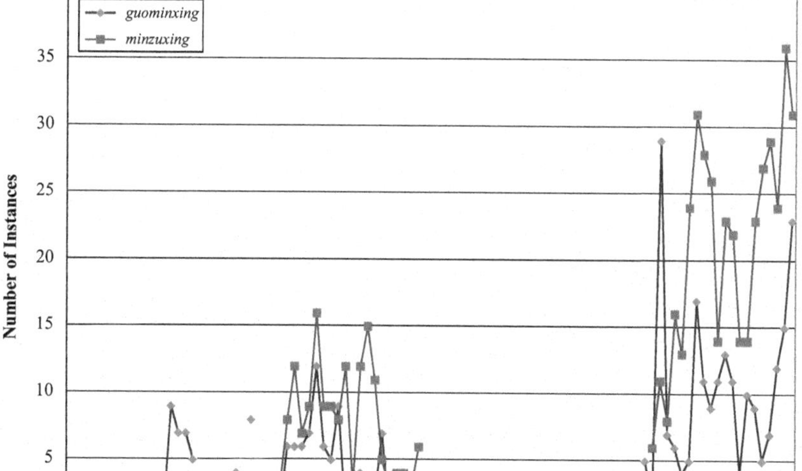

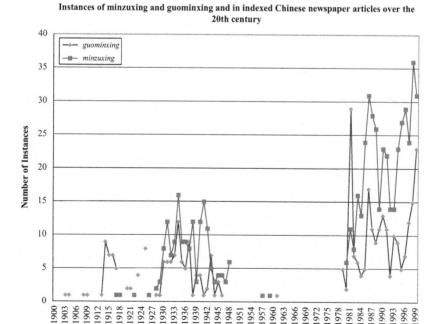

FIGURE 8.1 Instances of *minzuxing* and *guominxing* appearing in the National Index to Chinese Newspapers

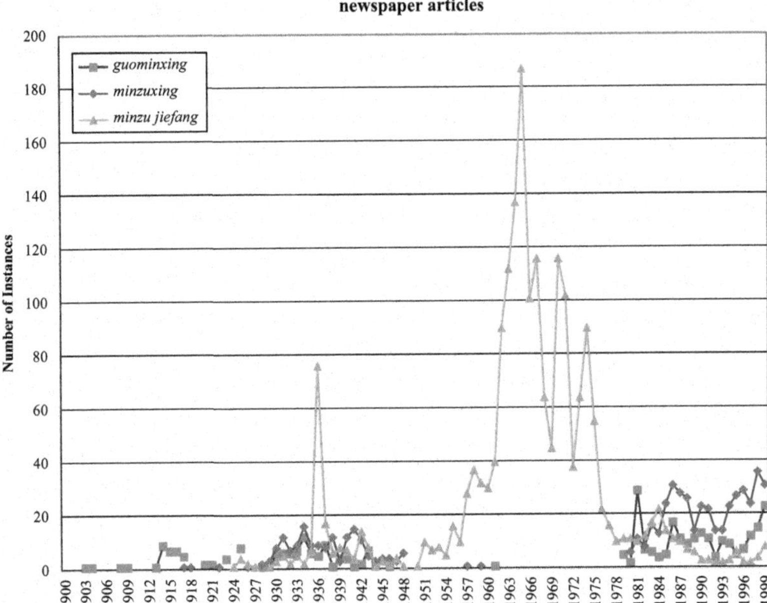

FIGURE 8.2 Instances of *minzuxing* and *guominxing* compared with the term *minzu jiefang* appearing in the National Index to Chinese Newspapers

China, and the role it would play as a manifestation and representative of the global Third World challenge against Euro-American capitalist hegemony.

Minzu has been intertwined with China's relationship with the West and has been shaped by the changing status of Western-oriented urban intellectuals, and in turn, linked with China's different relationship to the West and Global South. The compounds *minzuxing* ('national character') and *minzu jiefang* ('national liberation') show that the concept of *minzu* shifted over the course of the twentieth century from a hierarchical conception of people groups with different inherent characteristics that determine their destiny, to a conception of nations equally deserving freedom from domination and imperialism, and back to a hierarchical conception again. I argue that these shifts in meaning were intimately related to the changing social conditions for the production of knowledge and the social/class location of intellectuals.

The concept of *minzu* exemplified in the compound *minzu jiefang* pointed to the promise of a 'South-South' solidarity grounded in relations of equality. This in turn was facilitated both by the larger context of a global anti-colonial movement and by a set of social practices within China which undermined institutional bases of elitism, particularly in education, and an ideological program that repudiated hierarchical notions on both the national and international scales.

Notes

1 *Minzuxing* is used interchangeably with *guominxing* 国民性 (literally, the nature of the people of the country) in this discussion. They both denote a set of supposedly stable characteristics broadly shared among the entire population of the *minzu*.

2 Lu Xun himself was a complicated and deeply profound thinker, and by the late 1920s he had distanced himself from both the pro-Enlightenment, Western-oriented anti-traditionalism he had championed in the previous 10 years. Not coincidentally, he also ceased writing 'Ah Q'-style lampoons of 'traditional' rural people and other pronouncements on the deficient or flawed 'national character' supposedly rooted in the Chinese masses.

3 Rebecca Karl traces the beginning of a nonracialized anti-imperialist nationalism in China even earlier to Chinese writers and activists at the turn of the twentieth century (Karl 2002).

4 This process was not without setbacks, the most serious of which may have been China's conflict and border war with India, which was exacerbated by China's conflict with the Soviet Union among other factors (Prashad 2007).

Bibliography

Andreas, J. (2009) *Rise of the Red Engineers: The Cultural Revolution and the Origins of China's New Class*. Stanford: Stanford University Press.

Barlow, T. (1991) 'Zhishifenzi (Chinese Intellectuals) and Power', *Dialectical Anthropology*, 16, pp. 209–232.

Bulag, U. E. (2012) 'Good Han, Bad Han: The Moral Parameters of Ethnopolitics in China', in Mullaney, T. S. et al. (eds.) *Critical Han Studies: The History, Representation, and Identity of China's Majority*. Berkeley: University of California, pp. 92–109.

Chatterjee, P. (1986) *Nationalist Thought and the Colonial World: A Derivative Discourse*. Minneapolis: University of Minnesota.

Chen, X. (2003) *Occidentalism: A Theory of Counter-Discourse in Post-Mao China*. 2nd Revised & Enlarged edition. Lanham, Md: Rowman & Littlefield Publishers.

Cheng, Y. (2019) *Discourses of Race and Rising China*. Cham, Switzerland: Palgrave Macmillan.

Day, A. F. (2015) *The Peasant in Postsocialist China: History, Politics, and Capitalism*. Cambridge: Cambridge University Press.

Dikötter, F. (2015) *The Discourse of Race in Modern China: Fully Revised and Expanded Second Edition*. Oxford: Oxford University Press.

Dikötter, F. (2016) *The Cultural Revolution: A People's History, 1962–1976*. New York: Bloomsbury.

Ding, W. (2006) *Zhongguo minzuxing*. Xi'an: Shaanxi shifan daxue chubanshe.

Doak, K. M. (2007) *A History of Nationalism in Modern Japan: Placing the People*. Leiden; Boston: Brill.

Duara, P. (1995) *Rescuing History from the Nation: Questioning Narratives of Modern China*. Chicago: University of Chicago.

Feigon, L. (1990) *China Rising: The Meaning of Tiananmen*. Chicago: I.R. Dee.

Fennell, V. L. (2013) 'Race: China's Question and Problem', *Review of Black Political Economy*, 40(3), pp. 245–275.

Foster, P. B. (2006) *Ah Q Archaeology: Lu Xun, Ah Q, Ah Q Progeny and the National Character Discourse in Twentieth Century China*. Lanham, MD: Lexington Books.

Friedman, J. S. (2015) *Shadow Cold War: The Sino-Soviet Competition for the Third World*. Chapel Hill: University of North Carolina Press.

Goldberg, D. T. (1993) *Racist Culture: Philosophy and the Politics of Meaning.* Cambridge, Mass: Blackwell.
Goldberg, D. T. (2009) 'Racial Comparisons, Relational Racisms: Some Thoughts on Method', *Ethnic and Racial Studies*, 32(7), pp. 1271–1282.
Han, X. (2005) *Chinese Discourses on the Peasant, 1900–1949.* Albany: State University of New York Press.
Harrison, H. (2001) *China: Inventing the Nation.* London: Arnold.
Herzfeld, M. (2005) *Cultural Intimacy: Social Poetics in the Nation-State.* 2nd ed. New York: Routledge.
Hevi, E. J. (1963) *An African Student in China.* New York: Praeger
Jenner, W. J. F. (1993) 'The Discourse of Race in Modern China (Review)', *The Australian Journal of Chinese Affairs*, (30), pp. 199–200.
Jenner, W. J. F. (2001) 'Race and History in China', *New Left Review*, 11, pp. 55–77.
Karl, R. E. (2002) *Staging the World: Chinese Nationalism at the Turn of the Twentieth Century.* Durham: Duke University Press.
Kelley, R. D. G. and Esch, B. (1999) 'Black like Mao: Red China and Black Revolution', *Souls*, 1(4), 6–41.
Leibold, J. (2007) *Reconfiguring Chinese Nationalism: How the Qing Frontier and its Indigenes Became Chinese.* London: Palgrave Macmillan.
Levenson, J. (1965) *Confucian China and Its Modern Fate.* London: Routledge and Kegan Paul.
Liu, L. H. (1995) *Translingual Practice: Literature, National Culture, and Translated Modernity--China, 1900–1937.* Stanford: Stanford.
Liu, X. (1986) 'Weiji! Xin shiqi wenxue mianlin weiji', *Shenzhen qingnian bao*, 3 October 3, p.3.
Lu, H. (1977) *Selected stories of Lu Hsun.* New York: Norton.
Lu, X. (1981) *Lu Xun quanji.* Vol. 3. Beijing: Renmin wenxue chubanshe.
Lufrano, R. (1994) 'The 1988 Nanjing Incident: Notes on Race and Politics in Contemporary China', *Bulletin of Concerned Asian Scholars*, 26(1–2), pp. 83–92.
Matten, M. A. (2012) '"China is the China of the Chinese": The Concept of Nation and Its Impact on Political Thinking in Modern China', *Oriens Extremus*, pp. 63–106.
Mitchell, T. (1991) *Colonising Egypt.* Berkeley: University of California Press.
Müller, G. (2008) 'Are We "yellow" and Who Is "us"? China's Problems with Glocalizing the Concept of Race (around 1900)', *Bochumer Jahrbuch zur Ostasienforschung*, 32, pp. 153–180.
Peck, J. (2006) *Washington's China: The National Security World, the Cold War, and the Origins of Globalism. Culture, politics, and the cold war.* Amherst: University of Massachusetts Press
Prashad, V. (2007) *The Darker Nations: A People's History of the Third World.* New York: New Press.
Sautman, B. (1994) 'Anti-Black Racism in Post-Mao China', *The China Quarterly*, (138), pp. 413–437.
Smith, A. H. (1900) *Chinese Characteristics.* London: Oliphant, Anderson & Ferrier.
Stocking, G. W. (1987) *Victorian Anthropology.* New York: Free Press, 1987.
Sun, J. (2012) 'Blumenbach in East Asia: The Dissemination of the "Five-Race Theory" in East Asia and a Textual Comparison', *Oriens Extremus*, 51, pp. 107–153.
Teng, H. (1974) *Speech by Chairman of the Delegation of the People's Republic of China, Teng Hsiao-Ping, at the Special Session of the U.N. General Assembly, April 10, 1974.* Peking: Foreign Languages Press.
Trouillot, M.-R. (2002) 'North Atlantic Universals: Analytical Fictions, 1492–1945', *South Atlantic Quarterly*, 101(4), pp. 839–58.

Trouillot, M.-R. (2003) *Global Transformations: Anthropology and the Modern World*. New York: Palgrave.

Wang, S. (1961) 'Guanyu 'guominxing' wenti: du Lu Xun zawen zhaji', *Guangming ribao*, 16 October.

Wu, G. (2007) 'Injured Self-Image: Rethinking the Critique of Chinese National Character as an Intellectual Discourse', *The Chinese Historical Review*, 14(2), pp. 266–290.

Yan, H. (2008) *New Masters, New Servants: Migration, Development, and Women Workers in China*. Durham: Duke University Press.

Zarrow, P. (2006) 'Liang Qichao and the Conceptualization of "Race" in Late Qing China', *Zhongyang yanjiuyuan jindaishi yanjiusuo jikan*, (52), pp. 113–63.

Zhang, J. and Qu, G. (2016) Ah Q de tuxiang xipuxue fenxi. *Zhongguo wenzhe yanjiu tongxun*, 26(4), pp. 147–193.

9

KAVI

Shonaleeka Kaul

Kāvya is literature as art – highly aesthetic poetry and prose, composed chiefly in Sanskrit during the first millennium CE and after. The genre is marked by the use of ornamented, figurative language (*alaṃkāra*), and the evocation of various states of essentialized emotion (*rasa*), from the erotic and heroic to the calm and compassionate. Occurring in at least four subgenres including drama, biography, and tale, *kāvya* is most widely understood as epic poetry, *mahākāvya* – continuous, metrical, narrative verse. It is associated with some of the literary luminaries of the ancient Indic world like Kālidāsa, Śūdraka, Bāṇa, Māgha, Daṇḍin, and so on. The composer of *kāvya* was the *kavi*, the quintessential poet. It is the self-representation of the *kavi* in Sanskrit poetry and in the theory of its poetics that is the focus of this essay. In particular, the poet's claim to epistemic insight and authority that extended to knowledge of the past, as such positioning him as a historian par excellence and more, as we shall see.

This claim in premodern India on behalf of the poetic vision as a historical vision is important to underline because mainstream modern scholarship has not acknowledged *kāvya* as history but merely as the realm of aesthetics and rhetoric. Aesthetics and rhetoric, in turn, have been misconstrued as sterile, self-indulgent constructs rather than as semantic codes and symbolic investments, which is what I have argued elsewhere these were (Kaul 2010). One of the reasons for this situation is that after Leopold von Ranke (1795–1886), and the European Enlightenment more generally, the discipline of history came to hegemonically acquire enduring overtones of objectivism and scientism, automatically generating a distance from the humanities and in particular creating an unfortunate opposition vis-à-vis literature and poetry. Thus, the latter's figurative and subjective modes of apprehending and rendering reality and truth, such as intuition, symbolism, mythmaking, and didacticism, suffered a slide from recognition. And when positivism mingled with imperialism through the likes of James Mill

DOI: 10.4324/9781003273530-12

(1817) and others in the early nineteenth century, who influentially denied any sense of history or even rationality to colonized India and accused her literary traditions of failing to measure up to their Judeo-Christian counterparts, it ended up downgrading and delegitimizing indigenous Indian narratives of the past and traditional modes of history (Mantena 2007: 396–408).

Though recently there has been some scholarly interest in identifying and reclaiming such genres and modes from early India, it is a rather fraught process, and has barely taken on board a patently poetic genre like *kāvya*, and even less the *kavi*'s own take on history. (For a discussion of these recent positions on history writing in early India, see Kaul 2018a.) This essay attempts to redress this gap by demonstrating that a clear theoretical enunciation of poetry as history is to be found in Sanskrit poetics. And further, that the practice of this theory may have consisted in developing an ethico-political discursivity that frames the understanding of historical knowledge and defines, in a culturally specific yet potentially universal manner, what 'true' knowledge of time and human action may be.

Now, who or what is the *kavi*? The earliest work on Sanskrit etymology, the *Nirukta* by Yāska, fifth century BCE, gives the meaning of *kavi* as follows: *kaviḥ krāntadarśano bhavati*, or the poet is the true seer (1.12.13 in Sarup 1927). It is a testament to the continuity of this semantic tradition that even 1500 years later, the Kashmiri rhetorician Bhaṭṭa Tauta, the preceptor of the renowned Abhinavagupta, was explicating the idea of the *kavi* in identical terms:

> None a poet (*kavi*) but also a seer (*ṛṣi*). A seer is so called because of his vision (*darśana*), which is knowledge of the true nature of entities and their varied states of being. And it is because of his vision of the truth that the seer is declared…a poet. The conventional meaning of the word poet, for its part, is derived from his capacity for vision (*darśana)* as well as his powers of description (*varṇana*).
>
> *(432, translation by Pollock 2004: 53)*

Similarly, the great Rājaśekhara in his tenth century *Kāvyamīmāṃsā,* an influential text of the science of Sanskrit poetics (*alaṃkāraśāstra*), speaks of the power *śakti*) of true poets lying in their divine sight (*divyadṛṣṭi*) that enables them to perceive that which no one before them has ever seen. He also likened poetic power to spiritual omniscience, saying: 'Poets explore with their words that which *yogin*s see through the power of their spiritual accomplishments' (12. 62-63, translation by Granoff 1995: 364).

Thus, over a millennium of *kāvya* theory, the *kavi*'s special insight was a steady article of faith for generations of poets. But insight into what exactly? The true nature of entities and their varied, changing states, as Bhaṭṭa Tauta tells us. Or, witness the words of Kalhaṇa, the twelfth century Kashmiri *kavi* who, significantly, has been celebrated by modern scholars as the author of the only work of history proper in Sanskrit, the *Rājataraṅgiṇī*. Kalhaṇa, in a show of metadiscursive reflexiveness, says in the preamble to his iconic poem, that the talented *kavi* is able to truly see (*paśyet*) existences otherwise commonly known (*sarvasamvedyān bhāvān*) by virtue of his intuition and creative insight (*pratibhayā*), and that (somewhat circularly) this is an indication of the poet's divine sight (*divyadriṣṭitva kaveḥ*) (RT I.5). He thus claims for the poet a special ontic access to the reality of things, so much so that he says *satkavikṛtyam andham jagattvām vinā*, that is, the world is in darkness without the illumining work of the good poet (RT I. 47).

But before all this begins to appear overly metaphysical rather than this-worldly (which is what history relates to), a political component to the poet's vision and area of interest also emerges. Thus, transitioning from the seemingly abstract to the acutely political, Kalhaṇa states that it is particularly the deeds of kings that would be lost forever were it not for the poet who resurrects, vivifies, and embodies their glory (*yaśaḥ kāyaḥ*) through his words (RT I. 3, 45). He further writes:

> Renowned [and mighty] kings...would not even be remembered without the favour of the poet's work (*anugraham kavikarmaṇe*). To the art of the poet, which is sublime, we offer salutations.
>
> *(RT I.46. Translation by Pandit)*

Interestingly, this is precisely the self-projection that is found in the works of other Sanskrit poets as well, for instance, the eleventh century Bilhaṇa who composed the *Vikramāṅkadevacarita* (I. 26) and the twelfth century Ratnākara who wrote the *Haravijaya* (VI.8) (Slaje 2008: 216–17). An important difference remains that unlike the others, Kalhaṇa does not seem to have been a court poet. In any case, they all speak of the king's glory (*yaśaḥ*) being the work (*kṛtam*) of the *kavi*.

This assertion of the dependence of the king, the patron, on the poet rather than the other way around – deserves to be underlined. It contradicts the stereotype, cultivated by supercilious moderns, of the ancient poet passively prostrating before his courtly patrons, a mere 'housebird' of patricians as D.D Kosambi (1957) provocatively labeled the Sanskrit *kavi*. (For a critique of this collapsing of patron and poet, and of the elitist characterization of *kāvya* literature generally, see Kaul 2010.) Contrary to this characterization, ancient *kavi*s in fact emerge as self-assertive and opinionated vis-à-vis the political order vested in the monarch. For example, as we will see later in this essay, while Kalhaṇa's entire epic is a stellar critique of monarchical power, his compatriot Bilhaṇa demonstrates the condescension and contempt that a poet could display for his political master. Thus, he says of his patron, the eleventh century Western Chalukya king Vikramaditya VI of Kalyani, in the latter's own biography *Vikramāṅkadevacarita* which Bilhaṇa was commissioned to write:

> When their own accomplishments
> Are few and far between,

Why ever do kings gather around them
Poet laureates?
What need, indeed, would
Berry-wearing forest dwellers
Have for goldsmiths-in-residence?

(I.25, translated by author)

Though I appear to digress, these observations are germane to my argument, that is, to explicating the meaning and function of the *kavi*. I believe that his assumed superiority and autonomy vis-à-vis the world and even the king perhaps lent a greater force to the *kavi*'s authority, epistemic and otherwise.

What is more, it is in his indispensability to the royal project that we see the *kavi* approaching the proto-historic role of the poet as documenter, if not historian. But, as the poets also proceed to tell us, it is not just royalty but speaking of all matters past (*bhūtārthakathanam*) that is the job of the *kavi*. Kalhaṇa's successor *kavi* Śrīvara, who composed a sequel to the *Rājataraṅgiṇī* in the fifteenth century, puts the relationship between poetry and the past in crystal clear terms thus: '*kāvyadīpam bhūtavastuprakāśakam*'(I. 1, 4 in Kaul 1966) that is, *kāvya* is the lamp that illuminates matters of the past.

There can be no doubt that in these self-conscious statements we find a concrete assertion of the epistemic capacity of poets. But that is not all. The *kavi*'s access to the past is not merely by way of illuminating it. In a strikingly constructivist approach to the past and to the pursuit of its knowledge, the poet is understood to be not just the 'knower' but even the 'creator' of the past: *kavi-prajāpati* or *kavi-vedhas*, that is, poet-creator. Thus, Kalhana writes: 'Who else is capable of making visible (*pratyakṣatām*) bygone times except the poet-creator who can make delightful productions (*ramyanirmāṇa*)?' (RT I. 4). It should be noted that Kalhaṇa is merely repeating the understanding and usage in a host of poets and poeticians before him (Bāṇa, Ānandavardhana, Abhinavagupta, and Kuntaka).[1] Here again, then, is Sanskrit *kāvya*'s belief in the poet's creative ability to make the unobservable past perceptible – the quintessentially historical function – and indeed a statement on the past itself so rendered as a construction or production (*nirmāṇa*).

Equipped thus with complete authority over the past and over its 'true' nature and meaning, the *kavi* often proceeds to instruct the present, either directly or symbolically. Here is where the second component to the *kavi*'s engagement with history after the political – but not detached from the political – comes into the foreground, namely, the ethical-discursive or the didactic.

Now the didactic in Sanskrit *kāvya* has often been regarded as some conventional, rhetorical superfluity, or a residual symptom of the poet's Brahmanical allegiance to the concept of *dharma* (piety/socioethical order) – never as possibly a central part of *kāvya*'s mandate, not even when it is such a significant and recurrent strain in a deemed historical *kāvya* like the *Rājataraṅgiṇī*, as I will show. Sheldon Pollock, the leading authority on *kāvya* studies today, even as he argues for *kāvya* as a discourse of power, maintains that the didactic function was entirely subordinated to the aesthetic objective in *kāvya* (Pollock 2004: 49–50). I submit, on the other hand, especially but not only on the strength of the *Rājataraṅgiṇī*, that the didactic is inseparable from the aesthetic, and it is the combination that made *kāvya* so powerful a politico-literary phenomenon.

One look again at the theory of Sanskrit poetics will tell you why one takes such a position. As I have argued elsewhere, while *kāvya* may be distinguished by the highly aesthetic form of figurative language it cultivates, its objectives went beyond the aesthetic (Kaul 2010). Among its stated objectives was *lokasya anukaraṇa* or mimesis of the world, and *upadeśa* or instruction about worldly affairs, encapsulated in the concept of *trivarga*, which refers to *dharma, artha, kāma* – in other words, the entire spectrum of human goals and activities divisible into piety, power, and pleasure. As we will later see, this instruction could and did extend sometimes to the fourth goal, *mokṣa* or liberation through detachment as well. From Bharata in the second century who used the term *upadeśa* in the *Nāṭyaśāstra* (I. 111-13 in Kavi 1934), the first work on Sanskrit dramaturgy, and Bhāmaha in the fifth century who spoke of *vaicakṣaṇya* (understanding/expertise) in his *Kavyālaṃkāra* (I.2 in Sarma and Upadhyaya 1928), to Bhoja in the eleventh century who uses the term *adhyeyam* (lesson) in the *Śṛṅgāraprakāśa* (596 in Raghavan 1998), this contemplative-educative function of *kāvya* remained a constant refrain among rhetoricians. The point is most directly made by Abhinavagupta in his eleventh century commentary on the *Nāṭyaśāstra*, the *Abhinavabhāratī*. He writes in no uncertain terms that the end result of the savoring of poetry is instruction in *dharma* and the other ends of man (*Abhinavabhāratī* 1.261, 1.36, 1.292.20, and 1.276 quoted in Pollock 2017: 33).

Further, it is my belief that this didacticism framed not only the rhetorical but the historical agenda of *kāvya*. In fact, the coalescing of didactic with historical functions via poetry meant that the model of epistemic truth generated by *kāvya* was both transcendent, in invoking higher ethical ends, and contingent in so far as it was located in a referentially adduced, historical past.

Let me illustrate my hypothesis by the example of the one *kāvya* accepted as historical by modern scholars, albeit for objectivist reasons external to the text, and which had nothing to do with it being poetry at all. In fact, the modern positivist interpretation of Kalhaṇa's *Rājataraṅgiṇī* as history privileged qualities such as objectivity and causality but shunned and dismissed all aspects of figuration proper and integral to it as a traditional *kāvya*, such as rhetoric, didactics, and myth (see Kaul 2018a). I would argue that it is precisely through these poetic means and devices, which as a matter of fact constitute the bulk of the text, that the *Rājataraṅgiṇī* achieves historicality.

The *Rājataraṅgiṇī* is a twelfth century, sprawling dynastic account of the ancient kingdom of Kashmir from its putative origins till the poet's own time. Apart from recording all the different royal dynasties, it evaluates governance and kingship according to certain principles with which the *kavi* frames his composition (Kaul 2018a). This ethicized commentary runs through the text, unifying his account in a moral logic. It is this unity of plan, I argue, that characterizes the *Rājataraṅgiṇī* as a poetic and historical narrative. In his very first chapter, Kalhaṇa, in fact, declares the organizing principle of his vision, which happens to be both historical and ethical. He tells us:

> From time to time, due to the spiritual merit of the subjects, kings appear who organize a kingdom that is sunk deep in disorder (*dūrotsannasya maṇḍalasya yojanam kriyate*). Those who are intent on harassing their subjects (*prajāpīḍanam*) perish with their families; on the other hand, fortune waits on even the descendants of those who reinstate order where there is chaos. ...this [is] the feature of each tale given here (*prativṛttāntam lakṣaṇam*)...(RT I.187-89). Single-minded application in protecting the subjects is the sacred duty of kings (*prajānupālanenanyakarmatā bhūbhṛtām vratam*).
>
> *(RT II.47-48. Pandit's translation.)*

Ensuring these didactic aims were meant to be a series of qualities in the king: good conduct (*sadācāraḥ*), righteousness (*sat*), generosity/liberality (*dākṣiṇya*), discriminating intellect, encouraging men of merit, character, and learning, and the will to enforce justice (*dharma*) and absence of fear (*abhaya*) among the subjects (RT VII. 773, VIII. 2663, VI. 193, VII. 998, VIII. 122, 2034, V. 204-05, I. 350-58, III. 131-45, and 300-23). The *kavi* thus lays out a highly prescriptive list of personal and political values that draw on a conception of moral order to which the king's commitment is expected. Then, these values are plotted through a series of kings as exemplars excavated by the *kavi* in Kashmir's past. Further, he often arranges these exemplars in pairs, elucidating their comparative morality. Thus the hedonist Vibhīṣaṇa is succeeded to the throne by his son, Siddha the puritan; the violent Mihirakula by the righteous Baka; and the just Candrāpīḍa by the tyrannical Tārāpīḍa. And the debauched father and son, Kalaṣa and Harṣa, by the high-minded and high-souled Uccala (Kaul 2018a). These were all sets of historical kings separated by centuries but connected by the *kavi*'s hermeneutical scheme.

In fact, I argue that the title of the poem, *Rājataraṅgiṇī*, which means River of Kings, is an allusion to history as precisely this flow of ethical exemplars. This schematic organisation of the text articulating the poet's ethicized vision is striking when its didacticism and rhetoric are not dismissed. It is here that the *Rājataraṅgiṇī* displays what Hayden White (1973, 1987) has called narrativization or the configuration of historical 'facts' around a plot-structure that endows otherwise random data with a unified structure and meaning, thereby rising above mere seriality. Narrativity in the *Rājataraṅgiṇī* embodies the poet's vision of the past, endowing that past with culturally sanctioned meanings that etched a profound understanding of historicity in early India.

Even as he laid down a model for kingship in Kashmir in this fashion, so acute is *kavi* Kalhaṇa's didactic strain that it trains its guns on monarchy itself. Thus, though the text treats it as exalted, it also critiques monarchy, through a range of comments and parables, as an inherently and inevitably unreliable and fickle institution. As a matter of fact, this is how several classical *kāvyas* have regarded kingship, in ways more or less obvious, inscribing *kāvya*'s own intervention in the discourse of *artha* and *rājadharma* or politics and power (Kaul 2010). To remind you, I would argue that this was an integral part of *kāvya*'s mandate.

Building on this, Kalhaṇa offers a larger critique of power which rounds off and deepens the concern for the ethical and the discursive with which the *kavi* seeks to frame his meditative poem. Thus, drawing intertextually on popular mythology from the *Rāmāyaṇa* and the *Mahābhārata*, the two master epics of the Sanskrit archive, the following analogy at the death of a powerful king offers a corrective to the might of monarchy:

> The lord of Lankā, conqueror of the three worlds, suffered a rout at the hands of monkeys; the lord of the Kurus, paramount among kings, received a kick on the head. Thus, everyone has … a mischance stripping him of his exalted rank as if he were a commoner. Who indeed can afford to be high and mighty and, obsessed with oneself, persist in conceit?
>
> *(RT VIII.335 Pandit's translation)*

Again, in a moral and mortal take on power, Kalhaṇa has a Kashmiri king-protagonist soliloquize thus:

> There is perhaps no man who, having been at first shown favour [by Royal Fortune, the sweetheart of kings], has later not been harassed by her, as by the friendship of the vulgar … She, who is without affection, has never followed kings in death when they, without friends or provisions, are en route for the next world … Gold vessels of the banquet and other articles collected in the treasury rooms – how is it that those kings who have departed for the next world [no longer] own them? … Torn from the necks of those [enemies] about to die … the necklaces, accursed and unholy, for whom are they an attraction? Predecessors have left behind ornaments defiling them with hot tears of anguish when about to die; while touching them, who does not have a qualm?
>
> *(RT V.6-15. Pandit's translation)*

Elsewhere in the *Rājataraṅgiṇī* the *kavi* comments: 'Even after realizing the transient nature of existence, fools do not give up ambition, seduced as they are by the attractions of treacherous fortune' *(RT VI.146)*. But

> 'on the same path of death is every individual plunging headlong. I am the slayer and he the slain – the notion of a difference [between the two] lasts but a short while…He who but yesterday exults while slaying his foe, at the end sees an enemy gloating over him when he is himself about to be killed. How awful! Fie on this illusion!'
>
> *(RT VIII. 358-59, Pandit's translation)*

The *Rājataraṅgiṇī's* discourse on the themes of mortality and evanescence of human life and action was not just a critique of vanity and power but can be seen as a profound deposition on temporality itself and its ever-attendant quality, change – that recognizably historical characteristic. A recognition of this characteristic frames the text in that it begins, too, with describing itself as a balancing remedy, an antidote as it were, for kings who may be seized by change – prosperity or decline – across space and time (*nṛpāṇām ullāse hrāse vā deśakālayoḥ*) (RT I.21). A certain universality and inevitability, then, attach to the march of history in this poetic vision, as also a coming together of transcendent and contingent truths.

As for time in *kāvya,* it seemed to 'return' relentlessly, mirroring persistent patterns of human thought, action, and experience. It looped around deeply ethical moments or ruptures in history which connected with other such moments otherwise far apart from one another. In the *kavi*'s vision, time was a laboratory perhaps where personal and societal ideals played themselves out. Time could stretch, collapse, or return because so did patterns of human ethics and behavior. Hence, Sanskrit poetry's preference is not for linearity or diachronicity alone but for recursivity and synchronicity of a fashion alongside. This was not the much-lamented 'ahistoricity' of Indic civilization but instead a purposive, cultivated transhistoricity – a self-reflexive reworking of history to serve culturally specific functions and foreground values far removed from what Eurocentric modernity would allow. (For a detailed discussion of time in Sanskrit poetry and other pre-modern Indic traditions from the perspective of the Global South, see Kaul 2022, and of the Indic historical vision see Kaul 2018b.)

To sum up, literature does not merely reproduce the events it describes; 'it tells us in what direction to think about the events and charges our thought about them with different emotional valences' (see White 1987: 178; 1973). Likewise, *kāvya's* representation of the experience of historicality could operate in a way that was both literal in what it asserted about past events and figurative in what it suggested about the meaning of that experience.

Of course, a genre is by definition an umbrella term, gathering under it a wide variety of modes and practices. It is no one's case that all *kāvya*s did or would relate to the past in identical ways. However, as the case of the *Rājataraṅgiṇī* shows, whether in his normative prescription of power or in his philosophical critique of it, the *kavi* made masterly use of the fecundity of his chosen genre to spin out a discourse about the past. In emplotting the past around the principle of ethical order, he narrativized it, and it is in narrativizing the past that he historicized it, by lending shape and meaning to a vast stretch of time and the countless figures and events entailed by it. This involved centering a certain critical idealism (*dharma*) and call to action (*karma*) by the *kavi*. For him, writing history did not exhaust truth; moralizing reality was equally the object. Hence the larger project of creating ethical monarchy and governance, and, ultimately, unveiling the transcendent end of human life – detachment – not as a goal in itself but as a wider insight into the 'true' nature of time and human action, which led to liberation. It took a *kavi* to see and show all these truths.

Note

1 For more on the creativity of the *kavi*, though not with regard to history, see Granoff 2014.

References

Granoff, Phyllis. 1995. 'Sarasvati's Sons: Biographies of Poets in Medieval India,' *Asiatische Studien / Études Asiatiques*, 49 (2): 351–376.

——— 2014. 'Putting the Polish on the Poet's Efforts: Reading the Karnasundari as a Reflection on Poetic Creativity,' in Bronner et al., eds. *Toward a History of Kavya Literature: Innovations and Turning Points*, New Delhi: Oxford University Press.

Kaul, Shonaleeka. 2010. *Imagining the Urban: Sanskrit and the City in Early India*, New York: Seagull (2011).

——— 2018a. *The Making of Early Kashmir: Landscape and Identity in the Rajatarangini*, Delhi: Oxford University Press.

——— 2018b. 'Historical Methods,' in Pankaj Jain et al., eds. *Encyclopaedia of World Religions: Hinduism and Tribal Religions*, New York: Springer.

———, ed. 2022. *Retelling Time: Alternative Temporalities from Premodern South Asia*, London: Routledge.

Kaul, Srikanth, ed. 1966. *Rājataraṅgiṇi of Śrivara and Śuka*, ed. Srikanth Kaul, Woolner Indological Series: 8, Hoshiarpur.

Kavi, M. Ramakrishna, ed. 1934. *Nātyaśāstra*, Baroda: Oriental Institute.

Kosambi, D.D. and Gokhale, V.V., eds. 1957. *The Subhasitaratnakosa*, Harvard Oriental Series, vol 42, Boston: Harvard University Press, Boston, vol II, xlvi.

Mantena, Rama. 2007. 'The Question of History in Precolonial India,' *History and Theory*, 46 (3): 396–408.

Mill, James. 1817. *The History of British India*, London: Baldwin, Cradock and Joy.

Pandit, Ranjit Sitaram, ed. and translated, 2004 [1935, 1968]. *The River of Kings: Rājataraṅgiṇī, The Saga of the Kings of Kashmir*, New Delhi: Sahitya Akademi.

Pollock, Sheldon, ed. 2004. 'Sanskrit Literary Culture from the Inside Out,' in Sheldon Pollock, ed. *Literary Cultures in History: Reconstructions from South Asia*, New Delhi: Oxford University Press.

Raghavan, V., ed. 1998. *Śṛṅgāraprakāśa of Bhoja*, Harvard Oriental Series: 53, Cambridge: Harvard University Press.

Sarma, B.N. and Upadhyaya, Baladeva, eds. 1928. *Kāvyālaṅkāra of Bhāmaha*, Benaras: Chowkhamba Sanskrit Series.

Sarup, Lakshman, ed. and transl., 1927. *The Nighantu and the Nirukta*, Vol. 1 and 2, Lahore: University of the Punjab.

Slaje, Walter. 2008. 'In the Guise of Poetry: Kalhaṇa Reconsidered,' in Walter Slaje ed., *Śāstrārambha: Inquiries into the Preamble in Sanskrit*, Weisbaden: Harrassowitz Verlag.

White, Hayden. 1973. *Metahistory*, Baltimore and London: John Hopkins University Press.

——— 1987. *The Content of the Form: Narrative Discourse and Historical Representation*, Baltimore and London: John Hopkins University Press.

10

RAJO GUṆA

William R. Pinch

Sudipta Kaviraj has argued that while people in the West have generally turned to social theory to understand themselves in modernity, Indians have historically turned to literature. He makes the case for this by examining the writings of the Bengali intellectual and litterateur, Bankimchandra Chattopadhyay (Kaviraj, 1995; Kaviraj, 2000, esp. pp. 380–381). One might well quibble with the civilizational comparison, and – in the wake of the linguistic turn – the opposition of social theory and literature. But there is no doubt that literature has formed an important source for self-reflection and self-understanding in India – and the West, and indeed the West in India. To cite two prominent examples: Subhas Chandra Bose evidently thought of himself as a modern-day 'warrior ascetic', only to abandon that self-understanding when he fell in love and had a daughter with Emilie Schenkl during his second European sojourn in the 1930s (Chaudhuri, 1988, pp. 120–121). The ideal of the warrior ascetic from which Bose drew inspiration was first expounded, for modern Bengalis, by Bankim in his serialized novel *Anandamath* (Chattopadhyay, 1879–82). The novel and its appealing sprung-from-the-soil ascetic patriots profoundly influenced early twentieth-century Bengali patriotism, including revolutionary calls to violence, just as Bose was arriving at political consciousness (Bose, 1997, esp. pp. 20, 36–50). Bose's great rival, Jawaharlal Nehru, also looked to literature for self-understanding and was especially drawn, in his youth, to Rudyard Kipling's 1901 novel, *Kim*. Nehru includes *Kim* on a list of his 'great favorites' when he was a boy in Allahabad (Nehru, 1941, p. 28) and one frequently encounters the claim that he treasured the book long after. This may appear surprising, given Kipling's reputation as a defender of empire. However, Kim's insider–outsider status will have appealed to 'Joe' Nehru, given his elite, mainly English-language upbringing and the immense class distance that separated him from what Kipling (and Nehru himself) regarded as the *real* India of peasants and villages – 'India as it

DOI: 10.4324/9781003273530-13

was', not 'the India of books and old monuments and past cultural achievements' or the 'superficial modernism of [India's] middle classes' (Nehru, 1946, p. 37; see also Nehru, 1941, pp. 55; cf. Kipling, 1901, pp. 96–100). Further, Nehru's political discipleship to 'Mahatma' Gandhi, which first took him to the villages of eastern UP in 1920, will have resonated with Kim's discipleship to the lama.

In what follows, I explore a concept closely related to the self in modern and early modern India: the notion of sovereignty, or *rājya*. I do this via recourse to Bankim's *Anandamath* (Chattopadhyay, 1879–82; Chatterjee, 1906; Chatterji and Lipner, 2005), Rudyard Kipling's *Kim* (1901), and Gandhi's *Hind Swaraj* (Gandhi, 1909, 1910; Gandhi and Parel, 1997). I then place these texts alongside and in conversation with a little-known eighteenth-century Hindi (Brajbhāṣā) work of historical poetry, *Anūp-prakāś* by Mān Kavi (Mān Kavi, 1792). Whereas Gandhi and Bankim's works were formative expressions of Indian nationalist thought and Kipling's of British imperialism, Mān Kavi's late eighteenth-century poem is emblematic of the prenationalist and precolonial 'courtly' literature associated with the Rajput kingdoms of north India. Though a century of dramatic cultural and political change intervened between Mān Kavi and our later authors, it is nonetheless possible to discern some useful threads, especially between the themes of power, the self, political legitimacy, and asceticism.

~ ~ ~

Rāj, from which *rājya* is derived, possesses a range of meanings: from king, prince, and ruler, to realm, kingdom, and state. The more formal term *rājā* refers to the individual ruler or sovereign. As noted above, *rājya* usually refers to the abstract notion of sovereignty, though it can also be used to signify the kingdom or state as well as governance. *Rāj* can be rendered as a verb by adding *karna*, 'to do'. Thus *rāj karna* means to do the work of the state, to rule. The term is etymologically linked to the Latin cognate terms *rex/regis/reges*.

In English, *rāj* appears most often as 'The Raj', the British Empire in India, or the period 1858–1947 when India was subject to direct rule by the British crown – hence the term 'crown rule' and India's status as the proverbial 'jewel in the crown'. The century prior to 1858, during which the English East India Company power penetrated into the interior of the subcontinent from its coastal trading centers, is often referred to as the era of 'Company Raj'. We have a fairly good sense of what 'the Raj' meant to the British. It conjured up imperial pomp and grandeur, massive public works projects, railroads and irrigation canals and hill stations, the 'steel frame' of the Indian Civil Service, 'red tape', and (most of all) cantonments, the Indian Army, and the enlistment of the 'martial races' in the service of British global domination. In short, the Raj calls to mind an Indian underwriting of 'Rule *Britannia*' if not 'Pax *Britannica*'.

No one better evoked the Raj from the point of view of the British than Rudyard Kipling, and perhaps nowhere more evocatively than in his novel *Kim*. In *Kim*, the Raj emerged as both a military and informational network, an all-seeing system of governance designed as much to control and manage the chaotic diversity of Indian society as to rule Indians as such. Indeed, a unified India was perceived in *Kim* as something of an impossibility absent the British, and as a way of driving this point home, Kipling rendered Kim himself – 'friend of all the world' and master of disguise – as the only character capable of embracing the entirety of India, of being the only *true* Indian. In contrast, Kipling's tragicomic Bengali spy, Hurree Chunder Mookherjee, stood as a not-so-subtle condemnation of the very idea of the Indian nation.

A not-dissimilar conception of the Raj, if not Indian nationalism (though Bankim shared in the critique of the culturally compromised Bengali Hindu), may be seen in Bankim's writings, especially in his novel *Anandamath*. In the final chapter, the godlike figure of 'the Healer' informs a despondent Satyānanda, the leader of the *sanyāsī* rebellion, that despite the battle that had just been concluded, Indians actually need British rule:

> To worship three hundred and thirty million gods is not the Eternal Code [*sanatana dharma* in most editions]. That's a worldly, inferior code. Through its influence the real Eternal Code—what the foreigners call the Hindu rule of life—has been lost. The true Hindu rule of life is based on knowledge, not on action. And this knowledge is of two kinds—outward and inward. The inward knowledge is the chief part of the Eternal Code, but unless the outward knowledge arises first, the inward cannot arise. Unless one knows the gross, one cannot know the subtle.
>
> ... The outward knowledge no longer exists in this land, and there's no one to teach it; we ourselves are not good at teaching people such things. So we must bring in the outward knowledge from another country. The English are very knowledgable in the outward knowledge, and they're very good at instructing people. Therefore we'll make them king.
>
> *(Chatterji and Lipner, 2005, p. 229)*

Satyānanda objects, but the Healer continues:

> 'At present the English are traders. They're intent on amassing wealth and do not wish to take on the burden of ruling a kingdom. But because of the Children's rebellion, they'll be forced to take on the burden of ruling, for without this they cannot collect wealth. The rebellion came about to usher in English rule'.

As Partha Chatterjee has noted, Bankim's dim view of the Hindu ability to manage their own affairs, and the cause of their subjection to foreign rule, whether Muslim or British, was the result of their attitude to power, which in turn was grounded in *Sāṁkhya* philosophy and its emphasis on *vairāgya* or reclusion (which Bankim understood in terms of 'otherworldliness and fatalism'). In an essay on *Sāṁkhya* Bankim opined:

> It is because of this other-worldliness and fatalism that in spite of the immense physical prowess of the Indians, this land of the Aryans had come under Muslim rule. And it is for the same reason again that social progress in this country slowed down a long time ago and finally stopped completely.

He added:

> 'Knowledge is power': that is the slogan of Western civilization. 'Knowledge is salvation' is the slogan of Hindu civilization. The two peoples set out on the same road bound for two different goals. The Westerners have found power. Have we found salvation? There is no doubt that the results of our journeys have been dissimilar.
>
> Europeans are devotees of power. That is the key to their advancement. We are negligent toward power: that is the key to our downfall. Europeans pursue a goal which they must reach in this world: they are victorious on earth. We pursue a goal which lies in the world beyond, which is why we have failed to win on earth. Whether we will win in the life beyond is a question on which there are differences of opinion.
>
> *(Chattopadhyay, 1965, p. 226, cited in Chatterjee, 1986, pp. 56–57)*

We will return to *Sāṁkhya* in due course. Meanwhile, we get a remarkably different – though more apposite than opposite – image of the Raj, and of the West, in Gandhi's *Hind Swarāj* (Gandhi, 1909, 1910; Gandhi and Parel, 1997). In his well-known dialogue between Reader and Editor, Gandhi explained both the 'pitiable' condition of England and, behind it, the 'diseased' and 'degraded' nature of Western civilization. At this, the Reader asked, 'If civilisation is a disease, and if it has attacked the English nation, why has she been able to take India, and why is she able to retain it?' The Editor explained:

> The English have not taken India; we have given it to them. They are not in India because of their strength, but because we keep them. … They came to our country originally for purposes of trade. Recall the Company Bahadur. Who made it Bahadur? They had not the slightest intention at the time of establishing a kingdom. Who assisted the Company's officers? Who was tempted at the sight of their silver? Who bought their goods? History testifies that we did all this. In order to become rich all at once, we welcomed the Company's officers with open arms.
>
> *(Gandhi and Parel, 1997, pp. 30–40; see also Chatterjee, 1986, p. 85ff; Gandhi's account may be read as a prefiguring of the argument of Bayly, 1983)*

The Reader is readily convinced by this argument, but follows with a question on how the English are able to retain control of India given their evident weakness. The Editor responds:

> The causes that gave them India enable them to retain it. Some Englishmen state that they took, and they hold, India by the sword. Both these statements are wrong. The sword is entirely useless for holding India. We alone keep them. Napoleon is said to have described the English as a nation of shopkeepers. It is a fitting description. … Many problems can be solved by remembering that money is their God. Then it follows that we keep the English in India for our base self-interest. We like their commerce, they please us by their subtle methods, and get what they want from us. To blame them for this is to perpetuate their power.
>
> *(Gandhi and Parel, 1997, pp. 41)*

All this, of course, is but preamble to the main lesson conveyed in the text, about the relationship of individual self-rule, *swarāj*, and collective Indian sovereignty, *Swarāj*. In short, the Editor instructs the Reader, 'if we become free, India is free…. It is Swarāj when we learn to rule ourselves'.

It is difficult to imagine three more important authors for early twentieth-century Indian nationalism and the British Empire than Bankim, Gandhi, and Kipling. That Gandhi and Kipling's texts were written far from India – Gandhi wrote the first draft of *Hind Swarāj* en route to South Africa from London, on board the *SS Kildonan Castle* in the Atlantic Ocean, and Kipling conceived and wrote *Kim* while living in England and Vermont, and also South Africa – only underscores the global significance of India's subjection to the British. Of course, the audience for Kipling, which was mainly global imperial Whites (including Americans), was quite distinct from the Indian audiences to whom Bankim and Gandhi aimed their prose. But it is easy to push a racially bifurcated understanding of literary reception too far. Much of Kipling's poetry and prose would appeal to an elite English-educated Indian public (e.g., Nehru, noted above; Nirad Chaudhuri is another; for Kipling's profound influence on Indian nationalist and postnationalist writers, and grudging appreciation by postcolonial critics, see Moore-Gilbert, 2002) and of course Gandhi's writings drew upon and were read appreciatively by Western critics of British imperialism and industrialized modernity. And though there would have been considerable overlap between Bankim and Gandhi's audiences, especially as their respective texts rippled outward via translation into other Indian languages, these audiences would have varied considerably – not least because of the position that each author took on the appropriate use of violence in the service of the nation.

A second point requires emphasis. A central theme in all three works is asceticism. Kipling's Kim early on dedicates himself to a Buddhist lama – an autochthonous Indic ascetic returned to a homeland that has forgotten its own ancient wisdom (save for the director of the Museum in Lahore, modeled after Kipling's father, Lockwood). But Kim soon becomes a willing *chelā* to and protege of Colonel Creighton, a very different kind of all-seeing ascetic. The novel ends with Kim faced with a choice: whether to follow the lama back into the hills to be prepared for *nirvāna* or enter the imperial secret service alongside Creighton's other operatives Mahbub Ali and the 'babu', Hurree Chunder Mookherjee. (The liberal reading of the novel is that Kim is on the verge of opting for the former, or is at worst undecided, but there is a good case to be made that Kim was actually preparing to bid the lama goodbye and follow Mahbub Ali and Hurree Babu in the service of empire; see Trivedi, 2011, p. xxix.) Similarly, Bankim's Satyānanda is an ascetic guru to his soldier '*santāns*' (children-saints, married householders turned temporary warrior ascetics) and warrior *sanyāsīs*, but he is also a *chelā* to the mysterious Healer. As noted above, Satyānand heads for the Himalayas with the Healer, leaving his *chelās* (and Indians generally) in the hands of the British. And finally, Gandhi's sagacious Editor imparts guru-like instructions via a question-and-answer dialog to the young, energetic, and impressionable Reader. For Gandhi, the choice is clear: Indians need to adopt a personal ascetic discipline, to become *chelās* to truth and masters of themselves in order to qualify for and bring into being true political *and* cultural freedom for India. To drive home this point, Gandhi put himself forward as the paradigmatic ascetic ideal – an object example of non-sectarian national asceticism.

Finally, and most importantly, all three modern texts lay emphasis, either implicitly (in the case of Kipling) or explicitly (Bankim) or both (Gandhi), on the importance of a distinction between the interior and exterior. For Kipling, this is expressed via Kim's dual discipleship, which stands as a metaphor for the tension between his private quest (his search for his identity, 'who is Kim?') and his public destiny (as an imperial spy in the 'Great Game'). For Bankim, the inner–outer tension is articulated by the Healer: in India knowledge comes in two forms, both inward and outward, and for the former to be realized the latter must be inculcated. Indians had both, but in losing the one (the outward) they lost sight of the other (inward). The English can provide the outward knowledge; only then will Indian inward knowledge come back into focus. Gandhi inverts this formula to argue that inward knowledge, or rather self-rule, will lead immediately to outer self-rule, or freedom from foreign subjection – indeed, this inversion is at the core of Gandhi's 'critique of civil society' (Chatterjee, 1986, pp. 85–132). While Gandhi would thus disagree with Bankim's formulation, to say nothing of Bankim's apparent appreciation for English institutions of governance (Gandhi famously derided the British Parliament as a 'prostitute', a sentiment for which he later expressed misgivings), he would have agreed that Indians had lost sight of their inner selves, which as he understood it was their inner readiness for *swarāj*.

~~~
~~~

Let us now turn to Mān Kavi (this section references Mān Kavi, 1792). How did our eighteenth-century poet think about the distinction between interior being and exterior 'reality'? How did he conceive of power, politics, and sovereignty? As with Kipling, Bankim, and Gandhi, for Mān Kavi the question of asceticism was central to the discussion.

Some brief background is in order: Mān Kavi's *Anūp-prakāś* was composed in Brajbhāṣā (early modern or 'classical' Hindi), the main literary language of the Rajput courts, and it celebrates the military and political career of Anūpgirī Gusaīn (a.k.a. 'Himmat Bahādur'). Anūpgirī was a Saiva ascetic, a '*gusaīn*' who, in 1792, became the *de facto* ruler of Bundelkhand, an upland forested province ranged along the southern flank of the Gangetic Plain (see Pinch, 2006, 2012). In 1803, the year before his death, Anūpgirī would ally his army, which included thousands of *gusaīns* like himself as well as Rajputs and 'Hindustanis' of various ranks, with Company forces under Lord Lake, and thus facilitated the British capture of Delhi. *Anūp-prakāś* was composed in the 1790s, soon after Anūpgirī's defeat of the Rajput general Arjun Singh near Ajaygarh, a fortress stronghold in eastern Bundelkhand. Indeed, it was the 1792 victory that provided the occasion for the composition of Mān Kavi's work, as well as a related poem by the younger (and eventually more famous) Padmākar, *Himmatbahādur Virudāvalī*. (The translations that follow draw on Busch, Rajpurohit, and Pinch, 2024 [forthcoming]; for discussion of the historiographical, metahistorical, literary, and linguistic registers of the poems, see Busch, 2018; Pinch, 2018; Pinch 2022 [forthcoming]; and Rajpurohit, 2018.)

For Mān Kavi, the rise of a Saiva ascetic to the commanding heights of Rajput courtly power in Bundelkhand would have represented a conundrum. This conundrum may have had particular urgency given the rumors that circulated about this particular Saiva ascetic's uncertain origins: according to oral tradition collected by the Hindi scholar Bhagvāndīn in the early twentieth century, Anūpgirī and his brother had been sold as infants to their guru Rājendragirī by their destitute, widowed mother (Padmākar, 1930, ix). For Mān Kavi the challenge was to explain how such a 'yogi' had achieved kingship, *rājya*. Significantly, he makes no mention of Anūpgirī's youth. Rather, he takes up the issue of yogic kingship at the very beginning of his work, when describing Anūpgirī's guru, Rājendragirī, when he was a young *chelā* (disciple) in central Bundelkhand. It was Rājendragirī, according to Mān Kavi's account, who made the initial transition from yogi to warrior and king – a transformation that would culminate in the glorious career of Anūpgirī.

According to Mān Kavi, Rājendragirī possessed a distinguished yogic pedigree, a sequence of 12 sages beginning with one Sadānandgirī and ending with Dhyān Nāth, Rājendragirī's own guru, who had absorbed 'yoga knowledge' (*yoga vidyā*) from his predecessors and was (as his name suggests) 'expert in *dhyān*', or the meditative focusing of the mind (vv. 13–15). We first meet the young Rājendragirī outside of a 'womb-like' cave; inside is his guru Dhyān Nāth, steeped in meditation. Rājendragirī, who possesses the kingly quality of *raj* (*rajo guṇa*),[1] is guarding the cave and dutifully blocks the entry, when a mysterious stranger approaches (v. 16). This stranger turns out to be none other than Dhyān Nāth's guru, Nayan Nāth (v. 17). The elder sage is so pleased with Rājendragirī's steadfast loyalty that he offers the youngster a boon (v. 18). Rājendragirī replies, invoking the term *rajo guṇa*, 'I want to be like Raja Indra, to be a king among kings, so that other kings will obey my rule' (v. 19).[2] Nayan Nāth happily grants his wish.

Rājendragirī then experienced an inner transformation (v. 23) and soon was enjoying martial success (v. 24). Rājendragirī's guru, meanwhile, was disturbed by this turn of events. Meeting his disciple in Kulpahār (the supposed birthplace, incidentally, of Anūpgirī – though Mān Kavi does not mention this), Dhyān Nāth urged Rājendragirī to renounce all kingly power and pleasures and instead focus on being a yogi-lord (*jogīsh*) (v. 32). Rājendragirī complied with his guru's command and immediately renewed his meditation (v. 33). But as the *chelā* honed his mental powers, his martial cunning grew (v. 35).[3] Dhyān Nāth, content in the knowledge that Rājendragirī had his priorities straight, proceeded to Prayag. Upon reaching the spot where 'the dark and light waters look lovely [and] the three rivers meet;' (v. 44), Dhyān Nāth 'relinquished his spirit through his skull' (v. 45) and 'merged with the divine essence' (v. 46). As for the *chelā,* 'King Rājendragirī focused on *rāja yoga*' (v. 46).[4]

In short, according to the apotheosis of Rājendragirī in Mān Kavi's introductory chapter, whereas the life of a warrior-king may be incompatible with that of an ascetic, the mental discipline inherent to ascetic practices makes one more focused, intelligent, and powerful – qualities befitting a military commander and king. The poet thus resolves the paradoxical phenomenon of Anūpgirī, who would achieve yogi-king status, via reference to a transformation that was said to have occurred a generation earlier, in Rājendragirī's youth.

Key to this transformation is Mān Kavi's recourse to the concept of *rajo guṇa. Guṇa* is usually translated as quality, property, or inner nature. *Rajo* and the cognate terms *raj* and *rajas* connote action, enjoyment, greed, ambition, and passion – and also chaos. One who possesses, or is possessed of, rajo guna is naturally predisposed to restless and often destabilizing action – in modern parlance, they are 'change agents'. In some cases, if things go well, such individuals may aspire to *rājya*, kingship. Mān Kavi, in repeatedly pointing to Rājendragirī's *rajo guṇa*, was alluding to *Sāṁkhya* metaphysics – a system that was later central, it will be recalled, to Bankim's theory of power, or rather the Indian lack thereof. According to the *Sāṁkhya* system, all creatures are the product of the interplay between three deeply ingrained *gunas*, namely, *tamas* (destruction, darkness), *rajas* (action, ambition), and *sattva* (purity, harmony). While each of these *guṇas* is present in all living beings, it is their relative weight and the interplay between them that determines the character (and destiny) of an individual (see e.g., Ruzsa, n.d.). How that works in practice is the concern of philosophical

Yoga, which is closely linked to *Sāṁkhya* metaphysics (on the relationship of Yoga to *Sāṁkhya*, see Bryant, n.d.; also White, 2014). According to Mān Kavi, in granting Rājendragirī's wish to be a king, the mysterious Nayan Nāth simply put his thumb on the scale of the young chela's inner *rajo guṇa*. But this was not enough: crucial to Rājendragirī's final *rāj-yoga* apotheosis was his guru Dhyān Nāth's subsequent admonition to refocus on meditation, to be a yogi-lord.

As with Bankim and Kipling, Mān Kavi's tale of ascetic transformation implied a religious and philosophical canvas of vast temporal dimensions. After all, *Sāṁkhya* and Yoga are generally represented to be as old as India itself (Ruzsa, n.d.; Bryant, n.d.). And as with Bankim and Kipling, Mān Kavi's narrative combined literary truth with historical invention. Bankim repurposed the 'Sanyasi and Fakir Rebellion' of the late eighteenth century to explore pressing questions of Indian agency amidst imperial subjection in the late nineteenth century. Kipling similarly repurposed the 'Great Game' (his use of the term referred to spy-craft rather than the grand strategy it came to invoke) of the mid/late-nineteenth century to imagine British-Indian cultural hybridity amidst the hardening racial politics of imperialism at the turn of the twentieth century. Neither was interested in explaining the past, and neither viewed their work in terms of 'history'. Indeed, Bankim explicitly requested that his novel not be read as 'historical literature', even though in later editions of the novel he provided copious extracts from historical accounts of the insurgent ascetics and its backdrop, the Bengal famine of 1769–70 (Chatterji and Lipner, 2005, p. 43). And while there are good candidates for historical models for Kim (esp. the British slave-orphan described in Lang, 1859, pp. 157–92, first noted in Moore-Gilbert, 1986, p. 24; but see also the tonga-wallah of Lahore in Allen, 2009, pp. 214–215) and for iconic scenes in the novel, such as the Grand Trunk Road (Digby, 1998), Kipling thought of his work as 'a long and leisurely Asiatic yarn' (Kipling and Pinney, p. 11). Insofar as both authors sought to engage with history, it was to manage a disconcerting present via recourse to the not-too-distant past.

Mān Kavi may be read in much the same way. His disconcerting present, the problem to be solved in Bundelkhand in the 1790s, was a yogi's kingship – and not just any yogi, a *gusain* of uncertain antecedents. The challenge was to do so in a way that comported with Brahmanical sensibilities. Hence the recourse to *Sāṁkhya* and Yoga, Mān Kavi was engaging in historical invention is suggested by the picture of Rājendragirī's turn to military entrepreneurship provided in an 1807 letter from the Maratha *subedār* (commander-in-chief) of Jhansi, Rao Shiv Rao Hari Bhau. According to the *subedār*:

> When Naroo Shunker Rajah Behadur held the situation of Soobahdar of Jhansee on the part of the Peshwa, Rajinder Geer the master of the late Rajah Himmut Behadur resided in the town of Jhansee; he was then engaged in the business of a banker, by which means he acquired much influence and lived with respectability under the Rajah's government. It

> happened that some disturbances arose between the people of Rajinder Geer and certain turbulent persons, in consequence of which he became distressed in his mind, gave up his house and property to be distributed in charity, and resolved to leave the place. The Rajah from the regard which he entertained for him assigned to him the village of Moth for his residence. Rajinder Geer after putting the fort of this place in a state of defence began to excite disturbances in some of the Khalusa [personal] villages of the Rajah in consequence of which an army was assembled at Jhansee to quell them, and hostilities continued for some time. At length Rajender Geer made a proposal to the Rajah to resign the place and bestow it in charity which the Rajah aware of the importance of the possession of the fort on any terms was readily consented to. Rajender Geer being thus dispossessed of the place crossed the Jumna and went into the Nawab's country. [i.e., Awadh], and in the meantime, certain villages including Moth were conferred in jageer by the Peishwah upon Narroo Shunker.
>
> *(Soobadar of Jhansee, 1806)*

This biographical snippet of Rājendragirī by the *subedār* of Jhansi does not necessarily invalidate Mān Kavi's tale of Rājendragirī's yogic transformation; after all, Rājendragirī may have had his encounter with Nayan Nāth long before becoming a respectable banker of Jhansi. In any case, *gusains* were well known as merchants, bankers, and soldiers in the eighteenth and nineteenth centuries (see, e.g., Kolff, 1971; Leonard, 1981; Bayly, 1983). Nonetheless, it is telling that while Mān Kavi mentions the conflict with Nāru Shankar in *Anūp-prakāś*, he makes no mention of Rājendragirī's career in banking. The picture he paints of Rājendragirī is uncluttered by such mundane affairs. Rather, he focuses, like Bankim and Kipling, on the wider philosophical dimensions of asceticism for an individual's political destiny.

~ ~ ~

Mān Kavi is separated from Gandhi, Bankim, and Kipling by a century of profound transformations, in politics, literature, religion, and much else besides. The prospect of an Indian struggle for sovereignty in the British Empire, over which our later authors spilled so much ink and for which many Indians spilled so much blood, was barely visible on the poet's horizon. Indeed, insofar as imperial politics was an issue for Mān Kavi, it concerned the gradually intensifying grip of the Marathas over Bundela Rajput power centers in Bundelkhand.

In addition to the discursive gestures to *Sāṁkhya*, there are ground-level strands that bring these four texts into conversation. First, there is a historical thread: the mobile warrior-asceticism represented by Rājendragirī and Anūpgirī was the same ascetic-military phenomenon that gave rise to the 'Sanyasi and Fakir Rebellion' of the late eighteenth century in Bihar and Bengal, to which Bankim looked for inspiration in *Anandamath*. It is doubtful that Bankim knew much if anything about Anūpgirī, to say nothing of Rājendragirī, but he knew (or thought he knew) enough about the 'depredations' of wandering bands of armed ascetics from his reading of British accounts of the period to conclude that they embodied a form of sovereignty than paled in comparison to that which the British had evolved in Bengal the course of the nineteenth century. For Bankim, the limited political success of the insurgency was based on ill-gotten gains: he has the Healer tell the despondent ascetic-commander Satyānanda, 'do not grieve. It was mistakenly, by means of banditry, that you gathered wealth and won your victory. Wrongdoing can never produce holy fruit. So you will not be able to free the land' (Chatterji and Lipner, 2005, p. 229). Were we to put this in the *Sāṁkhya* metaphysics that our eighteenth-century poet would have appreciated, we could say that the achievements of Satyānanda's *santān* and *sanyāsī* rebels were built on *tamas*, that is, chaos and destruction. There was no place for the likes of Satyānanda in the new world being ushered in by colonial modernity. The new inward knowledge, the Healer (and Bankim) insisted, could only be nurtured by the internalization of the outward knowledge (read: an appreciation of power for worldly gain, *rajas*) for the unlocking of which the English seemed to hold the key.

Second, there is a yogic thread. The disciplining of the self that Gandhi's Editor urges upon the young Reader in *Hind Swarāj* shares much with the advice that Mān Kavi has Dhyān Nāth impart to his *chelā* Rājendragirī: one should not be taken in by the material pleasures of kingly power, rather, one should still the mind (cf. Tagore, 1925). Rājendragirī follows this advice, but the result is not a return to reclusive meditation, an abandonment of the world. Instead, Rājendragirī became a yogi-*rājā* par excellence, possessed of both material power and mental cunning – and, of course, lots of weaponry. Similarly, Gandhi's admonition to the Reader is to gain control over oneself, not to retreat from the world but to conquer it. This is *Sāṁkhya* metaphysics with a yogic twist. Or it would be more appropriate to read Bankim's rejection of *Sāṁkhya* metaphysics as the reading with a twist, or rather a twisted reading borne of his too-willing engagement with (or enslavement to) European post-Enlightenment thought, according to which asceticism is simply a form of religious renunciation that turns its back on power and worldly things (*pace* Chatterjee, 1986, 56–57). Mān Kavi makes clear, in contrast, that the true yogi had everything to do with power and world-conquest. There is nothing necessarily otherworldly or even fatalistic about Indian asceticism, Bankim (and Weber) notwithstanding. And as we know from popular responses to Gandhi across north India, many and perhaps most north Indians perceived the 'mahatma' in precisely such terms. When the *sanyāsī* and future peasant leader Sahajanand Saraswati encountered Gandhi at the Ahmedabad Congress gathering in 1921, he saw a thunderbolt-hurling second coming of Siva (Saraswati, 1952, p. 212; Hauser and Jha, 2015, p. 216). Peasants in rural Gorakhpur experienced Gandhi more or less along these lines, though with a more tantric inflection (Amin, 1984). These are indications that the popular understandings of *rāj yoga* that infused Mān Kavi's account of an earlier warrior yogi persisted well into the twentieth century.

Third, the discursive prominence of asceticism in these texts prefigured the 'nationalist asceticism' of the twentieth century. The 'nationalist ascetic' is the ideological obverse of what colonial officials derided as the 'political *sādhu*' in the early decades of the twentieth century who, by definition, were compromising their religious commitments by taking part in politics (cf. Pinch, 1996, pp. 5–11). Nationalist asceticism would take many forms after the turn of the century, in figures as ideologically disparate as Sarala Devi ('Devi Chaudhurani'), Aurobindo Ghosh, Lala Lajpat Rai, Bhai Parmanand, Bhagat Singh, Chandrashekhar Azad, and V. D. Savarkar. The wide appeal of these leaders had much to do with the fact that they were perceived as having subordinated their own wealth, worldly comforts, and (to varying degrees) family ties for the sake of the nation. The asceticism of nationalist asceticism is not an asceticism of religious reclusion (Bankim's *vairāgya*), a salvation-oriented retreat from the world. Rather, it is an emancipation from the home – the site of family – but also caste. This creates the condition of possibility to better apprehend, diagnose, and address, with an uncluttered mind, worldly concerns, concerns of the nation. Bankim's negative estimation of asceticism and *Sāṁkhya* tell us more about the scientific positivism of Comte, Mill, and Spencer to which he was devoted (Chatterjee, 1986, p. 58) than it does about the conception of sovereignty and its relation to self-mastery in precolonial (and postcolonial) India. For a glimpse of *Sāṁkhya Yoga* sensibilities free of post-Enlightenment scientism and reactions to it (e.g., Gandhi), Mān Kavi comes to our rescue.

Bose and Nehru, with whom we began, may also be understood in terms of nationalist asceticism. Certainly they endured much privation and hardship, including arrest and imprisonment – a kind of enforced asceticism – in the service of the nation. Like Kim, Nehru was torn between his personal loyalty to an anti-modern ascetic, Gandhi, and his public devotion to a secular modernist vision of progress for the nation-state. Unlike Kim, Nehru's choice was made easier by the assassination of Gandhi by Nathuram Godse. In any case, Nehru had long since made his statist preferences known, as indeed had Kim (though Kipling only hints at this at the end of the novel; see Trivedi's close reading). By contrast, Bose, who had abandoned the warrior asceticism of Bankim in the mid-1930s, seemed to return to it (at least partially) in the early 1940s, taking up the mantle of military leadership of the Indian National Army. But like Nehru, Bose's choice was an embrace of sovereign statism modeled on Western forms – though in his case it was focused on waging war rather than industrialization. Whereas Bankim's Satyānand had been convinced, albeit reluctantly, that the British should be allowed to rule so that Indians could learn the forgotten secrets of external knowledge, Bose decided that the modern state-building lesson was complete and it was time to remove the British by force. Both Bose and Nehru thus embraced industrialized forms of Reason to combat the evils of Western imperialism. According to this reading, Nehru lost the war even as he won the battle (Chatterjee, 1986, pp. 131–166). Bose lost both the battle and the war.

The story does not end with the rejection, or reworking, of nationalist asceticism by Bose and Nehru. Nationalist asceticism was at the heart of the creation in 1925 of the Rashtriya Swayamsevak Sangh (RSS), which melded the physical culture (*anūśīlan*) and patriotic sentiments of Bankim's warrior ascetics with British military drill. Central to this newer nationalist asceticism is the subordination of family loyalties and vows of poverty and celibacy, required for advancement to leadership positions in the RSS ranks. The dramatic growth of the RSS, particularly after Independence, and the rise to power of its political wing the Bharatiya Janata Party (formerly Jana Sangh) in recent decades, culminating in the prime-ministership of Narendra Modi (an RSS ascetic of long-standing), are evidence of the enduring popular appeal of nationalist asceticism. (This extends, of course, beyond the RSS ranks, as is clear by the meteoric political rise in recent years of a non-RSS-affiliated Hindu [or, more precisely, *Gorakhnāthī*] ascetic, Yogi Adityanath, in the BJP.)

The popular appeal of nationalist asceticism is due in part, I would argue, to an abiding discomfort with the enduring epistemological hegemony of an unreconstructed West in postcolonial political thought – that many Indians are all-too-aware that the winning of political Independence in 1947 has not led to the achievement of philosophical, theoretical, epistemological, and ontological independence even 75 years later. In Gandhi's terms, they have achieved *Swarāj* without *swarāj*. In Bankim's terms, they achieved outer knowledge but not inner knowledge. Or in Mān Kavi's terms, they have *rāj* but not yoga.

Notes

1 राजेंद गिर राजेंद गिर सो राज रजो गुण साज में
2 राजेंद्र गिर राजेंद्र लो अपने रजो गुण वासना
राजाधिराजा हों हुया ते राज मान शाशना
3 कछु काल मैं बल पाइ। दल पे सयान पठाई. This all occurs in vv. 30-35.
4 ब्रह्म अखंड मिलयौ सुमुनि धयान नाथ धरि धयान।
इत राज राजेन्दगिर राज जोग करि ग्यान॥

References

Allen, C. (2009) *Kipling Sahib: India and the Making of Rudyard Kipling.* New York: Pegasus.

Amin, S. (1984) "Gandhi as Mahatma," in Guha, R. (ed.), *Subaltern Studies: Writings on Indian History and Society*, vol. III. Delhi: Oxford University Press, pp. 1–61.

Bayly, C. A. (1983) *Rulers, Townsmen and Bazaars: North Indian Society in the Age of British Expansion, 1770–1870.* Cambridge: Cambridge University Press.

Bose, Subhas Chandra. (1997) *An Indian Pilgrim: An Unfinished Autobiography*, Bose, S. K. and Bose, S. (eds.). New York: Oxford University Press.

Bryant, E. (n.d.) "The Yoga Sutras of Patañjali," in *The Internet Encyclopedia of Philosophy*, https://iep.utm.edu/yoga/ (Accessed: 8 December 2020).

Busch, A. (2018) "The Poetics of History in Padmakar's *Himmatbahadurvirudavali*," in Williams, T., Malhotra, A. and Hawley, J. S. (eds.), *Texts and Traditions in Early Modern North India*. Delhi: Oxford University Press, pp. 260–281.

Busch, A., Rajpurohit, D, and Pinch, W. R. (2024) *Poems for a warlord: a translation and study of Padmākar's Himmatbahādur-virudāvali and Mān Kavi's Anūp-prakāś*. Forthcoming.

Chatterjee, B. *Abbey of Bliss*. (1906) Trans. Of *Anandamath* by Nares Chandra Sen-Gupta. Calcutta: Padmini Mohan Neogi.

Chatterjee, P. (1986) *Nationalist Thought and the Colonial World: A Derivative Discourse*. London: Zed Books for the United Nations University.

Chatterji, B. and Lipner, J. (2005) *Anandamath, or the Sacred Brotherhood*. New York: Oxford University Press.

Chattopadhyay, B. (1879–82) *Anandamath*. Bengali ser. Ed. Calcutta: Bangadarsan.

Chattopadhyay, B. (1965) *Bankim Racanabali*, 2 vols., Jogesh Chandra Bagal (ed.). Calcutta: Sahitya Samsad.

Chaudhuri, N. (1988) *Thy Hand Great Anarch!: India, 1921–1952*. Reading, MA: Addison-Wesley.

Gandhi, M. K. (1909). *Hind Swaraj*. Bengali ser. Ed. Natal: Indian Opinion.

Gandhi, M. K. (1910). *Indian Home Rule*. English ed. Natal: International Printing Press.

Gandhi, M. K. and Parel, A. J. (1997) *Gandhi's Hind-Swaraj and other writings*. Cambridge: Cambridge University Press.

Hauser, W. and Jha, K. C. (2015) *Culture, Vernacular Politics, and the Peasants: India, 1889–1950: An Edited Translation of Swami Sahajanand's Memoir*. Delhi: Manohar.

Kaviraj, S. (1995) *The Unhappy Consciousness: Bankimchandra Chattopadhyay and the Formation of Nationalist Discourse in India*. New Delhi: Oxford University Press.

Kaviraj, S. (2000). "Laughter and Subjectivity: The Self-ironical Tradition in Bengali Literature," *Modern Asian Studies* 34, 2: 379–406.

Kipling, R. (1901) *Kim*. New York: Doubleday, Page & Company.

Kipling, R. (1990) *The Letters of Rudyard Kipling*, ed. Thomas Pinney. Iowa City: University of Iowa.

Kolff, D. H. A. (1971) "Sanyasi Trader-Soldiers," *Indian Economic and Social History Review* 8, 2: 213–220.

Lang, J. (1859) *Wanderings in India: and other sketches of life in Hindostan*. London: Routledge, Warne, and Routledge.

Leonard, K. (1981) "Banking Firms in Nineteenth-Century Hyderabad Politics," *Modern Asian Studies* 15, 2: 177–201.

Mān, Kavi. (1792) "Anūp-prakāś," Mss.Hin.D.9a. London: British Library.

Moore-Gilbert, B. J. (1986) *Kipling and "Orientalism"*. London: Croon Helm

Moore-Gilbert, B. J. (2002) "'I am Going to Re-write Kipling's *Kim*': Kipling and Postcolonialism," *Journal of Commonwealth Literature* 37, 2: 39–58.

Nehru, J. (1941) *Toward Freedom: The Autobiography of Jawaharlal Nehru*. New York: John Day.

Nehru, J. (1945) *The Discovery of India*. Calcutta: Signet Press.

Padmākar. (1930) *Himmatbahādur Virdāvali* [sic], 2nd ed., Bhagvāndīn (ed.). Banaras: Kashi Nagaripracharani Sabha.

Pinch, W. R. (1996) *Peasants and Monks in British India*. Berkeley: University of California Press.

Pinch, W. R. (2006) *Warrior Ascetics and Indian Empires*. Cambridge: Cambridge University Press.

Pinch, W. R. (2012) "Hiding in Plain Sight: Gosains in Banaras, 1809," in Dodson, M. (ed.), *Benares: Urban History, Architecture, Identity*. New Delhi: Routledge India, pp. 77–109.

Pinch, W. R. (2018) "War and Succession: Padmakar, Man Kavi, and the Gosains of Bundelkhand, 1792–1806," in Williams, T., Malhotra, A. and Hawley, J. S. (eds.), *Texts and Traditions in Early Modern North India*. Delhi: Oxford University Press, pp. 235–259.

Pinch, W. R. (2022) "Who Killed Arjun Singh? Poetry and History in Bundelkhand," in Ahmed, M. (ed.), "*Circuits of Culture in Early Modern South Asia: Essays in Honor of Allison Busch*," special issue of *Comparative Studies of South Asia, Africa, and the Middle East* 42.2 (August).

Rajpurohit, D. (2018) "Making War Come Alive: Dingal Poetry and Padmakar's *Himmatbahadurvirudavali*," in Williams, T., Malhotra, A. and Hawley, J. S. (eds.), *Texts and Traditions in Early Modern North India*. Delhi: Oxford University Press, pp. 282–298.

Ruzsa, F. (n.d.) "Sankhya," in *The Internet Encyclopedia of Philosophy*. Available at: http://www.iep.utm.edu/sankhya/ (Accessed: 8 December 2020).

Saraswati, S. (1952) *Mera Jivan Sangharsh*. Bihta (Patna): Sitaram Ashram.

Soobadar of Jhansee. (1806) "Trans. of a statement of the particulars of Moth received from the Soobadar of Jhansee written on the 7 of Jumadooluwul 1221 [23 July 1806]," (1807) Enclosure no. 4 of no. 1 of 26 Feb 1807: John Baillie to Neil Edmonstone, secretary to the Governor General, dated 10 Feb. Bengal Political Proceedings. London: India Office Records, British Library.

Tagore, R. (1925) "The Cult of the Charkha," *Modern Review*, September.

Trivedi, H. (2011) "Introduction," to Kipling, R. (ed.), *Kim*. London: Penguin Classics, pp. xix–xliv.

White, D. G. (2014) *The Yoga Sutra of Patanjali: A Biography*. Princeton: Princeton University Press.

PART IV
The Social

11

ASABIYYA

Magid Shihade

Introduction

In this chapter, I will discuss briefly the responses in the Arab world to the imperialist aggression on states and societies, and suggest an alternative to that through a reading of Ibn Khaldun's concept of *asabiyya* – group solidarity.[1] I will first briefly discuss the current situation in the region, how it developed, and the impact of colonial, neocolonial, and imperialist interventions in the region. Second, I will discuss two current dominant trends in the region in response to Western hegemony and interventions. The first trend is that of a neoliberal character going along Western dictates, affecting negatively the poorest and weakest in the society, and entrenching self-interest and individualism rather than the interest of the collective. A second response that I will also discuss is of a nativist militant Islamist type that has further dismembered the societies in the region, and thus helped the global empire and hegemony in the region. After discussing both of these responses, I will outline the main ideas of Ibn Khaldun's concept of *asabiyya* (group/social solidarity) as a way to suggest a new approach toward the collective, common good, social solidarity that is crucial to fend off imperial aggression and hegemony, as well as a corrective to the two dominant responses in the region. Then, and by way of concluding the chapter, I will attempt to propose rethinking the concept of *asabiyya* as a concept that could be of use for the peoples of the Global South rather than a concept confined to a single society/state as it was articulated by Ibn Khaldun in the late fourteenth and early fifteenth century. The goal of attempting to rethink the concept of asabiyya as a framework for a possible future of the Global South is because in today's global hegemony of the West/North local *asabiyya* may not be a suitable answer for fighting the hegemony of the Global North. It requires the multitude of the Global South united around common interests and aspirations, and around

DOI: 10.4324/9781003273530-15

resistance to exploitation, interventions, and hegemony leveled against them by the West.

Imperialism, Colonialism, and Its Current State of Affairs in the Region

When thinking about the 'Arab world' as it exists now in the form of states in West Asia and North Africa, it is not an exaggeration to argue, as many have done before, that the region is the creation of the colonial era of Western colonial and imperial powers. Starting with the nineteenth century, states were charted on maps, regimes were created, and when colonial powers left the region, they left only symbolically. The economic system remained the same as during the colonial era; local resources remained the privilege of Western companies, with part of the wealth being enjoyed by few local leaders and their benefactors; and local markets remained hostage to Western products and were run according to conditions of the global market. The little that changed in the scene that lasted till the 1980s, was the entry of a few producing countries from the Global South into the same economic system. Industrialization, self-sufficiency in agriculture, and an independent economic system remained an illusion. Not only economically, but also militarily, states in the region have been, since their creation, dependent on imports of products from and military support provided by imperial states that have kept these states dependent on their Western patrons. The dream of Arab unity advocated by Gamal Abdel Nasser since the 1950s has fallen apart on account of the interventions and attacks of Western countries (including Israel).

What came to replace that period of hope for unity is the rise of petrodollar states in the Gulf (with the support of Western countries, especially the United States). With their increased power and role in the region came also the spread of their patronage system to accommodating regimes in the region, and the spread of a reactionary and militant Islamization wave that came to dominate the politics and societies in the region today. Any attempt by any state in the region (Egypt, Iraq, Syria, Libya, or Algeria, despite the critique that one can level against the regimes in these countries) has been faced with indirect and direct attacks by Western countries. Through the prevention of access to cash or technologies for industrialization, support for internal oppositions, support for reactionary, and militant Islamist groups, and or direct wars, these regimes that many hoped would bring about an end to dependency were crushed (Dreyfuss, 2005; Amin, 2012). They could not withstand the assault of imperial interventions and the imperial hold over the global economy and have succumbed to the dictates of the global economic center (Hamouchine, 2016)). Israel was created in 1948 through Western military, technological, economic, and diplomatic support. Since 1948, Israel has been dismembering Palestinian society and wreaking havoc on the neighboring states and societies that were flooded with Palestinian refugees, and who had to deal with constant Israeli attacks.

The result of all of that is that today, there is not one state in the region that one can describe with certainty as being a stable one. Far from it, what we witness is further internal instability, and the possible further breakup of states. Western intervention and hegemony, with the help of client regimes, has increased sometimes through direct wars (as it is seen in Libya, Iraq, and Syria) or indirect wars (as it is seen in Yemen) that further disrupted life in the region, displaced millions of people, dismembered these societies further, and destroyed much of the infrastructure in these states. The responses to this state of affairs in the region have been two-fold; neoliberal politics, and/or a nativist and reactionary Islamic militancy, to which I will turn next to discuss in brief.

Neoliberalism in Palestine and the Region

In light of the unmaking of the Soviet Union and the retreat of socialism and the left in general since the 1980s, and with the defeat of revolutionary movements, regimes in the region have collaborated with or succumbed to the World Bank's monetary policies and dictates as conditions for receiving loans. Among the measures have been the breaking down of protective measures to the local economy, the opening of markets further to global products, the cutting of subsidies to necessities that supported the poor in these countries, and the cutting of spending on social, health, and educational programs for the public. These states have become more dependent, and the weakest sections in these societies have been further burdened with higher living costs and with uncertainty. The richer section in these societies gained privileges and accumulated more wealth through their links to the global economy and or through direct links to specific states in the West (Amin, 2012).

Neoliberalism came to dominate life in the region not only economically. Unions were crushed, as also any political opposition to the policies of regimes in the region. Socially also these societies went through an alteration. Solidarity and revolutionary politics were replaced with accommodation to regional and global powers, a retreat of the sense of the collective, and self-interest overshadowed the collective interest. The hope that many in the region had after the waves of revolts in the region that took place starting 2010–11 were crushed sooner than later through the intervention of Western countries with the collaboration of reactionary forces in the region, including the militant Islamic forces that hijacked these revolutions. These forces were supported by both Western states and their local client states in the region (Shihade, 2012). In short, the picture today is that of a retreat of the state, except in its disciplinary and repressive internal power, as well as a retreat of the collective. This, while local elites (including the still colonial Palestine) continue to accumulate more wealth, collaborate with local regimes, and external hegemons. Repression and dictatorship have become the norm on the state level, as well as on the level of the smallest local institution. Any dissenting voice on a group or individual level is met with the harshest response (Hanafi and Tabar, 2005).

The neoliberal ideology that dominates states and societies in the region has led to an emphasis on self-interest over that of the collective. A sense of alienation from one another and materialism have become dominant in the region, resulting in diminished social solidarity, lack of interest in, and engagement with the common good, and diminished political organizing both in the form of old-style political parties and nonallied political organizing. This may be seen as reflecting a modern form of 'each on his own, and each for his own', a new form of a 'state of nature'. Even revolutionary regimes and revolutionary movements are busy selling out to the global neoliberal agenda, with a few accumulating personal wealth in the process, while many are left out, and an increase in poverty and insecurity, sense of despair and disillusionment with formal politics, political movements, and even with the state (Hamouchine, 2016). What Franz Fanon had warned us about in thinking about the postcolonial has become a reality, and in Palestine, it has become a reality before being in the postcolonial yet (Fanon, 1966). Fanon's call for the Third World to create a new humanity for the globe, to create continuously an independent economy, a new form of politics based on the active participation of the public, a new identity that is constantly born out of people public and active participation in politics, economics, and ideas, has fallen on deaf ears in the Arab world, and elsewhere in the Global South. Instead, we have more dependency, more poverty, alienation from politics, and stagnation in ideas. Rather than social solidarity, we have social divisions, infightings, and dictatorial regimes on the state level, as well as on the smallest level of public institutions.

Political Islam in the Region

The rise and dominance of political and militant Islam is best understood in the contexts of the atmosphere described in the previous two sections. Yet, long before the shift to neoliberal economy and politics, Islamist groups were supported by different Western countries, as also Israel (Mamdani, 2003; Dreyfuss, 2005; Amin, 2012). That support was aimed at helping to crush revolutionary movements and to crush regimes in the region that called for the end of dependency, as also for unity, and nonalignment in the global power competition between the United States and the Soviet Union at the time (Dreyfuss, 2005; Amin 2012). With the defeat of the so-called republican regimes in the region after the war of 1967, the balance of power in the region shifted to the Gulf States (Kerr, 1971). With this shift, and with the aid from petrodollar economies, political Islam and Islamic militancy spread further in the region. While these Gulf States aimed through their support for Islamist groups to gain further hegemony in the region, Islamist groups themselves aimed at taking over governments in the region, with the hope of creating Islamic political regimes connected to the patron states in the Gulf (Amin, 2012).

According to this ideology, in Islam, there is no separation between politics and religion, a true state for Muslims is an Islamic state, and creating one is the true path for Muslims. It is a return to the 'original' Islam of the past, a pure Islam not contaminated by the plague of Western secularism that separates religion and the state. This return would bring back the glory of the past and make Muslim countries/states more powerful and players on a global scale. Yet, these assumptions are based on a misreading of history. Religion was not the main reason for powerful states(s), and there was never an Islamic state in the past as these advocates argue (Hallaq, 2012; Shihade, 2016). Moreover, secularism (the running of states according to nonreligious principles or doctrines) was not created by the West, but has had a long history in the region, as elsewhere in the Global South. Running states and societies according to religion, a specific dogma or interpretation of it for that matter, can only divide societies further for it automatically excludes those who do not follow that specific interpretation including those who are Muslims themselves (Shihade, 2016).

By the way of summing up the previous two sections, one cannot but remember a concern that Fanon had; his fear of entrapment of postcolonial societies in the identities that were the making of the colonial world; nativist and reactionary identities, identities that are frozen in time. This impulse worked against what Fanon called for: the remaking of the identity of the postcolonial states to reflect the new spirit of freedom after decolonization. What we see in the Arab region now is a reactionary identity. Two trends have come to dominate Arab culture in the last few decades: one is a mimicry of Western culture; the other, a reactionary nativist Islamist culture.

There is a similarity between Fanon's warnings of mimicry and of adopting a frozen and rigid identity in the postcolonial world, and Ibn Khaldun's idea of mimicry (the weak/ruled mimicking the strong/ruler) and his concept of *asabiyya*, by which he meant a sense of a collective that must always be reformulated according to the changing conditions of the group. This is an important point to which I will turn next by discussing Ibn Khaldun's concept of *asabiyya*, by which I aim to detail what are the conditions that build and sustain a society. By bringing Ibn Khaldun into the discussion, the aim is to discuss one, among many other examples, of how 'Muslim' or Arabic (because it written in Arabic, and not all scholars were Muslims) scholarship from the distant past is different in the way it views and analyzes sociopolitical structures compared to the current Islamist view. The absence or marginalization of the Khaldunian thought, among many other great thinkers of the past, is in part due to nonknowledge, but more so in my view to the politicization of knowledge and to its colonization in the Arab and Islamic world in general (Shihade, 2017).

Ibn Khaldun's *Asabiyya*-Social/Group Solidarity

One of the main reasons, in my view, for the lack of group solidarity in the region is the lack of reading; the alienation or self-alienation of peoples in the region from local/regional knowledge. This is similar to conditions in other parts of the Third World/Global South. This is also in part due to the working of Western modernity and the geopolitics of knowledge that led to the marginalization of knowledge from outside the 'center', and to the devaluation of knowledge from the Global South through the hegemony of the Global North (Mignolo, 2009). Furthermore, the global empire was aided by an intellectual imperialism that created a conformity of thought in the North as well as the South (Alatas, 2000). In the Global South, and here I will restrict my discussion to North Africa and West Asia, scholars and intellectuals have mostly followed established Western knowledge, or claim to, without any modification, and without offering alternative knowledge. This is while it has been established that knowledge production and imperial conquest have been the twins of Western hegemony and its devastating impact on peoples of the Global South (Said, 1978; Mignolo, 2009). Furthermore, for the most part, scholars/intellectuals in the Arab world have participated in the devaluation of their own heritage and knowledge production from the past, through what has been called 'self-Orientalism' (Khalidi, 2006), in which local knowledge from the past has been cast in the Orientalist lens. These texts have come to be seen as of less value, of being particular to a specific time and space, unlike Western texts that are considered of universal value (Shihade, 2013).

Furthermore, scholars in the region for the most part, like Western scholars, have taken Arabic knowledge as a text to be studied, as an object of knowledge about the past, rather than a source of epistemology, an epistemology that can offer an alternative to the history of Western knowledge production that has been at least in part entangled with Western global dominance and violence (Raju, 2009). The result has been an alienation of generations of students and scholars from their own 'secular' knowledge, an alienation accompanied by a sense of defeat and weakness in the face of the Global North. This has produced a void that has been filled by nativist, and reactionary Islamist groups with their own particular religious narrative as the only response to the state of despair and weakness that may feel in the region. It has contributed to the dismemberment of group solidarity, because a group does not produce its own knowledge and only engages with knowledge produced in the past or relies on knowledge produced somewhere else, by other people with their own specific experience. They are engaged in copying, or mimicking (using Ibn Khaldun's term) the knowledge of globally dominant groups, and conforming to its parameters, methods, and even questions, without reflecting on the relevance of such knowledge to local histories and needs (Alatas, 2000, 2001).

Thus, this chapter is a modest attempt to push for a de-alienation from one's own heritage that not only can offer a challenge to the 'religious' reading of culture/heritage/past, but also can offer alternative to the neoliberal and devastating subject-hood/investment in individualism and self-interest offered and created by the Global North. In this context, the chapter will briefly engage with the concept of asabiyya – group solidarity as articulated by Ibn Khaldun in the fourteenth to fifteenth century in his *Al-Muqaddimah* (An Introduction to the History of Social Organizations), a multivolume text that explores the reasons for why people live together, and what conditions are needed for sustaining their dignified existence (Rosenthal and Dawood, 2005). This chapter is also a way to creatively read such work to make it relevant to local needs (as Syed Farid Alatas's work does), both to counter the state of alienation we are in, and to engage with questions that are relevant to local contexts, that provide an alternative to process of dismemberment of the societies in the region that we witness currently.

Ibn Khaldun and the Concept of *Asabiyya*: An Elaboration of the Aristotelian Concept that Humans by Nature Are Political

Ibn Khaldun argues that we often repeat established knowledge without either investigating its validity, or its accurate meaning. In his view, one of the crucial concepts that is often repeated without understanding its meaning is the concept that 'humans are by nature political'. In his view, this concept is crucial for understanding why social organizations are natural to humans. His goal in *Al-Muqaddimah*, he argues, is to understand the meaning of why humans are by nature political and live together in plurality, and what the conditions are for sustaining a together-living in multitudes in a way that guarantees both the individual's dignity life and the sustainability of the group.

Ibn Khaldun argues that the meaning of the idea that the 'human is by nature political', is that the human can not only live in a polis, the polis meaning directly a city, but also a space where a larger number of humans live together. Due to self-interests and needs, one needs the group to sustain a dignified life, and at the same time, this social organization needs to offer the individual a dignified life for the group to sustain itself. Thus, what we see here, is an early reading, if not an original idea, that one's freedom and dignity is guaranteed once one moves from the state of nature to human civilization (Rousseau and the social contract). In Ibn Khaldun's view, the concept of the state of nature is a hypothetical one as humans never lived in such a state of being. Rather, according to him, the difference is in the number, in the size of the group. The state of nature is the group with a small number of individuals, and the political–social organization is the larger social organization. In his view, the move from being/living in a small group into a larger one is natural to all human beings regardless of their religion or racial background (Shihade, 2013; Mamdani, 2017). That is because living in small social organizations, life is difficult and insecure not only economically but also physically (Shihade, 2015).

According to him, living in a larger social organization offers a move from one form of economic system to a different one. It is a move from a simple economic system based on agriculture and farming, exchange, and sharecropping, to a much more developed economic system that by the effect of there being a larger number of people in it, leads to a surplus of labor. The labor of many together, is larger than the sum of each on his/her own, which leads to a surplus of capital that gets invested in creating new products that both make life easier. It also creates the need for more labor, which is met by the coming of more individuals into that social organization, which leads to not only constant surplus of labor, further surplus of capital, and newer products that make life easier, but also to the generation of a much more developed and sophisticated urban life (ibn Khaldun, 2005: 43, 91ff, 119, 133ff, 143, 221, 241, 273ff, 276ff, 298ff, 308).

The question is whether this natural tendency of humans to live in larger groups is something different from what bound together individuals living in smaller social organizations, whose main link was the blood relationship. In larger social organizations, something different is needed for binding the individuals together, and preventing the dismemberment of the group, and here comes in the concept of *asabiyya* (ibn Khaldun, 2005: 26ff, 35, 71, 79f, 107ff, 111-15, 123, 132, 151f,169f, 183f, 230). In a smaller social organization, the blood relationship connected members of the group together, and this relationship was managed by an elder or elders of the group. In a larger social organization, a new spirit is needed to create a sense of unity among the people and a new form of governance is needed to manage both the relationship between the individuals in the group as well as the larger and more developed/sophisticated economy. So, what is that spirit that is needed to keep people together in a larger social organization, and what is the form/type of governance that is needed to regulate their life together and manage the economy?

While some might argue for religion to bind people together, according to Ibn Khaldun, a unifying religious spirit/feeling is unnatural to humans. Even if one is religious, one must admit that such cases are exceptional in the history of human social organizations, and it only took place with the existence/presence of a prophet and lasted only during his lifetime. The more natural and more common phenomenon in different historical periods and in different geographical locations (time/space) has been a history of human social organizations bound together through a different spirit: a nonreligious, 'secular' spirit. This is the binding together through asabiyya that both guarantees and secures the individual's dignified life, and consequently the survival/sustainability of the group (Shihade, 2016).

So, what guarantees the individual's dignified life? According to Ibn Khaldun, one is human only through thought and labor. That is, one can live and sustain a life only through labor (both physical and mental). For the individual to remain in a social organization, his/her labor must be fairly compensated, fairly in relation to the living costs of the place/city one lives in. Otherwise, the individual paid an unfair wage for his/her labor that does not allow her/him to sustain a dignified life, either cheats the system that treats him/her unfairly by putting in less labor contributing to the deterioration of that profession/sector of the economy. Sooner or later that sector of the economy disappears, and with it also disappears the surplus of capital that could have been accumulated if fair wages were paid. Thus, unfair pay for labor for the individual indirectly disaffects the well-being of the whole larger social organization, and its economic development. Another possibility if one is not paid fairly for one's labor is labor flight; that one moves to another location and into another social organization that might, or does, in fact, pay a fair wage. If this process were to continue without a government intervening on behalf of the individual, it would lead sooner or later to the destruction of that social organization. But that government has much more to do than merely guaranteeing a fair pay for labor to individuals under its rule (Shihade, 2013).

Governments/regimes must constantly work to infuse a sense of asabiyya, a sense of group solidarity among the individuals under its rule. This sense of group solidarity is not based on religious feelings, but on the material needs of the individuals in the group. For the internal cohesion of the group to be maintained, the government or regime, in addition to securing fair pay for the labor of each individual (regulating a fair pay for labor), must also avoid the presence of monopolies in the economy, for monopoly kills/destroys fair opportunity for all. The government/regime must avoid engaging in any sector of the economy, but should constantly, through taxes collected, keep working at creating more economic opportunities for the individuals in those social organizations. It must also offer them education; education that encourages critical thought and is not based on memorization and harsh punishment and offers space for learning skills needed in the economy. It must also offer health facilities, public health, management of, and planning for a healthy life in the city that avoids overcrowding, allows the flow of fresh air, and makes the health of the individuals more secure. Health and education can only help in sustaining the continuity of the group and its development (Shihade, 2013, 2017). It is only through these policies that a government/regime can guarantee a sustainable collective, and cohesion of the social organization, the sense of *asabiyya* – group solidarity. Without this, members in the group won't come together at times of external aggression, invasions, and or interventions from outside powers.

By Way of Conclusion: *Asabiyya* for the Global South

The times of Ibn Khaldun were times of a less connected global economy, and a less connected world. It was a world that did not have a global empire, based on a hegemonic aggressive capitalist system, a system that requires global interventions and domination and exploitation of humans and resources all around. Thus, the concept of *asabiyya* as articulated by Ibn Khaldun must be creatively rethought to fit this current globalized condition, a condition where the Global North has been accumulating wealth through the exploitation of labor of peoples in the Global South and through the repression of any possibility for any group in the Global South to carve for itself a dignified life (Wallerstein, 2004; Amin, 2012). As the Empire has become global, a certain counter global *asabiyya* among the peoples of the Global South must be the response for peoples there to start building a dignified life that guarantees/secures the wellbeing of each individual, and that guarantees the sustainability of the Global South as a whole. A form of new alliance and solidarity based on the common interests of the Global South to live without external aggression, intervention, and exploitation is needed. A sense of *asabiyya* that learns from past mistakes, from the pitfalls of the nationalism, and from the mistakes of the experiences in the so-called postcolonial/post-Apartheid states.

One can enumerate the reasons for why the Global South should sustain itself, create a dignified life where the wellbeing of each individual is secured, and why this approach/goal is the only way to fend off the naked violence of the global empire. It is also easy to argue that the nativist violence of the different groups in North Africa and West Asia only helps in destroying the Global South guaranteeing a longer life for the hegemony of the global empire. However, it is not easy, at least for me, and for now, to suggest how to organize/build a regime/leadership that can lead, organize the life and economy of the peoples in the Global South. For sure, neither neoliberalism nor a militant religious reactionary spirit can bring the kind of a collective spirit, a kind of global *asabiyya* that can bind people of the Global South together. Rather, it requires the critical analysis of past and present experiences in different parts of the Global South to organize and coordinate the efforts of peoples and states in the face of a global empire that by its very nature does its best to prevent the emergence of such alternatives.

The alternative cannot be by mimicking Western norms, nor by a reactionary and exclusionary identity. Following the main ideas suggested by Ibn Khaldun, it must put the dignity of the individual first; for without the individual the multitude cannot be. The dignity of the individual must include a fair pay for one's labor so that one is able to sustain a decent living. The multitude must find a new spirit, a new spirit that fits the current globalized world that is dominated by Western countries and led by the United States. It must include elements that unite peoples in the Global South, their aspirations, and their needs. It must reflect peoples' economic needs, secure, and critical education, a healthy living, a just living without oppression neither by the global empire nor by local rulers. It must be secular (not to confuse that with animosity to religion and spirituality). It must be concerned with people's physical health and necessary material needs. It must be attuned to nature and the fragility of the environment. If the Bandung spirit of the 1950s failed to achieve its goals, we might need to think of a reworking of that concept in a way that unites peoples around the world around the common good, common needs, and aspirations, a new form of *asabiyya* that fits our current time.

Note

1 *Asabiyya* is a term that has been used often by different scholars. Sometimes it is translated as strict allegiance to one's group united by blood or ancestry. In my view, so other scholars also argued, reading the Al-Muqaddimah as whole one clearly realizes that the term is much more flexible than such an interpretation. In the text itself Ibn Khaldun argues against strict interpretations of any concept, including the religious ones. The citations from *Al-Muqaddimah* used in this chapter are based on a translated and abridged version of Ibn Khaldun's monumental work *Al-Muqaddimah*: An

Introduction to History. One important note here about referencing Ibn Khaldun. His style of writing is cyclical and repetitive, and that is in part that Al-Muqaddimah is a collection of his lectures, in which he summarizes constantly what was said earlier and adds something new to the idea. So, one finds a discussion on the same topic all over *Al-Muqaddimah* always with new dimensions and additions.

References

Alatas, S.H. (2000) 'Intellectual Imperialism: Definition, traits, and problems', *Asian Journal of Social Science*, 28(1), 23–45.

Alatas, S.F. (2001) 'The study of social sciences in developing societies: Towards an adequate conceptualization of relevance', *Current Sociology*, 49(2), 1–19.

Amin, S. (2012) 'The Arab revolutions: A year after', *Interface: A Journal for and About Social Movements*, 4(1), 33–42.

Dreyfuss, R. (2005) *Devil's Game: How the United States Helped Unleash Fundamentalist Islam*. New York: Metropolitan Books.

Fanon, F. (1966) *The Wretched of the Earth*. Translated by Constance Famington. New York: Grove Press.

Hallaq, W. (2012) *The Impossible State: Islam, Politics, and Modernity's Moral Predicament*. New York: Columbia University Press.

Hamouchine, H. (2016) 'Fanon's revolutionary culture and nationalism', in Fanon, F. (ed.) *Voices of Liberation*, compiled by Leo Zeilig. Chicago, IL: Haymarket Books.

Hanafi, S. and Tabar, L. (2005) *The Emergence of a Globalized Palestinian Elite*. Institute of Jerusalem Studies and Muwatin.

Kerr, H.M. (1971) *The Arab Cold War: Gamal Abd Al-Nasser and his Rivals 1958–1970*. Oxford University Press.

Khalidi, A.M. (2006) 'Orientalism in the interpretation of Islamic philosophy', *Radical Philosophy*, 135, 25–33.

Mamdani, M. (2003) *Good Muslim, Bad Muslim: America, the Cold War, and the Roots of Terror*. New York: Doubleday.

Mamdani, M. (2017) 'Reading Ibn Khaldun in Kampala', *Journal of Historical Sociology*.30(1), 7–26.

Mignolo, W. (2009) 'Epistemic disobedience, independent thought, and de-colonial freedom', *Theory, Culture & Society*, 27(7–8), 1–23.

Raju, C.K. (2009) *Is Science Western in Origin?* Penang, Malaysia: Multiversity and Citizens International.

Rosenthal, F. and Dawood N.J. (2005) *Al-Muqaddimah: An Introduction to History*. Princeton: University of Princeton.

Said, E. (1978) *Orientalism*. New York: Pantheon Books.

Shihade, M. (2012) 'On the difficulty of understanding and predicting the Arab Spring: Orientalism, Eurocentrism, and Modernity', *International Journal of Peace Studies*, 17(2), 57–70.

Shihade, M. (2013) Ibn Khaldun: Writing from the margin—State of Nature, to remain there in Carlson, D.J. and Fox, A.R. (eds.) *The State of Nature in Comparative Political Thought: Western and Non-Western Perspectives*. Washington, DC: Lexington Books, Rowman and Littlefield.

Shihade, M. (2015) 'Global Israel: Settler colonialism, mobility, connections, and ruptures', *Borderlands*, 14(1), 1–16.

Shihade, M. (2016) 'Rediscovering religion and secularism: A critique of a critique', *Social Transformations*, 4(1), 3–25.

Shihade, M. (2017) 'Education and decolonization: On not reading ibn Khaldun in Palestine',*Decolonization: Indigeneity, Education & Society*, 6(1), 79–93.

Wallerstein, I. (2004) *World System Analysis: An Introduction*. Durham, NC: Duke University Press.

12

DADANI

Kaveh Yazdani[1]

Introduction

Dadan is a Persian verb meaning to give, deliver, or advance. However, the *dadani* system – which was prevalent in South Asia – did not bear the same name in Persia. A number of Persian words were absorbed in regions outside Iran and expanded into other languages. Needless to mention, some Persian words, that according to etymologists, entered other Asian and European languages (e.g., bazar, check, kiosk, pajama, paradise, etc.) did not disappear from the Persian lexicon and more or less retained their original meaning when adapted in different environments (Lewis, 2000, pp. 67–9, 71–2; Kluge, 1989 [1883], p. 371). But other names and terms with Persian roots did, in fact, change their significance with time and showed little resemblance to the terms from which they were originally derived (e.g., chicanery and magic).

In 1969, Irfan Habib wrote that in seventeenth century Mughal India 'the putting-out system was widely in use; and that both cash advances and the giving-out of the raw material were established practices' (Habib, 1969, p. 68).[2] However, most historians were of a different opinion and cast doubt on the alleged similarities between cash advances and putting-out (also known as '*Verlag*', 'outwork', or 'homework'). More recently, scholars have been even more articulate in either desisting or criticizing the equation of the Indian *dadani* system with the putting-out system (*Verlagssystem*) that emerged in Western Europe. Therefore, the main thrust of this piece is to get a better understanding of the *dadani* system through a comparative lens (especially with Europe but also with Persia and the Ottoman Empire). It is often through comparisons that the characteristics and specificities of certain phenomena and practices become more clear and distinguishable. Furthermore, as far as I am aware of, there is no work that has yet systematically compared the putting-out and *dadani* systems with each other.

DOI: 10.4324/9781003273530-16

The following is a preliminary attempt and outline of a larger project that intends to examine the *dadani* system in comparison to other forms of procurement and production, especially the European putting-out systems. *Dadani* took off in a critical phase in the development of commercial capitalism in India. Nonetheless, we still lack information on its exact genealogy and regional specificities in comparative perspective. Moreover, it is not entirely clear how far the rise of the *dadani* system was related to West Asian and European influences or whether it was an indigenous and more or less parallel development. Indeed, more research is needed regarding this very important development that might be characterized as pertaining to the lineage of the capitalist mode of production.

Thinking with and historicizing concepts and practices specific to and distinctive of spaces within the so-called East, Third World, or Global South not only help to better understand the particular regions under examination. They also promote the project of deconstructing Eurocentric myths and alleged Western exceptionalisms. When comparing these concepts and practices with those of other spaces (and time periods), they can also help identify similarities, differences, singularities and general trans-regional, intercontinental, and global trends.

Putting-Out and 'Proto-Industrialization'

There is no consensus regarding the definition of the putting-out system. Like others, I define it as a system of advance payment of raw materials and/or means of production by merchants or middlemen to artisans or peasants, mostly working in households, but also in workshops or manufactories. Apart from urban production (e.g., in thirteenth and fourteenth century Florence or seventeenth and eighteenth century Bologna and Lyons), resources were mostly put-out to rural areas producing textiles (wool, linen, cotton, silk, and blended cloth). The workers were not allowed to sell the finished product but had to deliver it to the putter-out in return for a sum of money. The putting-out system gained importance in the thirteenth century, probably becoming widespread from the fourteenth and fifteenth centuries onwards, especially in Northern Italy, Flanders, and parts of Germany. In the seventeenth and eighteenth centuries, it became even more prevalent, also accelerating in other parts of Western Europe such as the Low Countries, France, England, and Switzerland (Lis and Soly, 1979, p. 105; Holbach 1994).[3]

Some historians have argued that it belongs to an intermediate stage between the independent handicraft workshop system (*Kaufsystem*) and centralized manufactories or proto-factories. However, these different forms of labor organization also existed simultaneously and complemented each other. As Maxine Berg points out: 'Putting-out systems coexisted with artisan and cooperative forms of production, and all of these systems frequently interacted with some type of manufacture or proto-factory' (Berg, 2005 [1994], pp. 59–60; Dobb, 1950 [1946], pp. 342, 347–8). Thus, there was no unilinear development from independent artisan production to the factory system. The putting-out system usually rested upon domestic commodity production within households, cottages, and to a lesser extent in workshops. It was based on a certain degree of labor division, often implied detachment from agricultural activities, but was usually not subject to practices of surveillance, common in factory settings. Production was often transferred to rural areas in order to avoid guild restrictions and higher production costs. Significantly, putting-out implied an increased penetration of merchant capital into production and sale, and led to a greater dependency of producers on merchants and putters-out. As a result, the producers lost access to the market and could neither buy raw materials nor sell their goods independently. In some forms of the putting-out system, merchants even provided the necessary means of production.

In the 1970s, some scholars argued that practices of putting-out were part and parcel of Western Europe's processes of 'proto-industrialization'. 'Proto-industrialization' may be defined as 'the massive expansion of export-oriented handicrafts which took place in many parts of Europe between the 16th and the 19th centuries' (Ogilvie, 2008, p. 710). But since the 1980s it has been increasingly pointed out that 'proto-industrialization' is a misleading term, not least because of its linear and teleological implications. The hypothesis that 'proto-industrialization' is a preliminary stage and basic prerequisite for industrialization has widely come under attack.[4] Indeed, the mode of organization, the quality, and quantity of preindustrial rural manufacture do not seem to be crucial when it comes to identifying favorable conditions for an industrial breakthrough. By contrast, D. C. Coleman even argues that out of approximately ten English regions that went through processes of 'proto-industrialization', only four became industrialized. Furthermore, he notes that Northeast and South Wales took-off even though they did not possess 'any significant prior experience of what the theory recognizes as proto-industrialization, but both had coal and iron'. He also holds that theories of 'proto-industrialization' do not 'take significant heed of urban industry of either the domestic or the centralized variety, be it textiles, dockyards or soap-boiling' (Coleman, 1983, p. 443).

Dadani – Comparisons with Ottoman and Safavid Practices

The *dadani*, better known as the *dadni* system, was a practice of advance payment common in many parts of seventeenth and especially eighteenth century South Asia.[5] It consisted of a considerable portion of money or raw materials for an arranged price and quantity and quality of commodities. Contracts were based on verbal or written agreements and advances were given by merchants to artisans and cultivators related to manufacture in both urban and rural areas – often through the mediation of middlemen and brokers (*dallal, paikar*, etc.). In return, the artisans and cultivators were bound to supply the final product to those who had provided the advance, and in a noticeable number of cases they had to deliver the wares on predetermined dates. From the seventeenth century onwards, the

European East India Companies made ample use of the *dadani* system, contracting merchants and middlemen, often with compulsory measures (especially penalties for payment of dues in arrears and confinement).

Regarding the production and sale of textiles, there is little indication that there was a monopsony in the market. Instead, there was fierce competition between the European companies, Asian merchants, and local trade (Gupta, 2009, p. 292). One of the reasons for the spread of *dadani* contracts was the lack of money available to the artisans to adapt to the requirements of an expanding market. Furthermore, they gave the producers the necessary security to sell their products. It also safeguarded that artisans were bound to merchants who, as a result, could count on the delivery of a considerable amount of commissioned commodities (Singh, 2005, p. 55; Prakash, 2009, pp. 220–1).

The origins of the *dadani* system still remain in the dark. Some historians act on the assumption that it was introduced by the British or other European East India Companies. According to K. N. Chaudhuri, however,

> The Indian system was essentially based on the idea of Islamic jurisprudence. The law of *salam* [safety, security] sales, for example, derived its authority from the Koran itself and literally signified a contract involving a prompt delivery in return for a distant delivery. In the language of the law, it meant a contract of sale, causing an immediate payment of the price, and admitting a delay in the delivery of wares. According to Hanifa a salam sale was valid only if, among other conditions, it specified the period of the delivery and the rate of the capital advanced.
>
> *(Chaudhuri, 1978, p. 256)*

Al-Hidayah, a central source of Islamic law, written in the twelfth century by the leading Muslim jurist Burhan al-Din al-Marghinani (1135–97), contains a number of passages that describe practices of advancement. The *salam* (advance) contract was based on the supply of advanced money to be delivered at a future period (Hamilton, 1791, pp. 12–4, 94, 204–5, 318, 379, 415, 456, 491–2; Johansen, 2006, pp. 861–99). There is sufficient evidence that this practice was continued up to the nineteenth century. In Ottoman Cairo between 1600 and 1800, for instance, Nelly Hanna identified 'occasional references to *salam shari* agreements between a merchant and a weaver wherein the merchant paid in advance for future delivery of woven textiles' (Hanna, 2011, p. 93). However, more research is needed to determine the emergence and historical development of the *dadani* system, especially the role of the European East India Companies. To the best of my knowledge, *dadani* should not be reduced to the aforementioned practices of advance payment, as from the seventeenth century onwards it could also imply advancements of raw materials. Whether cash or raw materials were advanced depended on the particular region, time period, and branch of production. Tapan Raychaudhuri points out that,

> So far as our evidence goes, by the later years of the seventeenth century and surely by those of the eighteenth, both the European companies and Indian traders procured virtually every commodity for the market – from Bengal and Coromandel textiles and Bihar saltpetre to Bayana indigo, Kashmir shawls and even Bihar iron – on the basis of the dadni system, if not some even more direct system of control over the artisan.[6]
>
> *(Raychaudhuri, 1983, p. 23)*

Systems of procurement equally existed in the Ottoman and Safavid Empires. But with respect to advancements made by merchants, very little documentary evidence is available. In the Ottoman domains, there are a few known instances where merchants advanced raw materials to artisans between the sixteenth and eighteenth centuries in Bursa, Cairo, and Ankara. But the position of the state and state-appointed merchants was prevalent (Faroqhi, 1979, 1994a; Petmezas, 1990; İslamoğlu-İnan, 1994, pp. 235–6, 246–7). According to Suraiya Faroqhi,

> (…) if we include the Ottoman state in our model, we find that the latter played the role which putting-out merchants played in other economies, coordinating different stages of manufacturing and mobilizing labor, albeit by political rather than economic pressures. Moreover, the Ottoman state was only marginally concerned with profits, its central concern being the provisioning of the army, navy, and court.
>
> *(Faroqhi, 1994b, pp. 18–9, 38)*

In Persia, a similar practice was known by the name of *pish-furush* (advance payment) and was mostly confined to money payments in anticipation of future harvests. The shah (king) also offered presents (*pishkash*) to producers and suppliers. In the seventeenth century, the observations of the well-educated aristocrat and Italian traveler Pietro de la Valle, as well as reports that were penned by clerks of the English and Dutch East India Companies (EIC and VOC) indicate that the shah had a quasi-monopsony over silk. These accounts suggest that he paid the producers in advance and bought the silk at about half the price for which he sold it to the Armenian Julfan merchants. Although it was discouraged by the court, merchants were not entirely prohibited from purchasing silk from the producers directly, provided they paid royal dues (Matthee, 1999, pp. 250, 45, 102–5). According to Rudi Matthee, one of the main reasons behind Persia's differences with Western Europe, as well as the quasi-monopsony of the Persian king was 'the fragmented state of Iran's domestic market, which was dominated by peddlers' (ibid., p. 129). However, in the case of wool, Persian practices of *pish-furush* approximated some forms of the Indian *dadani* system.[7] In Mughal and post-Mughal India as well as Western Europe, the *dadani* and putting-out systems may have had a stronger footing amongst private merchants, both Asian and European, who sometimes hired 'wage laborers' in workshops and manufactories. It is significant to note, however, that Western Europe went further than the 'gunpowder empires' and post-Mughal India in centralizing production through the advance of raw materials and tools, and Western European merchants more often provided the workplace outside of the household than their Asian counterparts.

Differences with the Putting-Out System

A generation of academics such as Joseph S. Brenning, Sinnapah Arasaratnam, and Morris D. Morris was cautious in labeling the Indian practice as putting-out system (see e.g., Morris, 1983, p. 562). Indeed, in 1965, the Russian historian A. I. Chicherov pointed out that the system of money advances to weavers 'must have prevailed in India right up to the end of the 18th century' (Chicherov, 1971 [1965 pp. 165, 181]). In reaction to Irfan Habib's conflation of *dadani* and putting-out, Hamza Alavi argued that, in India, the system of cash advances did not imply the involvement by the merchant in the organization of production and provision of materials and equipment and that weavers could hardly become capitalists as a result of living in poverty and being squeezed by the merchants (Alavi, 1980, p. 379). Bhattacharya also argued that exploitation did not allow for higher levels of capitalist production (Bhattacharya, 1983, p. 287). The late Ashin Das Gupta argued that, in India, 'no one had succeeded in centralizing and directing production or controlling distribution' (Das Gupta, 2004 [2001], p. 72). Similar arguments have also been put forward by Chris Bayly (1983, pp. 193–4), Om Prakash (1998, p. 166), René Barendse (2002, pp. 241–2), Ruby Maloni (2003, p. 28), David Washbrook (2007, p. 106), Maxine Berg (2015, pp. 126–7) and Sushil Chaudhuri (2020, pp. 38–40, 179–80). Indeed, in India, the *dadani* system promoted control of merchant capital over the producer, but hardly over the process of production itself.

By contrast, in parts of Western Europe, the subjugation of artisans by merchants took an important step further. The advancement of raw materials prevailed and tightened the purchaser's check on production. As T. P. Liu points out: 'Successful putting-out required merchants to buy up as much yarn as possible to deprive direct producers of independent access to raw materials' (Liu, 1994, p. 66). As a result of the monopolization of raw materials by putters-out, weavers were forced 'to sell to or take commissions from them exclusively' (ibid., 69). Moreover, merchants increasingly switched over to providing production sites and tools. Similar to what Maurice Dobb argued in the mid-1940s, as well as Klima and Macurek in 1960, Jürgen Schlumbohm has more recently reiterated that:

> (…) where the putter-out owned the raw materials, capital had clearly begun to go beyond the sphere of circulation, i.e., of trade, and penetrated into the sphere of production. Some of the means of production no longer belonged to the direct producers but had been transformed into capital, i.e. into a value that was to create surplus value for its owner.
>
> *(Schlumbohm, 1981 [1977], p. 102)*

Concurrently, Schlumbohm warns that, the 'stages in the development of the relations of production (...) do not constitute a sequence in the sense that they necessarily *had* to follow each other (...) stagnation or even retrogression could occur' (ibid., p. 110). Indeed, Karl Marx had already contended that the putting-out system was a stepping stone. However, 'it cannot bring about the overthrow of the old mode of production by itself, but rather preserves and retains it as its own precondition' (Marx, 1991, p. 452). This has also been confirmed by recent research. As Adrian Randall points out,

> The theory of proto-industrialization assumes that *Verlagsystems* were more adaptable to transition to the factory than were the more 'backward' *Kaufsystems*. The English woollen industry does not bear this out. In fact, the opposite is correct. Just as the Domestic System had proved itself adaptable to rapid growth in the eighteenth century, with the onset of mechanisation it was able to absorb much of the new technology within the existing structure and advance still faster.
>
> *(Randall, 1991, p. 26)*

It is true that in Western Europe and especially Britain the putting-out system and 'proto-industrialization' – which were predominantly based on labor-intensive and rural cottage-manufacture with little technological innovation – hardly explain the emergence of the Industrial Revolution that took place in the urban areas of Northern England. Concurrently, the changes in the organization of production that were becoming dominant in the wake of the implementation of the putting-out system and 'proto-industrialization' should not be ignored and must be considered as important factors in the transition to the factory system. As Schlumbohm points out, capitalist production 'began within the putting-out system', as 'the "surplus product" fell to the capitalist entrepreneur' (Schlumbohm, 1981, p. 104).

In India, a considerable number of producers worked for several purchasers and possessed a certain degree of maneuverability in negotiating prices. Weavers were often in a position to cancel their contracts and pay back the given advance, not least due to a lack of legal suability. They sometimes wove additional pieces for sale in the market and delivered inferior quality goods when dissatisfied with the contract conditions. Furthermore, a number of artisans, most notably weavers, had the means to migrate to other regions, if they were dissatisfied. These aspects further increased their bargaining power (Chicherov, 1971 [1965], p. 165; Vanina, 2004, pp. 89–92, 163; Habib, 2002 [1995], p. 220; Chaudhuri, 1974, pp. 155–6; Hossain, 1979, p. 324; Subramanian, 2009, pp. 259-60; Gupta, 2009, pp. 296–7; Parthasarathi, 2001). But this also depended on the commodities produced and the particular region being studied. Whereas in Gujarat, peasants and artisans maintained their relative autonomy in the marketplace, especially due to fragmentation, in Bengal, the Coromandel Coast, and Mysore, they were subject to oppressive and exploitative relations in the wake of the centralization and monopolization of production processes. Nonetheless, detailed narratives about riots and flights as well as 'governance structure' and juridical aspects related to the enforceability of contracts, monitoring, and transaction costs need to be scrutinized in order to be able to conduct an in-depth analysis in comparative perspective (Williamson, 1985).

Similarities with the Putting-Out System

In Western Europe, the advancement of raw materials was more dominant than in Asia and tightened the purchaser's check on production. Moreover, merchants increasingly switched over to providing production sites and means of production. However, this process did not only occur in Europe. The rising demand for Indian textiles and cotton equally stimulated similar processes in South Asia leading to increased commercialization and the penetration of merchant capital (Perlin, 1983, p. 86; Nadri, 2015, p. 97; Yazdani, 2017, pp. 361–556). Indeed, throughout the seventeenth and eighteenth centuries, the demand for Gujarati cotton and textiles was very high and India remained the textile workshop of the world from the seventeenth up to the early nineteenth centuries. In spite of the obvious differences between the Indian system of advancement and the European *Verlagssystem* such as the geographical location of production, for example, it can be proposed that, similar to certain core areas of Europe, some advanced parts of India were in a transitory phase where merchant capital increasingly penetrated the domain of production (cf. Chicherov, 1971 [1965], p. 174). Importantly, some merchants in Asia even made advancements in raw materials and thus went beyond the *Kaufsystem*, where producers purchased their own raw materials and sold their goods in markets. This took place in parts of Eastern India, Gujarat, and Mysore, though rather marginally, to a lesser extent than in Western Europe and sometimes with considerable resistance by artisans and cultivators.[8] Most significantly, the spread of manufactories and the recruitment of 'double-free' wage laborers were much more pronounced in Western Europe.

In the late seventeenth century, the traveler John Fryer mentioned European advances in raw materials to the weavers of Gujarat, and Binoy Shankar Mallick's survey has confirmed this practice (Fryer, 1698, 86; Mallick, 1986, p. 38). However, we also know of a few instances where indigenous merchants had the same degree of control over production as their Western European counterparts. While nonagricultural production between 1500 and 1800 still largely remained in the hands of households that were producing for the market or on behalf of assignments, we can equally detect the presence of merchant *karkhanas* (centralized manufactories) in seventeenth and eighteenth century Gujarat, where 'wage laborers' like silk twisters, dyers, weavers, and embroiderers were working (Vanina, 2004, pp. 90, 87, 105). The contemporary historian Ali Mohammad Khan wrote that in the early eighteenth century, especially Gujarati silk merchants owned 'a multitude of karkhanas', where winders, dyers, and weavers worked as 'wage-laborers' (Chicherov, 1971 [1965], p. 213). In precolonial

Ahmadabad – the populous Gujarati city founded in the early fifteenth century – the majority of artisans in the locally owned paper manufactories were 'wage-laborers', while the employers provided the tools and the raw materials (Mehta, 1991, p. 121).

However, it remains unclear if this represented a long-established form of artisanal production or rather a rupture in the system. It is also worth mentioning that, in 1646, the British built a dyeing-house in Ahmedabad where privately owned workshops emerged. The hired workers were 'wage-laborers' and the tools belonged to the master (Gopal, 1975, pp. 210, 221). Therefore, Surendra Gopal holds that 'the traditional mode of production wherein the craftsman combined in himself the function of owner, worker and seller was slowly disintegrating' (ibid., p. 210). The European trading Companies seem to have played a crucial role in this process. Importantly, the dyers were not forced to work in the dyeing-house, as was often the case in the royal *karkhanas*. Indeed, Gopal notes that: 'From Ovington's assertion that the hiring of wage-labour was a usual practice at Surat, we can infer that work-force was freely available (…) Many skilled artisans could be hired for wages. The role of wage-labourers was certainly increasing in the productive system' (ibid., p. 228). But he also alleges that the number of wage-laborers was still small (ibid., pp. 221, 238). Significantly, Gopal points out that in seventeenth century Gujarat, a period marked by the rise of a wealthy and powerful merchant class, 'the process of exploitation of the direct producers, the craftsmen and the peasants was intensified (…) Only a thin line separated him from the position of a hired worker' (ibid., pp. 201, 235; Chicherov, 1971 [1965], pp. 165–7, 175-6). Similarly, K. N. Chaudhuri observes that, at the end of the eighteenth century, 'in some areas of India the textile workers had come perilously near to being wage labourers. Control by merchants had increased both in western and southern India' (Chaudhuri, 1974, p. 160). Ruby Maloni has recently confirmed that 'a considerable portion of the Surat population worked in the service sector or as wage labourers' (Maloni, 2003, p. 45).

Indeed, it is noteworthy that in Surat – the second largest Indian city of the mid-eighteenth century – there was a cheap and abundant workforce that could be hired for wages. In a number of cases, urban artisans had almost become genuine wage laborers, while in a few cases the merchants even entirely provided the means of production (e.g., in the paper and segments of the textile manufactures of Ahmedabad which were thriving export commodities). In short, the social structure of some manufacturing centers in Gujarat did not stand in opposition to capitalist social relations and offered potentialities for a transition toward proletarianization and factory work. The aforementioned suggests that parts of Gujarat had entered a transitory phase. These developments were part and parcel of Gujarat's increasing degree of regional market integration, especially in coastal areas, alluding to mechanisms of *Smithian growth*, characterized by increased specialization in the wake of expanding markets (Yazdani, 2017, pp. 361–556).

Conclusion

The Mughal and post-Mughal periods witnessed the rising importance of the *dadani* system. Indigenous, Asian and European merchants mostly advanced cash, but occasionally they also supplied raw materials and semiprocessed goods to artisans and cultivators via middlemen. In a few cases, though less pronounced than in Western Europe, the merchants also provided the means of production and employed 'wage-labor'. The fact that all these different forms of organization of production have been subsumed under the term of *dadani* has caused some confusion. Indeed, it would be helpful to distinguish between these different forms and shades that became prevalent in the transitional period of the seventeenth and eighteenth centuries and use different terms when describing advancements of cash in contradistinction to raw materials and tools.

There is some indication that despite the socioeconomic, political, cultural, and historical interconnections and similarities between the three 'gunpowder empires', the systems of advancement in the Ottoman and Safavid domains seem to have been rather state-centered; whereas, in the Indian subcontinent and Europe, merchants had a considerable share in controlling production and trade. In the case of South Asia, this was a result of the high demand for Indian commodities (i.e., cotton, textiles, handicraft, ships, and iron), favorable supply structures, and the activities of wealthy Asian merchants and the European East India Companies.

In urban Northwest India, forms of production sometimes went even beyond the *Verlagssystem*. Indeed, centralized manufactories emerged in Gujarat (e.g., in shipbuilding, textile, and paper production), where merchants sometimes provided the tools and raw materials for 'wage laborers'. These examples reflect the *formal subsumption* of labor to merchant capital. Merchants and merchant-like rulers such as Tipu Sultan were more and more capable of tightening their grip on the artisans and cultivators. This process effectively increased in the course of the eighteenth century. Advance payments in India reflected the increased importance of *exchange-value* and *absolute surplus-value*. This development did not lead to greater potentialities for industrialization and no forms of *real subsumption* and *relative surplus-value* came into existence, since too few technological transformations occurred that were capable of triggering an industrial breakthrough. It was not only a manifestation of the consolidation – but also the evolution – of commercial capitalism.[9] As Jairus Banaji points out, 'under commercial capitalism, advances were the major form in which capital circulated', while 'the transactions between merchants and artisans, etc. surpassed the scope of simple circulation' (Banaji, 2010, p. 276).[10] Concurrently, the focus on production obscures the importance of the organization of production which was equally crucial in the transition to industrial capitalism.

The differences between established textile manufacturing sites in the cities and the production units that flourished in villages between the seventeenth and nineteenth centuries, the role of the East India Companies as well as the relationship between and the mechanisms of the market, guild system, caste, and the state are important for understanding the totality in which these different forms of organization of labor and methods of production unfolded in Western Europe and India. In order to determine similarities and differences between Asian and European advancement systems, these aspects need to be examined accordingly.

Even throughout the nineteenth and twentieth centuries, the putting-out and *dadani* systems continued to be applied in certain segments of production in Europe, South Asia, and beyond. In the wake of the rise of machine-spun yarn in late eighteenth and early nineteenth century Britain, for example, there was 'an enormous expansion along traditional outwork lines, as a whole new army of men, women, and children were recruited to the handloom' (Bythell, 1978, p. 36). The production of consumer goods such as boots and nails also depended on outwork. Alfred Kieser is of the opinion that putting-out 'is obviously even passing through a renaissance. High quality knitware production in Modena [in the 1980s and 1990s] represents an outstanding example' (Kieser, 1994, p. 615). In Nepal too, for example, the *dadani* system is still prevalent today (Balikci, 2008, p. 183; Karki, DeWald, Shahi, 2010, pp. 9, 13).

These are vivid examples, showing that history is never a linear process and archaic features belonging to preindustrial socioeconomic formations sometimes survive, continue to exist, adapt to socioeconomic transformations, and may complement newer forms of production and exchange. While the putting-out and *dadani* systems emerged during a period of transition between a precapitalist and capitalist mode of production, they outlived the period in which they emerged, not in the least because they are related to certain forms of commercial capitalist development, that, when combined with modern machinery, could have a number of advantages for capital accumulation (especially via lower production and labor costs). Although they belong to a preindustrial period where capitalist laws of motion had not yet become dominant, it is not surprising that they still existed during the nineteenth and twentieth centuries and endure up until today.

Notes

1 I would like to thank Naima and Kimberly Bright and Anke Schwengelbeck for proofreading an earlier version of the manuscript, Sina Delfs for compiling the bibliography and Nasser Mohajer for his invaluable comments, editions, and instructive suggestions.

2 See also Singh, 2006, pp. 3, 14-5, 20-2, 145-156. In this paper, advance payments during the 19th century will not be examined in detail. There is a short reference to contemporary practices in the conclusion. For an overview of advance payments in 19th and early 20th century India and beyond, see Banaji, 2010, especially pp. 100-1, 113-5, 144-5, 148-50, 175-6, 271-2, 274-7, 294-8, 303-4, 313-4; idem, 2016, pp. 415-22. For the case of India, see also Haynes, 2012, pp. 140-6; Roy, 1999.

3 For attempts at defining and explaining the term, see, for example, Schmoller, 1901, pp. 424-8; Poni, 1985, p. 306; Wehler, 1996 [1987], pp. 94-102; Komlos, 1994, pp. 791-2; Ogilvie and Cerman, 1996, p. 4.

4 For an overview of debates with respect to 'proto-industrialization', see Ogilvie and Cerman, 1996, pp. 1-11. In the introduction, they define proto-industrialization as 'the expansion of domestic industries producing goods for non-local markets', while, usually manufactories 'expanded without adopting advanced technology or centralizing production into factories.' Mendels was the first to argue that the growth of 'pre-industrial industry' was 'part and parcel of the process of 'industrialization' or, rather, as a first phase which preceded and prepared modern industrialization proper.' (1972, p. 241). Levine has argued that proto-industrialization led to population growth and 'proletarianization' and Mokyr has suggested that not agriculture, but proto-industry provided for surplus labor (Levine, 1977; Mokyr, 1976, pp. 371-396). See also Kriedte, Medick and Schlumbohm, 1981 [1977]; Berg, 2005 [1994]; Žmolek, 2013. Ogilvie and Cerman summarize the existing literature, when they write that 'the factors which decided whether a proto-industrial region would industrialize or de-industrialize remained largely unclear' (1996, p. 11).

5 However, we know of instances of advances in both cash and raw materials as early as the sixteenth century. See, for example, Dale, 2002 [1994], pp. 75–6.

6 Interestingly, 'In the early eighteenth century there is no evidence that temples or kings – both of which for several centuries had been important sources of capital in the South Indian economy – were engaged in advancing money to weavers. However, later in the century, a number of South Indian states entered the cloth trade and provided advances to weavers in order to finance production.' (Parthasarathi, 2001, p. 12).

7 As Barendse points out, in 1722, the VOC wrote that under the Safavids 'there were two ways of procuring wool. The first was to hand cash advances in January to the wool pre-purchasers – mostly Armenians – who operated in closed rings and had previously agreed on a set price among themselves, who then would go to the villages throughout the district and would give the owners of the sheep an advance payment in return for which they would sell all their wool to the agent (...) It was also possible to purchase wool from independent peddlers who did not use advances to procure wool, but rather bought it [in] cash from the tribes and then sold it in the open market.' (Barendse, 2009, p. 311). In the second half of the 19th century, the governor of Kerman made 'the sale of the wool a government monopoly, and retaining the whole export trade of wool to India in his own hands, to realize such an income as to be able to relieve the people of the grinding taxation which prevails elsewhere.' (Markham, 1874, p. 402). Interestingly, between 1877 and 1882, Ziegler & Co. established an enterprise in Sultanabad (Arak) in western Iran and 'provided weavers with raw materials, including wool and patterns, and cash advances' (Bloom and Blair, 2009, p. 376). By and large, very little is known about practices of putting-out in Persia.

8 For the advancements of raw materials in Patna, see Singh, 2005, p. 55. For the advancement of raw materials by local Bengali merchants, see Ray, 2011, pp. 95-6. See also Habib, 1964, p. 400. For Mysore, see Yazdani, 2017, p. 188. In Sikkim (Nepal), too, cultivators received both goods and cash (Balikci, 2008, pp. 183-4, 378).

9 I shall define commercial capitalism as a combination of *Smithian* growth and social relations of exchange and production dominated by a merchant class that reinvests portions of profit into commerce and/or a certain degree of commodity production. However, I am aware that this is only one of several ways to define merchant capitalism. Moreover, in many historical phases, 'commercial capital is synonymous with the non-subjection of production to capital.' (Marx, 1991 [1894], p. 445, see also pp. 438, 442). For a recent conceptualization and history of commercial capitalism, see Banaji, 2020.

10 However, Banaji refers to the 19th and not the 17th and 18th centuries.

Bibliography

Alavi, H. (1980) 'India: Transition from Feudalism to Colonial Capitalism', *Journal of Contemporary Asia* 10(4), pp. 359–399.

Balikci, A. (2008) *Lamas, Shamans and Ancestors Village Religion in Sikkim*. Leiden: Brill.

Banaji, J. (2010) *Theory as History: Essays on Modes of Production and Exploitation*. Leiden: Brill.

Banaji, J. (2016) 'Merchant Capitalism, Peasant Households and Industrial Accumulation: Integration of a Model', *Journal of Agrarian Change* 16(3), pp. 410–431.

Banaji, J. (2020) *A Brief History of Commercial Capitalism*. Chicago: Haymarket Books.

Barendse, R. J. (2002) *The Arabian Seas: The Indian Ocean World of the Seventeenth Century*. New York: M. E. Sharpe.

Barendse, R. J. (2009) *Arabian Seas 1700–1763: The Western Indian Ocean in the Eighteenth Century*, Vol. 1&2. Leiden: Brill.

Bayly, C. A. (1983) *Rulers, Townsmen and Bazaars: North Indian Society in the Age of British Expansion, 1770–1870*. New York: Cambridge University Press.

Berg, M. (2005 [1994]) *The Age of Manufactures, 1700–1820: Industry, Innovation and Work in Britain*. London: Routledge.

Berg, M. (2015) 'The Merest Shadows of a Commodity': Indian Muslins for European Markets 1750–1800', in Berg, M. (ed.) *Goods from the East, 1600–1800*. London: Palgrave Macmillan, pp. 119–138.

Bhattacharya, S. (1983) 'Eastern India II', in Kumar D. and Desai M. (eds.) *Cambridge Economic History of India (CEHI), Vol. 2, c. 1757-1970*, Cambridge: Cambridge University Press, pp. 270–331.

Bloom J. and Blair, S. S. (eds.) (2009) *The Grove Encyclopedia of Islamic Art and Architec*ture. New York: Oxford University Press.

Bythell, D. (1978) *The Sweated Trades: Outwork in Nineteenth-century Britain*. London: Batsford Academic.

Chaudhuri, K. N. (1974) 'The Structure of Indian Textile Industry in the Seventeenth and Eighteenth Centuries', *The Indian Economic & Social History Review* 11(2–3), pp. 127–182.

Chaudhuri, K. N. (1978) *The Trading World of Asia and the English East India Company: 1660–1760*. New York: Cambridge University Press.

Chaudhury, S. (2020) *Spinning Yarns: Bengal Textile Industry in the Backdrop of John Taylor's Report on 'Dacca Cloth Production' (1801)*. New York: Routledge.

Chicherov, A. I. (1971 [1965]) *India – Economic Development in the 16th–18th Centuries*. Moscow: Nauka Pub. House, Central Dept. of Oriental Literature.

Coleman, D. C. (1983) 'Proto-Industrialization: A Concept Too Many', *The Economic History Review* 36(3), pp. 435–448.

Dale, S. F. (2002 [1994]) *Indian Merchants and Eurasian Trade, 1600–1750*. Cambridge: Cambridge University Press.

Dobb, M. (1950 [1946]) *Studies in the Development of Capitalism*. London: Routledge and Kegan Paul Ltd.

Faroqhi, S. (1979) 'Notes on the Production of Cotton Cloth in Sixteenth and Seventeenth-Century Anatolia', *The Journal of European Economic History* 8(2), pp. 405–417.

Faroqhi, S. (1994a) 'Labor Recruitment and Control in the Ottoman Empire (Sixteenth and Seventeenth Centuries)' in Quataert, D. (ed.) *Manufacturing in the Ottoman Empire and Turkey, 1500-1950*. New York: State University of New York Press, pp. 13–58.

Faroqhi, S. (1994b) 'Crisis and Change. 1590–1699', in Inalcik, H. and Quataert, D. (eds.) *An Economic and Social History of the Ottoman Empire, 1600-1914*, Vol. 2. New York: Cambridge University Press, pp. 459–587.

Fryer, J. (1698) *A New Account of East-India and Persia, in Eight Letters, Being Nine Years Travels, Begun 1672 and Finished 1681.* London: R[obert]. R[oberts].

Gopal, S. (1975) *Commerce and Crafts in Gujarat, 16th and 17th Centuries: A Study in the Impact of European Expansion on Precapitalist Economy.* New Delhi: People's Publishing House.

Gupta, A. D. (2004 [2001]) *The World of the Indian Ocean Merchant, 1500–1800: A Collection of Essays of Ashin Das Gupta.* New Delhi: Oxford University Press.

Gupta, B. (2009) 'Competition and Control in the Market for Textiles: Indian Weavers and the English East India Company in the Eighteenth Century', in Riello and Roy (eds.) *How India Clothed the World. The World of South Asian Textiles, 1500-1850.* Leiden: Brill, pp. 281–305.

Habib, I. (1964) 'Usury in Medieval India', *Comparative Studies in Society and History* 6(4), pp. 393–419.

Habib, I. (1969) 'Potentialities of Capitalistic Development in the Economy of Mughal India', *The Journal of Economic History* 29(1), pp. 32–78.

Habib, I. (2002 [1995]) *Essays in Indian History: Towards a Marxist Perception.* London: Anthem Press.

Hamilton, C. (1791) *The Hedaya or Guide: A Commentary on the Mussulman Laws*, Vol. 3. New York: Cambridge University Press.

Hanna, N. (2011) *Artisan Entrepreneurs: In Cairo and Early-modern Capitalism (1600–1800).* New York: Syracuse University Press.

Haynes, D. E. (2012) *Small Town Capitalism in Western India: Artisans, Merchants and the Making of the Informal Economy, 1870–1960.* New York: Cambridge University Press.

Holbach, R. (1994) *Frühformen von Verlag und Großbetrieb in der gewerblichen Produktion (13.– 16. Jahrhundert).* Stuttgart: Franz Steiner Verlag.

Hossain, H. (1979) 'The Alienation of Weavers: Impact of the Conflict between the Revenue and Commercial Interests of the East India Company, 1750–1800', *The Indian Economic & Social History Review* 16(3), pp. 323–345.

İslamoğlu-İnan, H. (1994) *State and Peasant in the Ottoman Empire: Agrarian Power Relations and Regional Economic Development in Ottoman Anatolia During the Sixteenth Century.* Leiden: Brill.

Johansen, B. (2006) 'Le contrat salam. Droit et formation du capital dans l'Empire abbasside (XIe-XIIe siècle)', *Annales. Histoire, Sciences Sociales* 61(4), pp. 861–899.

Karki, S., DeWald, J. and Shahi, M. (2010) 'Value Chain Finance and Nepal: Perspectives and Insights', Mercy. Retrieved from: https://nepal.mercycorps.org/pdf/ValueChainFinanceandNepal-PerspectivesandInsights.pdf.

Kieser, A. (1994) 'Why Organization Theory Needs Historical Analyses-And How This Should Be Performed', *Organization Science* 5(4), pp. 608–620.

Kluge, F. (1989 [1883]) *Etymologisches Wörterbuch der deutschen Sprache.* Berlin: Verlag Walter de Gruyter.

Komlos, J. (1994) 'Putting-Out System' in Stearns, P. N. (ed.) *Encyclopedia of Social History.* Bosa Roca: Taylor & Francis Inc.

Kriedte, P., Medick, H. and Schlumbohm, J. (eds.) (1981 [1977]) *Industrialization before Industrialization.* New York: Cambridge University Press.

Lewis, B. (2000) *A Middle East Mosaic: Fragments of Life, Letters and History.* New York: Modern Library.

Lis, C. and Soly, H. (1979) *Poverty and Capitalism in Pre-Industrial Europe.* Brighton: Harvester Press.

Liu, T. P. (1994) *The Weaver's Knot: The Contradictions of Class Struggle and Family Solidarity in Western France, 1750–1914.* New York: Cornell University Press.

Levine, D. C. (1977) *Family Formation in an Age of Nascent Capitalism, Studies in Social Discontinuity*. New York: Academic Press.

Mallick, B. S. (1986) 'English Trade and Indigenous Finance in Bengal and Gujarat in the Seventeenth Century: A Study of Dadni System and the Rate of Interest', *Studies in History* 2(1), pp. 31–45.

Maloni, R. (2003) *Surat: Port of the Mughal Empire*. Mumbai: Himalaya Publishing House.

Markham, C. R. (1874) *A General Sketch of the History of Persia*. London: Longmans, Green and Co.

Marx, K. (1991[1894]) *Capital. A Critique of Political Economy*, Vol. 3. London: Penguin Books.

Matthee, R. P. (1999) *The Politics of Trade in Safavid Iran: Silk for Silver, 1600–1730*. Cambridge: Cambridge University Press.

Mehta, M. (1991) *Indian Merchants and Entrepreneurs in Historical Perspective*. Delhi: Academic Foundation.

Mendels, F. F. (1972) 'Proto-Industrialization: The First Phase of the Industrialization Process', *The Journal of Economic History* 32(1), pp. 241–261.

Mokyr, J. (1976) 'Growing-up and the Industrial Revolution in Europe', *Explorations in Economic History* 13(4), pp. 371–396.

Morris, M. D. (1983) 'The Growth of Large-Scale Industry to 1947', in Kumar, D. and Desai, M. (eds.) *Cambridge Economic History of India*. Cambridge: Cambridge University Press, Vol. 2, pp. 552–676.

Nadri, G. (2015) 'The Dynamics of Port-Hinterland Relationships in Eighteenth-Century Gujarat', in Mizushima, T. et al. (eds.) *Hinterlands and Commodities: Place, Space, Time and the Political Economic Development of Asia over the Long Eighteenth Century*. Leiden: Brill, pp. 83–101.

Ogilvie, S. C. and Cerman, M. (1996) *European Proto-Industrialization*. Cambridge: University Press.

Ogilvie, S. C. (2008) 'Protoindustrialization', in Durlauf, S. N. and Blume, L. E. (eds.) *The New Palgrave Dictionary of Economics*. Basingstoke: Palgrave MacMillan, pp. 710–714.

Parthasarathi, P. (2001) *The Transition to a Colonial Economy: Weavers, Merchants and Kings in South India 1720–1800*. New York: Cambridge University Press.

Perlin, F. (1983) 'Proto-Industrialization and Pre-Colonial South Asia', *Past & Present* 98(1), pp. 30–95.

Petmezas, S. D. (1990) 'Patterns of Protoindustrialization in the Ottoman Empire: The Case of Eastern Thessaly, ca. 1750–1860', *The Journal of European Economic History* 19(3), pp. 575–601.

Poni, C. (1985) 'Proto-industrialization, Rural and Urban,' *Review (Fernand Braudel Center)* 9(2), pp. 305–314.

Prakash, O. (1998) *European Commercial Enterprise in Pre-Colonial India*. Cambridge: Cambridge University Press.

Prakash, O. (2009) 'From Market-Determined to Coercion-Based: Textile Manufacturing in Eighteenth-Century Bengal', in Riello and Roy (eds.) *How India Clothed the World. The World of South Asian Textiles, 1500-1850*. Leiden: Brill, pp. 217–251.

Randall, A. (1991) *Before the Luddites: Custom, Community and Machinery in the English Woollen Industry. 1776–1809*. Cambridge: Cambridge University Press.

Ray, I. (2011) *Bengal Industries and the British Industrial Revolution (1757–1857)*. New York: Routledge.

Raychaudhuri, T. (1983) 'The Mid-Eighteenth Century Background', *CEHI* 2, pp. 3–35.

Roy, T. (1999) *Traditional Industry in the Economy of Colonial India*. Cambridge: Cambridge University Press.

Schlumbohm, J. (1981 [1977]) 'Relations of Production - Productive Forces – Crises', in Kriedte, et al. (eds.) *Industrialization before Industrialization*. Cambridge: Cambridge University Press, pp. 94–125.

Schmoller, G. (1901) *Grundriss der Allgemeinen Volkswirtschaftslehre*. Leipzig: Duncker & Humblot.

Singh, K. A. (2006) *Modern World System and Indian Proto-industrialization: Bengal 1650–1800*, Vol. 1. New Delhi: Northern Book Centre.

Singh, V. (2005) *The Artisans in 18th Century Eastern India. A History of Survival*. New Delhi: Concept Publishing Company.

Subramanian, L. (2009) 'The Political Economy of Textiles in Western India: Weavers, Merchants and the Transition to a Colonial Economy', in Riello and Roy (eds.) *How India Clothed the World. The World of South Asian Textiles, 1500-1850*. Leiden: Brill, pp. 253–280.

Vanina, E. (2004) *Urban Crafts and Craftsmen in Medieval India (Thirteenth-Eighteenth Centuries)*, New Delhi: Munshiram Manoharlal.

Washbrook, D. (2007) 'India in the Early Modern World Economy: Modes of Production, Reproduction and Exchange', *Journal of Global History* 2(1), pp. 87–111.

Wehler, H. U. (1996 [1987]) *Deutsche Gesellschaftsgeschichte Vol. 1: Vom Feudalismus des alten Reiches bis zur defensiven Modernisierung der Reformära*. München: C. H. Beck.

Williamson, O. E. (1985) *The Economic Institutions of Capitalism*. New York: Free Press.

Yazdani, K. (2017) *India, Modernity and the Great Divergence: Mysore and Gujarat (17th to 19th Century)*. Leiden: Brill.

Žmolek, M. A. (2013) *Rethinking the Industrial Revolution: Five Centuries of Transition from Agrarian to Industrial Capitalism in England*. Leiden: Brill.

13
MARUMAKKATTĀYAM

Mahmood Kooria

Transferring ideas into single words is a difficult task, as neither ideas nor words can summarise or encompass one another. Even a simple term that one might assume has a generally agreed-upon meaning could denote a complex idea carrying different connotations or be incomprehensible in a different spatial and temporal context. This predicament of words, ideas, and concepts has been a core concern of several disciplines such as linguistics, philology, literary, cultural, and translation studies dominated by the Eurocentric frameworks. Western epistemology has constructed a largesse of vocabularies for social and natural sciences that the intelligentsia all over the world has been struggling to translate into different cultural and language contexts. As this volume endeavours to break away from this hegemonic discourse in the social sciences and humanities in order to suggest alternative concepts from the Global South, this chapter explores the potential(ity) of such attempts *in the context of transregional, transcultural, and multilinguistic fields* on the basis of a conceptual term from coastal South Asia. On the basis of my research expertise in global history, I argue that any concept rings true in the global context only when it has a philosophical and analytical appeal beyond its *original* empirical context. Otherwise, the concepts become a parochial representation of spatial and temporal idiosyncrasies with less appeal to a scholarly society outside of its immediate locus. This aspect presents the most challenging task for a student of global history who explores areas beyond specific regional, national, and continental boundaries.

The term I analyse is *marumakkattāyam*, a Malayalam word that connotes a social system in which lineage, property, and power are vested in and transferred through women. Looking into its historical, etymological, and jurisprudential meanings as they evolved over time, I argue that not only the duality of dialectical essence of a concept but also the symmetry of binaries is dissolved in its meaning-making process and related praxis within a specific community that

DOI: 10.4324/9781003273530-17

understands and conceptualises the words and customs through multiple meanings. A search for the *original meaning* of a concept is a futile exercise, as much as the search for its origin, for the fact is that one cannot be puritan about social processes in which ideas and vocabularies evolve collectively. I try to unravel how one can comprehend the social system of a concept or a specific term, that of the *marumakkattāyam*, beyond its immediate contexts in order to see how its connotations of family forms, kinship, and lineage complicate the dominant paradigm of the patrilineal family in the West and elsewhere.

In historical experience, the nuances of the women-centred social system have been different from place to place and time to time. But three major elements continued to constitute its prime anchorages: matriliny (lineage), matrilocality (residence), and matriarchy (power). In the existing literature, these concerns and terms are far complicated with additional terminologies such as matricity, matrilaterality, and matriarchate, but I tend to group all these terminologies under an overarching adjectival phrase, *matriarchal culture*, for the sake of brevity and conveyance of the idea. Calling it exclusively *matriarchy* is, however, problematic, because it invites all sorts of different concerns even though there is no consensus among scholars on what constitutes matriarchy. Scholars have rejected the idea that matriarchy is patriarchy with an "m", and they have suggested various theories on the borders, promises, premises, and prehistories of such a social order, on the convergences and divergences of the system and its norms. I argue that most terms/concepts are insular in their narrowest nodes and it is the choice of a scholar to decide with which concept/term one should go. Divides such as "South-North" or "East-West" are problematic in the transregional and transcultural contexts, as most of the concepts become *foreign* beyond their empirical setting. Within that setting itself, the concept/term as such is understood differently with variations in its meaning, relevance, and familiarity although the concept might remain nearly or distantly with the same name. The words emerge into a space of foreignness as soon as they attract wider attention.

Visible Custom, Invisible Name

Across the Indian Ocean world, many societies have historically followed women-centred social systems or the systems in which power, property, inheritance, and/or lineage was vested in women. Although at present their presence is visible among Muslims in some parts of Indonesia, India, Malaysia, Sri Lanka, Mozambique, the Comoros, Ghana, Tanzania, and Malawi, such systems were historically even wider and deeper in many more countries of Asia and Africa. There are significant differences in its practice and conceptualisation from community to community and region to region, but the worlds of the Indian Ocean and Islamic praxis unite them.

Scholars who studied native American communities had initiated an argument for the existence of matrifocal systems in prehistoric periods all over the world. The very birth of social anthropology as a discipline was entangled with the question of matriliny/women-centredness of prehistoric/ancient societies and heated debates peddled across the nineteenth and twentieth centuries. Based on an extensive study of ancient Greek literature and myths, Johann Jakob Bachofen put forward a prototype of such arguments. In his *Mutterrecht* published in 1861, he argued that in ancient Greek society, kinship was traced through the maternal line alone. Only daughters possessed the right of inheritance, women's status was correspondingly high, and fatherhood did not matter much since it was unascertainable. The umbrella term he used was *mutterrecht* (translated as "mother right"), which also appears in the title of his book, but he also used conceptual adjectives related to matriarchy such as "matriarchal age/culture/system/genealogy/forms". He argued that the "mother right is not confined to any particular people but marks a cultural stage. In view of the universal qualities of human nature, this cultural stage cannot be restricted to any particular ethnic family. And consequently what must concern us is not so much the similarities between isolated phenomena as the unity of the basic conception" (Bachofen, 1973, p. 71).

This thesis of matriarchal primitivity was advanced by Lewis H. Morgan (1871; 1877) on the basis of his ethnographic research among the Native Americans, particularly among the Iroquois of New York. Even before Bachofen published his work, Morgan had noticed matrilineal practices among the Iroquois and other Native Americans and had written about them on various occasions in the 1850s. However, he developed the idea of a prehistoric existence of matriliny across the world in his magnum opus *Systems of Consanguinity and Affinity of the Human Family*, published in 1871. Analysing the transitions of humanity from barbarism to civilisation and the existence of a communal family system among the Native Americans, he observed that "the union of effort to procure subsistence for the common household, led to communism in living" and that "most barbarous nations at the present time … are now organised into such families, and practice communism as far as the same can be carried out in practical life" (Morgan, 1871, p. 488). However, he was very conscious to avoid such terms as matriarchy and matriliny in his both books, instead, he suggested these practices indirectly in his analysis of the classificatory system of universal families where he enlisted patriarchy as the eleventh stage in the long history of "consanguinity and affinity" and as the third stage of the family. The stages before this, he implies to be matriarchal. In his extensive observations on the historical priority of the matrilineal clan over patriliny and nuclear family, he uses related terms such as maternal bond, mother's gens, and female gens.

Many scholars of the time thus accepted the Bachofen–Morgan scheme according to which descent systems invariably underwent a historical change from matriliny to patriliny and not the reverse. On this scene, came Friedrich Engels with his controversial yet influential work where he highly praised Morgan's thesis and went so far as to state:

> The repeated discovery that the original maternal "gens" was a preliminary stage of the paternal "gens" of civilized nations has the same signification

> for primeval history that Darwin's theory of evolution had for biology and Marx's theory of surplus value for political economy

[, and]

> the maternal "gens" has become the pivot on which this whole science revolves[.] Since its discovery we know in what direction to continue our researches, what to investigate and how to arrange the results of our studies.
> *(Engels, 1909 [1884], p. 24)*

The fashionable term of his time was maternal gens or matriarchal gens (German: "Muttergens") but he also uses terms such as mother-right, following Bachofen, along with usages such as maternal law. He went on to articulate how matrilineal communities demonstrated an ideal state of the society in which the whole family communistically shared the wealth and women had the control over property and men were supposed to do their part. To quote him: "It is one of the most absurd notions derived from eighteenth century enlightenment, that in the beginning of society woman was the slave of man". And

> The downfall of maternal law was the historic defeat of the female sex. The men seized the reins also in the house, the women were stripped of their dignity, enslaved, [and became] tools of men's lust and mere machines for the generation of children.

From then onwards, many social anthropologists endeavoured to name and identify women-centred social systems in different places and periods and they followed the argument that the original form of family of humankind was matriarchal, matrilineal, and matrilocal. Their theses found followers in the late nineteenth and early twentieth centuries in archaeology, classical studies, antiquity studies, etc., and the arguments became ideological during the Interwar and early Cold War periods, when Soviet scholars upheld the system as an ideal form of socialist family. Social anthropologists and social historians of England, influenced by Victorian ideas of morality, criticised the theories from the 1930s onwards. The Polish-British anthropologist Malinowski categorically rejected the idea through his research to the "sexual lives of the savages" and argued that the family has always been monogamous and men the head of the family. He said that those who argue otherwise in support of matriliny are proposing the idea of an organised brothel system. These conflicting notions of prehistoric communistic matriarchy and organised brothels circulated among scholars up until the 1960s.[1]

In this long debate, various names and concepts emerged to identify the specific social systems such as gynarchy, gynocracy, gynecocracy, matrifocality, and gynocentric, matricentric, matristic, or matrilocal societies. Transformations within the European discourses were reflected in the names that emerged at each point, from mutterrecht to maternal gens to matriarchy to matriliny. These discourses also were reflected in the judgements and arguments of colonial jurists, administrators, and scholars of British, Dutch, Portuguese, and French origin with direct implications on the women-centred societies in the colonies under their control.

In the postcolonial period, anthropologists used different names by categorising the practice prioritising terms such as matriliny, matrifocality, and, to a lesser extent, matriarchy.[2] Matriliny, however, was established as a general term among scholars of the late twentieth century such as Kathleen Gough (1954), Leela Dube (1969), and Franz and Keebet Benda-Beckmans, to name only a few. Still, some scholars grappled with varying conceptual terms, such as Jeffrey Hadler (2008) who uses the archaic term matriarchate because it provides "a nod to local terminology and an acknowledgment that matriarchy is often more a utopian ideal than an ethnographic reality". In the local vocabulary of the Minangkabau people, the word matriarchate emerges from the Dutch word *matriarchaat* and connotes the institutions of matrilineal descent and inheritance and matrilocal residence.

By the 1970s, theories of prehistoric matriarchy were popularised by the feminist spiritual movements of North America as well as through the archaeological and linguistic analyses of such scholars as Marija Gimbutas (1974; 1989; 1991) who promulgated the idea of a European matristic prehistory in Palaeolithic and Neolithic periods. Such theories found wide popularity among the feminist middle-class white women of North America and these narratives gave them a belief that it was their past, and it was meant to empower them. Following this trend, several African-American, Asian-American, African, and Asian scholars also endeavoured to trace the origins of the matriarchy in Africa and Asia – as Cynthia Eller (2001; 2011) argues in her two fascinating studies. She has categorically rejected all these arguments by saying that there is no solid evidence to prove that any prehistorical societies were exclusively matriarchal, and she has argued that all such theories were based on assumptions and theories that do not help at all to empower feminist causes. However, recent researches in kinship studies and related fields argue, once again, that the matriarchal and matrilineal forms must have been the major characteristic of family in the prehistoric period. They base their arguments on genealogical and biological researches and kinship studies of the last one decade, and some of them revisit the original arguments of Morgan and Engels.[3]

In the context of our present focus on the concept and a name for the women-centred social systems, these prehistoric-matriarchy theories demonstrate the diversity of related intellectual engagements across disciplinary, geographical, and chronological boundaries. While the very birth of social anthropology was implicated with questions on the existence and characteristics of matriarchal communities, disciplines such as legal history, cultural studies, philology, philosophy, archaeology, and prehistoric studies contributed to the debate variously. Many of these disciplines evolved very much around the question of women's role in prehistoric societies, materialising to some extent what Engels had prophetically argued: "the maternal 'gens' has become the pivot on which this whole science revolves".

There are two major issues with these debates, however: first, none of these scholarly debates took into account the concept in which the local/indigenous matrilineal/matriarchal communities understood themselves and their praxis at large. Such an enquiry forms the core of this chapter. Secondly, most of the scholarly engagements have been on the prehistoric communities, whose histories are hard to substantiate. It is almost impossible now to understand how these communities comprehended their system through one or two concepts – besides the rejection in some academic quarters of the very existence of such a praxis among them. Against this background, what is intriguing to us is the historical and living communities who are capable of telling us about their conceptions of themselves as well as their universe at large, their understandings of their past, and the ways in which they named and identified themselves as well as by outsiders.

There is hardly any concrete *historical study* on the institution of matriarchy and its prevalence in *premodern* times, especially among Islamic communities who have been following the system for centuries. Several historians dealt with the period after around 1800 (Hadler, 2008; Bonate, 2007; Alpers, 1972), but they themselves have hardly nuanced the term/concept "matriliny" despite their constant use of it and their explorations into the relationality between the concept and the communities. Hadler is an exception as we mentioned above; he finds the existing terms such as matriliny and matriarchy unsatisfactory, and returns to the term "matriarchate" and redefines it in order to meet the specific case of the Minangkabau.

Now, none of these terms is indigenous to the communities. The system definitely existed, and we have various historical references from the ninth century onwards in the forms of epigraphic and textual materials. But what did those people call the system? As we try to explore the "indigenous" names used to re/present the system in order to see the translatability and commensurability, what I find interesting is that many languages do not have a specific umbrella term to denote the system as such. Most of the languages in these contexts do not relate the practice with a single term as many people asked me in Sri Lanka what matriliny is (except Makkathar Vappa who was familiar with the term and described himself as a matrilineal Sufi, for he was aware of an anthropological study about him [McGilvray, 2014]), although they undoubtedly agree with the praxis and their women-centred social system. Rather, the communities use descriptive or generic words such as in Malay (*adat perpatih*) and Bahasa Indonesia/Minang (*adat, matriarchate*), or contentious dimensions such as in Arabic (*manʿ al-uṣūl wa al-furūʿ*, mentioned by two nineteenth-century jurists Ahmad Khatib and Sayyid Bakri; the former was from a matrilineal region). This absence of an indigenous umbrella term, defining and definite term, in Bahasa Minang, Bahasa Indonesia, Malay, Arabic, and Swahili, is very telling.

Southwest Indian coast seems to be the only place in the Indian Ocean littoral that presents us with a name. Malayalam, Jazari, Tulu, and Kannada, the Dravidian languages spoken and used in southwest India, have definite and defining words and terms for the social system. In Malayalam it is called *Marumakkattāyam*; in Tulu and hence in Kannada it is called *Aḷiyasantānakaṭṭu*; and, *Veḷḷiyāḻca-swattu* in Jazari of the Lakshadweep Islands. In many other areas, there are terms coined in the nineteenth century by colonial jurists in order to address the rising juridical concerns around property and inheritance rights, but those terms catered for the specific legal-cum-economic priorities and they connoted less the system as such.

Through *Aḷiyasantāna*, the Kannada and Tulu relate a term with a wider system that is very crucial for several Tuluva groups in their socio, economic, and cultural regimes in different levels. Such Tuluva subgroups as Bunts, Billavas, Kulalas, Devadigas, and Mogaveeras follow the practice of transferring property through the mother's line and the lineage identity is inherited in the form of mother's *gōtra* (tribe) or from her ancestral house. The senior-most member, whether male (*ejamān*) or female (*ejamānatti*), is in charge of family management and property. This is different from what is evolved as the general Kerala and Lakshadweep systems in which only the senior-most male (*kāraṇavan*) had control over the management of the property and the senior-most female (*kāraṇavatti*) got control only in the absence of any adult male members. It stood closer to the system followed by the Muslim *marumakkattāyam* system in Arakkal royal family of Kannur in northern Malabar where also the headship was transferred irrespective of gender. The joint household, similar to the system in Kerala, was not impartible until the enactments in the early twentieth century supported alienation if all members agreed. The most important legislative act for this system was the Madras Aliyasantana Act of 1949. *Marumakkattāyam* in southwestern India had a long history and I explore this trajectory before I present how contradictory and complicated its meanings are.

Historical Roots of a Term: *Marumakkattāyam*

In southwest India, the practice has long existed but the absence of a term in premodern sources has motivated historians to question the presence of the system before the fourteenth century or so.[4] The absence of a term does not mean the absence of the practice as much as it also does not mean that the practice *did* exist. On the basis of the existing narratives, there is fragmentary evidence of its presence back to the tenth century. M.G.S. Narayanan, a prominent historian of ancient Kerala, says that there is epigraphic evidence of this system at the time of the Perumal dynasty of Mahodayapuram, with references to *nāyattiyār* and *marumakkaḷ*.[5] He says that, for example, the Tiruvalla Copperplate inscriptions (published in *Travancore Archaeological Series* (*TAS*), vol. 2, part 3, p. 203) mention the succession-rights of Nayars and their *marumakkaḷ*.[6] Earlier than this, the Parthivapuram Inscription of 922 CE and the Stone Inscriptions of Trivandrum of the tenth century also have related usages (*TAS*, I, pp. 403-404 and *TAS*, III, pp. 45-46). *Śāṅkarasmṛti* or *Laghudharmaprakāśikā*, a Sanskrit text ascribed to *Ādi Śaṅkara* (d. eighth century), mentions the matrilineal practice of inheritance as a specific custom prevailing in the region. The historical authenticity of the ascription is disputed but certainly, it was circulating in the region by the middle of the second millennium (Aiyer, 1953, pp. 104-105; Davis, 2013).

The nature of succession and lineage between mothers-to-daughters and uncles-to-nephews are not immediately evident in the inscriptions, but we can see how the term *marumakkaḷ*, a lemma for *marumakkattāyam*, appears in the tenth and eleventh centuries, the period of these inscriptions. The term *marumakkaḷ* becomes recurrent in the following centuries in various epigraphic and literary (such as Maṇipravāḷam) sources and it mainly connoted the sister's children (and on a few occasions, sons-in-law) (Retnamma, 1994; Davis 2013; Gopalakrishnan, 2013). Even so, a term for the system *marumakkattāyam* as such did not develop until much later and the custom and the system did flourish in various forms as we see in various accounts. Some historians believe that the system started after the Chera–Chola wars in the eleventh century, as Nayars lost most of their men during the war (Menon, 1924). The foreign travellers, Benjamin of Tudela and Marco Polo, have written about the system and related customs in the thirteenth century. About 50 years after them, Ibn Baṭṭūṭa (1987) who visited the region also made similar remarks. Once we come to the sixteenth century, there is a plethora of sources by the authors like John Huyghen van Linschoten (1885), Duarte Barbosa, Zayn al-Dīn al-Malaybārī (MS. Islamic 2807e; 1833; 2005), and Tomé Pire (1944). Interestingly, *none of them give the system a definite name.*

The name appears in the sources much later, notwithstanding the possibility of its occurrence in several unpublished Dutch, Portuguese, French as well as Malayalam sources. Once it appears and becomes ubiquitous, does it indicate the same praxis as we know of it today? It is difficult to say as the sources that give a name and describe the custom contradict each other in detail. As most of them make their statements on the basis of their familiarity with a particular region or a community, they tend to define the system on the basis of this particular group's customs while ignoring the larger picture in which those customs would not appear at all or would carry the opposite meanings. It needs further analysis, for the moment suffices it to say that from the initial definitions of the term, we have completely different meanings for the root word *marumakkaḷ*.

A Term with Opposite Meanings

As the term *marumakkattāyam* proves to be widely used in the early nineteenth century onwards, how was it defined and translated historically? We do not get an immediate answer from premodern sources but early dictionaries are good sources to understand the multiple layers and transformations of meanings, as an archaeology of words reveals different stratifications of the meaning-making process in the society. In the case of *marumakkattāyam*, interestingly, we see the meanings being entirely opposite and contradictory. Below, I describe and analyse this conundrum along with related words and concepts in order to see how the word takes different meanings, and the concept has great fluidity.

One of the main purposes of the *marumakkattāyam* system was to secure the property within the household, and not to pass it on to anyone who became a part of the household through marital relations alone. A father did not have any right over the property of a *taravāṭu* (matrilineal household), and vice-versa. The father's property did not go to his wife or children, rather it went back to his family, to his sister(s) and her (their) children. This systematic exclusion of husband/father/son-in-law from the *marumakkattāyam* inheritance is foundational to its property regime. However, the etymology of the term does not allow that, because the root word "marumakkaḷ" means not only sisters' children but also sons- and daughters-in-law. The inheritance regime of the *marumakkattāyam* is designed to exclude children-in-law from succession, but the ambiguity in its episteme and etymons questions the very foundations of the practice. This contradictory nature of the term *marumakkaḷ* is evident in a number of Malayalam dictionaries since the nineteenth century. The dictionaries accommodated the term *marumakkattāyam* limitedly, but they also gave double meanings of *marumakkaḷ* with both groups being part of its limit. When we read different lexicographers, we find that translations of both *marumakkattāyam* (the system) and *marumakkaḷ* (some of its members) along with a few other related terms are changing and expanding over time.

Among the earliest known dictionaries of Malayalam, Benjamin Bayley (1846; 1849) did not deal much with the terminologies related to *marumakkattāyam*. In his first dictionary (from English to Malayalam), which came out in 1846, he describes *marumakkattāyam* as "inheritance in the female line, a custom among Sudras, Cshetrias and some other classes". In this translation-cum-definition, he uses the larger categories of the north Indian Brahmanical *jāti*-system and avoids the local *jāti*-hierarchies and names. He also does not refer to the existence of the system among Muslims as well as some Brahmin households in the region. For the counterpart term *makkattāyam*, he does not give such class- or caste-explanations, rather he only identifies it as "inheritance from father to son" (Bayley, 1846, p. 597). For the root word in male form *marumakan* and feminine form *marumakaḷ* he gives both meanings (nephew and son-in-law, niece and daughter-in-law, respectively) (Laseron, 1856, p. 103). The terms thus stand for meanings of both *matrilineal* and *patrilineal* systems: *marumakkattāyam* and *makkattāyam*.

Three years later in 1849, he published the Malayalam-to-English dictionary, a less interesting work for it does not convey the diversity of kinship terms that he presented in the Malayalam part. In this, he contradicts his own Malayalam dictionary for he translates "aunt" exclusively as *ammāvi* whereas in the Malayalam one he had differentiated between *ammāyi* ("aunt"; also "mother in-law or wife's mother") and *ammāvi* ("the wife of a maternal uncle", without a word on "aunt").[7] Further interestingly, he also does not bring here any terms related to matri (lineal/archy), etc. Therefore, we get a rather flattened and undiscursive image of kinship terms for Malayalam. It is also noteworthy that how he does not define the *marumakkattāyam*-related words the way he defined *marumakkattāyam*: for example, he translates *taravāṭu* as "family" and "house", *taravāṭṭukāran* as "householder" and "a man of family", and *taravāṭṭu mutal* as "family property", and there is no *tāvaḻi* in his list of words despite it being a crucial term in the *marumakkattāyam* context (Bailey, 1846, p. 335; for the absence of *tāvaḻi*, see p. 339). Once we come to the Malayalam to English dictionary, all this diversity has been forgotten and the word "family" is used for the generic "*kuṭunpam*" and "*taravāṭu*" and the term "house" does not translate as "*taravāṭu*" (Bailey, 1849, p. 178).

Just ten years after Bayley's first dictionary, Rev. E. Laseron published a Malayalam-to-English and English-to-Malayalam dictionary in a single volume where he copies almost all the same words and meanings from Bailey's dictionaries. He follows the same meanings for *marumakkattāyam*, *marumakan* and *marumakaḷ* in its Malayalam section (Laseron, 1856, p. 103)[8] and we can see the same contradictions for *ammāyi/ammāvi* vis-a-vis aunt (Ibid, pp. 5, 103) as we saw in Bayley. The words related to *taṟavāṭu* are ignored in the English-to-Malayalam section, and the word "family" is reduced to the generic "*kuṭunpam*" and "*vaṁśam*" and does not include any reference to *taravāṭu* as such, being slightly different from Bailey (Ibid, pp. 64, 163). Beyond these remarks, this dictionary does not present anything much different from Bailey with regard to matriliny.

The most important dictionary, widely used both inside and outside Kerala for a long time, has been Hermann Gundert's *A Malayalam and English Dictionary*. Published more than two decades after both of Bailey's dictionaries, this work takes a rather nuanced and comparatively detailed take on *marumakkattāyam*. Although it also gives both meanings for *marumakan* (that it means sister's son as well as a son-in-law), it defines *marumakkattāyam* as "inheritance in the female line as practiced" by different groups in Kerala. He enlists 17 communities including the Brahmins in Payyanur as well as Ksatriyas and Pisharadis, Variyans, Nambis, Teyambadis, Nedungadis and Vallodis (Gundert, 1872, p. 793). In this long list, he does not however mention Muslims; to the contrary, he mentions "Mussulmans" under the term *makkattāyam* which he defines as "the right of sons to inherit" (Ibid, p. 769). In this list of male-succession groups, he also gives names of more than 25 such patrilineal groups in the region. He also nuances the kinship terms such as *ammāyi* and *ammāvan* with diverse meanings (Ibid, p. 43). His elaboration of these kinship terms as well as the succession patterns among various groups (notwithstanding his unfamiliarity with the Muslim *marumakkattāyam* despite his long stay in Thalassery where the majority of Muslims had historically followed the system) comes from his familiarity with the local tradition and culture. He had authored several works on the history and culture of Kerala before he published this dictionary, and therefore he was more committed to searching for and expounding the diversity of Kerala communities. It is not surprising that he was not aware of the life of matrilineal Muslims closer to his residence in Thalassery, for he had a rather distorted idea of scriptural, historical, and cultural Islam possibly because of the missionary engagements he was committed to.[9]

About a half-century after the dictionaries of Bailey, Laseron, and Gundert who all came to the region as part of the European Christian missions and studied the language, a native speaker of Malayalam, Tobias Zacharias, published his English-Malayalam dictionary in 1907. Unlike his predecessors, Zacharias had access to a larger repository of local lexicons immersed in cultural peculiarities and linguistic diversities. Possibly, this was the first known English-Malayalam dictionary prepared by a Malayali and the biggest dictionary in the language published until then.[10] Because of its comparative lateness, the author also could consult the dictionaries that came before him: he consulted and cited the published dictionaries such as of Bailey, Gundert, Collins, and the unpublished dictionary of Rev. F. Matthissen. He paid closer attention to the nuances of the matrilineal words that his predecessors had missed. This dictionary can be read as an ethnographical archive and a process of ethnographical translatability, for he was from north Kerala, a place where he must have been very familiar with the prevalent *marumakkattāyam* system.

In comparison to Bailey's (and Laseron's) translation of aunt simply as *ammavi*, Zacharias (1907, p. 36) gives several meanings to the word: (1) *iḷayamma*, *iḷayacci*; (2) *mūttamma*, (3) *ammāyi*, *ammāvi*. For the English headwords "mother" and "grand-mother", he gives a plethora of meanings and he translates the latter term as *mūttacci*, *mūttācchi*, *ammāma*, *valiyamma* (Ibid, p. 557). The grandmother in Malayalam is therefore not only mother's mother or father's mother, but also the elder sister of mother, elder sister-in-law, etc. The multi-layered and confusing meanings of such kinship terms among matrilineal communities have been a core concern of social anthropology from the time of Morgan and Engels themselves who noticed the fact that the mother (and grand-mother) was not a single person, rather all the sisters and several other female members of the matrilineal clan were identified with the same or similar wordings. The same pattern goes for the words such as nephew, niece, and uncle (Ibid, p. 576 [nephew] and p. 580 [niece]). They become complicated terms for Zacharias as it appears below for the cornucopia of Malayalam meanings he gives for the word "uncle":

> (n.) *acchanṟe jyēṣṭhan*; *muttappan*, *muttacchan*, *achanṟe anujan*, *iḷyappan*, *iḷayacchan*, *ciṯṯappan*. (S.) *pitr̥vyan*; 2. *ammayuṭe āṅṅaḷa*, *ammōman*, *ammāman*, *ammāvan* (S), *kāraṇavan*, *kuññiyacchan* (N.), *mātulan*; 3. *mūttammayuṭe bharttāvu*, *muttappan* 4. *iḷayammayuṭe bharttāvu*, *iḷyappan*; 5. *paṇayattil paṇam kaṭam koṭukkunnavan*, *paṇamiṭapāṭukāran*.
>
> *(Zacharias, 1907, p. 1218)*

This multiplicity of meanings and individuals cannot easily be communicated to a non-Malayalam speaker and/or a person from a non-matrilineal context. Even so, this passage illustrates the diversity of meanings that a simple word can bring in, especially as *the institution* of maternal uncle became very important in the matrilineal communities during and after the colonial period. He thus became a definite and defining member with hierarchies of power, which of course was arduous to translate to English. Zacharias catches this "confusing diversity" of a women-centred social system that his predecessors had missed. Through such an exercise, he not only points towards the direct untranslatability of several matrilineal terms in Malayalam into English, but also highlights the potential meanings that an English word such as mother, grandmother, aunt, or uncle can couch within.

Despite Zacharias' attention to these matrilineal vocabularies, what is even more striking is that we do not find any English words that directly or indirectly connotes *marumakkattāyam* as such. What comes closer is his translation of the term "matriarch", which he translates as (1) *kuṭunpavāḻiyamma* and (2) *marumakkattāya (prakāramuḷḷa) nāṭuvāḻi*. In this second meaning in Malayalam, he uses the adjectival form of *marumakkattāyam* in order to connote a ruler who follows that system, whereas the first meaning is simply about the clan matriarch or female head of the family. He also provides two related terms further: matriarchal and matriarchate. He translates the former as *mātr̥vāḻikkuḷḷa* and *mātr̥uvāḻikōymayuḷḷa*, and the latter as *mātr̥vāḻikkōyma, mātr̥vāḻca* (Zacharias, 1907, p. 516). In all these four terms, the important term he combines with other terms is a Sanskrit word for mother (*mātr̥*).[11] These terms do not contain much to connote the *marumakkattāyam* as a system, a word, or a concept. Neither does he address the main beneficiaries connoted usually through the *marumakkattāyam* system, such as individual nephews. It is worthy of note that he depends on the Sanskritised terminologies to define a concept that stands much closer to the culture and customs of the region. This is despite the fact that he complains at the beginning of the dictionary about a general tendency among Malayalis to use Sanskrit words to translate English words. Nevertheless, we cannot help but notice different names, concepts, and usages related to matriarchate he brings in, especially on the translatability of the matriarchate. The Malayalam usages such as *kuṭunpavāḻiyamma* indirectly takes its cultural premise from the *marumakkattāyam* praxis.

The above discussion demonstrates the ways in which the authors comprehended the concept of *marumakkattāyam* and its associated vocabularies. This shows that the word *marumakkattāyam* necessitated a treatment of a concept (and the lexicographers defined it, instead of translating it) while other words were mainly translated through single-word counterparts. In this attempt to find single-word counterparts, the devil was in the details, and we see how the lexicographers take different stands in translating particular terms (such as *ammāvi* and *marumakan*). In the early and some later dictionaries, we also see how the terms such as *marumakan* have been conflated by including both nephew and son-in-law while *marumakkattāyam* as a system wanted to exclude the latter from its regimes of lineage, inheritance, and property.

Defining and Translating: One-Sided Acts

Until the nineteenth century, what we had were descriptions of the *marumakkattāyam* without reference to a specific name. Premodern authors differentiated between the practices, the communities, and the regions and gave some descriptions, yet they somehow refrained from naming it. In the nineteenth century, however, there were significant attempts to define, understand, translate, transmit, and limit the concept and the system legalistically and analytically.[12] At the height of colonialism, numerous people approached the court with requests to delineate rights over *marumakkattāyam* properties. They had different reasons, some of which were direct outcomes of colonial interventions into the realms of family. Consequently, various legal acts and reports sought to control, regulate, and ban many aspects of the system. In the process of judicial definition, they limited its potentials and made it more Brahmanical and patriarchal (Arunima, 2003). The very act of defining was an act of patriarchy. Diverse meanings of *marumakan/ḷ*, for example, were systematically forgotten and it was used exclusively for the sisters' children, while people (mainly in matrilineal but also in patrilineal contexts) continued to use it also for children-in-law.

The major legislative enactments related to the social system tried to define *marumakkattāyam* from the nineteenth century onwards through different reports and acts. The Malabar Marriage Commission Report of 1891 discussed the nuances of *marumakkattāyam* in detail, but it refers to the earlier works on its foundational characteristics (*Report* 1891, p. 10). In other words, it refrains from defining the conceptual word in spite of calling it "the *Marumakkatthāyam System*". Similarly, the Malabar Wills Act of 1898 pertained to the *marumakkattāyam* and *Aḷiyasantāna* systems, yet it did not define what was meant by these laws of inheritance. Through its act of making laws, it made boundaries for the system and thus indirectly defined it. Following this, the Madras Marumakkattayam Act of 1932 briefly defined *marumakkattāyam* as a system of inheritance in which descent is traced in the female line; *marumakkathayi* as a person governed by the Marumakkathayam Law of Inheritance; and *tarawad* as a group of persons forming a joint family with community of property governed by Marumakkathayam Law of Inheritance. The Act differentiated the term *tavazhi* in relation to the female and in relation to the male. In the case of the former, it is a group of persons consisting of that female, her children, and all her descendants in the female line. In the case of the latter, it is defined as the *tavazhi* of the mother of that male.

Relatedly, the Travancore Krishnavaka Marumakkathayee Act (VII of 1115) and the Cochin Marumakkatayam Act, XXXIII of 1113 have defined the system with slight yet important variations.[13] The influence and impact of these acts need further study as they show the legalistic exchanges across political and cultural borders on the relatable social systems. Almost two decades after the Kerala state was formed in 1957 based on independent India's reorganisation of provinces, a major regulation against the *marumakkattāyam* was brought out by the Kerala legislative assembly entitled Kerala Joint Hindu Family System (Abolition) Act, 1975. This act formally abolished the practice of *marumakkattāyam* joint family system among the Hindus. In the abolition, it did not define what it meant by the *marumakkattāyam*, rather it referred to the earlier acts passed in the princely states of Travancore and Cochin and in the colonial district of Malabar, thereby conforming to the definitions already constructed during the colonial period and evading the responsibility of explaining what would have been some foundational questions on the system.[14]

It should be noted that the Kerala Act did not ban the *marumakkattāyam* among Muslims for they were ruled from the colonial period onwards by different bills and acts such as the Malabar Partition Bill of 1910, Mappila Succession Act of 1918, and the Mappila Marumakkathayam Act of 1939. The judicial predicaments of the *marumakkattāyi* Muslims were rather complex, for their legal status was not recognised in the colonial courts until much later. They were initially ruled by the Anglo-Muhammadan law, against which the Malabar Muslims litigated by asserting their legal school of Shāfiʿīsm as distinct from the Ḥanafī school predominant in the subcontinent. Further, within this fight of Shāfiʿīs, the *marumakkattāyi* Muslims asserted their social and cultural distinctions of a women-centred system. After a long judicial debate, their social system was recognised, yet it was bound to the pre-existing definitions of *marumakkattāyam* in the Nayar context.

There were distinctions within the Muslim and Nayar praxis of a similar system, but the nuances were flattened and were "Nayarized" in the definitions and judgements. For example, the Mappila Marumakkathayam Act defines "marumakkathayam" as a system of inheritance of which descent is traced in the female line; the *anandaravan* as "any member of a tarward or tavazhi, as the case may be, other than the karanavan"; and the *karanavan* as

> the oldest major male member of a tarward or tavazhi, as the case may be, in whom the right to management of its properties vests or in the absence of such a male member the oldest member; or where by custom or family usage the right to such management vests in the oldest major female member, such female member.

In these definitions, an informed reader can easily find out how the Muslim praxis was rendered in the terms of a perceived monolithic Nayar tradition, especially by side-lining some Islamic legal notions of inheritance peculiar to the *marumakkattāyi* Muslims. Linguistically, it is also notable that the *marumakan* as a term is side-lined and the emphasis is on the term *anandaravan*, which was rarely used among Muslims.

The colonial and postcolonial judiciary made several attempts to clarify definitions, and to define the system in their own way. It needs more space and time to elaborate how the judgements differed from the legislative enactments in a number of cases (Duncan, 1966; Shukkur, 2007). For the moment, it suffices to say that the judiciary, as well as the participant lawyers and plaintiffs, had different definitions of what *marumakkattāyam* meant for them. This was more so as the existing enactments oscillated between definitions of the term as a social concept. In several judicial proceedings, the plaintiffs and defendants often drastically questioned the wearisome governmental and judicial definitions. Under the umbrella of law and governance, defining the practice as a coherent social system and custom itself was a mode of limiting the fluidities and flexibilities of unwritten norms and variances from place to place, time to time, and groups to groups. Through definitions and translations, the colonial and postcolonial patriarchal governments subjugated the matrilineal, matriarchal, and matrilocal customs of southwest India as a whole. In all these definitions, we can see how the colonial law refers to itself as the sole authority on defining multiple institutional and individual entities, and how its own acts and rules became the baseline definitions. The postcolonial state reaffirmed this colonial attempt especially as it sought to dismantle the whole system. Hence laws and rules enacted by the governments became authoritative and authentic codes, while people's definitions and conceptualisations themselves lost their meanings and relevance in the rooms of law and lexicons.

Conclusions

There are four main conclusions emerging from the above discussion on the term *marumakkattāyam* as a concept from Global South: two are specific to the empirical contexts, and two are pertinent to the larger conceptual engagement.

In the lexical, linguistic, and legalistic analyses of the term, we see how the inheritance system of the *marumakkattāyam*, designed to exclude children-in-law from succession, presents us with an ambiguous terrain. Its etymology questions the very foundation of the practice, yet one meaning was preferred over the other in the lexicons of law and later language. This nuance demonstrates that definitions and translations of particular words and related concepts have been instrumental in the colonial and postcolonial patriarchal systems to subjugate the matrilineal, matriarchal, and matrilocal praxis. Defining and translating any praxis is loaded with one's own ideology, predispositions, and ethnographic familiarity. In the case of *marumakkattāyam*, such preconceptions facilitated limiting its fluidities through fixed translations and definitions.

Because of its distortion in the realms of law and language while couching a contradiction in its own etymology, the *marumakkattāyam* is a problematic concept as to what it is meant to represent. Scholars and broader communities differ on whether *marumakkattāyam* has any appeal in contemporary society. While a few negate any relevance for the term and understand it only as a memory of old times, others find it a peculiar and proud aspect of their identity (Abraham, 2017). One would doubt if the term is useful at all to describe the present or past praxis, not to mention its usability in a non-Kerala context, such as in Lakshadweep islands where people contest this term as foreign to their social system, despite its use and application in many colonial and postcolonial judgements to identify their social system. This is more so as the jurisprudential import from the mainlands of synonyms to the diverse practices in the islands has exterminated their own understandings with regard to the system.

If this is the intellectual trajectory of an *indigenous* term such as *marumakkattāyam*, how about other "foreign" terms used by the women-centred communities to describe their system? The terms starting with "matri" such as matrilineal, matriarchate, and matrilinear have somewhat been in use in some of the societies. Are these purely anthropological constructs, and used only by ethnographically informed people? Not really. The persistence of the Dutch word *matriarchaat* in Minangkabau is definitely connected to their engagements with European epistemologies. Even so, the word has been *indigenised* and *localised*, with its own fluidities in the meaning-making processes by the local users. Such terms as "matriliny" have thus become a local term in Indonesia, as is the case with any word that has borrowed to any language from a different origin, distant or nearer, north or south, inland or outland, in-law or outlaw. The words find meaning in the worldview of their users who contribute to their wider life, profile, and journeys. These multiple lives and travels of the words and concepts should be acknowledged without judging them on the basis of their origins. Words travel and find their own meanings; concepts differ, words merge, and usages change.

Marumakkattāyam demonstrates the paradoxes of any concept when we begin to universalise for our convenience. The generalising potentiality flattens transtemporal and transregional nuance and precipitates a move to identify specific systems or notions in an essentialist manner. This does not pertain to just the issue of analytical terms and concepts alone, but of any words for that matter. In that sense, the use of concepts from the Global South as much as from the North is equally rewarding as much as threatening to the idea of nuance and texture. The questions thus should not only be addressed to the terms and terminologies, but also to the epistemologies and ontologies of our approaches. When reading the anthropological literature, one thing that I always find amusing is how ethnographers pick a few terms from the field and analyse the whole system around those terms even as their analysis is deeply rooted in epistemological frameworks foreign to that field. This is not a productive intellectual exercise; the larger project should be about the knowledge systems and frameworks from the South. One should not only change wines and bottles, we also should think about changing the ambience, the venue, and even the manners and purposes of knowledge production and circulation.

Notes

1 For example, see the debate between Bronislaw Malinowski and Robert Briffault, broadcasted on the BBC Radio in 1931, and published in 1954. On the status of the debate in the 1950s, see the introduction by Ashley Montagu (1956).
2 By the 1970s, a scholarly consensus emerged on the absence of matriarchy (Ortner, 1974). However, scholars like Peggy Reeves Sanday (2004) stood for the usage of the term with redefinition.
3 See for example, the contributions by Chris Knight, Julia Lehmann, Kit Opie, and Camilla Power in Allen et al. (2008).
4 This was the prevalent opinion among early historians of Kerala (for example, see Menon, 1924, pp. 87–91).

5 MGS Narayanan's commentary in a documentary Marumakkattayam, dir: P.T. Kunjimuhammad https://www.youtube.com/watch?v=9VnfAwJWa0Q&t=507s (last accessed on 24 December 2021), starting from 7:10. Also, personal communication at his residence on 5 December 2018.
6 For the original inscription, see Rao, 1920, p. 203. I am thankful to Lekshmi Chandran for this and the following references.
7 For Malayalam words, see Bailey, 1846, p. 39; for the English counterpart "aunt", see Bailey, 1849, p. 22; for "aunt", he also mentions that it means the sister of mother or father. For the absence of any words related to wife's mother and wife of a maternal uncle, see p. 537, and for the translation of mother-in-law as *ammāyamma* (and not as *ammāyi*), see p. 306.
8 It is notable that he identifies these groups not as castes, but as "classes" (in "other classes"), despite the currency of the term "caste" in mid-nineteenth century colonial Indian contexts.
9 For his understanding of the scriptural and historical Islam, see Gundert (1844). His *Mahamata caritram* is a polemical text from a Christian priest's viewpoint.
10 Shiju Alex, "English Malayalam śabdakōśam", https://shijualex.in/an_english-malayalam_dictionary_1907/ (last accessed on 24 December 2021); It had about 1400 pages, whereas the previous dictionaries were less than half of its size (Bailey: 545pp and Muller: 365pp; Gundert being an exception with 1116 pages).
11 He combines this Sanskrit word with Dravidian terms for rule and power such as *vāḻuka*, *vāḻca*, and *kōyma*.
12 For example, see the earliest and repeated litigations in Travancore in the first decade of the nineteenth century (*Travancore Law Reports*, 1808, passim).
13 These are the major moments in defining the concept of *marumakkattāyam* through the law of legislatives. A few more enactments discussed the same and used the same definitions in their individual acts. Some of these regulations are the Travancore Nayar Act; the Travancore Ezhava Act; the Travancore Nanjinad Vellala Act; the Travancore Kshatriya Act, and the Cochin Nayar Act.
14 The marumakkattāyam acts it specifically repealed are Madras Marumakkathayam Act, 1932; the Travancore Nayar Act, 11 of 1100; the Travancore Ezhava Act, 111 of 1100; the Nanjinad Vellala Act of 1101; the Travancore Kshatriya Act of 1108; the Travancore Krishnavaka Marumakkathayam Act, VII of 1115; the Cochin Nayar Act, XXIX of 1113, or the Cochin Marumakkathayam Act, XXXIII of 1113; and the Madras Aliyasanthana Act, 1949.

References

Abraham, J. (2017) "Setting Sail for Lakshadweep: Leela Dube and the Study of Matrilineal Kinship", *Indian Journal of Gender Studies* 24(3), pp. 438–54.

Aiyer, Ulloor S. Parameswara. (1953) *Kēraḷa sāhitya caritram*. Vol. 1. Trivandrum: University of Travancore.

al-Malaybārī, Zayn al-Dīn, "Tuḥfat al-mujāhidīn fī Baʿḍi Akhbār al-Burtughāliyyīn", British Library, IOR, MS. Islamic 2807e.

Alex, S. "English Malayalam śabdakōśam", https://shijualex.in/an_english-malayalam_dictionary_1907/ (last accessed on 24 December 2021).

Allen, N.J. et al. eds. (2008) *Early human kinship: from sex to social reproduction*. London: Royal Anthropological Institute; Oxford: Blackwell Publishing.

Alpers, E. (1972) "Towards a history of the expansion of Islam in East Africa: the matrilineal peoples of the southern interior", in Ranger, T.O. and Kimambo, I.N. (eds.) *The historical study of African religion*. Berkeley: University of California Press, pp. 172–201.

Arunima, G. (2003) *There comes papa: colonialism and the transformation of matriliny in Kerala, Malabar, C. 1850–1940*. New Delhi: Orient Longman.

Bachofen, J.J. (1861) *Das mutterrecht: eine Untersuchung über die Gynaikokratie der alten Welt nach ihrer religiösen und rechtlichen Natur*. Stuttgart: Verlag von Krais und Hoffmann.

——— (1973) *Myth, religion, and mother right: selected writings of J.J. Bachofen*, trans. Ralph Manheim. Princeton: Princeton University Press.

Bailey, B. (1846) *Dictionary of high and colloquial Malayalam and English*. Cottayam: Church Mission Press.

——— (1849) *Dictionary: English and Malayalam*. Cottayam: Church Mission Press.

Bonate, L. (2007) "Traditions and transitions: Islam and chiefship in Northern Mozambique, ca. 1850–1974", Ph.D. Dissertation, University of Cape Town.

Davis Jr., Donald R. (2013) "Matrilineal adoption, inheritance law, and rites for the dead among Hindus in medieval Kerala." In Steven Lindquist (ed.) *Religion and Identity in South Asia and Beyond: Essays in Honor of Patrick Olivelle*. London: Anthem Press, pp. 147–164.

Dube, L. (1969) *Matriliny and Islam: Religion and society in the Laccadives*. Delhi: National Publishing House.

Duncan, D.J. (1966) *Shares taken by females in Marumakkattayam family property: a conflict of full bench decisions in Kerala*. Ernakulam: Law Times Press.

Eller, C. (2011) *Gentlemen and Amazons: The myth of matriarchal prehistory, 1861–1900*. Berkeley: University of California Press.

——— (2001) *The myth of matriarchal prehistory: Why an invented past won't give women a future*. Boston: Beacon Press.

Engels, F. (1884) *Der Ursprung der Familie, des Privateigenthums und des Staats*. Hottingen-Zurich: Schweizerischen Volksbuchhandlung.

——— (1909) *The origin of the family, private property and the state*, trans. Ernest Untermann. Chicago: Charles H Kerr & Company.

Gimbutas, M. (1974) *The gods and goddesses of old Europe, 7000 to 3500 BC: myths, legends and cult images*. London: Thames and Hudson.

——— (1989) *The language of the goddess: Unearthing the hidden symbols of Western civilization*. San Francisco: Harper & Row.

——— (1991) *The civilization of the goddess: The world of old Europe*. San Francisco: Harper.

Gopalakrishnan, N. (2013) *Early middle Malayalam*. Trivandrum: Dravidian Linguistics Association.

Gough, K. (1954) *The traditional kinship system of the Nayars of Malabar*. Cambridge, MA: Harvard University Press.

Gundert, H. (1872) *Malayalam-English dictionary*. Mangalore: C. Stolz, Basel Mission Book and Tract Depository.

——— (1844) *Mahāmmata caritṟam*. Manglore: No press mentioned.

Hadler, J. (2008) *Muslims and matriarchs: Cultural resilience in Indonesia through Jihad and colonialism*. Ithaca: Cornell University Press

Ibn Baṭṭūṭa (1987) *Riḥla: Tuḥfat al-nuẓẓār fī gharā'ib al-amṣār wa-'ajā'ib al-asfār*, ed. Muḥammad ʿAbd al-Munʿim al-ʿUryān and Musṭafā al-Qaṣṣāṣ. Beirut: Dār Ihyāʾ al-ʿUlūm.

Laseron, E. (1856) *A dictionary of the Malayalam and English and English and Malayalam languages with an Appendix*. Kottayam: CMS Press.

McGilvray, D. (2014) "A matrilineal Sufi shaykh in Sri Lanka", *South Asian History and Culture* 5(2), pp. 246–61.

Menon, K.P.P. (1924) *History of Kerala written in the form of notes on Visscher's letters from Malabar*, 2 vols. Ernakulam: Cochin Govt. Press.

Montagu, M.F.A. (1956) *Marriage: past and present, a debate between Robert Briffault and Bronislaw Malinowski*. Boston: Porter Sargent Publisher.

Morgan, L.H. (1877) *Ancient soceity or researches in the lines of human progress from savagery through barbarism to civilization*. London: MacMillan.

——— (1871) *Systems of Consanguinity and affinity of the human family*. Washington: Smithsonian Institution.

Ortner, S. (1974) "Is female to male as nature is to culture?", in Rosaldo, M.Z. and Lamphere, L. (eds), *Woman, culture, and society*. Stanford: Stanford University Press, pp. 68–87.

Pires, T. (1944) *The Suma oriental*, ed. and trans. Cortesão, A.N. London: Hakluyt.

Rao, T.A.G. (1920) *Travancore Archaeological Series*, vol. 2, part 3. Trivandrum: Government Press.

Report of the Malabar Marriage Commission. (1891) Madras: Lawrence Asylum Press.

Retnamma, K. (1994) *Early inscriptional Malayalam*. Trivandrum: Dravidian Linguistics Association.

Sanday, P.R. (2004) *Woman at the center: Life in a modern matriarchy*. Ithaca: Cornell University Press.

Shukkur, S. (2007) "Scope and application of Muslim family law in Kerala and Lakshadweep: A study of legislative provisions and distinct local laws". PhD Dissertation, Tamil Nadu Dr Ambedkar Law University.

TAS (in full *Travancore Archaeological Series*) (1910-1921) vols I to III. Trivandrum: Government Press.

The Travancore Law Reports (1808) vol. 15. Trivandrum: Travancore Government.

Van Linschoten, J.H. (1885) *The voyage of John Huyghen van Linschoten to the East Indies: From the old English translation of 1598*, ed. Arthur Coke Burnell. London: Hakluyt Society.

Zacharias, T. (1907) *An English-Malayalam dictionary*. Mangalore: Basel Mission Book and Tract Depository.

PART V

Words in Motion

14

RANTAU

Saarah Jappie

In November 1786, Dutch East India Company officials summoned an elderly Southeast Asian exile by the name of Noriman, for questioning at the Castle of Good Hope. Noriman's name had arisen in court proceedings related to an attack on a farm in the Swellendam district of the Cape, some two hundred kilometres from Cape Town proper. The attack had taken place two months earlier, when a group of six enslaved males escaped from their owners' homes in Cape Town and began a journey through the hinterlands, which they hoped would eventually lead them out of VOC-controlled territory. The group stopped at a number of farms on the journey, armed with a forged permit which allowed them to travel and ask for assistance from nearby farmers. They eventually arrived at the farm Honingklip, where they had heard the owner had "many goods and cash" (Worden and Groenewald 2005, p. 551). In need of such wealth, the men decided to take control of the house and, in the middle of the night, launched a violent attack and robbery, which involved the murder of at least six people, many of them slaves. The group eventually fled before being caught, transported to the town of Swellendam, and eventually sentenced to gruesome deaths (ibid., pp. 547–555).

Noriman was not among the six accused, yet he had been implicated in the attack, for one of the accused claimed to have received a "small square lead disc" covered in "Malay" writings from him. The object in question was an amulet against evil and danger, and possibly against pursuit (Worden and Groenewald 2005, p. 549). He was therefore called in for interrogation, to determine his involvement with the guilty runaways. Noriman had long been involved in VOC networks, having been banished to the Cape from Batavia by Company officials 16 years earlier for crimes unknown (Laffan 2017, p. 51). As an exile, he belonged to a large subaltern class of individuals, the majority of them enslaved, who had arrived at the Cape by force from diverse locations around the Indian

DOI: 10.4324/9781003273530-19

Ocean basin. While he denied it during questioning, archival records and popular memory alike indicate that Noriman served as a kind of Muslim spiritual guide and healer, and was even termed a "Mohammedan priest" (Worden and Groenewald 2005 p. 539; Laffan 2017, p. 41).

Despite his previous dealings with the authorities, and therefore his inclusion in VOC records, during the interrogation Noriman was obliged to provide background information, including when he was banished from Batavia and why. His interrogators also asked for basic biographical details such as his age, and his place of birth. To the latter, he responded that he was born in "Marantu." He thereafter gained the Dutch toponym "van Marantu."

There is no known place in West Java, where Noriman was reportedly from, called "marantu" (Laffan 2017). Equally, there is no known island in the Indonesian archipelago by that name (Koolhof and Ross 2005). Rather, marantu was most likely a Dutch rendering of the term *merantau*, which, in its essence, means "to wander." Noriman van Marantu was essentially ridiculing his interrogators, using their lack of cultural and linguistic knowledge to turn "nowhere" – or "everywhere" – into a presumed "somewhere."

Merantau might not be a specific place, but it is a key element in a complex of terms related to specific understandings of place-making and mobility in Island Southeast Asia. These terms are all generated from the term *rantau* – the base word from which specific understandings of movement, mobile figures, and place, all emerge. In this chapter, I explore the genealogy and derivatives of *rantau* within their Indonesian context, and discuss them in relation to other, distinct understandings of mobility in this setting. I also reflect on the terms' proximity to, yet distinction from, terms like migration and diaspora commonly used in English. In so doing, I draw on examples from across the archipelago, and across time periods. I then examine the term's potential to account for ideas of place in contemporary reimaginings of specific, historical Afro-Asian connections, which base themselves on the experience of itinerant, early modern figures like Noriman van Marantu.

Land, Water, Language

Before unpacking the concept, it is important to sketch out the regional and linguistic context in which it emerges. Referred to in patriotic terms as *tanah air* – literally "land and water" – Indonesia is the world's largest island nation, accounting for 1,826,440 square kilometres of land and 2.8 million square kilometres of water (Cribb and Ford 2009, p. 1). The archipelago consists of 18,108 islands, which stretch across the equator and collectively bridge the Indian and Pacific Oceans. The vast majority of these islands remain uninhabited and unnamed, and the various landmasses range in size from 1,600 km in length, in the case of Papua, to small, uninhabited islets only known locally. In terms of inhabitants, current country estimates place the total population at 261 million people, making it the world's fourth most populous country and the most populous Muslim-majority country. Most Indonesians live on the archipelago's fifth-largest island of Java, which accounts for just over half of the country's population. While the Javanese are ethnically and linguistically dominant, they exist as Indonesians alongside 300 distinct ethnic groups and over 500 different languages and dialects. The national motto of *bhinekka tunngal ika* (unity in diversity) thus speaks to this great diversity, and also the fragility of the oneness that underlies the national identity.

According to linguist James Sneddon (2003), the most important element in the unification of these hundreds of ethnic groups, and the development of a national consciousness, was the emergence of Indonesian as the national language (p. 5). Indonesian, or Bahasa Indonesia, as an official language has its roots in early twentieth-century political movements, which sought to unite peoples across the archipelago in opposition to Dutch colonial domination. Its status as the collective tongue was proclaimed in October 1928, when delegates at the Second Indonesian Youth Congress in Batavia proclaimed: one motherland, one nation, one language. This language was a specific variant of Malay that had been used as a lingua franca in the archipelago for centuries. In 1945, its status was elevated to that of the official national language and since then it has undergone several programmes of standardisation.

Malay is of course not limited to Indonesia; it holds the status of national language in Malaysia, Singapore, and Brunei, and is also spoken amongst the Pattani of southern Thailand. The choice of Malay was strategic, and intended to prevent any potential ethnic favouritism or domination, for only 5% of the Dutch East Indies population spoke it as a native language in the early twentieth century. Therefore, efforts to achieve national linguistic unity would be relatively equal throughout the archipelago. Furthermore, Malay conjured up memories of centuries of inter-island connection, facilitated by migration, trade, and regional court culture.

The first Malay speakers emerged in south and southeast Sumatra. As powerful maritime navigators and traders, they controlled the nearby Malacca Strait, which served as a gateway into the archipelago. Their language spread through insular Southeast Asia, developing local dialects and contributing to the creation of new coastal creoles. By the 1500s, there were two main variants of Malay, namely indigenous and non-indigenous styles. Following the 1824 Anglo-Dutch Treaty, two standardised versions of Malay emerged – one in the English sphere of influence of the Malay Peninsula and the other in the Dutch East Indies. For their part, Dutch colonial officials encouraged the use of Malay as a lingua franca within its island colonies, for ease of communication. Ironically, it was this same language that nationalists then promoted in their anti-colonial struggle.

The lexical and grammatical make-up of what became modern Indonesian reflects the region's many histories of migration and foreign contact. It is an Austronesian language, of the Malayo-Polynesian branch, developed by descendants of early Austronesians who arrived in Island Southeast Asia from Formosa as early as 3000 BCE. It therefore belongs to the same language family as Samoan and Tahitian, as well as Tagalog and Malagasy. Indonesian also reflects the influence of centuries of interregional contact through migration, trade, and colonialism, for it includes significant borrowings from Sanskrit, Arabic, Portuguese, and Dutch. Respectively, these words and grammatical features correspond to the early Hindu-Buddhist kingdoms of Sumatra and Java, the spread of Islam from the thirteenth century, Portuguese dominance in the spice trade from the 1500s, and Dutch commercial and then colonial domination from the 1600s until the mid-twentieth century. The growing influence of English has also manifested in new lexical borrowings in recent decades, most evident in contemporary Indonesian pop culture. The term rantau thus emerges from a watery landscape, in which inter-island and interregional circulation, along with contact with many kinds of *other* form the fabric of the language itself.

A Genealogy of Rantau

In its earliest usage, the term *rantau* referred to place, specifically "shoreline" or riverbank" (Echols and Shadilly 2007, p. 449-–450). It thus signified the meeting of land and water, as well as the fringes of known, inhabited spaces, which are, in island contexts, framed by the sea. Rantau, at some point, came to mean crossing over the terrestrial threshold of riverbank and shoreline in order to travel with the water by moving upstream, or crossing the shore in order to wander. It is this element of wandering to and beyond the fringes – this sense of adventure and coming of age – that *rantau* is still largely associated with.

In its shift from signification of place to process, *rantau* as a concept reflects understandings of the shoreline as a place of opportunity – a threshold rather than a barrier. By travelling across the shore, or by going upriver, the wanderer will find wealth and life experience. The ocean thus becomes a space to engage with rather than to avoid, and it becomes a route to personal development rather than a vehicle of uncertainty. To "shoreline" is to grow.

Such conceptions of the littoral as a gateway to elsewhere and of the ocean as a space of opportunity is prevalent in island societies like those of Indonesia where the sea plays a dominant role as a source of wealth both on its surface, as a carrier of trade, and beneath it, as a source of valuable marine products. This emphasis on the sea as a space of livelihood-seeking is most clearly seen in the lifestyle of the seaborne Sama-Bajau, who inhabit various regions in the eastern half of Indonesia, as well as the southern Philippines. The widely dispersed Sama, sometimes erroneously described as "sea nomads," famously make a living from the sea, temporarily fashioning homes in small wooden canoes from which they travel to collect diverse marine products for trade. As Celia Lowe's work (2003) has shown, for the Sama, the sea is not an empty space simply to be traversed in order to arrive at other terrestrial places. Rather, it is "intimately known and precisely inventoried" both generically and specifically (Lowe 2003, p. 116). The Sama are in many ways an anomaly in their own regional context, and to wander in the context of *merantau* does not necessarily mean to live at sea. However, the concept demonstrates understandings of mobility in an archipelagic environment, where movement often entails water, and adventure necessitates looking across the shoreline and sometimes even beyond the water's surface.

From Place to Process: Merantau

So, what does it mean when place becomes process? What does the act of *merantau* encompass? And how have scholars accounted for it? In its most widely accepted academic definition, established by sociologist Mochtar Naim (1973), *merantau* is the departure from one's cultural homeland which is voluntary, limited in timeframe, and usually undertaken with the expectation of return. The process thus entails wandering subject to certain conditions. It is to wander, but not forever. It involves migration, but not permanent settlement, although this factor is in practice negotiable. Because of the emphasis on return, social scientists have sometimes neatly glossed *merantau* as "circular migration," particularly in the context of labour migration (Hugo 1982). Others have translated the term as "out migration" (Hadler 1998) or simply "emigration" (Lineton 1975).

The act of *merantau* has also signalled belonging to a specific ethnic group and partaking in that group's rites. On an archipelago-wide scale, the tradition has been associated with communities known as the region's wanderers and adventurers or, according to a colonial census from 1930, as "wanderlust" (cited in Hugo 1982, p. 69). Most often, the term conjures up images of the matrilineal Minangkabau of West Sumatra, where in line with custom, young men must leave the homeland to "make their fortunes and feed their spirits" in order to return to the village with newfound prestige and worldly experience (Salazar 2016, p. 25). By gaining experience, education, and wealth, a young man would increase his social status and his appeal as a potential son-in-law. One consequence of generations of *merantau* is that Minangkabau communities are found scattered throughout Indonesia and, increasingly, in Indonesian diasporas across the world. Another consequence, suggested by historian Taufik Abdullah, is Minangkabau openness to external ideas and socio-cultural models (2007). However, Jeffrey Hadler (2008) has pointed to the cultural idealism underlying such claims, particularly given that "other Indonesian ethnic groups migrate with greater frequency than the Minangkabau do" (p. 2).

Other communities historically known for traditions that might be considered versions of *merantau* include the Achehnese of North Sumatra, the Banjarese of Kalimantan, the Bantenese of West Java, and the Bugis-Makassar communities of South Sulawesi (Salazar, 2016 p. 23; Hugo 1982 64–66; Lindquist 2008, p. 29). For their part, Bugis and Makassar speakers have moved outwards from Sulawesi to other parts of the archipelago and sometimes beyond, in waves that date back centuries. Jacqueline Lineton has pointed out that the majority of the earliest wanderers, known as *pasompe* in Buginese, were most likely nomadic traders, "roaming the archipelago in search of trade in accordance with the direction of the prevailing monsoon, returning to Sulawesi for only a few months of each year to refit and repair their praus" (1975, p. 174). However, with the fall of the kingdom of Makassar in 1669, large-scale migration to other areas began in response to unstable political and economic conditions back home. Lineton has argued that the choice of movement to far-flung areas rather than intra-regionally was supported by the existing prau technology and established widespread Bugis trade networks. The former enabled the movement of large groups of people, and through the latter, the Bugis had contact with and knowledge of social and political conditions elsewhere (1975, p. 175). Further waves of migration occurred in later centuries such that, as with the Minangkabau, Bugis settlements emerged widely, including in various parts of Kalimantan, Java, and Sumatra. In another parallel with the Minangkabau, the Bugis have become identified with the wanderer-figure, gaining a sense of cultural pride from it (Lineton 1975) and, according to some, a sense of freedom (Kompas 2008).

The Bugis–Makassar case of motivations for and forms of outward migration shifting over time illuminates how the wanderer pattern exists alongside and sometimes blurs into other forms of inter-island movement. In the Javanese context, we see that *merantau* as a concept exists alongside at least five other terms that denote specific kinds of movement. These include *pindah*, for permanently moving locations, *nyinep* or staying over in a different place for a set amount of time, and *nglaju*, which involves travel to a different place and return within the same day (Hugo 1982, pp. 63–64). These examples both further highlight the specificity of *merantau* and the myriad mobility-related concepts that have long existed in parts of Indonesia and continue today.

Adrian Vickers (2004) has called for attention to such multiple forms of mobility in Indonesia's past as a way to contextualise contemporary processes, in particular labour migration and urbanisation, rarely viewed in the context of the region's broader history. As he argues, such processes fit into a longer history of mobility in the region that has occurred in forms and "layers than can be traced back to early modern Indonesia" (2004, p. 305). These layers include origin tales of elsewhere, where a community's ancestors are said to have arrived by boat from a distant land, and movement due to political upheaval, as in the seventeenth-century case of the Bugis-Makassar or eighteenth-century Java. There is also a wealth of historical tradition related to wandering aristocrats and religious pilgrimage, as well as patterns of movement that have driven labour mobility. This includes the intensification of labour migration from villages to local urban centres, beginning in the twentieth century, and even to other countries, as in the case of Indonesian domestic workers in other parts of Asia and the Middle East today. As Vickers points out, *merantau* remains the "most famous of these traditions" in the broader scheme of Indonesian history (2004, p. 305).

The Impact of the Perantau

Through the temporary circulation of *merantau*, whether early modern male, like Noriman or contemporary female domestic worker, the subject takes on the status of *perantau*. Not quite a migrant, and not simply a traveller, this figure carries the prestige of having lived and learned elsewhere, and the respect of having adventured. He or she also carries the burden of living between two places. The *perantau* is thus a middle figure and intermediary, who opens up the provincial space of the hometown or village to the outside world. A clear illustration of both the desirability of *perantau* status and the role played by *perantau* in translating the outside world emerges in the autobiography of Minangkabau journalist Muhammad Radjab (1995), particularly in his reflections on his childhood in West Sumatra. Radjab describes his own desire to leave the bounded space of his home village, inspired by the good fortune of his peers who were able to travel to Java. As he relates, these young men were able to "see all the odd and remarkable conditions there ... making the acquaintance of the inhabitants there ... noting all the progress, clothes, *adat* customs and foods" and then return home to tell the tale (1995, p. 310). He goes on to explain how men who returned from the *rantau* acquired exclusive social status and often chose to socialise only with other *perantau*, the shared experience both bringing fellow wanderers together and distancing them from those who had stayed behind (ibid., p. 311).

While some, like those described by Radjab, tend to return to and settle in the same village they grew up in, there are other cases of the *perantau* as a more broadly itinerant figure, who moves between different parts of the expanded world, making secondary homes and even new families as they do so. An early modern example of this kind of figure is Shaykh Yusuf Taj al-Khalwati al-Makassari (1626–1699), remembered today as a Sufi saint and anti-colonial hero in both Indonesia and South Africa. Encouraged to pursue a religious education from a young age, Shaykh Yusuf left his home in Sulawesi, at the age of 18 and only returned to the East Indies two decades later. During this time, he undertook the hajj and then travelled through the Middle East, studying with renowned scholars from Yemen to Damascus and maintaining his connection to the homeland by engaging with other Southeast Asian sojourners in his midst. Shaykh Yusuf returned to the archipelago with a new family and the reputation of a revered scholar. He chose to settle not in South Sulawesi, but in the court of Banten, West Java where he served among the most influential advisors to the sultan and as the kingdom's highest religious authority (Azra 2004, pp. 90–96). This choice reflects a broadened sense of the homeland's boundaries. Yet, Shaykh Yusuf's time in the archipelago then came to an end for, as with Noriman van Marantu, he was eventually exiled by the VOC, first to Ceylon in 1684 and then in 1694 to the Cape of Good Hope, where he died five years later, at the age of 68.

The prestige of *merantau* exists alongside the risk of failure, in the form of becoming "destitute in the *rantau*," (*melarat di rantau*), or being lost and forgotten by those back at home (Mrazek 1994, p. 11). Entangled with these misfortunes are the dangers of moral corruption abroad, as described in a late eighteenth/early nineteenth-century Achehnese poem of social critique, *Hikajat Ranto* by Leube' Isa of Pidie (Drewes 1980). According to the author, the *rantau* is a place of misery, where the wanderer loses all Islamic values and may become "wild and crazy" in spite of any good intentions he might have left the homeland with (1980, p. 13). The poem further warns against the evils that individuals may be drawn to in this desolate place, including partaking in opium, gambling, and plundering, as well as the loneliness of *merantau* (1980, p. 11).

This historical Achehnese text speaks only of risks in the male *perantau* experience. Since at least the 1990s, the prevalence of female *perantau* has increased, and these wanderers face additional social and economic pressures. Johan Lindquist's research on migrant labourers on the island of Batam (2004; 2009) sheds light on the role of shame and embarrassment (*malu*), in the experience of female *perantau* factory workers and sex workers. According to Lindquist, *malu* "becomes the emotional link between the *kampung* and the *rantau*, as the demands of what it means to be a moral person haunt the migrant" (2004, p. 488). This is especially so since, through migration, the individual is confronted with more problematic social interactions than they would be back home (Lindquist 2004, p. 489). Rachel Silvey (2000) has documented similar pressures regarding morality and sexuality for female migrant labourers in South Sulawesi. As both researchers demonstrate, while all *perantau* face economic failure as the dominant source of shame, for women there are added stresses related to sexual activity and its links to perceived morality.

Although we often think of *merantau* as a process of Indonesians moving within or outside of the archipelago, we might also think of foreign *perantau* communities in the Malay-speaking world. One such example is the Arab diaspora, many of whose members settled in Southeast Asia directly from the Hadhramawt via other parts of the Indian Ocean world in the seventeenth and eighteenth centuries, and then directly from Yemen from the mid-nineteenth century (see Mandal 2018, Yahaya 2020). Members of this creolised community have maintained links with the Hadhramawt, some historically moving back and forth between the homeland and the *rantau* for religious and educational purposes (see Mobini-Kesheh 1999). In these cases, especially with locally born individuals of mixed Indonesian and Arab descent, the question is whether Indonesia represents the homeland or the *rantau*. Chinese Indonesian communities present additional examples of a considerable diasporic presence within Southeast Asia. Here, we might question if – or when – "diaspora" is an appropriate synonym for *perantau*, the crucial factor perhaps being the presence or absence of the intention of return.

Rantau as Place-making

The process of *merantau* sets in motion multiple layers of place-making. On the one hand, it involves the establishment of secondary, temporary homes in new places. On the other hand, due to its emphasis on return, the practice reinforces the notion of an original home or *kampung halaman*. In his discussion of migrant workers in Batam, Lindquist (2009) has explained how *merantau* is defined by home, in that the process is "about the relationship with home" (p. 7), perhaps more so than with the outside world. Furthermore, the temporality of the *perantau* is marked by home, for as long as they are in the *rantau*, they occupy the in-between state of having "not yet" returned home (ibid). Rudolph Mrazek (1994), reflecting on Minangkabau worldviews, pointed out that the *rantau* is "meaningless without the 'heartland'," and that while it has long been encouraged for men to explore the *rantau*, the decision to not return home would be a bad one (p. 10).

In recent years, the Indonesian government has leveraged the significance of home to attract *perantau* and their descendants back to the archipelago, as members of what officials have termed a global "Indonesian Diaspora." The Indonesian Diaspora Network (IDN, est. 2012), emerged during the term of former president Susilo Bambang Yudhoyono (2004–2014), as a way to encourage "brain gain" from those who had left the country. Appealing to this notion of a shared home despite time and distance, Yudhoyono addressed delegates at the fourth IDN congress held in Jakarta in August 2013, proclaiming that, "So long as in your head, heart and blood there is Indonesia, you will always be a part of Indonesia's extended family" (Hussain 2013). According to *The Jakarta Post*, in 2012–2013 alone, 55 diaspora chapters were founded in 26 countries (Yudono 2013). Furthermore, since the project began, numerous diaspora network meetings have brought together prominent overseas Indonesians to celebrate their diasporic ties, to share their know-how, and ultimately to consider contributing to the nation's economy. For instance, the IDN's seventh congress in 2017 attracted the likes of Barack Obama, who spent part of his childhood in Jakarta, as well as leaders from communities descended, at least in part, from Indonesians banished as slaves and exiles to former Dutch colonies such as Suriname and South Africa. While the IDN project has leveraged the idea of a shared home, it is yet to secure rights to dual citizenship for overseas Indonesians, many of whom have had to relinquish their Indonesian citizenship (see Dewansyah 2019).

In addition to foregrounding home, the process of *merantau* creates new kinds of places, at the level of both lived personal experience and the collective imaginary. It creates a third space that lies somewhere between foreign land and place of origin, for although wandering transforms previously unexplored territory into the familiar space of *rantau*, that space can never take on the status of home. It is simply *rantau*. While *rantau* is a lived experience for migrant workers, students, and seasonal traders, it becomes what Noel Salazar terms a "realm of imagined familiarity" for those who remain back home (Salazar 2016, p. 26). For, by sharing stories of the *rantau* on their visits back home, the *perantau* familiarises his or her family, friends, and neighbours with Java, Melbourne, or Abu Dhabi. Although these people might never travel to those lands themselves, they are in fact able to speak about the *rantau* as a part of a vicariously explored geography that connects the village or hometown to the rest of the world. In contrast to Anderson's "imagined communities" (1983) those non-*perantau* may not necessarily feel part of a broader community, but rather simply aware of these elsewhere and those others. Muhammad Radjab's autobiography illustrates this vicarious familiarity, describing late-night conversations with older people who had returned from the *rantau* and would relate tales of Bandung, Solo, and Malang. For Radjab, it was not enough that "only these stories would come into [his] brain," and that "[he] would have to live on these tales in the village" until he died, without ever witnessing what those stories were about with his own eyes (1995, p. 311). For some, the imagined familiarity is insufficient on its own and acts rather as motivation to enter the *rantau* oneself.

Engaging with Rantau of the Past: Afro-Asia Connections

This realm of imagined familiarity generally manifests in the context of *merantau* during one's own lifetime. That is, someone in Sulawesi who may never have set foot in Kalimantan may feel connected to it, and as if they intimately know it, because they have immediate contact with people who have lived there and returned home to share their experiences. It is in this direct dialogue that perceived familiarity emerges. However, how would connections between one's homeland and the *rantau* prior to one's lifetime impact such senses of familiarity? And what role does collective memory of historical *merantau* play in creating a similar feeling of connectedness with that part of the outside world? My research into the afterlives of early modern exile between the Dutch East Indies and the Cape of Good Hope offers some preliminary insights into the matter. This research, which focuses on South Sulawesi and Cape Town, indicates that popular knowledge of past circulations between these places has fuelled new imaginings of the *rantau* as well as desires to connect with a long-lost community that has been stuck there.

As mentioned earlier, movement between the Indonesian archipelago and Southern Africa occurred in the seventeenth and eighteenth centuries, through networks of forced migration within the VOC world. Through these channels, tens of thousands of slaves, as well as political exiles and convicts from around the Indian Ocean basin were banished to the Cape. Certainly, this movement was outside of the official bounds of *merantau*, since it was in no way voluntary and very rarely offered the prospect of return. However, of the elite figures banished as exiles to the Cape from the Indonesian archipelago – whose life stories were far better documented than that of the enslaved – many would have been considered *perantau*, who had sought knowledge and positions of power within the archipelago. They might even have been self-proclaimed *perantau*, like Noriman. The most well-known story of a *perantau* that ended up at the Cape is that of the aforementioned Shaykh Yusuf of Makassar. His story is particularly significant since he eventually returned to the *rantau*, albeit five years after his death. While the story has been disputed, VOC records and popular memory alike record that the king of Makassar requested that Shaykh Yusuf's remains be exhumed and repatriated in 1704 (Jappie 2018). Consequently, two tombs belong to the Shaykh: one close to Makassar and the other on the outskirts of Cape Town.

In South Sulawesi, much like in Cape Town, Shaykh Yusuf is considered a saint and in both locations, his tomb serves as an important pilgrimage site. Bugis-Makassarese reverence for Shaykh Yusuf revolves around the breadth and depth of his religious and spiritual knowledge, and the astounding journeys he embarked on in order to gain such knowledge, and then ensure that it flowed back to the homeland. As Thomas Gibson has pointed out, Islam in South Sulawesi is fairly cosmopolitan, with roots in the many parts of the *rantau* that Shaykh Yusuf, and other itinerant scholars, circulated within (Gibson 2001). Although Shaykh Yusuf was stuck in the *rantau* for much of his later years, his life story and teachings reached South Sulawesi through the oral testimonies and writings of his disciples and children who returned from the mid-seventeenth century. His disciples established the *Tariqa Khalwatiyya Yusuf* – a branch of the Khalwatiyya Sufi order specific to Shaykh Yusuf – which remains active in various parts of Sulawesi today. Through the retelling of these stories, the circulation of his texts, and the passing down of his practices, knowledge of Shaykh Yusuf's life in the *rantau* spread through the generations.

Arguably, the most widely dispersed of these texts was the hagiographical *Riwayaqna Tuanta Salamaka ri Gowa* (hereafter referred to as the Riwayat). Originally circulated in manuscript form and performed to audiences at important religious events, the text was so popular that in the 1930s it was eventually translated into Indonesian and published, although many early manuscript editions remained (PaEni 2003). The text has since been reprinted and retranslated, and continues to circulate today (e.g. Basang 1981; Manyambeang 2014). The Riwayat relates the story of Shaykh Yusuf's transoceanic circulations, integrated with Sufi mythology, and in so doing, records the geography of the *rantau*. Alongside passages about miracles performed in Mecca and Medina and a rise to political prominence in the Sultanate of Banten, the hagiography mentions Shaykh Yusuf's time spreading Sufism in Ceylon and in a place named *Kopah*, which is most likely a rendering of the Dutch term *Kaap*, i.e. the Cape. Although the Riwayat does not account for Shaykh Yusuf's exile and provides an alternative order of events, it clearly includes the Cape in its depiction of the fringes.

Therefore, it appears that since at least the 1700s, Southern Africa held a place, however marginal, in some Bugis-Makassarese understandings of the *rantau*. Vague knowledge of a place called Kaap, which their spiritual ancestor had travelled to, trickled down the generations of Khalwatiyya Yusuf followers. Those who encountered the Riwayat, either through its performance or as a written text, would have known of the place, if only by name. However, no substantial contact – and no further circulations – arose between South Sulawesi and the Cape of Good Hope for centuries. This rupture owed to a variety of shifts over the years, including changes in colonial domination in each place and Indonesian national boycotts of South Africa as an apartheid state.

However, in 1994, 219 years after Shaykh Yusuf's posthumous repatriation, contact resumed. The motivation to revive the realm of Shaykh Yusuf's *rantau* emerged from Muslims in South Africa, in the form of a committee organising a festival to commemorate the 300th anniversary of Shaykh Yusuf's banishment to the Cape and, as they saw it, the anniversary of the establishment of Islam in the region (Jeppie 1996). As a part of the planning process, organisers reached out to Malaysian and, later, Indonesian diplomats in a bid to connect with Shaykh Yusuf's homeland. After months of diplomatic correspondence, a delegation from South Sulawesi eventually travelled to Cape Town, following their spiritual great grandfather's footsteps as they did so (Jappie 2018).

This initial, momentous return of diplomats, scholars, and journalists from the homeland to the ancestral *rantau* received wide coverage in the local and national news in Indonesia. The media coverage, in turn, sparked a broader reimagining of the historical, wandering spirit of Makassarese people, as well as curiosity about long-lost cousins who, as a result of Dutch colonial domination, had been stuck in the *rantau* for centuries. This moment of "reconnection" also motivated increased diplomatic contact in the form of sister-province agreements between South Sulawesi and the Western Cape governments. It also served as the basis for increased tourism between the two regions in the form of roots-finding tours through Indonesia and exhibitions of Makassarese culture in South Africa.

Renewed circulation led to the spread of new impressions about the *rantau*, in its contemporary state, to South Sulawesi. This was so much so that during my months of fieldwork in Makassar, on numerous occasions locals would engage me in conversations about Cape Town and recount stories about the city to me. These included descriptions of the lay of the landscape such as the Eerste River, along with tales of its supposed healing properties, and remarks about the "flat-topped" mountain, in reference to Table Mountain. Some commented on the "*kampung* Makassar," in a reference to the suburb of Macassar close to Shaykh Yusuf's tomb, and recounted the legends they had heard about the tomb there. Others wondered what the current day Makassarese descendants there might be like. In all of these cases, none of my interlocutors had been to South Africa. Rather, they had heard stories and impressions from relatives who had journeyed there, not quite as *perantau*, but nonetheless inspired by a wandering ancestor. This imagined, distant Makassarese outpost located across many shorelines formed part of the collective realm of imagined familiarity.

Conclusion: Conceptualising from the Shoreline

In translating the complex of terms associated with *rantau* into English, meanings are lost or at best blurred. This is in part because there are no direct equivalents for the terms *merantau*, *perantau*, and *rantau* in English, yet words like "migration" and "fringes" may seem close enough. Moreover, as the nature of transregional circulation and overseas settlement change over time, the scope of *rantau* itself expands to include additional forms of movement closer to more common understandings of migration. People might live away for much longer periods of time and with less expectation of return, for instance. Nevertheless, *rantau* and its derivatives maintain a specificity that is helpful for unpacking the nuances of mobility and of relationships to place.

The term *merantau* denotes a particular understanding of outward movement for an individual's personal and professional growth, where the expectation of return is ever-present and the importance of an original home is underscored. *Merantau* as migration, at least in intention, is therefore never a uni-directional, permanent movement, and return is *as* important as leaving. As scholars have outlined, the act of *merantau* is place-making: it creates a third space between the home and the unknown, outside world. While a migrant land may never be home, it takes on a new, more familiar status as *rantau* – an imagined extension of the homeland's boundaries – both for those who undertake *merantau* and for those who get left behind. The process also creates new identities, for the migrant becomes a new kind of person, the *perantau*. While abroad, they are adventurer-foreigners who intend to eventually go home, and then upon return to the homeland, they maintain a distinction from the non-*perantau*. Once he or she leaves for the fringes, the wanderer is forever changed.

These terms enable us to ask helpful questions of migration's overlooked aspects and consequences, for which terms may not exist in English and other languages. For instance, what status does home hold for diasporic communities? How do migrants translate other worlds, for both the communities in their places of origin and in the places they relocate to? And in which other contexts do societies perceive migration to be a form of collective "brain gain" rather than a "brain drain"?

Rantau also draws our attention to the importance of the environment in both driving and conceptualising social and cultural processes. As we have seen, the shoreline lies at the root of this set of concepts. Indeed, *rantau* may resonate in island and coastal contexts well beyond Southeast Asia. For instance, Trinidadian writer, Nicholas Laughlin has remarked that:

> "To belong to an island is to look outwards, understanding that the horizon is not simply a boundary between what is visible and what is invisible, what is known and unknown, but a challenge: to imagine, to yearn, to leave, to search, to return.". (Laughlin 2018, p.10)

In this same spirit, the Malay–Indonesian term *rantau* demonstrates how in littoral societies, the end of terra firma may not necessarily present the limits of the known and potentially knowable world. The shoreline marks a threshold rather than a barrier, and water facilitates both movement outward for personal growth, and the necessary return home.

Bibliography

Abdullah, Taufik. (2007 [1972]). 'Modernization in the Minangkabau World: West Sumatra in the Early Decades of the Twentieth Century', in Holt, C. (ed.) *Culture and Politics in Indonesia* (Singapore: Equinox), pp. 179–245.

Anderson, B. (1983). *Imagined Communities: Reflections on the Origin and Spread of Nationalism*. London: Verso.

Basang, D. (ed., trans.) (1981). *Riwayat Syekh Yusuf dan Kisah I Makkutaknang dengan Mannuntungi*. Jakarta: Departemen Pendidikan dan Kebudayaan, Proyek Penerbitan Buku Sastra Indonesia dan Daerah.

Cribb, R.B., & Ford, M. (2009). 'Indonesia as an Archipelago: Managing Islands, Managing the Seas', in Cribb, R.B. & Ford, M. (eds.) *Indonesia Beyond the Water's Edge: Managing an Archipelagic State*. Singapore: ISEAS Publishing, pp.1–27.

Dewansyah, B. (2019). 'Indonesian Diaspora movement and citizenship law reform: towards 'semi-dual citizenship', *Diaspora Studies* 12(1), pp. 52–63.

Drewes, G.W.J. (ed.) (1980). *Two Achehnese Poems: Hikajat Ranto and Hikajat Teungku di Meuke*. The Hague: Martinus Nijhoff.

Echols, J.M., & Shadily, H. (2007). *Kamus Indonesia-Inggris: An Indonesian-English Dictionary*. 3rd ed. Jakarta: Gramedia.

Gibson, T. (2001). 'The Legacy of Shaykh Yusuf in South Sulawesi', Paper presented at the workshop 'Traditions of Learning and Networks of Knowledge' in the series 'The Indian Ocean: Trans-regional Creation of Societies and Cultures'. Institute of Social and Cultural Anthropology, Oxford University, 29–30 September.

Hadler, J. (1998). 'Home, Fatherhood, Succession: Three Generations of Amrullahs in 20th Century Indonesia', *Indonesia* 65, pp. 122–154.

Hadler, J. (2008). *Muslims and Matriarchs: Cultural Resilience in Indonesia through Jihad and Colonialism*. Ithaca, NY: Cornell University Press.

Hugo, G.J. (1982). 'Circular Migration in Indonesia', *Population and Development Review* 8 (1) (March), pp. 59–83.

Hussain, Z. (2013). 'Homecoming for Indonesian Diaspora', *The Jakarta Post*, 22 August, accessed February 23, 2016. Available at: http://www.thejakartapost.com/news/2013/08/22/homecoming-indonesian-diaspora.html (Accessed: 20 October 2018).

Jappie, S. (2018). *Between Makassars: Site, Story, and the Transoceanic Afterlives of Shaykh Yusuf of Makassar*. PhD Dissertation. Princeton University.

Jeppie, S. (1996). 'Commemorations and Identities: The 1994 Tercentenary of Islam in South Africa', in Sonn, T. (ed.). *Islam and the Question of Minorities*. Atlanta: Scholars Press, pp. 73–91.

Kompas (2008). 'Merantau Bagi Orang Bugis untuk Kebebasan', 10 June. Available at: https://nasional.kompas.com/read/2008/06/10/20422993/merantau.bagi.orang.bugis.untuk.kebebasan (Accessed 15 October 2018).

Koolhof, S., & Ross, R. (2005). 'Upas, September and the Bugis at the Cape of Good Hope: The Context of a Slave's Letter', *Archipel* 70, pp. 281–308.

Laffan, M.L. (2017). 'From Javanese Court to African Grave: How Noriman Became Tuan Skapie, 1717–1806', *Journal of Indian Ocean World Studies* 1, pp. 38–59.

Laughlin, N. (ed.) (2018). *So Many Islands: Stories from the Caribbean, Mediterranean, Indian, and Pacific Oceans*. London: Telegram.

Lindquist, J. (2009). *Anxieties of Mobility: Migration and Tourism in the Indonesian Borderlands*. Honolulu: University of Hawaii Press.

Lindquist, J. (2004). 'Veils and Ecstasy: Negotiating Shame in the Indonesian Borderlands', *Ethnos: Journal of Anthropology* 69 (4), pp. 487–508.

Lineton, J. (1975).'Pasompe' Ugi': Bugis Migrants and Wanderers', *Archipel* 10, pp. 173–201.

Lowe, C. (2003). 'The Magic of Place: Sama at Sea and on Land in Sulawesi, Indonesia', *Bijdragen tot de Taal-, Land-, en Volkenkunde* 159 (1), pp. 109–133.

Mandal, S. (2018). *Becoming Arab: Creole Histories and Modern Identity in the Malay World.* Cambridge: Cambridge University Press.

Manyambeang, A.K. (2014). *Syekh Yusuf dalam Perspektif Lontaraq Gowa.* Ed. Rahman, N. Makassar: Badan Perpustakaan dan Arsip Daerah Propinsi Sulawesi Selatan & La Galigo Press.

Mobini-Keshseh, N. (1999). *The Hadrami Awakening ; Community and identity in the Netherlands East Indies, 1900–1942.* Ithaca: Cornell University Press (SEAP).

Mrazek, R. (1994). *Sjahrir: Politics and Exile in Indonesia.* Ithaca: Cornell University Press.

Naim, M. (1973). *Merantau: Minangkabau Voluntary Migration.* Ph.D. dissertation. National University of Singapore.

PaEni, M. (ed.) (2003). *Katalog-Induk Naskah-Naskah Sulawesi Selatan.* Jakarta: Arsip Nasional Republik Indonesia kerjasama dengan Ford Foundation, Universitas Hasanuddin [dan] Gadjah Mada University Press.

Radjab, M. (1995). 'Village Childhood (The Autobiography of A Minangkabau Child)', in S. Rodgers (ed.) *Telling Lives, Telling History: Autobiography and Historical Imagination in Modern Indonesia.* Berkeley: University of California Press, pp. 149–320.

Salazar, N. (2016). 'The (Im)Mobility of *Merantau* as a Sociocultural Practice in Indonesia', in Bon, N.G. & Repič, J. (eds.) *Moving places: Relations, Return, and Belonging.* New York: Bergahn Books, pp. 21–42.

Silvey, R.M. (2000) 'Stigmatized Spaces: Moral Geographies under Crisis in South Sulawesi, Indonesia', *Gender, Place and Culture* 7(2), pp. 143–161.

Sneddon, J.N. (2003). *The Indonesian Language: Its History and Role in Modern Society.* Sydney: UNSW Press.

Vickers, A. (2004). 'The Country and the Cities', *Journal of Contemporary Asia* 34 (3), pp. 304–317.

Worden, N., & Groenewald, G. (2005). *Trials of Slavery: selected documents concerning slaves from criminal records of the Council of Justice at the Cape of Good Hope, 1705–1794.* Cape Town: Van Riebeeck Society for the Publication of South African Historical Documents.

Yahaya, F. (2020). *Fluid Jurisdictions: Colonial law and Arabs in Southeast Asia.* Ithaca: Cornell University Press.

Yudono, J. (2013). 'Kisah Para Pengembara', *Kompas*, 20 August. Available at: http://nasional.kompas.com/read/2013/08/20/2024240/Kisah.Para.Pengembara (Accessed 10 October 2018).

15

MUSĀFIR

Mahvish Ahmad

> To live, I must be a musāfir, a traveller.
>
> – *Hammal, Balochistan's capital of Quetta, southern Pakistan*

Hammal sits cross-legged next to Pervaiz on a patch of grass at the University of Balochistan. They are both political organisers with the Baloch Student Organisation – Azaad or Freedom, a banned separatist collective of ethnic Baloch active in southern Pakistan's Balochistan province. As young, male, Baloch students, they and those who look like them are also primary targets of the Pakistani state's forced displacements, disappearances, kill-and-dumps, extrajudicial killings, and army raids. They meet me to speak about life in this site of all-encompassing violence; they end up telling me that life is only possible when lived as a musāfir, a traveller. They say that travel allows them to escape attempts by the state to eradicate all opposition to its rule. "I need to run far away," says Pervaiz, "so I can live." And, through travel, they encounter people who can become potential sympathisers, allies, organisers, or friends. The divide-and-rule policies of the state transform meetings with strangers into transgressive encounters; through them, networks of opposition can be built to counter the violence of the state. "If I am talking about changes, if I say that I am trying to build a movement, then I must move around among people who are my own," says Pervaiz. For Hammal and Pervaiz, politics, even life, is only possible when they embody the figure of the musāfir, the traveller.

This chapter is about the musāfir as it was invoked and embodied by people like Hammal and Pervaiz. In 2016, I spent ten months in and around sites of contemporary, state violence in Balochistan, as part of a more expansive study into the historically and geographically shifting modalities of sovereign violence that states deploy to solidify their rule. I combined this ethnographic

DOI: 10.4324/9781003273530-20

investigation with a historical and archival analysis of two other moments of violence: a 1918 military expedition deployed by the British against people in northwestern Balochistan who refused conscription into the imperial army, and a 1973–77 counterinsurgency campaign targeting those protesting the dismissal of Balochistan's first democratically elected provincial government. The musāfir lurked behind all three moments of violence. In 1918, colonial telegraphs reference roaming Kandahari and Peshawari mullahs; secret Ottoman, German, and Russian spies; and underground, communist Baloch inspired by the 1917 Russian Revolution. During the 1973–77 counterinsurgency campaign, the musāfir emerged through travelling networks of sympathisers, allies, and members of political organisations among urban leftists and socialists from other, marginalised ethnicities across the country. They were part of a mobile opposition that circulated political pamphlets, food supplies, and medical aid despite state attempts to censor news and activity critiquing and opposing its violence. And in the contemporary moment, Hammal and Pervaiz were not the only ones who referenced the figure of the musāfir. A female student organiser said she escaped the confines of her home through travels with the BSO-Azaad. Organisers of the Voice for Baloch Missing Persons (VBMP) spoke of their un-ending trips to police stations, courts, and morgues, and a 100-day, 3,000 kilometre-long march they carried out in 2014 to protest and reverse ongoing state kidnappings. And, a son and nephew of a slain separatist leader, whose mothers now feared for their lives, explained how they navigated their city to avoid being seen by security forces.

Musāfir was, of course, not the only term invoked to explain movement in a place and time of violence. Ruzhun, another BSO-Azaad member, said her family had been turned into khāna badosh, a Persian word for nomad which literally means "those who carry their homes on their shoulders." Born and raised in Karachi – her family was forced there after a 1928 crackdown by Reza Shah Pahlavi in Irani Balochistan – nomadic life indexed unwanted dislocation in a site of violence, against her ethno-nationalist desire for a settled nation. Similarly, in his study of fishermen living on the coast to the Indian Ocean in southern Balochistan, Hafeez Jamali (2014, 144, 147) says Baloch described themselves as peoples darbadar, or displaced, and forced underground. In fact, a prolific writer on all things Balochistan, living in Quetta, told me not to read too much into the word: "musāfir is just musāfir," he explained. A Baloch separatist living in exile in London declared that this romantic, musāfir figure was an Urdu notion that had sullied the imaginations of younger Baloch, and should really be excised from any analysis of their existence. Rather than be dissuaded by the unevenness, ordinariness, and "miscegenation" of musāfir in Balochistan, this chapter unpacks musāfir through attention to the universe of terms alongside which it was used, the rote and redundant ways it was deployed and embodied, and the meanings it evoked specific not just to Balochistan, but the expansive geography within which the term circulates. Musāfir is not *just* an Urdu term, but a word used in Arabic, Swahili, Persian, Hindi, Kurdish, and – to the consternation of some Baloch separatists – even Balochi. Its extensive use is a reminder of how languages are infinitely entangled.

By doing so, I take seriously Dilip Menon's (2018) assertion in his abstract of the 2018 *Concepts of the Global South* conference: namely, that we "cannot go on as we are doing: southern fact, northern theory, as it were." This is particularly true of Pakistani Balochistan, a region hard hit in the post-9/11 moment, and a site of immense imperial and national violence since the state first emerged there through colonial conquest in 1839. Balochistan's geostrategic position next to Iran, Afghanistan, and the Indian Ocean; its mineral wealth including gold, zinc, and copper; and its extraordinary levels of poverty (two-thirds of its population live beneath the poverty line), means that state powers interested in it have overdetermined how its places and peoples have been made sense of, including within the academy. Disciplines like political science and security studies have understood its places and peoples and the violence they have been subjected to through top-down categories like tribal" and "civilised," citizen and traitor, or "terrorist" and civilian. Though anthropologists have already shown how such categories are undone in sites of violence – where terrorists are also civilians, citizens also traitors (Taussig 1992; Scheper-Hughes and Bourgeois 2003; Aretxaga 2005) – concepts emergent from such sites rarely figure in their untranslated form as theorisations of the sovereign violence to which those who use it are subject. Unlike canonised theories on sovereignty and violence, e.g. Weber's idea of the state as that which holds a monopoly on violence, Agamben's idea of the state of exception and bare life, or Arendt's insight into the banality of evil, a concept like musāfir is rarely mobilised to understand sovereign violence, either in Balochistan or *elsewhere*, in other parts of the world. This chapter asks: what happens when we mobilise a term like musāfir, so frequently invoked and embodied in Balochistan, as a concept through which to understand not just the places and peoples from which it emerged, but others further afield? What happens when we refuse to translate this term to the English "traveller" – rejecting equivalence and commensurability – but keep it in its original language(s), and focus on the excess of uncontainable, untranslatable meanings embedded within the term? Or, when we keep the term in a form where it is part of a time and space entangled but nevertheless separate from Europe and North America – a time before the coming of colonialism, and a geography stretching from northern and eastern Africa, the Middle East, and Central and South Asia?

To answer these questions, the chapter returns to contemporary Balochistan. I begin by describing the terrain across which musāfir moved, through a conversation I had with another student who poignantly described what violence felt like in the everyday. This sets the scene for considering the various invocations and embodiments of musāfir in Balochistan. After describing how the movement has always been central to a selection of mostly nomadic, only recently settled, Baloch communities, I tell four stories from my ethnographic fieldwork, indexing four different forms of movement in this moment of violence. Based on these insights, I argue that musāfir at a time of violence indexed *travel* made necessary/

possible through displacement and political organising – and *enlightenment*, which emerged from the unexpected encounters that take place when people move slowly, in directions the state does not desire, and in ways they did not plan. And, I argue that a similar duality is mirrored in musāfir that emerged in earlier moments of violence, and in broader invocations of the term in South Asia and its regions of circulation. I end with an observation that what concepts travel, and what concepts do not travel, has been a central preoccupation in the *Concepts from the Global South* conferences held in 2016 and 2018. This is one among many concerns that musāfir can shed light on – alongside comparable but not replaceable terms like *rantau* (from the Malay/Indonesian archipelago), *noga molateng* or the underground serpent (from Afrikan mythology and the Zimbabwean poet, Dambudzo Marechera), fugitivity and maroons (from Black Studies), and the figure of the guerrilla (among Kurdish, Naxalbari, and Baloch territories), all of which describe movement in places outside Europe and North America, and journeys sought obstructed by power (Jappie 2018, Letswalo 2018).

The Musāfir in Balochistan and Beyond

I once sat with a boy called Mushtaq on a bench in Quetta, who recounted to me the ways he was going to die.

I will die a Pakistani patriot; a Baloch nationalist martyr; a martyr for Islam. Or, I will die sitting at home, with my mother, when the forces raid our home.

The environment has become a burden.

It was a summer afternoon and he was trying to cajole the university administration to accept his registration papers so he could start his courses in the coming academic year. In the face of his impending death, of which he was so thoroughly convinced, such a mundane chore provided refuge from a life defined by a long, never-ending, low-intensity war.

I begin with Mushtaq's story to capture the terrain upon which he, and others, were forced to navigate. For Mushtaq, death was a guarantee. He was young, strong, well-educated, male, Baloch, and a member of a tribal formation, the Marris, with a history of taking up arms against state power. He fitted perfectly with the Pakistani nationalist public sphere's imagination of the Baloch "traitor." The only way people like him could render themselves legible to the state, and to their peers, was by subjecting themselves to one of the three, pre-determined categories: that of the Pakistani patriot, the Baloch separatist, or the Islamist militant. Though the import of these categories shifted depending on whether the person was a woman or man, from the cities or the villages, or from this or that "tribal" formation, they were everywhere present. While the categories, which everyone exceeded and transgressed, were patently absurd – unable to capture the plurality of any site or person anywhere – they also exercised a violent social force. The result is, as Mushtaq reminds us, an environment which is burdensome: where positions outside of these three forced subjectivities are nearly impossible because they are illegible both to the state and to the society within which they live. Since most people did not fit easily into any one category, they frequently described everyday life as enwrapped in a haze or a fog. For example, one public school teacher explained life as an *andha dhund*, an Urdu word for a blind, directionless fog where violence is indiscriminate. Of course, the category into which one is cast, or which one decides to join or perform is not of equal consequence. To become a Baloch ethno-nationalist carries enormous risk. The charge of separatism has justified extraordinary violence.

This is the terrain upon which the musāfir emerged: as a figure that must travel upon a ground where people are violently identified, and where refusing subjection to imposed categories risks living in a blind, directionless, and violently indiscriminate fog. Of course, travel, journey, and a certain unsettledness have always permeated Baloch communities.[1] While regular movements are sometimes replaced by more permanent migratory waves of Baloch (like the 1928 crackdown in Iran which led to Baloch settling in Karachi), migration circuits are a historically integrated part of life. The Baloch regularly travel between the sovereign borders of Pakistan, Iran, and Afghanistan. Baloch settled along the western borders look towards, and are integrated into, the labour and trade circuits in Iran. Baloch living in the northeastern districts of Dera Bugti and Kohlu are linked, by road, to the Pakistani provinces of Sindh and Punjab in the east, and into an old migration route that links them to Kandahar in Afghanistan to the west. And, Baloch along the southern Makran coast are part of migration circuits linking them to the Gulf, the eastern coast of Africa, and the western coast of India. The state's imagination of this place as a strategic border territory populated by marginal state subjects sits oddly, or against, the mobile lifeworlds among the people who live within and through this place. It is this misfit between, on the one hand, the state's attempts to "capture and fix" territory and subjects through "anti-nomadic techniques" and, on the other hand, older lineages of mobility and movement, that has played a key role in repeated explosions of sovereign violence (Foucault 1975a, 189, 218).

During a period characterised by extraordinary sovereign violence, however, travel takes on a different valence. It matters that the terrain upon which travel takes place has shifted under the very feet of those who once moved around so easily. I contend that it is the state-induced friction that travellers once unobstructed (or less obstructed) face is what forces the musāfir to emerge so strongly as a figure necessary for the continuation of life and politics.

Of course, the modes of travel that I came across among people targeted in violence indicated that the musāfir was embodied in qualitatively different ways. Hammal and Pervaiz were among the musāfir who travelled to weave together disparate places and peoples within one movement, the movement for Balochistan. Much like their sangat, or comrades, they spoke of working towards articulating a zehen, nafsiyat, shaoor, or zameer (roughly translated: a mind, psychology, consciousness, or ideology) that could *counter* the violence of the state through the politics of Baloch ethno-nationalist separatism. Yet, there were other musāfir who travelled with other purposes. Nasrullah and Mama Qadeer, the faces of the VBMP who, unlike Hammal and Pervaiz, did not counter, but rather *engaged*, the state through its own institutions, travelled to take on the state within its own institutions, including its police stations, courts, and hospitals as they represented the families of those subject to enforced disappearances. Meanwhile, Mohsin and his cousin Arsalan in Karachi, the son and nephew of the slain separatist leader whose mothers wanted them safe, moved through the city merely to *avoid* being seen, heard, or felt by a state so ready to categorise, or miscategorise, them. Another young man living in Quetta, who I met at a missing persons camp, told me that he would regularly travel only part of the way to his home village by road. He would always make sure that he got off the main road before the checkpoints started, making his way through paths in the mountains known by his friends. And, finally, people like Tokli decided to *submit* to the state, by moving in ways that were easily legible. When he faced accusations of sympathy and membership of Baloch separatist groups, he joined the Tabligh-e-Jamaat, an Islamist organisation that is given space and support by state security forces around Pakistan. With the Tabligh, he carried out chillas, a 40-day missionary tour, rendering his movements legible to a state on a terrain where refusal to cooperate could mean disappearance and death.

Running through each mode of movement (travel to counter, engage, avoid, and submit to the state) were the dual themes of displacement and consciousness. On the one hand, the figure of the musāfir was invoked alongside that of the khāna badosh and the experience of being darbadar. This affect of being a forced nomad, on-the-run, dislocated, and illegible was a direct result of constantly experiencing illegibility because of the reductive, state-induced categories of the citizen, Baloch insurgent, and the Islamist. On the other hand, the figure of the musāfir was directly related to the emergence of consciousness, or what Hammal, Pervaiz, and many other members of their student organisation called zehen, nafsiyat, shaoor, or zameer. This was particularly stark in the experience of female separatists, whose political commitments forced them out of places they had earlier been confined. Ruzhun, an organiser in Karachi, explained how the head of the BSO-Azaad, Kareema Baloch, had politically inspired her with the extensive travels of her imagined nation of Balochistan. "Kareema carried her entire life in her purse, and refused to settle with a man in a marriage because of her love for Balochistan. I want to be like her, and like other women revolutionaries, like Leila Khaled." Ironically, Ruzhun, who was the one who had used the Persian word for "those who carry their homes on their shoulders" – khāna badosh – was now romanticising the nomadic experience she had earlier eschewed as necessary to the emergence of political consciousness. "When I travel to meet people, I remember that I cannot just live for myself but must live for others," she said.

Ruzhun's invocation of Leila Khaled and Kareema Baloch referenced forms of wilful travel which move against those sanctioned by capital or state. Khaled, known for the Trans World Airlines Flight 840 hijacking in 1985 as a member of George Habash's Popular Front for the Liberation of Palestine (PFLP) redirected the flight towards a political goal of Palestinian emancipation. Kareema Baloch transgressed spaces rarely moved around by women without male guardians, and against the threats of the state. The power of Kareema Baloch's transgressive movement continued after her untimely and shocking death in December 2020, while living in asylum in Canada: when her body was returned to be buried in her home town of Tump by the border to Iran, it prompted Baloch women to travel so they could carry and bury her casket, acts that transgressed masculinist rituals of mourning and burial where only men, not women, could bid farewell to that final travel between this world and the next.

The lives of figures important in the 1918 military expedition and the 1973–77 counterinsurgency campaign also gesture towards the figure of the musāfir and the embedded duality of displacement and consciousness. In 1918, Misri Khan Khetrani was named as one of the primary "ringleaders" of the "rising" in telegraphs sent from the office of the Attorney to the Governor-General (AGG) and the General Headquarters (GHQ) coordinating the expedition. Operating just a year after the 1917 Russian Revolution, Misri Khan identified as a communist who had been influenced by spies, mullahs, and others interpellated by what the AGG's office called "democratic intrigue." Against the colonial ideas of difference and war between ethnicities and "tribes" in Balochistan and other parts of the colonial frontier, Misri Khan travelled underground, hiding with communities that local political agents had declared as different and at war with Misri Khan's own tribal formation, the Khetranis. He eventually escaped over the border to Afghanistan, where he was given exile, and attended the Soviet-funded 1920 Congress of the Peoples of the East in Baku in contemporary Azerbaijan. Similarly, in 1973–77, sympathisers from other ethnicities, including urban leftists, around Pakistan regularly travelled to Balochistan as a part of their political education. One of these allies, Murād Bhabha – whose father had settled in Karachi after escaping South Africa because of his involvement with the African National Congress (ANC) – regularly worked with Baloch and their sympathisers to receive travellers and take part in travel for the purposes of political consciousness-making. For example, in the 1970s, he arranged for 40 members of the Baloch Popular Liberation Front (BPLF) to train with the PFLP.

The duality of displacement and consciousness in this use of musāfir mirrors definitions and invocations of the term in South Asia and around the Muslim world, where travel repeatedly emerges as central to personal and collective growth.

Though its etymological root – s f r – is usually associated with the word it spells, *safr*, or travel, it is also connected to another universe of meanings according to Hans Wehr's 1961 *Arabic-English Dictionary*: that of unveiling, shining, glowing, disclosing, achieving, ending, and bringing to a close. Or, that moment when something is revealed. In fact, in the Qur'an, s f r, refers not just to travel, but to the act of unveiling a matter or a thing, of brightening, or of bringing light. This duality of travel and enlightenment embedded in the etymological roots of musāfir is markedly different from the duality embedded in the English word, travel: English "travel" has its roots in "travail" from the Old French "trepalium" which means "instrument of torture" and "stake."

More importantly, the duality embedded in the etymology of musāfir – its reference *both* to the act of journeying *and* to the act of unveiling a matter or a thing – surfaces as a recurrent theme in poetic and religious invocations of the musāfir across South Asia and the broader region in which it circulates.

For example, in his poem, "dil man, musāfir man" or "The Mind is a Traveller," which Faiz Ahmed Faiz wrote while in voluntary exile in London, he speaks about the experience of being lost in a city of strangers, trying to find his way home. He opens by saying:

> My heart, my fellow traveler
> It has been ordained again
> That you and I be exiled (watan-badar)
> We call out in every street,
> We scour every town.
> In order to find a code
> To a messenger of love
> We ask every stranger
> The address of our old home.
>
> *(as published in Yaqin 2013)*

The fishermen in Jamali's 2014- study spoke of becoming darbadar, or displaced, while in this poem Faiz speaks of becoming watan-badar or expelled, banished, and ejected from his watan or abode, nation, or country. Though the experiences are qualitatively different – Faiz was in voluntary rather than forced exile, and his class position as an elite Pakistani from Lahore is in no way commensurable to that of the fishermen of southern Balochistan – the relationship between travel or displacement and a longing for reunion with a collective, higher self where those around one are not strangers but friends is palpable. Elsewhere – in poems like "dasht-e-tanhai" – Faiz repeatedly returns to the theme of safr or travel and longing for union in other ways, most notably through an invocation of hijr, which means separation but also refers to the emigration of Muslims from Mecca to Medina. Aamir Mufti argues that "the significance of Faiz's repeated use of hijr and its derivatives is that it imbues the lyric experience of separation from the beloved with a concrete historical meaning – the parting of ways or leave taking that is Partition." (Mufti 2007, 223) Amina Yaqin (2013, 11) goes on to argue that this state-induced separation which resulted in the violent travels of Partition is simultaneously imbued with the need for wisāl or reunion to a "utopian Indian national identity that normalizes the Muslim" finally giving it space to live within the broader political community of a united Indian subcontinent. In such poetic invocations of musāfir and its parallel terms, journey and revelation come forward through the reality of exile and a longing for wisāl or reunion for an elsewhere that is not ahead in the future, but behind in the past in the figure of an imagined, formerly united India. Namely, not a new destination, but an imagined, collective Hindustani self has already been and been lost.

Ideas of travel in Islam gesture towards a similar duality. In his book, *Islam and Travel in the Middle Ages*, Houari Touati argues that "Muslim men of letters" travelled in pursuit of "intimate self-knowledge." They travelled not out of a desire to confront alterity at the limits of geography or to know the "other" – as Touati says medieval European travelogues aimed to do – but rather to know a collective self living within the "abode," "house," or "territory" of Islam, namely dār al-islām. Muslim travel within this dār al-islām became equivalent to the pursuit of intimate *self*-knowledge, rather than knowledge about an unknown *other*. It is also apparent in some understandings in Sufi thought of the safr. Here, believers journey upwards without moving instead of outwards to a geographical other place. This ascendant journey towards fanaa or annihilation with the divine is followed by a descent back into the world, where the believer must tell others about what awaits them if they, too, choose the path of self-annihilation. This journey towards self-knowledge, or knowing a higher self, emerges also in Urdu travel writing in the form of safrnamas. Daniel Majchrowicz (2015) argues that travel, though always integral to social life in the Indian Subcontinent, emerged in the nineteenth- and twentieth-century Urdu writing as a necessary end in itself. "The imagined virtues of travel," he argues, "hinged on two emergent beliefs: that travel was a requisite for inner growth, and that travel experience was transferable." This positions them as different from colonial travel writings, which were carried out with the explicit purpose of rendering societies legible in order to govern them better, as well as the writing of foreign correspondents who similarly prioritise a knowing of the collective other rather than the collective self.

I suggest that these dualities, between exile and reunion (Urdu poetic reference in Faiz) and travel and self-knowledge or revelation (Islamic and Sufi references; Touati and Majchrowicz) point to sedimented meanings of musāfir and parallel ideas of travel, journey, and movement that are retained when the concept is invoked by Baloch in a site of violence. It also indicates that a reference to the figure of the musāfir in a site of sovereign violence has embedded within it a critique of how states obstructing travel also try and obstruct the possibility of reunion, self-knowledge, revelation – or the knowing of a higher and collective self through the development of what Baloch ethno-nationalist students called zehen, nafsiyat, shaoor, or zameer. More importantly, it is a reminder that despite attempts at strangling the circulation of people and ideas, these circuits persist in ways illegible to a state intent on controlling its territory and subjects. It is when such movements happen that encounters take place across state-induced lines of difference – of ethnic, "tribal," ideological, gendered, and other divides – breaking open the possibility to forge relations which are not ordered according to a state seeking hegemony, breaking open the possibility for imagining another way to live together. It is no wonder that today the Pakistani state does not wish anyone to go to Balochistan. Such a regulation of travel and movement means that new imaginations of political collectivity will struggle to emerge. That is why the now deceased human rights advocate, Asma Jahangir, presented such a risk to the state; when they asked her why she kept on going to Balochistan, she answered, "This is my country, I will go wherever I like." And that, I suggest, is why Hammal and Pervaiz and the many others I spoke to attached politics, even life itself, to the figure of the always-moving musāfir.

Conclusion: Musāfir and Other Subaltern Movements

What travels, and what does not, has been a central preoccupation at the two *Concepts from the Global South* gatherings held to date. In the abstract circulated in the run-up to the 2018 conference, Dilip Menon (2018) observes:

> Concepts from a European history, such as secularism, individualism, and rationality in all their singular brightness have travelled well … What travels from the spaces of Asia, Africa are ideas like dharma, karma, yin, yang etc. which derive from an Orientalist understanding of spaces of civilisation which exist in a premodern aspic. Or, if one thinks about the Middle East, ideas such as jihad, fatwa, talaaq which signal a recalcitrant resistance to the modern.

I would add that concepts travel out of their point of origin because they are carried around by travellers, travelling by flight on routes they can afford or along well-paved roads built to connect North to South, or metropole to colony (less often, South to South or colony to colony). It is no coincidence that western yogis and DC security analysts are so central to the circulation of terms like karma and jihad. This was brought home at the first conference in 2016 when Magid Shihade from Palestine's Birzeit University was unable to attend because he had been held up at three checkpoints on his way to the airport, where he missed his flight. It is brought home when Shehzad Akbar, a lawyer representing drone victims and now a member of Imran Khan's cabinet, was blocked from entering the US in 2013 to speak about those targeted by the CIA. And it is re-asserted when the Pakistani government places political dissidents on Exit Control Lists to ensure their ideas do not circulate in a wider global debate.

Given the conference's preoccupation with words that do not travel, it is telling that so many words or concepts that continuously emerge from the sites this project seeks to centre deal with movement in places outside of Europe and North America, or among people whose movement is actively obstructed by power. At the 2018 conference, Saraah Jappie introduced the Malay/Indonesian word, rantau, which she argued recalled "notions of place and of movement beyond the oceanic frontier." In its various instantiations, she explained that the "concept and practice of the verb form, merantau, occurs in societies across the Indonesian archipelago – from Sumatra to Sulawesi – and, in each of these contexts, [indicates that] to advance in one's life necessitates engagement with the sea." She was followed by Gabriel Morokoe Letswalo who analysed the figure of the noga, or serpent, as a moving and watching being molateng or underground in the poetry of the Zimbabwean writer Dambudzo Marechera. Gabriel explained how the noga "in Afrikan mythology was a contradictory figure" – both dangerous and vulnerable, "a thing to kill and an object of care … a sign of sadness and a symbol of resistance" – and how it had to move underground in order to live. As a result, he gestured towards another kind of duality from that of the musāfir in Balochistan, embodying another form of movement in another site of historic and contemporary violence. In his presentation on the noga molateng, Gabriel was gesturing towards another figure that has emerged from the margins: that of the fugitive in Black Studies. Through a study of figures like the maroons or runaway slaves, the fugitive emerges as that which has not only been expelled from the norm, but that which chooses this expulsion and the underground/undercommons because they "refuse to be a subject to a law that refuses to recognize" them (Campt 2014). Similar figures – on-the-run, illicit, and criminal – emerge in the figure of guerrillas across the world, from the female guerrilla fighting in the Women's Protection Units (YPJ) in Kurdish territories to the figure of the sarmachar (literally, the one who is willing to sacrifice their head) who roams the mountains of Balochistan to the Naxalbari in West Bengal (Dirik 2018; Shah 2017; Ahmad 2019).

Within the academy, a series of practices – like presenting at conferences, publishing books and journal articles, holding annual lectures, and so on – inadvertently differentiate between two types of concepts: institutionalised ones, and "vernacular" or "popular" ones. Sometimes, the latter have been processed through the mill of academic practices to emerge as institutionalised concepts. Anthropologists have played a particularly large role in this kind of migration, bringing terms like mana, shamanism, totemism, potlatch, and taboo which emerged from anthropological fieldwork into the halls of the academy, subjecting each of these terms to rigorous debate by thinkers relatively removed from their embedded use in societies further away. This chapter is calling for something different. Rather than trying to institutionalise musāfir as an analytical concept within the halls of the academy, it is calling for attention to how musāfir and its related words are *already* concepts, albeit ones that we do not recognise as such. The point is not to articulate a "new" concept from an older vernacular one – an articulation that reproduces this division between institutionalised (and therefore superior) thinking and that which is outside the walls of the institution (and therefore inferior) – but to recognise that the vernacular, everyday, ordinary, collective use of terms is already a site of theory-making.

Indeed, it is telling that such roaming, illicit, on-the-run figures emerge repeatedly on the global margins, in sites of violence, and in places where power attempts to obstruct movements. This chapter's focus on the musāfir is therefore not just a focus on the term itself and all its particular, embedded meanings as it emerged in Balochistan, South Asia, and the broader region within which it circulates. The emergence of musāfir as a recurrent theme in Balochistan parallel to the emergence of terms like rantau, noga, the maroon/fugitive, or the guerrilla is a reminder that despite attempts to obstruct the circulation of people and ideas from the Global South – a project which the university as an institution can be complicit in –they move around anyway. Inadvertently, therefore, this chapter calls for attention to how people and ideas move around, despite attempts to obstruct them, and despite the lack of recognition of these ideas by the academy – or how politics, life, and movement persists even when institutions of power try to ensure that they are excluded, contained, even destroyed, in acts of marginalisation and violence.

Note

1 A popular nationalist origin myth, which describes them as a nomadic tribe that settled in the area between contemporary Iran and Pakistan after leaving Aleppo, recalls this theme of constant movement. Subsequent epic ballads recall stories of Baloch heroes who conquered territory not to rule, but to expand the remit of Baloch migratory circuits. See Baloch, Inayatullah. 1987. *The Problem of Greater Baluchistan: A Study of Baluch Nationalism*, pp. 67–68; Lutfi, Ameem, "Conquest without Rule: Baloch Portfolio Mercenaries in the Indian Ocean" (PhD diss., Duke University), 2018.

References

Ahmad, M. (2019) *Destruction as Rule: Containment, Censuring and Confusion in Pakistani Balochistan* (Doctoral thesis). https://doi.org/10.17863/CAM.38970.

Aretxaga, B. and Zulaika, J. (2005) *States of Terror: Begoña Aretxaga's Essays*. Reno: Center for Basque Studies, University of Nevada.

Baloch, I. (1987) *The Problem of Greater Baluchistan: A Study of Baluch Nationalism*. Hamburg: Beiträge zur Süudasienforschung.

Campt, T. (2014) "Black Feminist Futures and the Practice of Fugitivity." Helen Pond McIntyre'48 Lecture, Barnard College, October 7. Available at: http://bcrw.barnard.edu/blog/black-feminist-futures-and-the-practice-of-fugitivity. Accessed 7 Sep. 2018.

Dirik, D. (2018). *Competing Concepts of Freedom: Kurdish Politics between 'Housewifization' and 'Struggling Woman'* (Doctoral thesis). https://doi.org/10.17863/CAM.55612.

Faiz, F. A. *mere dil, mere musāfir*. Available at: https://www.rekhta.org/ebooks/mere-dil-mere-musafir-faiz-ahmad-faiz-ebooks.

Foucault, M. (1975) *Discipline and Punish: The Birth of the Prison*. Translated by Alan Sheridan. New edition. London: Penguin.

Jamali, Hafeez. (2014) "A Harbor in the Tempest: Megaprojects, Identity, and the Politics of Place in Gwadar, Pakistan." PhD diss., The University of Texas at Austin, 2014.

Jappie, S. (2018) "Rantau" at Concepts from the Global South Conference. University of Cape Town.

Letswalo, G. M. (2018) "Noga Molateng" at Concepts from the Global South Conference. University of Cape Town.

Lutfi, A. (2018) "Conquest without Rule: Baloch Portfolio Mercenaries in the Indian Ocean." PhD diss., Duke University Press.

Majchrowicz, D. (2015) "Abstract. Travel and the Means to Victory: Urdu Travel Writing and Aspiration in Islamicate South Asia." PhD Dissertation, Harvard University.

Menon, Dilip. (2018) "Abstract: Concepts from Global South." Witwatersrand University.

Mufti, Aamir R. (2007) *Enlightenment in the Colony: The Jewish Question and the Crisis of Postcolonial Culture*. Princeton and Oxford: Princeton University Press.

Scheper-Hughes, N. and Bourgois, P., eds. (2003) *Violence in War and Peace: An Anthology*. 1 edition. Malden, Mass.: Wiley-Blackwell.

Shah, A. (2020) *Nightmarch: Among India's Revolutionary Guerillas*. London: Hurst Publishers.

Taussig, M. (1992) *The Nervous System*. New York/London: Routledge.

Yaqin, A. (2013) "Cosmopolitan Ventures during times of crisis: a postcolonial reading of Faiz Ahmed Faiz's "Dasht-e tanhai" and Nadeem Aslam's Maps for Lost Lovers." *Pakistaniaat: A Journal of Pakistan Studies* Vol. 5, No. 1, pp. 12–13.

16

FEITIÇO/UMBANDA

Iracema Dulley[1]

> When the king dies or is deposed, the one who will substitute him invites an *ocimbanda* to remove everything that was part of his predecessor's *umbanda*, for it is said that the king's *umbanda* cannot be substituted. At the gate where the hoe stands the new hoe with its *umbanda* is placed.[2]

> what is only a substitute for the being of the thing itself, a fetish. … a simulacrum, a prosthesis … (a wooden leg that one can dance gracefully with) … a simulacrum, a prosthesis, a fetish.
>
> *(Derrida 2009, p. 293)*

This chapter reflects on the disseminating chain of substitution that includes but is not limited to terms such as *feitiço*, *fetisso*, *fetiche*, "fetish," *Fetisch*, *fétiche*, "fetishism," *feiticismo*, *umbanda*, *owanga*. The borders that define what is translation and what is transliteration are both porous and political. It is therefore no simple matter to say to what "language" each of these terms "belongs." But lest the reader be at a complete loss, one could tentatively say that *feitiço* is a Portuguese word; *fetisso* and *fetiche* were produced in the encounter between Portuguese and African traders on the Mina coast; "fetish" is the translation/transliteration of this Creole word derived from *feitiço* into English; *Fetisch* and *fétiche* are translations/transliterations of the same word into German and French, respectively. *Umbanda and owanga* are words in Umbundu, the main language spoken in the Central Highlands of Angola during colonial rule and the *lingua franca* employed in trade in surrounding regions. *Umbanda* is also the name that gives unity to a set of religious practices in Brazil. These terms have been translated, or transliterated, back and forth from and into European languages in connection with the attempt at generalization implied by theories of fetishism and the "fetish." The last two terms in this chain relate to translational efforts

DOI: 10.4324/9781003273530-21

involving speakers of Umbundu and speakers of European languages who were mostly missionaries (Dulley 2010, 2018) during the Portuguese colonial rule in Angola.[3] If one includes terms in Umbundu in the chain of substitution whose most familiar terms – "fetish" and its iterations in European languages – derive from the Portuguese word *feitiço*, what appears to be an effort of theorization from "Europe" about the religious practices of "others" (and the economic practices attributed to "oneself") is displaced as the most visible part of a chain of substitution that is governed by dissemination (Derrida 1981). By dwelling on the iteration of the above-mentioned signifiers – for which it might be accused of "methodological fetishism" (Appadurai 1986, p. 5) or of "fetishism [as] a principle of reading" (Morris 2017b, p. 276) – this chapter interrogates the relation between translation and the "fetish."

One may approximate the "fetish" and translation on the grounds that both aim at fixation. Yet, in the "fetish," as in translation, fixation is accompanied by instability. Writing on fetishism according to Marx, Rosalind Morris (2017b, p. 188) calls our attention to the translational transformation of *Fetischcharakter*, roughly "fetish-like," into "fetishism," which is made apparent, for instance, in the translation of "*Der Fetischcharakter der Ware und sein Geheimnis*" into English as "The Fetishism of Commodities and the Secret Thereof." I would like to add another translational displacement to this one. When Marx writes about "*den Fetischismus, der den Arbeitsprodukten anklebt*" (Marx 1987, p. 103) ["the fetishism which attaches itself to the products of labour" (Marx 1992, p. 165)], *anklebt* is translated as "attaches itself." The verbal form is maintained and points to the act of attaching, which is the first step in fixation. In the passage in which Marx affirms that when the proportions in exchange "have attained a certain customary stability, they appear to result from the nature of the products" (Marx 1992, p. 167) [*Sobald diese Proportionen zu einer gewissen gewohnheitsmäßigen Festigkeit herangereift sind, scheinen sie aus der Natur der Arbeitsprodukte zu entspringen* (Marx 1987, p. 105)], "stability" is the translation offered for *Festigkeit*. A couple of lines further, when the way in which the "character of value" fixes itself is addressed, *befestigt sich* is translated as "becomes established." Thus, the action implied in *befestigt sich* is rendered qualitative and final in English, as the character of having value does not "fix itself" (this would be the more literal translation of *befestigt sich*) but "becomes established."

What translational displacement does above is to insist on the becoming-fixed of that which is affected by fetishism. And it does so through mimesis. The sequence culminates in the rendering of *der Warenwelt anklebenden Fetischismus* (Marx 1987, p. 112), more literally, "the fetishism that attaches itself to the world of commodities," simply as "the fetishism *attached* to the world of commodities" (Marx 1992, p. 176, my emphasis). My point is not to criticize the translation of Marx but to provide us with one familiar instance in which translation, like fetishism, operates through contagion. This very brief comment on Marx, whose work is part of the disseminating chain that includes *Fetisch* and *Fetischismus*, intends to summon his specter to haunt what follows by calling our attention to the fixation that occurs in the English translation of his description of how the "fetish" becomes stable. For translation, like fetishism, operates through displacement (Derrida 1985).

This chapter focuses on instances of such iterative displacement. *Feitiço*, transliterated as *fetiche*, *fétiche*, *Fetisch*, "fetish," disseminates into fetishism, *fetichismo*, *feiticismo*, *owanga*, *umbanda*, and the open chain of substitution called forth by these terms. Thus, the relation between translation and the "fetish" as one of juxtaposition is questioned, as both translation and the "fetish" point to the possibility of othering that is contained in displacement. I argue that terms such as *feitiço*, *umbanda*, and *owanga*, "concepts from the Global South" with which the following engages, cannot be described in themselves, based on a conceptual particularity grounded in the emic gesture (Dulley 2019). Rather, because conceptuality, like translation, depends on displacement, with its continuities and ruptures, *feitiço*, *umbanda*, *owanga*, "fetishism," and the "fetish" only make sense in the chain of their dissemination.

Feitiço, Feiticismo, Fetichismo

As we learn from Pietz (1987), the term "fetish" and its variations in European languages are transliterations of the Creole word *fetisso*[4] derived from the Portuguese word *feitiço*, itself a vernacularization of the Latin term *facticius* or *factitius*, past participle of *facere* (to make), which might be glossed as "fictitious," "artificial," "false," or "deceptive." Thus, *feitiço* became *fetisso* on the Western coast of Africa as a result of the encounter between Portuguese and African merchants, and it is this word, which for Pietz bears the "origin of the idea of the fetish" (1987, p. 39), that was transliterated into European languages as "fetish," *fétiche*, *Fetisch*, *hechizo*, and so on. *Feitiço*, variously translatable as "spell," "charm," "incantation," "bewitchment," and "fetish," is a noun that shares the root of *feitiçaria*, commonly translated into English as "sorcery." *Feitiço* can also mean "sorcery," in a conflation of that which is done (to cast a spell, bewitch, enchant) with sorcery as a general concept. Thus, *feitiço*, like *facticius*, points to the indeterminacy between particularity and generality, "propriety and promiscuity" (Morris 2017a, p. xi), and the "undecidable bond to contraries" (Derrida 1986, p. 227) that characterizes the simulacrum.

Yet, the iteration of these transliterations of *feitiço* does not produce nonhierarchical equivalence between the signifiers in this chain. For translation, like the "fetish," "implies substitution without equivalence and relation beyond reciprocity" (Morris 2017b, p. 273). If the Portuguese term, *feitiço*, is not to be understood as pertaining to the order of the emic, i.e., it pertained to no one specifically but was employed in the generalization of what was understood to be the universality of sorcery, what is important about it is not its origin but its openness to alterity. Sansi-Roca advances the argument that "in the Atlantic world, sorcery [*feitiçaria*] was a particularly efficient method for appropriating objects, people and discourses from elsewhere, objectifying them, and "attaching" them, so to say" (Sansi-Roca 2007, p. 132). The origin of the word in this historical encounter was, according to the author, lost due to the uneasy place of Portuguese colonialism and the Lusophone world when it comes to European modernity and civilization.

I wish to retain two ideas from Pietz and Sansi-Roca before focusing on Angola. The first one is Pietz's claim that the "fetish" is historical in that it fixates "an original event of singular synthesis or ordering" (Pietz 1985, p. 10). If this is the case, the iteration of *feitiço* into *fetiche* and "fetish" depends less on its supposed origins than on a history of commensuration. Yet, according to this author, the emergence of the "fetish," and thus of "fetishism," "was related to the triangulation, on the Mina coast, of "Christian feudal, African lineage, and merchant capitalist social systems" (Pietz 1985, p. 6). The lure of origins is an effect of the "fetish," for it "retains the foreign as foreign and yet with the promise of possession of it" (Siegel 1997, p. 245). The translations of *feitiço* in Angola do not reveal any supposed originality that might have been lost. For this transliteration, apprehended as a process of multiple translations, i.e., of transposition of meaning between languages conceived as different, is one marked by supplementarity (Derrida 1997).

The second idea that I would like to retain is Sansi-Roca's (2007) observation in "The Fetish in the Lusophone Atlantic" that the force of the "fetish" resides in its alterity. According to him, the Portuguese term *feitiço* was used on the Mina coast to refer to magic that operates through fixation whereas *mandinga*, a term from the Western African coast, was used in Portugal to mean something very close to the idea of *feitiço*. It is therefore not merely coincidental that one of the Umbundu words translated as *feitiço* in Angola names a set of religious practices called *umbanda* in Brazil. And although *umbanda* was recognized as an Afro-Brazilian religion in the 20th century (Montero 1985), it is nonetheless frequently accused of being akin to *feitiço*. It seems that the "fetish," in translation, is governed by a hierarchy that promotes othering. For, as Siegel reminds us, with "the acceptance of the foreign as foreign, the fetish disintegrates" (1997, p. 253).

The process Sansi-Roca describes is one of the successive generalizations and particularizations, in which the "fetish" arises as the most abstract concept and its iterations as *feitiço* are deemed particular. The idea of "fetishism" as the highest concept organizes this hierarchy. Yet, it is not always to be found in Lusophone ethnographic records. What follows revolves around displacements of the "fetish" in translation: as *feitiço*, as "sorcery," as the doing and undoing of fixation. Such displacement is intimately related to acts of transposition, such as translation and transliteration, between various languages: Portuguese, English, French, German, and the vernaculars into which *feitiço* was translated in Angola. If this process relates to the hierarchization of "fetish-like" practices, this hierarchy is intimately connected with the generalization and particularization entailed in translation, itself a "fetish-like" process.

A curious term is frequently found in colonial sources on Angola: *feiticismo*, something in-between *feitiço*, *feitiçaria*, and *fetichismo*. Twentieth-century missionary ethnographies in Portuguese on Central Angola rarely use the term *fetichismo*, the Portuguese equivalent of "fetishism" (Estermann 1983; Valente 1973, 1974). In ethnographic writing, the term *feiticismo* is preferred as the generalization that classifies religious practices considered to be at odds with Christianity. *Feiticismo* retains *feitiço*, and not *fetiche*, as a root, but is supplemented by an "ism" (*ismo*), as in fetishism. It sounds like something in-between sorcery (*feitiço*; *feitiçaria*) and the Portuguese equivalent of fetishism (*fetichismo*); and it does so in a particularizing way, i.e., in a way that erases the universal aspiration that marks fetishism as a concept and iterates a more localized relation with the "fetish" through the apposition of an "ism" to a term that refers to sorcery. Now, the way in which *feiticismo* is used, frequently in an accusatory mode, erases *feitiço* as the supposed originator of "fetishism," but does so in what one might hear as the transliteration of the word "fetishism" (*fetichismo*) into Portuguese. Because *feiticismo* resonates both *feitiço* and *fetichismo*, it can be heard as a reverberation of the awkward place of the Portuguese language in the iterative history of the concept of "fetishism."

Translations of the "fetish" and its chain of substitution in 20th century Angola are informed by this erratic history of displacement. However, *feitiço* was then no longer the universalizing category it was when Portuguese merchants reached the Guinea coast; rather, it was now employed to mark African specificity and alterity (despite the Portuguese root of the word). But if *feiticismo* and *feitiço*, as they appear in colonial sources, aimed at generalizing local practices, they did not have the same generalizing capacity as the (almost absent) concept of "fetishism." In embracing *feiticismo*, and not *fetichismo*, as a descriptive category, the subalternity of the Portuguese language was marked vis-à-vis the languages in which "fetishism" had been fixed as a general concept to talk about practices considered non-Christian. The attribution of inferiority to others in Portuguese is thus marked by the inferiority of the language into which it is translated. The choice of a term that is connected in a distanced way to the intellectual debate in the broader world of colonialism reflects Portugal's position within it (Messiant 2006).

In *On the Modern Cult of the Factish Gods*, Latour (2010) reproduces an anecdote that has become familiar in the anthropological and historical literature dealing with discourse on "fetishism" and "sorcery" in the colonial encounter. In a report sent by a Korean court official to Chinese authorities in the mid-18th century, "the peoples of fair skin" are said to worship their gods in a very particular way: after destroying fetishes in hidden rituals that confer them power, they restore the same fetishes after they feel the void of guilt. Anecdotes of this sort were also told in Angola by Protestant missionaries, who considered Catholics to be as fetishistic as local people. By the same token, the Protestant Bible was included in the divining basket of the *ovimbanda* (plural of *ocimbanda* or "medicine man") so that they could find out the misdeeds of Christian believers, in a performative critique of the Protestant attempt to ground its anti-fetishistic discourse in the Bible. The expression *feitiço do homem branco* (cf. Figueiredo 2009), translatable as "the white man's fetish," "the white man's spell," or "the white man's charm," points to a designation that ensued from the encounter between Portuguese colonizers and local people, a kind of translation into Portuguese of the strangeness that inheres in magic.

In the early 20th century, communication in the Central Highlands of Angola depended on interpreters because very few Umbundu speakers were fluent in Portuguese. As the dictionarization of Umbundu was in progress, the equivalences between Portuguese and vernacular expressions were unstable. Records of linguistic exchange involving Portuguese and Umbundu at the time are not vast. Available sources usually address the missionary effort to systematize the vernacular and translate doctrinal material into it. These sources seem to indicate that no term of comparable generalizing capacity was used in Umbundu to describe the set of practices that were classed under the rubric of *feitiço* in the colonial encounter. *Feitiço*, a kind of floating signifier, indexed an encompassing power while simultaneously othering the practices it named. Thus, the different terms used to refer to different actions in the vernacular, among which *umbanda* and *owanga* acquired prominence, came to be understood as instances of *feitiço. Feitiço* was assimilated to the hierarchization that governs colonization, but its juxtaposition with the vernacular categories that it came to encompass was not smooth.

Feitiço, Owanga, Umbanda

In colonial Portuguese–Umbundu dictionaries (Alves 1951; Guennec and Valente 1972), no entries for *fetiche*, *fetichismo*, and *feiticismo* are to be found. The only term in the series to appear as an entry is *feitiço*, which, as we have already noted, contains both concreteness and abstraction. *Feitiço* is presented as the term that translates into Portuguese all its imperfect equivalents in Umbundu. But it is not simply presented as the more abstract term for which one gives as examples concrete instances; rather, translation seeks to contain the proliferation of its possible empirical instantiations by choosing two concepts in Umbundu, *owanga* and *umbanda*, to be placed at approximately the same level of abstraction as *feitiço*.[5] This is the case to the extent that *feitiço* is understood to be that which the *feiticeiro* ("sorcerer") possesses, whereas *owanga* belongs to the *onganga* (the medicine man in its anti-social version, frequently translated as *feiticeiro*) and *umbanda* belongs to the *ocimbanda* (the *adivinho*, or "diviner," often understood to act on behalf of the community).[6] In the commensuration of these figures and their powers, *feitiço* is doubled as it is assigned a good and an evil dimension. But this doubling unsettles the specificity of *feitiço*, for in Portuguese it is something one does for one's own benefit. Thus, *feitiço* loses its specificity in translation and disseminates into the infinite practices it indexes to sorcery and magic.

One such manichaeistic equivalence is attempted in Bishop Alves's *Instruction to Catechists*, in which he equates *umbanda* with *curativos* ("remedies") and *awanga* (the plural of *owanga*) with *malefícios* ("evil deeds," "spells," or "charms") (Alves 1954, p. 68). Catholic missionary-ethnographer Valente states that *umbanda* is "any and all *feitiço*," whereas *owanga* is "a *feitiço* for harming a given person" and "might lead to death" (Valente 1973, p. 428). Yet, despite such attempts to index *owanga* to an evil side of supernatural power and *umbanda* to a positive and more encompassing one, this frontier is easily blurred. In Alves's Umbundu–Portuguese dictionary, positive and negative aspects of magical power are to be found in both entries, *umbanda* and *owanga*. One of the entries for *anga*, which is the root of *owanga*, defines it as "poisonous power" and an "evil doing [*malefício*] (which sorcerers cast during the night)" but also states that a good elder is measured by his *feitiço*:

> ANGA (ow; ovaw, aw)
>
> I. From *o / hanga (wanga)* = prolonged act, effect of / to be cast (active, awake). (…) Possibly from *o / hanga (wanga* and now *vanga)* = something of / packing (poisonous powder).
> II. S. Evil doing [*malefício*] (which sorcerers cast during the night).
> III. "*Itjiva tiyalonga vatjiseteka l'ongandu; ekongo liwa valiseteka l'owanga*" = A deep lake is measured by the crocodile; a good elder is measured by his *feitiço* (Alves 1951, p. 38).

The verbal entries for *mbanda* revolve around the subject of annihilation whereas the one corresponding to the noun *umbanda* includes "something of the medicine man," "evil doing, *feitiço*, medical science," "magic art," and "sorcery":

> MBANDA (u; ovo)
>
> I. From *u / 'mbanda* = something of / medicine man.
> II. S. Evil doing, *feitiço*; medical science.
> III. 1. "*Okûpako umbanda*" = To remove *feitiço* = To drink the first sip.
> 2. "*Okwinisa umbanda*" = To make swallow the magic art = To initiate in sorcery [*feitiçaria*] (Alves 1951, p. 660).

In the entries above, both *owanga* and *umbanda* are translated as *feitiço*. In the last one, *umbanda* is also translated as *feitiçaria* (sorcery). *Feitiço* appears as an act, an effect, a powder, the result of evil deeds, something one (the *ocimbanda* or *onganga*) can possess, and an art. It cuts across different grammatical categories and moral appreciations. It is as if the translation of all these things as *feitiço* were an attempt to control the dissemination of magical forces. *Umbanda* and *owanga* are also rendered as *feitiço* by Valente (1973, pp. 14, 27) in his collection of Umbundu proverbs. However, Umbundu expression responds to this contention drive with proliferation. This is how *feitiço* is translated into Umbundu in the dictionary put together by Valente and Le Guennec:

> ***Feitiço***, m.n. The sorcerer's evil doing [*malefício do feiticeiro*], *ondyangu, osilo, ochilungula, owanga, ulyangu, umbanda*; ... represented, *ombonha, ochihemba, ochiteka*; science of..., *umbanda, unganga*; various *feitiços* for: lovers, *ekulo, ochinjolele, onjole*; weapons, *ochiholo, ochiyoyo*; hunters, *elenge, ohuvi, syamemba, nuhanga;* fields, *olufuko, ochiñguma-ñguma*; rain, *upuli wombela*; money, *ekovo, ngeve, ofundi, oluhongo, osamba, otulundumba*; slave, *osamba*; wounds, *olonanda*; pregnancy, *olombamba*; inflammation, *olombando*; madness, *ochingalu, uyalwi*; rhetoric, *ochitunda, emaluvo*; prisoners, *eseleho*; wealth, *ehungu, namusungila, oluhongo, ombungu, onjawu*; kingdom, *ochimba*; traveler, *uvindiki*; to teach the art of ..., *+yambisa*; to remove a ..., *__nasi umbanda, +upa umbanda.*
>
> *(Valente and Le Guennec 1972, p. 276)*

In Lecomte's 1899 instruction to Umbundu-speaking catechists, the same difficulty in finding a general term arises:

> *Umbanda uâliapu umbanda upi?*
>
> *Umbanda uâliapu: âuanga, okuloua, okuliangula, okutaha, lokulimbingila lokunhua ombulungu.*
>
> What is magic art?
>
> Evil deeds and sortileges, the various types of divination, evocation of the dead, the poison ordeal, etc.
>
> *(Lecomte 1899, p. 32–33).*

Through the question "What is magic art?" Lecomte wishes to let people know which actions are forbidden by the Catholic church. But the question he asks in Portuguese and the answer he provides are not easily translated into Umbundu. In the first place, the translation does not convey the negative meaning that is immediately implied by such a question in Portuguese. Thus, the solution Lecomte finds is a double one: in order to render "magic art" in Umbundu, he resorts to the term *umbanda*, which is one of the two terms that have become the most general in translation, and adds to it the qualification *uâliapu*, i.e. "of the devil," *eliapu* being the Umbundization of *diabo*, the Portuguese word for "devil." In Umbundu, the question would read approximately like this: "What are the *umbanda* of *eliapu*?," i.e., the *umbanda* of the devil, *eliapu* being not that widespread a figure at that time and *umbanda* not necessarily applying to all the items in the enumeration the answer provides. The enumeration is not as lengthy as the above-mentioned one in Valente's dictionary but also includes disparate elements: in it, *âuanga* (pl. of *owanga*) is encompassed by the term that will later be classed as the more benign one: *umbanda*.

Feitiço, like the "fetish," disseminates in translation. *Feitiço* seems to be whatever one does to obtain something one lacks or desires. One can use it to harm others; obtain lovers, weapons, money, and wealth; be successful in hunting; make rain; heal wounds; get pregnant; obtain protection for one's travels; escape slavery; escape madness or make someone mad; and even become a distinguished orator or make someone lose the capacity to speak meaningfully. *Feitiço* is purpose-oriented. Moreover, each *feitiço* has a name, and names of *feitiços* ("fetish" names?) commonly mime the work that is done to achieve their purposes. According to fetishism, in the "fetish" one seeks to conflate language and the world through reification. But the concept of fetishism, as an "ism," both opens the gap between language and the world in order to be able to point out the arbitrariness that connects speech and action and sutures the very gap it opens. The response of the "fetish" to the abstraction of "fetishism" is dissemination. It is not witchcraft or sorcery in general that explains every event; rather, each *feitiço* accounts for one kind of event. And if success is thus explained, so is failure; for the "fetish" is marked by the indeterminacy of its result.

In colonial Angola, there was much discussion about the translation of God, the holy spirit, and sin, to name but a few (cf. Dulley 2009). Translations were kept or rejected depending on the effects they seemed to have on the behavior of those that colonial power and Christian missions wished to convert to Christianity and its underlying morality. Yet, the translation of *feitiço* into so many vernacular equivalents remained uncontested. Practice seems not to have revealed many incongruities. I contend that this is because *feitiço* was already a hybrid concept, formed in historical encounters not only on the Western coast of Africa but also in Europe. It, therefore, contained a sedimented history of displacement that made it permeable to dissemination. The "fetish" accommodates desire in its promise to stop the flow of contingency. Translation does something similar.

The "Fetish" in Translation

Like the "fetish," translation is magic that operates through coupling, contagion, and fixation. Both are marked by undecidability and therefore must be tested. Fixity arises from a process of commensuration that, when concluded, looks like it was always meant to be. If language precedes and exceeds the work of commensuration that translation supposes, it is also true that such work is never finished, for what is translated necessarily escapes fixation. The equivalent of the materiality that resists being reduced to the abstraction of fetishism might be, in translation, the multiplication of meaning entailed by the juxtaposition of concepts. Hence the dissemination that governs every chain of substitution.

The transliterative iteration in which *feitiço* becomes *fetisso*, *fetiche*, *fétiche*, *Fetisch*, "fetish" is followed by the apposition of a similar suffix (*ismo*, *isme*, *ismus*, "ism") to these instances of materiality. This supplement marks the addition of abstraction to a practice that is defined by its relation to concreteness. Nevertheless, as supplements, such iterations in the form of "isms" depend on the materiality of the "fetish" for their existence. As in fetishism, one insufflates a concrete noun with abstraction in the hope that it might reach transcendence, but the supplement depends on that which it aims to surpass. Conversely, it is only possible to name "fetishes" because one has already supplemented them in abstraction.

In the set of translations above, "fetishism," as an abstract universal, sutures in a ghostly way. It is rarely apparent in its own name. Rather, it operates in the name of the "fetish." But it does appear in a modified form, not as fetishism (*fetichismo*) but as *feiticismo*, an accusatory description that seeks to bridge the gap between the concrete concept and the abstract universal. In so doing, it attempts to dilute the borders of the "fetish" (uneasily equated with *feitiço*) and of unmentioned "fetishism." It introduces spacing between them but does not quite create another concept that might be added in-between. This is probably the case because the Portuguese language was not one in which one could aspire to universal universalism. Universalism, within Portuguese colonial rule, was restricted to the particularity of its own uncertain borders. Thus, the concepts employed in the othering of colonial subjects lacked the apparent fixity of fetishism's "ism." The spacing *feiticismo* introduces between the concrete concept and the abstract universal promises to suture by means of translation. But this attempt at commensuration is lost in that vernacular expression is deprived of the possibility of aspiring to the universal. What is translation, if not the "fetish" of suture? It promises the possibility of equivalence but can hardly contain dissemination.

Notes

1 I thank Rosalind Morris, James Siegel, Maria José de Abreu, and Evanthia Patsiaoura for their comments and encouragement. The research based on which this text was written was funded by FAPESP (The São Paulo Research Foundation), for which I am very grateful.

2 "*Osoma nda ya fa pamue va yi tundisako, u o vialako o pañinyavo ocimbanda caye oku pongolola ovina viosi viovombanda vokuavo, momo hati, Ka ci tava oku piñala kovombanda vosoma yiñi. Vombundi yetemo mu enda etemo liñi lumbanda waco*". In: *Customs of the Ombala (Capital) of Bailundu*. The source, available at the Archives of the American Board of Commissioners for Foreign Missions, Houghton Library, ABC 15.1, v. 44, was transcribed, commented and translated by Julino Didimo and the author (Dulley 2021). The text from which the quote was extracted was registered in Umbundu at the Bailundo Mission in the Central Highlands of Angola in the beginning of the 20th century. It is an account of ritual practices in Bailundo prior to the establishment of colonial administration. Its author is not named.

3 Portuguese presence in the Central Highlands dates back to the slave trade (Candido 2013), but the region was only submitted to colonial rule after the 1902-1903 Bailundo war. Before this, foreigners depended on the permission of local rulers to trade and settle in this region.

4 De Brosses (2017, p. 48) takes *fetisso* for the Portuguese word.

5 In the Kongo region, Laman seems to have found one word in Kikongo to stand for the idea of the "fetish": *nkisi*, which he then divided between *nkisi mi nloko* and *nkisi mi bimenga*. Yet, as MacGaffey's article shows, attempts to contain dissemination through the translation of the former as "cursing charms" and the latter as "blood sacrifice charms" failed, for "[a] charm with the same name and function did not always appear in the same form" (MacGaffey 1977, p. 176).

6 In an ethnographic text titled "*O que é um feiticeiro*" ["What is a sorcerer"], in which Estermann considers aspects related to sorcery throughout Angola, he affirms that "the *onganga* is the possessor of *owanga*", translated as "*feitiço*, supernatural force" (Estermann 1983, p. 346–351). For him, *ouanga*, or *wanga*, is "a harmful magic power whose purpose is to cause disease and death among men, and rarely among domestic animals" (Estermann 1983, p. 331). He attributes the vagueness of his definition to the fact that "the blacks themselves" (*os próprios pretos*) have no clear notion of such a mysterious force whose effects are disastrous. The *ouanga* has the power to kill (Estermann 1983, p. 31), and it is through killing ("eating") others that one becomes a powerful *onganga*. The *kimbanda* is, according to Estermann (1983, p. 314), imperfectly translatable as *sorcier*, medicine man, or *Zauberer*. All translations from Portuguese are mine.

References

Alves, Albino. 1951. *Dicionário Etimológico Bundo-Português*. Lisbon: Silvas.

———. 1954. *Directorio dos catequistas*. Huambo: Tipografia da Missão do Cuando.

Appadurai, Arjun. (ed.). 1986. *The Social Life of Things: Commodities in Cultural Perspective*. Cambridge: Cambridge University Press.

Candido, Mariana. 2013. *An African Slaving Porto and the Atlantic World: Benguela and Its Hinderland*. Cambridge: Cambridge University Press.

De Brosses, Charles. 2017. "On the Worship of Fetish Gods". In: Morris, Rosalind & Leonard, Daniel (eds.), *The Returns of Fetishism: Charles de Brosses and the afterlives of an idea*. Chicago: University of Chicago Press.

Derrida, Jacques. 1981. *Dissemination*. Chicago: University of Chicago Press.

———. 1985. "Des tours de Babel". In Graham, Joseph (ed.), *Difference in Translation*. Ithaca: Cornell University Press.

———. 1986. *Glas*. Lincoln: University of Nebraska Press.

———. 1997. *Of Grammatology*. Baltimore: Johns Hopkins University Press.

———. 2009. *The Beast and the Sovereign. Volume I*. Chicago: University of Chicago Press.

Dulley, Iracema. 2009. "Notes on a Disputed Process of Signification: The Practice of Communication in Spiritan Missions in the Central Highlands of Angola". In: *Vibrant* 5(2): 231–255.

———. 2010. *Deus é feiticeiro: prática e disputa nas missões católicas em Angola colonial*. São Paulo: Annablume.

———. 2018. "Angola". In: Lamport, Mark (ed.), *Encyclopedia of Christianity in the Global South*. Lanham: Rowman & Littlefield Publishers.

———. 2019. *On the Emic Gesture: Difference and Ethnography in Roy Wagner*. London and New York: Routledge.

———. 2021. "Chronicles of Bailundo: A Fragmentary Account in Umbundu of Life Before and After Portuguese Colonial Rule". In: *Africa* 91(5): 713–741.

Estermann, Carlos. 1983. *Etnografia de Angola (Sudoeste e Centro). Coletânea de artigos dispersos. Volume II*. Lisbon: IICT.

Figueiredo, João. "'Feitiço do homem branco': ruptura e continuidade na concepção de 'feitiço' nos diários de viagem de António Brandão de Mello (1909–1915)". In: *Mneme* 10(26).

Guennec, Grégoire e Valente, José Francisco. 1972. *Dicionário português-umbundu*. Luanda: Instituto de Investigação Científica de Angola.

Latour, Bruno. 2010. *On the Modern Cult of the Factish Gods*. Durham: Duke University Press.
Lecomte, Ernesto. 1899. *Ondaka ia suku ou Doutrina Christa em umbundu e portuguez*. Luanda: Imprensa Nacional.
MacGaffey, Wyatt. 1977. "Fetishism Revisited: Kongo 'Nkisi' in Sociological Perspective". In: *Africa: Journal of the International African Institute* 47(2): 172–184.
Marx, Karl. 1987 [1867]. *Das Kapital: Kritik der politischen Ökonomie*. Berlin: Dietz Verlag.
———. 1992 [1867]. *Capital*. Volume I. New York: Penguin.
Messiant, Christine. 2006. *1961. L'Angola colonial, histoire et société*. Basel: Schlettwein Publishing.
Montero, Paula. 1985. *Da doença à desordem: a magia na umbanda*. Rio de Janeiro: Graal.
Morris, Rosalind. 2017a. "'Fetishism (Supposing That It Existed)': A Preface to the Translation of Charles de Brosses's Transgression." In: Morris, Rosalind & Leonard, Daniel (eds.), *The Returns of Fetishism: Charles de Brosses and the afterlives of an Idea*. Chicago: University of Chicago Press.
———. 2017b. "After de Brosses: Fetishism, Translation, Comparativism, Critique." In: Morris, Rosalind & Leonard, Daniel (eds.), *The Returns of Fetishism: Charles de Brosses and the Afterlives of an Idea*. Chicago: University of Chicago Press.
Pietz, William. 1985. "The Problem of the Fetish, I". In: *RES: Journal of Anthropology and Aesthetics* 9: 5–17.
———. 1987. "The Problem of the Fetish, II: The Origin of the Fetish". In: *RES: Journal of Anthropology and Aesthetics* 11: 23–45.
Sansi-Roca, Roger. 2007. "The Fetish in the Lusophone Atlantic". In Naro, N. P., Sansi-Roca, R. & Treece, D. (eds.), *Cultures of the Lusophone Black Atlantic*. London: Palgrave MacMillan.
Siegel, James. 1997. *Fetish, Recognition, Revolution*. Princeton: Princeton University Press.
Valente, José. 1973. *Paisagem africana (uma tribo angolana no seu fabulário)*. Luanda: Instituto de Investigação Científica de Angola.
———. 1974. *Namussunguila, a Ceres umbundu*. Luanda: IICA.

PART VI

Rooted Words

17

NONGQAYI/NONGQAI[1]

Hlonipha Mokoena

> Asibonanga – ngani: Kwati – tu nduli yimbi ka Xakeka, eyatsho saxakeka ngenyani: Amahashi o Nongqai esiza kuti kanye enga sapali etsiba izihogo – : Zabaleka Inkokeli zona engekafiki nokufika lomahashiapo e Gantolo: Zati ziyoyika ngokumhlophe azafihla: Kuba ziluvile "Utyikityo olwenziwe ngo Nongqai e Fidasdolopu ngezolo …
>
> *(Mgqwetho 2007, 253)*

> What did we see? Another hill. Difficulty suddenly confronted us, scattering confusion. Tinpot cops on horseback charged us down, at full tilt, like bats out of hell. Our leaders took to their heels before those horses reached the Fort. They made no bones about their fear, saying they'd been pounded by the Tinpots at Fordsburg the day before.
>
> *(Mgqwetho 2007, 252)*

This vignette from Nontsizi Mgqwetho's short account titled "Yintsomi yo Nomeva/The tale of the wasps", is about a pass protest that occurred in Johannesburg in 1919. It is an indictment of political leaders who abandon their followers as soon as they are confronted by the police. This account would not have been significant since it could be read as one among many such accounts of a clash between protesters and the police. However, what is striking about her account is that she used the word "Nongqai". She thereby indicates that the word was also used by Xhosa-speakers (and hence not a specifically Zulu word) and also that as a poet who was publishing her work in newspapers, she preferred to use what was the Anglicized spelling of the word. This helps to establish the fact that "Nongqai" may not have been the invention of white police officers but that it was also used by literate Nguni-speakers. Secondly, her use of this word confounds the translators (Jeff Opland and Phyllis Ntantala) in that they choose the term "tinpot cops" as

DOI: 10.4324/9781003273530-23

an equivalent to "Nongqai". By giving the word an overtly political meaning, the translators forgo the etymological problem that confronted lexicographers and the military when attempting to define or appropriate this word.

This chapter is about those difficulties – the linguistic, cultural, and militaristic difficulties of a word that became associated with black men in uniform but whose provenance is debatable and even controversial. It would be an exaggeration to claim that this chapter is somehow going to resolve these difficulties; that is not its purpose. Its purpose is to stitch together what seem to be discrete and separate realms – the world of policing and the world of lexicography, as an example – into a speculative argument about why this word gained so much power. When Mgqwetho was writing her account in the 1920s, she was living in Johannesburg, an urban setting in which one would have expected a different vocabulary for "the police" and yet, she resorts to what could be thought of as the rural diction that her mother or even grandmother may have used. From her urban location, she also reveals the antagonism that existed between the educated black literati and what was presumed to be the illiterate and boorish class of men who became policemen. The translators, in some ways, exaggerate this antagonism (as might be expected) by exactly translating "Nongqai" into "tinpot" as if these policemen were inauthentic versions of something else (presumably white policemen) when in fact, as the chapter hopes to show, white policemen were using "Nongqai" as an idealization of what they wanted to be.

The Zulu Raconteurs and their Kindred

Linguistically, dictionaries are the readily available source for checking the provenance or etymology of a word. Although this may seem uncontroversial enough in the case of English, for example, the matter becomes a little more complicated in the case of *isiZulu* (even writing the name of the language in this manner is a contestable choice). This is because Zulu lexicography as it exists today owes its origins to missionaries and their desire to translate the Bible into indigenous languages. As such, there is always, therefore, the suspicion that their religious motives clouded their intellectual capabilities as scholars. In qualitative terms, however, "the missionary era" of lexicography and book publishing represents the high-point of indigenous language publication precisely because it was done at local printing presses using the skills of indigenously trained printers and typesetters. This means that the final product was not actually the outcome of the singular efforts of "the missionary" but in fact the product of a team of workers many of whom were African. This latter point is often lost in debates on indigenous languages since there is a presumption that texts produced by missionaries inevitably had a religious bent to them when in fact they didn't. The "bent" that such texts actually had is that they in fact presented the language in question as "pure" and uninfluenced by regional dialects, or by cognate languages. Thus, in advertising his Zulu–English dictionary, John William Colenso drew a line in the sand and separated "pure Zulu" from its dialects and accents. He wrote:

In making use of this Dictionary, the following points should be noticed by the Student.

1. It is a *Zulu*-English Dictionary; and, therefore, is meant to contain, as far as possible, only pure Zulu words, and not such words as belong to the amaXosa Kafirs, and to the other kindred tribes, which inhabit the Southern part of this Colony.
2. It does not contain peculiarities of dialect, which are heard among different tribes, such as those which *tefula* or *tekeza* in their speech (*Grammar*, 5, 6, 7), or that of the abaNtungwa, who insert a *guttural* between the *nasal* and *click*, where others do not, as *ngcono* for *ncono*. (Colenso 1861, iii)

By adding the emphasis in italics, Colenso was not only reminding the reader of the *Zulu* as an ethnic group, but he was also spatially separating them from their "kindred" whom he located south of the colony of Natal. Nearly half a century later in 1905, A.T. Bryant printed his *Zulu–English Dictionary* and he even goes further in the assertion of the purity of the Zulu language. He asserts that the copious vocabulary that Zulus are exposed to is not only an expression of an expansive imagination but that the Zulu speaker is as "active" in their exercise of language as the European.

> We present it [the Zulu language] in this work in its primeval purity. Of the 20,000 words herein contained, not more than a couple of dozen will be found to be exotic importations. This may be a startling announcement to those who, mindful of the assertion that the daily speech of the average English peasant does not embrace more than a total of a few hundred words, had concluded that the vocabulary of a savage race must be equally small. The fact shows that the brain of the African black, of whose thoughts these words are the tangible manifestation, is, in so far as language can be a criterion (a point clearly to be noted), not a whit less active and capable than that of the average European.
>
> *(Bryant 1905, 7)*

This comparative mode becomes one of the tools of Zulu lexicography and both Colenso and Bryant deploy several such tactics in order to place Zulu in a global polyglot world in which all languages are inherently "transparent" and translatable. Thus, from this perspective, the missionary printing and publishing of books is not as earth-shattering as their claim that they were doing so in the name of "pure languages". This assertion of unadulterated and discrete languages belies the presence of the already existing linguistic otherness in which "non-dominant" groups spoke variations of the "pure" language. The point of criticism is that the missionaries didn't think that such marginalization actually impoverished the very languages that they were claiming supremacy for. The word "Nongqayi" thus becomes one of those words that represent the pure versus impure fissure created by the missionary lexicographers. In this way, the word takes its first incarnation as a talisman, protecting the missionary lexicographer from being accused of being outside the Zulu language and therefore unable to grasp the nuances of the language. We could go so far as to argue that the missionary, by virtue of his act of sifting the language of foreign detritus, was already asserting that the word "Nongqayi" belonged to some intrinsic and immutable language vault which only the Zulus had access to. Thus, in his 1905 edition of his dictionary, Bryant classes "u-nongqayi" as a word that represents the Zulu language's ability to innovate by forming new words for new concepts and realities. It is worth quoting him at length since he makes statements that do more than explain what words mean but, in fact, speculate about the destiny of the language itself. He thus writes,

> Owing to its unrivalled onomatopoetic capabilities, it provides both a medium of lifelike expression that the cleverest European raconteur could never aspire to, and offers an ever-ready means for the coining of endless new words. That a language is possessed of abundant inherent qualities allowing the facile coinage of new words is a strong and healthy characteristic showing that it is capable of responding to much further intellectual growth and material progress on the part of the people speaking it. Now, the Zulu possesses this characteristic to a truly remarkable degree. Indeed, in certain respects it is probable that no living European language, if left only to its own resources and unable to borrow from other languages, could even compare with it; for, given merely a sound or a peculiarity of motion – and sound and motion include a good deal – the Native can coin nouns and verbs with ease and to an unlimited degree, dignified in form and expressive to life. Quite a large number of the older words have undoubtedly been formed in this way – names of birds, names of beasts, names of actions of every description, and a multitude of verbs. Nor is this power and process already dead. As witness of this, we have the words *u-mbayimbayi* (cannon), *m-ntuluntulu* (maxim gun), *u-nongqayi* (policeman), *u-noxaka* (iron-trap), *u-boziyembe* (shirt-front), and quite a number of other modern and intelligently formed nouns, invented, not by missionaries, but by the raw, uneducated Native."
>
> *(Bryant 1905, 7–8)*

Thus, the word "u-nongqayi" not only represents the fissure drawn between the pure and the impure; it is also a testament to the onomatopoeic capacities of Zulu speakers. However, what seems like contemporaneity – the "average" Zulu being compared to the "average" English peasant – is a scale of civilization in which the Zulus are stumbling for words in search for an index of the modern. As would occur elsewhere in missionary scholarship, the Zulus' facile dexterity with language becomes both proof of their fossilized and antiquated ethnic typology while at the same time, opening up the space for linguistic and cultural upgrading. Thus, what is notable about the Zulu vocabulary is that it is being constantly renewed not by the efforts of the missionary but by the "raw, uneducated Native".

By situating the word "u-nongqayi" within a continuum of other modern nouns, Bryant positioned Zulu speakers as being both exceedingly modern and irreversibly backward. This is because what starts off as a compliment – praising the language for its onomatopoeic capacities – ends with the stereotype of the "raw, uneducated Native" who is perhaps "accidentally" tripping over words in the search for concepts and ideas capacious enough to capture the rapid and unrelenting arrival of the modern world. Thus, what may seem at first to be linguistic contemporaneity – the comparison of your "average" Zulu with your "average" English peasant – becomes a scale of civilization in which the Zulus (and by implication their language) are constantly approaching modernity but can never reach it. The word "Nongqayi" is therefore being positioned, even before its lexicographic entry is presented, as a novelty; a word that has arrived in the Zulu language together with other modern objects and nouns whether it is cannons or shirt fronts. The actual meaning of the word is, therefore, already anticipated in its categorization as "modern", a word of the impure or tainted Zulu. Through this double bind, the missionary invented a dilemma that would continue to haunt future debates on indigenous languages while at the same time placing the Zulu policeman in the crosshairs as an undefinable contamination.

The work of the lexicographer is, therefore, to draw the boundaries of this taint or at least to limit its damage by posting warning signs around it, as Bryant does. However, the actual entries for the word introduce new complexities rather than solve the original complexity, namely, is it a Zulu word or not. Again here, Bryant and Colenso are exemplary. For Bryant, the word actually deserves two entries, the first the contemporary meaning and then the second the historicized meaning. Under "u-Nongqayi" he gives the following explanation: "Name given to the Natal Police; also to Zululand Native Police" (Bryant 1905, 440). To our contemporary mind, such an explanation does not make sense since it seems to localize the meaning of the word rather than tell us what the word refers to. The two geographies of "Natal Police" versus "Zululand Native Police" also don't make sense. This distinction will become clearer once we examine the military and policing history of the Nongqayi. For now, it is sufficient to point out that what Bryant is referring to is the "colony" of Natal and the balkanized Zulu kingdom which became "Zululand". The implication is that both the "raw" Zulus and the "colonized" Zulus are using the same word for "police". However, what Bryant does not tell us is how this word has traveled. Is it a word that was coined in the colony and then moved to the Zulu kingdom or vice-versa? By presenting the traffic of words as a historical fact and yet failing to explain how it happens, Bryant created yet another lacuna into which the work of policing could remain shrouded in mystification and mythology. As if to compensate for exactly this lacuna in meaning, Bryant offers the reader an alternative reading of the word by adding at the end of the entry, "see gqaya". In other words, Bryant is suggesting that the noun "u-nongqayi" is derived from the verb "gqaya". The presentation of two meanings opens up the chasm that Bryant had already presented between "new" and "old" words, the pure and the impure. Importantly, this diversion or redirection places the burden on the readers. If the reader really wants to know what the word means, they have to page to a different part of the dictionary to find the meaning there. As it turns out, Bryant's strategy is useful since as stated above, his entries introduce complexity rather than resolve it. Thus, under "gqaya", Bryant inserts, "Look at observingly (almost obsolete)" (1905, 197). So, the implication is that the word "u-nongqayi" comes from the Zulu verb for close observation; a "nongqayi" is, therefore, a close observer. The unobservant reader would not see that a few entries down, Bryant has inserted another word which is neither referred to in the entry on "u-nongqayi" nor under "gqaya". Hidden in plain sight is the entry, "u-Gqayinyanga n. Night-watchman, for guarding the *isi-Godhlo* in the royal kraals = *i(li)Vakashi*". The immediate question then is what is the difference between "u-nongqayi" and "u-Gqayinyanga" since the two words come from the same verb "gqaya" a connection which Bryant neglects to make? More importantly, why does Bryant fail to point this out to the reader? Why, in other words, is "u-Gqayinyanga" given an entry that connects it to no other words in the Zulu language while "u-nongqayi" is given as a derivative word? The possible explanation is that in his eagerness to separate "old" from "new" words, Bryant has misread the "nightwatchman" as being conceptually different from "policeman". This is further demonstrated by his willingness to link "u-Gqayinyanga" with the old practice of Zulu kings of keeping a "harem" *(isi-Godhlo)* and thereby give the word a sheen of antiquity which it may not deserve.

Through this sleight of hand, Bryant turns two words that are actually synonymous into two opposing narratives – the one is a narrative of how policing is a "foreign" imposition while the other is the idea that Zulu kings exercised their power over women by placing them under the observing eye of a nightwatchman. For Bryant, it is a case of two words, two concepts, two histories. The excessive historical burdening of the word is completely absent in Colenso, who (using a different orthography) has an entry under "uQainnyanga", and he gives the definition as, "Sentinel, night-watch, (one who gets the first glimpse of the moon)". (Colenso 1861, 410). By not attempting to historicize the word, Colenso normalizes the meaning and function of the night watch; they are soldiers who keep watch while others sleep, hence his universalizing gesture of equating "uQainnyanga" with "Sentinel". Unlike Bryant therefore, Colenso seems to be suggesting that the Zulu word for nightwatchman is already in the world of the "universal"; there is no bifurcation necessary.

This brief discussion of dictionary entries from two missionary scholars – A.T. Bryant and John William Colenso – is not exhaustive and many other dictionary entries could have been included. The objective was not to provide a survey of nineteenth-century Zulu dictionaries but to point to the disagreements (voluble and tacit) between different authors about what a "policeman" in the Zulu language is or was. The disputed word "uNongqayi" appears in different guises in different dictionaries and the obvious question to ask is what kind of evidence does this constitute? Importantly, does the dispute between missionary lexicographers equal a dispute between native speakers? What if this is just a case of another word that is being "lost in translation"? Although these are all possibilities; this discussion wasn't meant to resolve the question of what the word "uNongqayi" means; it was merely meant to indicate that dictionaries can generate more questions than they answer and that lexicographers are often responsible for opening the already existing yawns between "old" and "new" words, "pure" and "impure" words by their act of selective listening and "reading" of a language. Thus, what seems to separate Bryant from Colenso is their willingness to draw a historical line that links a Zulu "watchman" and a colonial "policeman".

The Zululand Native Police

The military history of "uNongqayi" follows the same thread as the etymological history since it is also prefaced with the search for meaning. Thus, in his 2001 *uNongqayi: A History of the Zululand Native Police*, Cubbin provides no less than 12 definitions and guesses as to what the word means. Thus, even before telling us what the policing or military unit that was given the name "Nongqayi" was about, he warns that the multiplicity of potential meanings renders the "onomastics" (his heading) of the word elusive. He tells the readers, "You may be disappointed with my suggestion that "Nongqai" means neither more nor less than 'Police', but unfortunately grammar is sometimes less romantic than conjecture." (Cubbin 2001, 11). Although intent on simplifying his narrative on the history of the Nongqayi, Cubbin fails to actually explain whether the Nongqayi were a military or police corps. But before discussing this, it may be useful to give a brief history of when the corps was established and disbanded. According to Cubbin's history, the uNongqyayi corps was established in 1883, "under the name of the Reserve Territory Carabineers as a bodyguard for the new Resident Commissioner and Chief Magistrate of Zululand, Melmoth Osborn" (Cubbin 2001, 12).

Although informative, this description obscures the historical context of this establishment, namely, that it occurred as a consequence of the end of the Anglo-Zulu War, the exile of the Zulu king Cetshwayo, and the dismemberment of his kingdom. The term "reserve" was used to define the territories that were now under the control of Cetshwayo's opponents, especially his contrarian relative Zibhebhu who was an ally of the British. Thus, the Nongqayi were formed as an expression of the British empire's desire to curb and restrict the power of the *uSuthu* (the Zulu royal house and nobility) rather than as a regular policing force. What is notable about the force is that it was armed and trained to use rifles (Cubbin 2001, 15). This latter fact is what precipitated their disbandment since beginning with the Police Act of 1894, Natal's settler politicians expressed and enacted legislation that gave the colony more control over black soldiers and police. Although it took a decade to be effected, the Nongqayi were eventually disbanded in September of 1904 (Cubbin 2001, 35). This was after their illustrious service during the Anglo-Boer War, now called the South African War, between 1899 and 1902. Ironically, when the Bhambatha rebellion broke out in 1906, the force had to be reconstituted (Cubbin 2001, 35–36). It is this latter moment that crystallized the image of the Nongqayi as "traitors". Rather than focus on the events that occurred between 1883 and 1906, it may be more useful to present descriptions of who the Nongqayi were and why they were brought into existence.

In the aftermath of the Anglo-Zulu War (1879), the defeat of Cetshwayo by the British opened a political and spatial vacuum that led to the creation of "Zululand" which was an extension of the Natal colony without being a British colony (the official colonization of Zululand only took place in 1897). In order to manage the partition of the Zulu kingdom and the borders of the Zulu Native Reserve (which was created to apportion territory to Cetshwayo's enemies), the colonial officials recruited men from Natal. From the historian's perspective, this becomes doubly important since what was being created was a black anti-uSuthu military force that was then imported into Zululand. Thus, Jeff Guy expresses this manipulation of "Zuluness" as a form of mendacity on the part of the colonial government:

> Soon permission was obtained to place "Government men" (that is, Natal Africans) armed with rifles on the boundary of the Reserve to keep a check on who was crossing into Cetshwayo's territory ... Under two white officers these men were to form the core of the Zululand Native Police, the notorious *Nongqayi.*
>
> *(Guy 1994, 188)*

The reason why it is important to underscore the notoriety of the Nongqayi is that it supports the idea that these men were "imported" or "Natal" Zulus who were therefore amenable, due to their proximity to colonial governance and power, to being used to undermine an indigenous ruler. This is the moment in which it could also be said that, as with the missionary lexicographers, the word escapes its confinement as either "foreign" or "indigenous" and is left open to capture by the Resident Commissioner who, no doubt, wished to elevate himself to the position of a "Zulu" potentate. In Guy's description, the implication is that the Nongqayi's lack of loyalty to the Zulu kingdom was due to the spatial and ideological remove from the kingdom. However, in his book on the Bhambatha rebellion of 1906, the same historian presents a slightly nuanced reading of the position and function of the Nongqayi. He notes that,

> In times of conflict the names that one side give to the other are often more than descriptive – they also reveal strong feelings of antagonism. Thus the men who opposed the government were known as rebels, or *umShokobezi*,

> after the white coattails they wore – an insignia of the royal house. Africans fighting on the colonial side were known as "levies", "loyal" by the troops and *amambuka* (traitors) by the rebels. They played an important role in putting down the rebellion, not only in the drives in to the forests, but also in pursuing those who attempted to escape, and in burning homesteads and looting cattle. The military also held them responsible for its failures and blamed its African allies when reports of atrocities reached the press. The *Nongqayi* were the armed Zulu Police. They were used by the colonial authorities but also feared – a fact that explains their history. Founded in 1883 they fought on the colonial side in the civil wars of the 1880s and for the British in the 1899–1902 war with the Boers, but were broken up by the Natal government in 1904. They were formed again in 1906 to fight against the rebels – and retrenched again when rebellion was over and they were no longer needed.
>
> *(Guy 2006, 90)*

The second description of the Nongqayi places them in a continuum of positions between "loyalty" and "betrayal" rather than forcing them into the binary position of being "traitors". The nuanced interpretation creates more of a space for multiple readings of who these men were. Notwithstanding such a generous interpretation, it should not be forgotten that the manipulation of the boundary between "loyalty" and "betrayal" was also part of the colonial discourse. Thus, in praising the work of the Nongqayi, Cubbin cites Colonel George Mansel who praised them in the following terms:

> Their instincts are wholly military. When you enlist a Zulu you have a ready-made soldier, all his tendencies are martial. All you have to do is teach them how to handle a rifle. This you can do in three or four months .... He is, as a rule, the best tempered, easiest-managed man in the world, understands discipline by instinct, is docile, plucky, proud of himself and his Corps, kindly disposed towards his officers, full of mettle and capable of enduring extremes of marching and hunger. His almost only failure is that he sometimes overstays his pass. The trained Zulu works splendidly with white men in the field. I may add that, though the Zululand Police were often fighting against their own kith and kin, not a single case of treachery or breach of faith ever occurred.
>
> *(Cubbin 2001, 39–40)*

Thus, from a military perspective, the working assumption was that the Nongqayi were being employed because they were "Zulus" and, therefore, natural soldiers and also because they could be relied upon to fight their own "kith and kin". The enduring attractiveness and allure of this notion of a "martial" tendency are seen in the fact that when the Natal Police created a magazine in 1907, they named it *The Nongqai.* This magazine was published in Pietermaritzburg, Natal from 1907 to 1913 when it became the official magazine for the unified South African Police Force. The magazine retained its name until 1961 when it became *Justitia.* The irony is that although this magazine was given a Zulu name, its pages were dedicated to the interests of white officers and only occasionally would there be a photograph of black policemen or a letter from one of them.

Conclusion

The stereotype of the African levy as a traitor is a standard starting point for describing the world of black men in uniform. In the case of South Africa, the term "askari" represents the manifold histories of the co-optation of black men into military service. Out of this history of traitors and turncoats, the word "Nongqayi" emerges as a forgotten and receding history. To begin with, the confusion was created at a linguistic and lexicographic level when missionary scholars attempted to define the world of the nightwatchman by referring obliquely to his origins as a sentinel of the Zulu king's "harem". Alternatively, the missionary scholar would suggest that the uNongqayi was an interloper, a tainted and foreign intrusion introduced to the Zulu language by the plasticity of the Zulu imagination. The traffic from word to concept would, however, elude the missionary scholars who more often than not preferred to leave the word alone to float and be appropriated by those who wanted it to mean either "nightwatchman", "policeman" or "traitor".

This chapter has attempted to bring the Nongqayi into the foreground as men who had an ambiguous status even while they were being deployed as the allies of the British empire. Their ambiguity lies in the fact that they were neither soldiers nor police and they were also "foreign" Zulus from Natal. The chapter has presented the basic argument that both the "nightwatchman" and the "police" are concepts that confounded lexicographers and military officials and that the ultimate benefactor was perhaps the latter. Although there is a fine line between recovering the Nongqayi's histories and an apology for colonial brutality, this chapter is not an attempt to rehabilitate their reputation. Rather, it is part of a larger work on the visual history of black men in uniform the aim of which is to show how military clothing seeped and suffused popular culture in the nineteenth century and how the "Zulu policeman" became an emblem for this type of sartorial colonialism.

Note

1 The variations in the spelling and orthography of this word make it impossible to choose a title that uses only one spelling thus the use of the two most common spellings.

References

Bryant, A.T. 1905. *A Zulu-English Dictionary with Notes on Pronunciation: A Revised Orthography and Derivations and Cognate Words from Many Languages; Including Also a Vocabulary of Hlonipa Words, Tribal-names, Etc., a Synopsis of Zulu Grammar and a Concise History of the Zulu People from the Most Ancient Times*. Maritzburg and Durban: P. Davis & Sons.

Colenso, John W. 1861. *Zulu-English Dictionary*. Pietermaritzburg: P. Davis.

Cubbin, Tony. 2001. *UNongqayi: A History of the Zululand Native Police*. Eshowe: Zululand Historical Museum.

Guy, Jeff. 1994. *The Destruction of the Zulu Kingdom: The Civil War in Zululand, 1879–1884*. Pietermaritzburg: University of Natal Press. Original edition, 1979.

Guy, Jeff. 2006. *Remembering the Rebellion: The Zulu Uprising of 1906*. Scottsville: University of KwaZulu-Natal Press.

Mgqwetho, Nontsizi. 2007. *The Nation's Bounty: The Xhosa Poetry of Nontsizi Mgqwetho*. Translated by Jeff Opland. Johannesburg: Wits University Press.

18

NAAM

Amy Niang

This chapter is concerned with the historical and the ideological fundaments of the *Naam*, a concept that was central to the history of state-building in the pre-colonial Voltaic region (present Burkina Faso, parts of Ghana, Niger, and Mali) between the 16th and the 19th centuries. It is part of a long-term research project in state and social formation in Africa using the Mossi states system as a case study. The Mossi states system emerged in the 16th century in a context of regional effervescence that gave non-centralised societies a geopolitical frame within which to position themselves, vis-à-vis centralised groups. The decline of the greatest empire around the Niger Bend, namely the Songhai Empire, inaugurated critical transformations compounded by intensified commercial relations with Europeans, particularly Portuguese entrepreneurs. At the same time, the Fulbe expansion reorganised trading structures and networks in West Africa in a way that created opportunities for groups outside centralised zones to capitalise on economic relations with states and state actors.

A very common story goes that horse-mounted conquerors subdued the first-comer groups across the Voltaic region in the early 16th century thanks to their technological and civilisational superiority but also because of the apparent disinterest in things political by the "first-comer" communities. These first-comer communities and their ritual leaders (tengbiisi or tengdanas) were gradually marginalised in favour of a new political elite and a new political system characterised by its bureaucratic structures, its military apparatus, its hierarchies, its institutional language, and its demarcation of various socio-professional categories. The ritual leaders became confined to the task of preserving the moral order and things spiritual. There were many stateless groups on the fringes of the expanding Mamprugu–Dagbon–Mossi states. In Mossi accounts, non-Mossi groups are represented as a generic grouping of the nyonyonse (indigenous) made up of Gurunsi (Kibse), Lobi, Kusasi, Nankani, Builsa, Busasi, Nabdam, Kasena,

DOI: 10.4324/9781003273530-24

and so forth. However, in alternative, non-Mossi accounts, Mossi rulers emerged in contexts of fragmented specialisation and were typically "invited" to act as conflict mediators and rainmakers. This meant that their power was always going to be limited in practice and according to specific purposes.[1]

The concept of the Naam implies a definition of power that is in part linked to a notion of political authority, but more so to a number of diffuse elements having to do with rog-n-miki (customs, cultural heritage). Although coming from dominant accounts of those that conquered the Voltaic region for centuries (the Mossi), the Naam denotes a history of interdependence between different groups that came into contact through commercial and religious transactions, migration and conquest as well as matrimonial exchanges. In Moogo (literally the "world"; it refers to the boundaries of the land of the Mossi), rog-n-miki embodies the body of rules and the source of legal authority that govern society. As such, it is that "(…) force that perpetuates the past (and) … enacts history" (Bazemo, 1993, pp. 199–200). Deviation from it was, therefore, a fundamental cause for decline, disorder, and anxiety. But rog-n-miki was primarily a set of customs, elaborated over time by non-Mossi (first-comer) groups as the normative framework that presided over their actions. Mossi rulers, however, saw in pre-moaga society a permanent state of mess and in the Naam ideology the source of order that could "emancipate" pre-moaga society from the dominium of "nature". In reality, state ideology was merely superimposed on relatively flexible stateless communities characterised by an egalitarian economic orientation and political organisation.

In deploying the Naam as a principle of authority across Moogo, state proponents intended for it to restructure the social order and by extension the whole world (Moogo). In the context of the emergence of the state in the Voltaic region in the 16th century, the operative mechanisms of the Naam help trace and assess the parameters of state-making and related transformations in pre-colonial West Africa. The Naam as state ideology is a rather open and vague concept. The extent of its institutional reach, its institutional arrangements, its normative consensus, its structural coherence, and transgenerational continuity are usually recognised as key characteristics. I do not, however, treat these as intrinsic properties of the Naam. Instead, I treat the functions of the Naam as fundamentally problematic. The conditions for the consolidation of the Naam structures are thus important, historically, for a better understanding of the multiple connections in historically changing and unevenly bounded social alignments.

More importantly for the history of state formation in the Voltaic region, the Naam was a reordering principle that crystallised the state around its ideology. The Naam made the state and determined its historical trajectory. It provided the state the arguments and justifications to intervene beyond its conventional remit. From a Mamprusi (place of origin) blueprint, it was constructed around a model that took on a number of local specificities but maintained the defining dichotomy between the Naam (secular rule) and *Tênga* (divine rule) on the one hand and the principle of expansion through fission of political authority on the other. Thus, the overall political system was unified by derivation of the Naam and its periodic return to the place of origin (Mamprusi) either metaphorically or ritually. In all this, the Naam ideology was deployed to maintain the proper orchestration between the Naam and Tênga, between the sphere of political rule and the sphere of divine rule. Although problematic, such a distinction provided an ideological basis for the imposition of ideas associated with the Naam against social and political practices associated with Tênga and which were presented as fundamentally illogical and irrational. Against this backdrop, the Naam became a technological innovation and the impetus that precipitated state formation, and Mossi migrations the forward drive that provided the dynamism for the reproduction of a model of political authority across the entire Voltaic region (Niang, 2018, pp. 20–21).

The methodology that guides this project draws broadly from structuralist and hermeneutical readings of the historical process and social action and their various representations. On the one hand, a structuralist approach helps to read and to decode signs, moral codes, symbols and symbolic relations, metaphors, and connections as they shape and are produced by structures and processes. It, therefore, helps in the interpretation of political action in broader social configurations. On the other hand, a hermeneutical analysis of the formation of power and authority can help show how the operations of structures are articulated in relation to the operations of culture. It further allows the deconstruction of social symbols on the basis of performing agents (who elaborates them?), intent (for what purpose?), and effects (with what consequences?). Such an approach is applied to the idea of "belief" as a flexible container that enacts human experience in its various political, moral, normative, and cultural expressions.

In the following, I propose to explore the discursive work of the Naam, but also the areas of resistance that make apparent the many tensions between the Naam/Tênga. I propose to examine the Naam ideology as an emerging sociopolitical referent and a framework of order that was promoted as qualitatively different and therefore imposed on pre-moaga communities (singular for Mossi).

What Is the Naam?

The Naam literally means, "that which allows someone to lead". It is also an ambitious ideological project that enunciates a new historical order, which at once subsumes and erases all pre-existing orders and symbols of power. As state theory and discourse of legitimisation, the Naam rested upon the necessary assumptions of the following structure. The vocation of every Moaga (an individual member of the Mossi group) is to exercise power, in other words, to hold a naam, therefore to become a Naaba (king) and rule over people; this entails having a rule (*solem* or authority).[2]

Despite some divergences in the various dynastical accounts, Mossi traditions generally trace a Mossi vocation for political rule back to the very beginning of History, that is the history of political formation. The common ancestor of all Mossi, Naaba Ouedraogo, son of the legendary princess Yennenga, was the crafter of the Naam, a technology of power he passed on to his offspring. In this sense, state authority derived from the Naam was very much grounded in the segmentary logic of the Mossi group and was never totally divorced from its rationality even when Mossi state rulers began to seek to sever the link between kingship and kinship through strategies of alienation of successive incumbents' kin.

The ideological basis of the political system thus rested on the exclusive character of the Naam and the idea that nakombsé (sing. nakombga, member of the extended royal lineage) were born with an intrinsic right to rule people, in other words, to possess a naam. The Naam's ideational construction promotes the importance of blood affiliation as the basis for the structuration of the state. The chapter introduces the notion of the Naam as initially envisaged as the theoretical foundation of a nascent and expanding state, the Mossi state or Moogo.

The Mossi state was constructed so as to establish a strict congruence between lineal history and territorial history at the junction of which a mechanism of power devolution, a system of social categorisation as well as the consolidation of the state's moral orientation would be established. This, however, remains a purely theoretical framework whose function is limited to informing initial attempts at political engineering in a given society. The guiding principles of the Naam system point to a hypothetical model; Mossi rulers maintained that the Naam structures were stable and timeless; that political rule was fundamentally bound to the possession of the Naam; and that Mossi-ness was an intrinsic quality that described the way of the moaga. The reality was that a great amount of flexibility and institutional distortions were possible, and were in fact implemented over the course of territorial expansion and political centralisation. Faced with recurrent internal upheaval and endless conflicts among different naam lineages, state rulers were to introduce a number of alterations in the devolution system of the Naam. The political framework turned out to be rather fragile, particularly from the middle of the 18th century, both in Ouagadougou and Yatenga. The Naam ideology was adapted through a continuous elaboration of the principles of political rule and the vagaries of identity, culture, and social change.

The Realm of Ideas and the Realm of Ideals

The binary opposition between the Naam/Tênga is the cornerstone of state-building and society-making in Moogo. However, the familiar construct reveals, beyond the homogenising discourse of assimilation and appeased resentment put forward by the Mossi ruling class, a number of contradictions and the persistent dilemma of an "imperial" concept. State conquest in Moogo was not just an endeavour to subdue "first-settler" communities; it was primarily an attempt to control Tênga, the religious domain of the first-settler communities and the earth divinity. This goal was never fully realised, even when it seemed that proponents of the Naam had managed to gain acceptance amongst indigenous societies. In reality, Tênga remained out of reach to the holders of the Naam. For this reason, the Naam has been confined to the realm of ideas, those in particular that advance state ideology, abstracted from real society yet juxtaposed to social structures framed under the concept of Tênga. The all-encompassing status of the Naam is in fact widely contested, both openly and implicitly, for sovereignty was never the exclusive prerogative of a ruler but rather something that existed first and foremost within the realm of Tênga.

The initial contact or "pact" concluded between autochthonous (future earth priests) and Mossi migrant-conquerors (future chiefs), at least in Mossi accounts, seems to give the pride of place to the latter. However, what is clear from oral traditions is that state-building was a common project, a co-produced process between Mossi and non-Mossi groups, including blacksmiths, indigenous Nininsi and the Fulse, and many other social categories. On the one hand, the future "earth priests" had the advantage of the number for Mossi conquerors were a small number of migrants. They also had the advantage of territorial grounding in the sense that they had settled for a long while in the valley of the Volta rivers. On the other hand, the future chiefs could count on their material advantage and a past "experience" of political institutions, both of which were key ingredients in staging a revolution. According to Michel Izard, they "they have the capacity to subject (others) to the conduct of a project of which they have a clear representation… and the modern means of war" (Izard, 2003, pp.140–141).[3] The joint initiative was, therefore, to result in a socio-political revolution of an internal kind. The Nakomsé might have thought of themselves as the inventors of the idea of a political ideal embodied by the Naam. However, the development of the Mossi state in many ways belies the principle of a single-handed and unilateral formation bearing the initial characteristics of its foundation. As it turned out, there was not one single idea of the Naam but ideas of it, adapted and altered by its holders through a series of structurations of power across Moogo.

The chapter seeks to argue that the Naam has more to do with the sources of power than the capacity to influence specific outcomes. In contrast to the Weberian understanding of power, the Naam does not necessarily stress capacity but the dynamics, perceived and lived, which underlie and enable that capacity. The Naam introduces elements of perception in the interaction of power holders and those over which power is exercised. In looking at the implications of the contradistinction between the Naam and Tênga, the political versus the ritual realm, the chapter seeks to demonstrate that this demarcation had to bear a degree of flexibility in order to effect a process of assimilation that required interpenetration for the expansion of the Moos buudu (a group that comprises all descendants of Ouedraogo, the founding ancestor of the Mossi). The Naam/Tênga antagonism was a construct that derived from the Naam's own logic of state formation, office formation, and the transmission of rule, and does not, therefore, reflect a view, from the perspective of the operations of Tênga, of political possibilities understood in a non-linear way. Put differently,

> "the construct Naam/Tênga as a working pair of antagonistic references and life-worlds cannot be understood as delineative of distances but rather

> as productive of positionalities and relationalities which are indissociable from the projection of [specific] mental charters.
>
> *(Niang, 2018, p. 138)*

The many virtues attributed to the Naam principle by Mossi rulers suggest that the latter's initial intent was to re-create history, a comprehensive thrust in historical perspective, what Izard referred to as a totalisation process (Izard, 1985, p. 20). The Naam runs through the conceptual history of the Mamprusi–Dagomba–Mossi states as an overarching yet unstable concept. It is built on a uniform projection of power, at all local and decentralised levels of governance. In other words, it conveys, regardless of the spatial and temporal circumstances, an idea of a well-devised and completed system-government, modelled upon an original format, then refined, exported, and standardised across local territories. The proponents of the Naam thus took a comprehensive approach to state-building and society-making geared towards the accomplishment of a community of purpose. How they achieved their goal is a long process of institutional initiatives and a combination of circumstances wherein lineage politics and the resistance of social forces played an important role.

On the other hand, from the perspective of the Naam holders, the social grammar of power has to be conceived in terms of elder/youngster, generation of an old/new stock, centre/periphery in its spatial conception, whereas such semantics do not fit in the ideals of equilibrium recognised in the realm of Tênga. Tênga is its own core as much as it is its own periphery and the politics of kinship do not derail the ritual mission that places it apart from the logic of power. In fact, political rulers' framing of the differentiation between conquerors and autochthons is not readily transferable to Tênga's framing of social action, mainly in terms of professional practice, whether it is land-tilling, farming, blacksmithing, and so on. From this perspective, the importance of Tênga has to do with the preservation of the cosmic balance and its re-restoration where it has been disrupted. For Tênga designates the space that provides a place of dwelling and a source of livelihood to people, all people. It is the place that connects people to ancestors and mediates access to the sources of their personhood (Niang, 2018, p. 143). Here might reside the explanation for the Mossi's unsuccessful project of unification. Throughout the Mossi conquest across the Voltaic region between the 16th and 19th centuries, unification was never achieved but remained at the level of representation. Whilst many first-settler communities became assimilated as "Mossi" in conquered societies, the discourse on the Naam has very much remained the discourse of rulers as vanguard figures.

Discourse of the Universal and the Violence of Discourse

The effectiveness of the Naam lay in its translation of a Mossi identity into structures of authority that extended beyond the political into structures of belief and social organisation. However, the internal discourse on the Naam is far from being coherent. Neither is it always consistent with stated goals. The Naam does not "evolve", so to speak, in its natural milieu: it has to break the temporal barriers of history and the spatial bounds of "pre-civilisation". By abolishing Tênga's prerogatives over the orientation of its own history, the Naam holders introduced a conceptual rupture that was never entirely overcome by the uniformising effects of a state discourse.

In so far as discourse, through speech, words, and moral references (as opposed to bare violence) seeks to persuade, it is eminently political. The power of ideology to steer and to justify action when it is against the interests of wider society is taken to be a sign of maturity in the practice of politics. From this on, violence appears to be a pre-political phase; in the Mossi case, it corresponds to pre-moaga society. If the ethics of the Naam constitutes an encompassing framework within which contradictions and opposing tensions are resolved as a matter of necessity to project a unifying morality, in the realm of tênga, the basis of ethics resides in the very existence of parallel discourses that cohabit but do not cohere as a homogeneous body of knowledge. If these were not always strident, they could result in flight. Mossi and non-Mossi alike escaped the stifling grip of the state simply by migrating. As Asiwaju contends, migration, as a form of resistance, was widespread in pre-colonial West Africa and its colonial and postcolonial versions were also the expression of dissatisfaction to oppressive rule by ordinary people. As he saw it: "exodus is the weapon of the weak"[4] and it could be a powerful one in a context whereby people were considered to be a state's greatest of resources.

On the other hand, the têngbîise tend to adopt a silent treatment, a combination of disdain and avoidance, rather than open complaint, towards the nakombsé. This, however, never meant that têngbîise – and non-Mossi groups more generally – resigned themselves to being subjected to Mossi rule. If the Naam's universalising discourse was merely the manifestation of an ideology of domination, "acceptance" could be explained through the effects of the ritual alliances the Mossi contracted, particularly in the union Wende/Tênga (sun and earth divinities) as they became sedentary. But alliance alone was never sufficient. In reality, beyond alliance, the Naam acquired its legitimacy from tênga through the ringu or enthronement voyage, harvest festivals, and other ritual celebrations.[5] In "asking" to be accepted, the Naam holders deploy their own reference, which is historicity, contrasted and juxtaposed to the reference of tênga which is a form of control over the forces of nature. The terms of such alliance can be seen as unequal only if one considers political rule as more valuable than, say farming, herding, or the performance of rituals and the preservation of cosmic stability. The perspective of the guardians of tênga could well be that political rule was only one element in a vast social mosaic in which men are identified with what they do.

If we assume the existence, in every state system, of a dualistic structure of violence [coercion] and consent, one could envisage the Mossi state as an example of state ideology that "constructs" and makes consent "out of violence". It is what Izard refers to as "coercion of consent". In other words, "It is the expansion of the world, and of society on the basis of ideological encodings" (Izard, 1980, p. 970).[6] If the Mossi state's capacity to exert violence is relatively low,

> "it is precisely in virtue of an adjustment of means to ends; a form of state violence that is well calibrated and that requires limited consent. It was a moderate form of violence indeed for the violence of moaga rule, of the Naam, even of pânga, is not exerted evenly upon the whole population; … even less upon the population living in the extended territory of the kingdom."
>
> *(Izard, 1980, p. 967).*[7]

The operations of the state were not necessarily derailed by the existence of forms of public disorder that could otherwise have been disruptive in a different context. In fact, political consolidation of state structures could be successfully carried amidst fragmentary violence and disorder. This feature was very much determined by the dynamics between "core" and "periphery" as well as the level of autonomy afforded to lineage groups. The very logic of political formation by fission meant that the state could, and did encourage the creation of autonomous formations answerable to the centre. In places where the state did not interfere with the operations of autonomous polities, forms of violence could go hand in hand with a relatively "appeased" state. Centralisation was, therefore, more about the consolidation of a structure of rule than it was a systematisation of violence.

If power is to be conceptualised in terms of concentric circles that indicate the direction of its radiation, it is easy to see how its intensity weakens as one moves away from its core. The discourse of power is first directed to those closest to its operation, namely royal dignitaries, captives close to the Naaba, other members of the royal household, then warriors, and nakombsé (the extended ruling class). State violence in question is very much a result of extraversion of the Naam in the form of pânga, it is generally confined to the groups enumerated above, in the exception of the têngbîise who might be summoned to provide ritual sanction to political rule. Beyond what could be called the limits of relevance of the discourse of the Naam, the articulation of such discourse becomes tedious and ineffectual. The Naam's articulation of order over "peripheral" disorder was, therefore, an uneven strategy. In so far as consent-making was a process, the articulation of the Naam discourse had to be balanced with the requirement of territorial expansion and the necessary incorporation of non-Mossi actors in the state apparatus.

In fact, the Mossi state did not have control over alternative and peripheral ideologies that coexisted with the Naam ideology. Tênga specifically was the main area of elaboration of alternative ideologies, the Yarse and Maranse traders are strangers to the moaga world, and the blacksmiths live on the margins of society. Another way, therefore, to understand the acceptance of the Naam by indigenous groups is to ask whether the latter actually understood the language of the Naam. Everything in the discourse of the Naam points to Nakombsé – generally – as main interlocutors. It is, therefore, possible to argue that, in so far as the discourse of the Naam was neither explicitly articulated nor, in fact, directly addressed to the world "outside" that of the Naam, the issue of acceptance is of little relevance in understanding how the state weaved consent. The world of the Naam is closed over itself; there are only fragments of it that penetrate the alien world of Tênga. Têngbîise, on the other hand, may not be privy to the discourse of the Naam but they know that the latter could neither make the rain to fall nor bring good harvest. This may sound contradictory, particularly with regards to my discussion, above, of the Naam as encompassing all modes of formulation and of Moogo as encompassing the entire world, that over which it has an actual grip as much as the world over which it had little or no control. Thus, for the Mossi, controlling the world comes down to essentialising it to the world of the Mossi.

There were two ways in which the expansionist tendencies of the Naam were derailed by practices that prevailed in the realm of Tênga. Firstly, the ritual union between Naaba Wende (sun divinity) and Napagha Tênga (earth divinity) was devised as an answer to the Naam holders' pursuit of an entry point into the field of rituals, spirits and natural forces. Such a deficit is, however, partly transacted by the Naam's ideological representations which make the ritual sanction of power, namely through the ringu (enthronement voyage), an important moment of its legitimation process. Secondly, Mossi rulers' attempt to draw guardians of Tênga into the state logic by making their collaboration seem like full consent in reality concealed a specific anxiety. Ritual officers' capacity to manipulate indecipherable languages was seen as a direct threat to state power. Thus, even when indigenous forms seemed to fit into dominant structures, they were highly subversive, albeit in a non-confrontational but subtle manner.

Articulating Order, Controlling Disorder

The Mossi see pre-moaga society as disorderly and needing to be reordered. The idea that greater political order should prevail was based upon a further assumption, that is that disorder was an indication of political immaturity. In Izard's reconstruction of Mossi conception of time and space, ancestrality is the expression of the temporal continuity of human existence from birth to death: the ancestor is a former person as much as the (human) person is derived from an ancestor. Such continuity is transacted, in the sphere of power, by the short interregnum of the na-poko (literally woman-chief, first daughter of a deceased chief) at the death of her father at the same time that the kurita, her male counterpart, is sent away in exile as if to exorcise departure seen as transacting discontinuity. On the other hand, the kinkirga ("spirit") is the expression of the spatial discontinuity of human existence: the kinkirga confers to the person his/her individuation in so far as it contextualises the circumstances of his/her birth (differentiation) whereas the ancestor is the reference of identity. Within such a configuration of representations, continuity (time) is an instance of order intrinsically opposed to discontinuity (space) as an occurrence of disorder: "Time is opposed to space in the manner of a sequencing of order (as ordering, ordination,) in relation to disorder" (Izard, 1986, 230–231).[8] However, the two instances are not entirely exclusive as they both socialise the individual within a society that conceives of birth and death in stages, at once biological, sociological, and symbolical.

For all its "disorderliness", however, pre-moaga society offered to the Naam ideology the conditions of its realisation. Thus, as the Naam holders sought to substitute pre-existing social codes with new (naam) structures, they had to rely on the social structures and the contextual knowledge of first-settler communities in order to advance their objectives. This was done in such a way that the familiar dichotomy between the Naam/tênga, between therefore the realm of power and the realm of rituals ceases to be an adequate frame in apprehending state/society dynamics. As Fairley notes, "ideological innovations of a religious nature were tools of change in their own right rather than merely means of maintaining existing political stability" (Fairley, 1989, p. 92). Even when state rulers succeeded in imposing an idea of the state as an extended Moos Buudu, such a representation could not obliterate the contradiction Naam/Tênga. State power was always tangential and sketchy, incomplete and yet omnipresent in the abstract but in reality the state struggled to maintain control or hegemony over the domain of tênga. For the Naam never succeeded in transcending the kin order as reference, and it never entirely resolved primary, dual assumptions that placed it in a position of competition with the structure of tênga.

Theoretically, however, the interpenetration of power with the ritual realm created consubstantiality between power and sacrality whereby the ritual appeared as a settled, in fact, an "appeased" form of power.

The pursuit of hierarchical power by the ruling class was achieved through the rationalisation of the parameters of culture held as socio-cultural objectives in collective mentalities. Whether this was a form of indoctrination is open to question. As collective mentalities were "made" to subscribe to the universal norms enacted by the state ("cultural" norms in disguise), the latter could not be seen as encroaching upon these norms, and by extension upon its "contract" with cultural communities. One has to see the Naam's well-structured framework as coextensive with a system of values, indigenous in kind, which operate according to their own logic despite the subversive intervention of Mossi conquerors.

In reality, Mossi chiefs had to contend with pre-moaga social rationalities whose logic undermined the universalising discourse of the proponents of the Naam. The state, therefore, had to build into the decentralising practices of office transfer a mechanism to keep at bay the predatory inclination of nakombsé. The condition of the nakombga was symptomatic of the dilemma of power: if he [nakombga] exercised power and violence, violence was also, primarily, exercised upon him. The tension between coercion and consent was in many ways more acutely felt, and more significantly meted upon the nakombsé – as holders or aspirers of power – than other groups. In this sense, the universalising discourse of the Nanamse has to be understood as also an attempt to transcend the effects of the binary Naam/Tênga discourse in political practice. In other words, the purpose of state discourse was to transcend a historical reality by adopting key characteristics of social morality of first-settler societies. It did so more or less successfully.

The action of the nakombga often went against the orientation of the state. The nakombga is said to operate with a pre-state mindset; in other words, he does not conceive of the state as the ultimate end of his action. His is an itinerant life lived at the tip of the sword, that of the restless warrior in the search for wars to fight. The nakombga is, therefore, something of an oddity in the state, rejected from a history-making process that accounts for the figure of the Naaba who is a sedentarised warrior, and earthpriests as technicians of the sacred who invest the resources of tênga to sanction the legitimacy of political rule. As much as nakombsé pursue a logic of anarchy and destruction rather than consolidation, their action can be read in parallel to that of royal captives who serve in the frontlines of the state's centralisation endeavour. Captives (pasdemba) create mayhem, assault and persecute, and steal and confiscate in the name of the Naaba, therefore, in the name of the state. Their ethics is indissociable from that of the state, but the ethics of nakombsé is also supposedly that of the Naam. Here, of course, a contradiction is discernable in the distinctive commitments of these two groups. They both serve the Naam but in different ways: whilst nakombsé symbolise the temerity of the frontiermen, captives very much symbolise the lucidity of power.

In many ways, therefore, it can be said that pasdemba are the mediating agents in the transformation of the Naam from a principle of legitimate rule to a logic of political power. This serves to reassert the principle that the Naam's function is to bridge a gap between crude power/violence and legitimate rule. There was a simple, practical reason for this. Horses could not, for instance, be kept for a long time and no state could prevail if it did not have a sedentary base; domination without actual control had its obvious limits and Mossi (horse-mounting warriors) had the ambition to achieve their purpose which is to establish state rule.

In redefining the place of power, the Mossi state sought to displace its source as much as its effects. The (new) place of power under the framework of the Naam is the place of those that serve the state regardless of the configuration of its legitimacy and the basis of its rule. It is also the place from which radiates the essence of pânga. The pasdemba (holders of pânga or "the people of force") thus assembled embody a particular aspiration whereby political centralisation hinges upon their ingathering as a social category appended to the state institution. As state servants, "the people of force" thus occupy a very ambiguous spatiality that emerges at the very place (of birth) of power; their spatiality is different from that of both autochthons and conquerors; it exists outside of the ordinary frame of lineal and social reproduction.

Where different temporalities are seen to operate within the sphere of the Naam and the sphere of pânga, this comes out of the state's attempt to "stabilise" the latter at the expense of the former and this inevitably leads to permanent struggle. The society that develops out of this process is an association and/or incorporation of indigenous groups or first-settler societies. In effect, the statisation process is of progressive replacement, of a blood nobility (nakombsé) by a functional nobility (tasobanamba); it is also, to an extent, a process of renaissance that seeks to erase history by purging the state of its constitutive elements (nakombsé). It is almost as if the state had to fold history in order to become history.

In a social structure hinged on the distinction between "strangers" and "autochthons", between the realm of political power (over people) and that of the ritual control (over land), the articulation of identity became a way to assign social functions to groups according to settlement histories, patterns of migration, and most importantly, people's lineal affiliation (Vinel, 2000).

Identity, Culture, and Meaning-making

Culture, identity, and similar concepts do not possess intrinsic coherence always and all the time. Both culture and identity appear to be a set of ideological rationalisations that serve purposive aims. Furthermore, these notions often go through a process of (re)construction of meaning that seeks to establish familiarity and acceptance. In order, therefore, for the proponents of the Naam to be able to define identity and impose "Mossi culture" as a standard of culture, they had to reconfigure the reality within which these terms were to be apprehended. According to Wolf,

> meanings are not imprinted into things by nature; they are developed and imposed by human beings. (…) The ability to bestow meanings – to "name" things, acts and ideas – is a source of power. Control of communication allows the managers of ideology to lay down the categories through which reality is to be perceived.
>
> *(Wolf, 1982, p. 388)*

In addition to naming things, the Naam holders had to describe pre-moaga society as devoid of a recognisable culture and identity. Proponents of the Naam put forward the latter as a superior disposition that provided them with an argument to delegitimise actors that did not fit into, or comply with, its internal hierarchies. In fact, the very expansion of the Naam ideology and the replication of Mossi state structures across the Voltaic region, in other words, the "Mossi model", was premised upon the belief that areas of expansion were bereft of any institutional or political history. They were a tabula rasa. But the "frontier" was a social construction of the Mossi ruling class, in other words, an imagined reality that had to be emptied of its content and populated with "novel" ideas. As Wolf aptly puts it, such a process "(…) entail[ed] the ability to deny the existence of alternative categories, to assign them to the realm of disorder and chaos, to render them socially and symbolically invisible." (Wolf, 1982, p. 388). And that is exactly what the Naam ideology attempted to achieve:

> In the rough-and-tumble of social interaction, groups are known to exploit the ambiguities of inherent forms, to impart new evaluations or valences to them, to borrow forms more expressive of their interests, or to create wholly new forms to answer to changed circumstances. Furthermore, if we think of such interaction not as causative in its own terms but as responsive to larger economic and political forces, the explanation of cultural forms must take account of that larger context, that wider field of force. "A culture" is thus better seen as a series of processes that construct, reconstruct, and dismantle materials, in response to identifiable determinants.
>
> *(Wolf, 1982, p. 387)*

When everything has been said, cultural unification remained entangled, centuries after the creation of Moogo, in the intricate dynamic between political centralisation and kin-politics (segmentarity), between a concern for the "proper" reproduction of the governing model and the increasing narrative dissonance carried from "peripheries" of the Naam and that challenged the Mossi master narrative as a tale of the successful hunter. Ironically, what was meant to be a clash of identity between the Naam/Tênga morphed into a marginalisation process of kasemnâmba or lineage elders. So much so that, it would be fair to say that in the Mooga world, all political processes were defined and shaped by the deployment of the Naam for its own sake. As the Naam came to occupy the status of an all-encompassing state ideology, naam offices held by nakombsé warriors and state elders were further marginalised and kept at a distance from the state project. In this process, the ultimate purpose of politics came to be understood as the assertion of the Naam over all other possible social and political frameworks. The Naam was the beginning and end of everything. Such essentialisation had to contend with lineal conservatism which opposed an ambiguous kind of resistance to the pragmatic, yet encompassing politics of centralisation.

In all this, a crucial point needs to be made. It is that the Mossi, in particular the nakombga struggle with cultural placement, was never entirely resolved as identity continues to stir dissenting memories and emotions in contemporary Burkina Faso. On the other hand, a notion of specialised practice applied to politics and other "professional" sectors of activity becomes important in accounting for the ambivalence of identity in the context of a dominant ideology that seems to be resistant to historical correction.

Conclusion

State processes in Moogo can be conceived as a series of historical denials, a continuous process of construction and reconstruction of models of orders. This dynamic remodelling has to be understood within epistemological reconfigurations that are inbuilt, so to speak, in the procedures of the Naam. The Mossi conception of its "peripheries" was, therefore, the outcome of a necessity to construct disorder in order to articulate a new form of order. At the heart of this process, is arguably the question about the extent to which the state can subsume the parameters of the political. Strategies to "tame disorder" are both a recognition of the dynamics of the political outside of the state sphere and a struggle to erase them.

There is a marked tendency, in the Mossi literature, particularly in Mossi-centred accounts, to insist on the differentiated nature of the political sphere and the ritual sphere as discrete categories of action of different political valence; they may overlap sometimes but have different rationalities. In this context, one of the aims of political discourse is to reduce, even eliminate, the discrepancies between political power as external practice and the sacred as domain of pre-state Moogo. Mossi state ideology was quite successful in drawing the realm of rituals into the sphere of power by interlocking, so to speak, ancestrality and autochthony (Tênga) in surveying the sources of political legitimacy.

However, the introduction of pânga marked a turn in the use of violence in state-building. The separation of kinship from kingship produced specialised, professional bodies within the state structure. As political rulers created different bodies that proliferated the work of the state, they also created avenues of inequalities that disrupted the unifying potential of state discourse. As a consequence, the increased disjunction between power and the sacred, the "political" and other spheres of action is also about the dilemma of the state form caught up between authority and "force" (violence)[9] and thus meant to produce winners and losers.

However, people's adherence to state justificatory framework was facilitated by an open system of government; the despotic tendencies of some of the power holders did not seem to discourage participation in the logic of power at its most oppressing aspects for the fact that the creation of a new political structure required the incorporation of aspects of state ideology in the collective articulation of customs and beliefs. This stretched the possibilities of state discourse beyond rhetoric and propaganda. At the same time, it grounded the state institution as an adequate basis for social organisation. Such ambition could only be achieved through a decentring of state authority that was translated in the application of a segmentary system across territorial, political, and social entities.

From the point of view of critiques of western conceptions of the political, in particular, a critique of the Westphalian state model, the relevance of concepts such as the Naam is double-fold. Firstly, they help show the limited naturalisation of European experiments of government in formerly colonised societies despite their enduring character. Secondly, beyond critique, they allow to explain the root causes of institutional failure in postcolonial societies in general, and in Africa in particular, through a reconstitution of social practices informed by distinct common sense and moral dispositions, different belief systems, different regimes of social interaction, and different material interests. Where modern government logics were built against these practices, the political system continues to be at odds with people's capacity to construct meaning through the institutions that represent them.

Notes

1 This section is based on A. Niang (2018) *The Postcolonial African State in Transition. Stateness and Modes of Sovereignty*. New York and London: Rowman and Littlefield.
2 I use "Naam" to refer to the ideology of rule that informs the Mossi state model and "naam" as decentralised power/office granted to members of the ruling class.
3 "*disposent de la capacité d'assujettir à la conduite d'un projet dont ils ont une claire représentation l'emploi des moyens modernes de la guerre.*"
4 On politically motivated migration in precolonial West Africa, see Archives nationales, Abidjan Direction A.N.A. (D): Serie IV-46/11-3304, Rapport de M. L' administrateur en Chef Itier, Inspecteur des Affaires Administratives sur les exodes en Gold Coast, Rapport No. 87 du 1ier aout 1936, p. i6. In A. I. Asiwaju (1976) "Migrations as Revolt: The example of the Ivory Coast and the Upper Volta before 1945," *The Journal of African History*, 17(4): 577–594, p. 579.
5 For an extensive treatment of the enthronement ritual (*ringu*) as political reference, see Niang (2014, pp. 77–89; 2018, pp. 157–182).
6 [«c'est la massification à coup d'encodages idéologiques du monde et de la société.»]
7 ["c'est précisent en vertu d'une adéquation des moyens aux fins: une violence étatique bien tempérée qui demande un consentement limite. Violence tempérée : la violence du pouvoir mooga, du *naam*, de *pânga* même, ne s'exerce pas également, on l'a vu, sur toute la population du royaume, moins encore sur toutes les populations vivant sur le territoire du royaume"]
8 "(...) la durée s'oppose à l'étendue comme une instance d'ordre (d'ordonnancement, d'ordination) à une instance de désordre"
9 The differentiation, in French, between "pouvoir" and "force" makes the conceptual difference between *naam* and *pânga* more apparent than the differentiation between between "power" and "violence" in English.

References

Asiwaju, A. I. (1976). "Migrations as Revolt: The Example of the Ivory Coast and the Upper Volta before 1945." *The Journal of African History* 17(4): 577–594.

Bazemo, M. (1993). "Captivité et Pouvoirs dans l'Ancien Royaume de Ouagadougou à la Fin du XIXe Siècle." *Dialogues d'Histoire Ancienne* 19(1): 191–204.

Fairley, N. J. (1987). "Ideology and State Formation: The Ekie of Southern Zaire." In I. Kopytoff (ed.) *The African Frontier: The Reproduction of Traditional African Societies*. Bloomington: Indiana University Press.

Izard, M. (1980). *Les Archives Orales d'Un Royaume Africain. Recherches sur la Formation du Yatenga*. Paris: Laboratoire d'Anthropologie Sociale.

Izard, M. (1985). *Gens du pouvoir, gens de la terre: Les institutions politiques de l'ancien royaume du Yatenga*. Paris and London: Cambridge University Press and Editions de la Maison des sciences de l'homme.

Izard, M. (1986). "L'Etendue, la Duree." *L'Homme* 97–98: 225–237.

Izard, M. (2003). *Moogo: L'Emergence d'un Espace Etatique Ouest-africain au XVIe siècle*. Paris: Karthala.

Niang, A. (2014). "Reviving the Dormant Divine: Rituals as Political Reference in Pre-colonial Moogo." *Journal of Ritual Studies* 28(1): 77–89.

Niang, A. (2018). *The Postcolonial African State in Transition. Stateness and Modes of Sovereignty.* New York and London: Rowman and Littlefield.

Vinel, V. (2000). "Etre et devenir 'Sikoomsé': Identité et Initiation en Pays Moaaga." *Cahiers d'Etudes Africaines* 40(158): 257–279.

Wolf, E. R. (1982). *Europe and the People without History.* Berkeley and London: University of California Press.

PART VII
Indeterminacy

19

PAJUBÁ

Caio Simões de Araújo

On 10 November 2020, Brazil's President Jair Bolsonaro lamented that many of his fellow citizens still feared infection by COVID-19. On the occasion, he claimed that death was both universal and inescapable, a destiny from which it was futile to try to escape. What Brazil needed instead was some virile courage: "we need to stop being a country of *maricas*" (Chaib, 2020), he claimed, in his familiar belligerent tone. What is interesting about this case is how his words travelled, as they made headlines around the world. Bolsonaro was accused of deploying a homophobic slur, and *maricas* was translated as "sissy" (Farzan and Berger, 2020), or "fag" (Radio France Internationale, 2020). But *maricas* is not synonymous to male homosexual. In fact, in a dictionary of the late eighteenth century, *maricas* (listed as the same as *maricão*), is defined as a "womanizer" (*mulherengo*) (Silva, 1789, p. 270). In another dictionary, of the nineteenth century, *maricas* is the adjective for an "effeminate man" (Silva Pinto, 1832). In its contemporary usage, the word has various meanings: "an individual with effeminate manners", a "homosexual", or a "coward" (Michaelis, 2020).[1] The etymology of the term comes from the proper name Maria, to which is added the diminutive suffix "ico", in the plural female form ("icas"). If Maria is a metonym for "women", then "little women" is the etymological basis of *maricas*. If we take all these definitions and linguistic trajectories into consideration, then *maricas* is less a reference to sexual orientation than a marker of performative gender identities. In all its uses, what is at stake is the boundaries of respectable manhood, or of what scholars have called "hegemonic masculinity" (Connel, 2000, pp. 10–11).

I am raising this particular etymology to allude to a rather familiar argument about the mutually constitutive – entangled even – nature of categories and hierarchies of gender and sexuality emerging in the wake of European colonial capitalist modernity (McClintock, 1995; Stoler, 1995; Lugones, 2007). Colonial histories are surely inscribed in the global circulation of *maricas*, too,

DOI: 10.4324/9781003273530-26

as the term travelled from the Iberian Peninsula to Latin America and Africa (in both its Portuguese and its Spanish version – *maricón*). As in Brazil, today in Angola and Mozambique, the term is also used as a marker of dissident male sexualities and minoritized, non-hegemonic, masculinities. But in telling this story, I also want to stress the performative powers of words. Speech acts are rooted in (and are routed through) gendered and sexualized imaginaries and meanings. As such, they can serve to reify and naturalize identity categories and social positionings that are otherwise constructed, mediated, unstable. But words, terms, and, broadly speaking, practices of naming and self-inscription, can also be subversive: they can call into question normative discourses and expose the arbitrary, constructed, nature of hegemonic systems of meaning and attribution of (social and cultural) value. If Bolsonaro was ready to use such a historically dense word, it is also true that sexual minority groups in Brazil, as in so many other locations, have for long engaged in processes of linguistic experimentation and re-appropriation. "Pajubá", as this linguistic style is called[2], is built on lexical borrowings of various kinds, but particularly from the Yoruba language. First articulated by *travestis*,[3] today it has not only been popularized to other LGBTIQ groups in Brazil, but some of its words have also entered the mainstream vocabulary as well.

Of course, this will be no news to scholars working on the intersecting fields of socio-linguistics, linguistic anthropology, or sociology of language, to name just a few perspectives of relevance to this debate. Indeed, since the 1940s, scholars have worked in mapping out the linguistic practices and lexical constellations associated with various forms of a "homosexual slang" or "argots" (Cameron and Kulick, 2006, pp. 15–18). Since then, a growing scholarship in the field of language and sexuality research has suggested that gay and lesbian speakers – as members of other marginalized or "deviant" social groups – resort to specific linguistic styles and lexical constellations as modes of self-expression, identity formation, community-making, and, in other words, forms of socialization and self-emplotment into sexuality and dissident desires (Bucholtz and Hall, 2004). In addition to the work done on gay and lesbian linguistics (also known as *lavender* linguistics), in the last decades, scholars have also built and expanded on Judith Butler's influential argument that gender is performative, in the sense that it is produced, instantiated, and reified through linguistic and discursive practices (Butler, 1990). In this perspective, queer approaches to language – or the field of "queer linguistics" – have tended to reject any fixed identity categories of gender and sexuality, interrogating, instead, how (hetero)normative orders are built and cemented, and how "difference" gets inscribed onto non-normative bodies through language practices (Hall, 1997; Leap, 2012).

The "queer turn" in linguistics is important if one is interested in excavating the forms of elocution and political articulation emerging in and around dissident sexualities and desires in the Global South. After all, the very concept of "homosexual" (and heterosexual) as a fixed subjectivity is inseparable from its historical emergence within the disciplinary formations of European modernity in the late nineteenth century (Foucault, 1981). Through colonialism and, later, neoliberal globalization, modern European discourses of (homo)sexuality travelled, carrying with them their epistemic categories and lexical constellations (Boone, 2014; Tellis and Bala, 2015). The (post)colonial itineraries and uneven cartographies of sexuality have already been the object of research and criticism. As scholars have argued, the hetero/homo binary, so crucial to European notions of sexuality, is not universal, and often find a difficult accommodation and only a precarious translation into the vernacular vocabularies and the desiring practices of the (post)colonial world (Khanna, 2007; Dutta and Roy, 2014; Pelúcio, 2012; Pereira, 2019). Likewise, queer scholarship has pointed out that the hegemonic Euro-American narrative of gay and lesbian liberation places the white, middle-class, subject as its normative protagonist, therefore excluding people of colour, the working classes, and other marginalized or "deviant" positions from what basically becomes a (neo) liberal political project (Duggan, 2002; Stryker, 2008). Moreover, mainstream queer politics can be appropriated, co-opted and deployed in name of a civilizational narrative in which the Global South is (mis)construed as a homophobic – and hence barbaric – space that needs Western aid and intervention in order to achieve sexual liberation (Massad, 2007; Puar, 2007).

Both the words "*maricas*" and "queer", thus, are representative of two forms of uneven linguistic circulation and globalization. The first follows the cartography of Iberian colonialism and its imposition of the Portuguese and Spanish languages in South America and Africa. The second speaks to a more contemporary iteration of the age-old "centre-periphery" problematic, in which the "pioneering" academic production of the Global North gets to travel Southwards and shape scholarship in the (post)colonial periphery. Of course, this process is not without its contestations, and in recent years, scholars have increasingly been devising epistemologies and theories of, and from, the (decolonial) Global South (Comaroff and Comaroff, 2015; Santos, 2018; Santos and Meneses, 2019; Ndlovu-Gatsheni, 2020). Yet, unlike other English-language, Western, terms that circulate globally, in my view, "queer" carries with it the potentiality of its own displacement. Particularly because queer theory puts much emphasis on the performativity of identity and its production in and through language, it also calls into question, problematizes, the possibility (or even desirability) of its transparent translation and transplantation elsewhere. It is not coincidental that queer scholars in the Global South have not shied away from a critical engagement with the term, often resorting to new modes of writing – such as in the Portuguese spelling "cuir" (Inácio, 2018) or the Taiwanese appropriation "ku'er" (Lim, 2008) – or devising alternatives to it altogether, such as Pelúcio's "cu theory", which subversively engages "cu" – the Brazilian slang word for the "asshole", the anus – as a place of theorization (Pelúcio, 2014). Scholars have also begun to challenge linear narratives of Euro-centric dissemination – of one-sided transfer from North to South – to argue instead that under conditions of globalization of queer cultures and lives, messier movements of transposition, appropriation, and cross-cultural engagements and coalitions take place (Cruz-Malavé and Manalansan, 2002, pp. 5–7).

In this context, scholars have looked not only into how hegemonic linguistic formations – such as "gay English" – are unevenly circulated, appropriated, and re-territorialized in various locations, but also into how vernacular and indigenous modalities of queer linguistic expression have engaged with, and resisted, neoliberal globalization and its dominant sexual culture (Leap and Boellstorff, 2004). Here, there has been a continued academic interest in mapping out how sexually minoritized and gender-non-conforming groups have devised modes of articulation in the Global South, including Bahasa gay in Indonesia (Boellstorff, 2005), Gayle and IsiNgqumo in South Africa (Maclean and Ngcobo, 1994; Cage and Evans, 2003; Rudwick and Ntuli, 2008), Swardspeak in the Pilipino diaspora (Manalansan, 2003), or the linguistic idiosyncrasies of the hijras in India (Hall, 1996, 1997).

In this chapter, I want to intervene in this debate, from the standpoint of "pajubá" – also commonly known as Brazil's "gay language" – a queer linguistic practice that is still relatively underexplored in the literature in English. While I do take queer linguistics' suspicion of essentialist identities seriously, my approach here is grounded on my own (inter)disciplinary position, as I write from the standpoint of history and anthropology. In fact, it has already been pointed out that queer theorizing tends to be "highly abstract and general" (Bucholtz and Hall, 2004, p. 492), as it has relied on the analysis of "literary and philosophical texts" rather than on "the particulars of lived experience" (Lewin and Leap, 2009, p. 6), be that historically or ethnographically registered. Taking this critique into account, in what follows, I will explore *pajubá* as a concept naming a queer linguistic practice of deep histories and multi-layered temporalities. As I will argue, *pajubá* is so promising within an intellectual and political project invested in thinking concepts "from the Global South" because its biography eludes the linear narrative of dissemination of Western categories of gender and sexuality. Rather, *pajubá* is rooted in and routed through the southern itineraries of the Black Atlantic and its postcolonial iterations.

"Memory Is Not a Secret": *Pajubá* as Queer Articulation of the Black Atlantic

> Memory is not a secret,
> To be locked or hidden.
>
> (3 Uiaras de SP City, *2018)*

In 2018, the nation-wide high school exam ENEM[4], which students throughout Brazil take hoping to get ahead in the competition for a university spot, included what was, to many observers, a puzzling question concerning the linguistic particularities of *pajubá*, here defined as a "language of Yoruba origin" and "the 'secret dialect' used by gays and travestis". Noticing that many of its words already circulate online and that even a dictionary had been published in 2006, including more than 1300 entries, the question required exam-takers to identify what gives *pajubá* its "status as a dialect", as "linguistic heritage". The correct answer here, to be marked from a multiple-choice list, was that *pajubá* is "consolidated through formal objects of register" (Eler, 2018). This was a general question; whose goal was to determine students' competence in reading and interpretation. As such, it did not demand any familiarity with, or specific knowledge of, *pajubá* itself. Yet, in the midst of the conservative political wave that had led Bolsonaro to electoral victory, that a question involving LGBTIQ issues was included in a national exam made headlines, especially after the members of the Bolsonaro family spoke out against it. Eduardo Bolsonaro, a congressman for Rio de Janeiro and one of the president elect's four sons, tweeted that "it is not a requirement that the Minister of Education knows about the dictionary of travestis or feminism" (Globo, 2018), in a snide comment to the fact that ENEM is prepared by the Ministry of Education. Bolsonaro himself, who was preparing to take office roughly two months later, on 1 January 2019, noted that the question on *pajubá* had no use, it "did not measure any knowledge" and only served to "force our youth into being interested for such issues in the future". He promised that under his administration, the ENEM exam would be reformulated to include "useful knowledge" (Folha de São Paulo, 2018).

I am telling this story to point out the obvious frictions between *pajubá*'s constitution as a "secret [*queer*] dialect", on the one hand, and its public exposure and translation in popular culture and political debate, on the other. This is not surprising if one considers that the tension between "the closet" – as a space of intimacy and secrecy – and the "public" sphere of politics and citizenship has been a distinctive trait of homosexual subjectivities in the West (Segdwick, 1990). Secrecy too, is entrenched into the histories and meanings of *pajubá*, although in a very different manner. As some studies have suggested, *pajubá* is a word rooted in the Yoruba-Nago languages of West Africa, originally meaning "secret" or "mystery" (Barroso, 2017, p. 17), but re-signified, in its mobilization by queer speakers, to mean "news" or "gossip" (Barroso, 2017, p. 20; Camarano, 2020, p. 76). Yet, it is difficult to determine the soundness of these assertions. Indeed, *pajubá* is absent from a recent dictionary of Yoruba–Portuguese, which nevertheless lists various words to mean "secret" and related terms, such as "mystery" (awo) (Beniste, 2009, p. 139); "privacy" (ikoko) (Beniste, 2009, p. 369); "private matter" (asiri) (Beniste, 2009, p. 129); or something told in confidence (eke) (Beniste, 2009, p. 233). Moreover, most studies of *pajubá* have been silent of the etymology of the term, which may suggest that there is no legible trajectory here: in this sense, *pajubá* has no specific meaning preceding and outside of the queer language practices that it names. Yet, I want to suggest that the connotation of *pajubá* with "secret" and "mystery" may be productive if interpreted in relation to its social history, rather than as a result of its linguistic genealogy. Indeed, it is interesting that the ENEM question to which I alluded above, while noting that we "don't know for sure when this language surfaced, it is known that there is a clear relationship between pajubá and African culture, in a seam that started during the colonial period" (Globo, 2018). I find this statement to be both provocative and intriguing, because it claims an African ancestry for *pajubá* while, at the same time, questioning any clear or transparent point of origin, which remains a "mystery", or a historiographic "secret".

Surely, one must remember that the selective celebration of the country's African roots is a relatively new position in Brazilian social thinking and public culture, having gained space only in the 1930s when new narratives of a racially miscegenated nation gradually displaced a long-standing intellectual tradition still predicated on racial thinking, eugenic science, and the "whitening ideal" (Skidmore, 1993; Nascimento; 2003). The work of the anthropologist Gilberto Freyre was influential in recasting the national narrative in this direction by painting a celebratory image of the racial and cultural mixing of Portuguese, Indigenous, and African elements in the making of a harmonic "Brazilian civilization" (Freyre, 1986). Once boasted as progressive by Brazilian elites invested in the new variant of nationalist thinking, the "fable of the three races" has been the object of intense criticism in the last decades, especially because it "camouflaged" the reality of white supremacy under the disguise of racial miscegenation (*mestiçagem*) as a national virtue (Nascimento, 2003, pp. 55–56). Underlying this exclusionary narrative, moreover, lied the romantic notion of the sugar plantation as the cradle of the nation; which only served a politics of forgetting the foundation of Brazil in slavery and rape (Isfahani-Hammond, 2008). Besides cementing a white, elitist, and patriarchal standpoint, this national imaginary was, too, shaped by a blatant heteronormative orientation. For instance, an article published in the newspaper *Jornal do Brasil* in 1970, in discussing aspects of Freyre's work, mentioned that colonial-era plantation owners encouraged in their sons the "precocity of stallions", pushing them to "deflower" and "impregnate" slave women. From this, it followed that no family would want to be known for having "maricas" and "effeminate" sons (Jornal do Brasil, 1970). In this view, the (post)colonial national project in Brazil has been fundamentally white, male, and heterosexual, based on the nuclear family, and invested in the marginalization of the "other", whose "difference" was marked in terms of race, gender, and sexuality (Miskolci, 2012). *Pajubá* has no place in this history, as its speaker, the sexual dissident, is an "impossible subject" (Manalansan, 2014), out of sight.

To understand *pajubá*'s formation – and its claims to African origin – one must depart from these exclusionary narratives of the nation and resort to a different intellectual project and historical imagination altogether; one attentive to the expressions of subaltern transnationalism and diasporic thinking that Paul Gilroy (1993) has influentially called the Black Atlantic. In this perspective, scholars of Brazil have challenged the territoriality of national and colonial histories to explore instead the making of Brazilian society in the space of passage, circulations, and cross-cultural exchange between the multiple shores of the Atlantic world (Ferreira, 2012; Alencastro, 2018). Building on the foundational and traumatic moment of the slave trade, this scholarship has been interested in its cultural afterlives, thus following how transnational flows of people, goods, and ideas shaped Brazilian society, from the influence of African languages in Brazilian Portuguese (Castro, 2005) to the emergence of Afro-Brazilian religions such as Umbanda and Candomblé. Referring to the latter, J. Lorand Matory (2005, pp. 7–8) uses the term "Black Atlantic religion" to capture a complicated history of African survivals and (dis)continuities amid "multifarious" transnational confluences.

Indeed, Candomblé has been a major channel through which African linguistic and cultural forms survived in Brazil's post-colonial landscape, even if immersed in discontinuous movements of re-invention and re-imagination (Capone, 2007). This includes an engagement with African languages of Yoruba or Bantu origin, fragments of which are used in the practice of the religion routinely, thus shaping both rituals and the social life in the *terreiro*[5] more broadly (López, 2004, pp. 122–129). Candomblé has been recognized, too, as the medium through which Brazilian queers gained knowledge of the lexical universe of the Black Atlantic (Lima, 2017, p. 56). Since the 1930s, Candomblé has had a reputation for attracting gay people, a view that has since been popularized by practice but also by the circulation of anthropological writing on the matter (Matory, 2005). More recent anthropological research has demonstrated that this aura of tolerance indeed invites sexual dissidents who do not find space in other faiths, or in society at large, to reach out to the *terreiros* as spaces of sanctuary and support (Fry, 1982, p. 74). In addition, Matory (2005) has pointed to the relationship between spiritual possession in Candomblé and notions of sexual/gender roles in Brazil, whereby the position of initiates in the religion, ritualistically considered to be wives of the *orixás*,[6] can be taken by "passive" gay men, to be "mounted" by the deity in spiritual possession rituals. Peter Fry also suggested that the connection between homosexuality and magic in Candomblé relates to their similar position at the "margins" of society, as both are construed as dangerous to the dominant social structure (Fry, 1982, p. 79). Other scholars have argued that Candomblé has offered *travestis* a space to explore their spirituality and the "sacred", while also exercising a femininity moulded after the deities they worship (Pelúcio, 2009, p. 201; Pereira, 2019, pp. 38–39). Originating in this dense, multi-layered terrain, *pajubá* can be thought of as a practice of queer articulation proper of the Black Atlantic.

If the *terreiros* were spaces of contact and learning, where, arguably, queer practitioners could absorb the Yoruba lexicon, *pajubá*'s origins as a living language is positioned elsewhere, on the streets. Indeed, as a linguistic style and as a practice of resistance, it has been, reportedly, first mobilized by *travestis* in the context of the military dictatorship established in 1964 (Lima, 2017, p. 58; Araújo, 2018, p. 134). As Quinalha (2017) has observed, until recently the military period had been narrated, in the historiography, as a moment of severe political repression, but of relative leniency on questions of sexuality and public morality; a view that has been disputed by the Truth Commission created by Lula da Silva in 2009. In its report published in 2014, the Commission submitted that even though there had been no coherent "policy of extermination", the regime's ideology was homophobic, as it represented homosexuals as "harmful, dangerous, contrary to the family, to prevailing morals, and to 'good manners'". In doing so, it legitimized direct homophobic violence and the violation of rights, while prohibiting any form of LGBTIQ political organizing (Comissão Nacional da Verdade, 2014, p. 301). Moreover, the report refers to police operations carried out to "cleanse" the city of São Paulo by arresting, under the pretext of vagrancy, various marginal figures, such as *travestis*, prostitutes, homosexuals, pimps, and the like (Comissão Nacional da Verdade, 2014, p. 309). It is in this context that *pajubá* emerges as a "secret language", or yet an "anti-language", that is, "a coded way [of speaking] which is designed to exclude outsiders [and is used] by those who have reason to be secretive" (Cameron and Kulick, 2006, p. 15). As the *travesti* activist Keila Simpson recalls, *pajubá* was a language forged on the streets, from the nightly practice of sex work and the lived experience of struggle: as such, it allowed in-group communication while ensuring that outsiders, and particularly the police, would not "understand what we are saying" (*apud* Araújo, 2018, p. 134). The "secrecy effect" of *pajubá*, as Florentino (1998, p. 76) identified for another context, could be achieved through various linguistic strategies of illegibility, of devising a clandestine and creative system of meaning, including the use of the African lexicon, the invention of hybrid words, the resort to slang, and the re-assembling of these elements through figures of speech, therefore resulting in the multiplication of possible meanings. In this perspective, the mobilization of *pajubá* under the military regime was also a political act of resistance, of escaping the repressive tentacles of the state (Lima, 2017, p. 59).

The political opening of the mid-1980s, which resulted in the transition to constitutional democracy in 1990, created the opportunity for the formalization of LGBT political organizing, a process that had already started in the late 1970s, albeit timidly, with the publication of a gay newspaper, *Lampião*, and the creation of small gay and lesbian organizations (Green, 1999, pp. 430–432). In this wave of institutionalization of sexual-queer politics, in the 1990s, the first *travesti* organization in Brazil was founded, named *Astral-Associação de Travestis e Liberados* (Astral-Association of *Travestis* and the Liberated). In 1995, *Astral* published a glossary of 232 words used by *travestis* in the everyday, titled *Diálogo de Bonecas* (Dialogue of Dolls).[7] As Gabriella Araújo (2018, pp. 52–53) has argued, in the context of increasing NGO-ization of politics driven by international funding priorities (the publication was financed by Swedish cooperation), the glossary was produced primarily to promote the legibility of the "target group" and to facilitate the access to it in the framework of HIV/Aids health interventions. The main contradiction here is that, for its speakers, the social currency of *pajubá* is predicated on its secretive, and elusive, character, which resists easy attempts at standardization and crystallization. In her conversation with *travesti* interlocutors, Araújo (2018, p. 134) observed that their insistence in affirming the secret status of the language has to do less with a concern with linguistic exclusivity and more with *pajubá*'s role as an important marker of group identity. Carlos Lima (2017, p. 32) reaches a similar conclusion, when he stresses that *pajubá* is not only a lexical repertoire, but also lived "performativity": its uses involve tones, rhythms, gestures, mannerisms, bodily motions, facial expressions, etc., and not words alone. Likewise, the transformative, subversive, powers of this language, he suggests, reside on the radical solidarities and sociabilities it creates around itself, amongst its speakers (Lima, 2017, p. 31). Even if fragments of its vocabulary and forms of speaking have been popularized, gone mainstream, through the internet, popular culture, or *telenovelas* (soap operas), new words, combinations and forms of codification emerge, and the language is in constant re-invention (Lima, 2017, p. 32). In the context of globalization, marked by increasing *travesti* migration (Vartabedian, 2018), words in European languages, especially English, are being incorporated into *pajubá*'s Atlantic repertoire (Lima, 2017, 57–58; Araújo, 2018, p. 127).

It is important to note that even if projects of collection and systematization of *pajubá*, such as *Diálogo de Bonecas*, risks disclosing the secret status of the language, the interlocutors with whom Araújo spoke are agreed that these initiatives are important to preserve the "history and memory of Brazilian *travestis*" (Araújo, 2018, p. 130). This is interesting to me because it speaks of a desire for legibility and self-inscription not in the linear language of the nation and constitutional citizenship, but as a minoritized subject position that resists assimilation into the norm, be that of gender, class, race, or sexuality. What is at stake here is the possibility and the desirability of approaching *pajubá* not as an object of social history, but as a living archive. As already mentioned, *pajubá*'s queer originality lies in its orality and performativity, and not in its incremental repertoire of words. As such, it is singularly unsuitable for incorporation in the conventional archive form, dependent as it is on the evidentiary authority of the written record. *Pajubá*'s absence from the narrative archive and its textual forms is not a "lack" in any negative sense; but it perhaps pushes us to think in terms of "ephemeral evidence", of queer acts akin to memory and performance (Muñoz, 1996, p. 10). Looking at memory, or at "practices of intense memorialisation", by rejecting any claims to authoritative history, affords one the opportunity of exploring dissidence in the histories "that people are already telling themselves" (Rao, 2020, p. 23). Pajubá's southern itineraries, which I outlined above – its crossing of the Black Atlantic, its entrance in the *terreiros* of Candomblé, its dissemination through urban street corners – are all forms of (performative) memorialization, insofar as they are histories that queer people are already telling themselves: the claim of African origins; the spiritual experience of the *terreiro*; and the political life of the non-gender-conforming body a site of resistance. Powerful moments of memory and performance are reflected in the work of the *transvestigênere*[8] playwright Ave Terrena Alves, in her play *3 Uiaras de SP City*, of 2018. Set during the last years of the military regime, the play follows the misadventures of Miella and Cinthia, two *travestis* trying to "make it big" as performers, while also struggling to evade the repressive machinery of the state, as embodied in the character of Police Deputy Rochetti, a "cis macho" obsessed with cleaning the street of "SP City" from "sodomites, travesties, prostitutes", etc. The play brings Yoruba terms from Pajubá and prayers to *orixás* in conversation with references to feminist slogans and class struggle, demonstrating the multiple temporalities and geographies in which queer lives unfold.

Based on the documents recovered by the Truth Commission on episodes of state violence against *travestis*, the play is a memorialist performance. Towards the end, after they manage to escape from prison, Miella utters: "the battle is not over, for centuries we will still need to fight". To which Cinthia replies: "memory is not a secret, to be locked or hidden" (*3 Uiaras de SP City*, 2018). This is such a rich moment, in my view, because it speaks to the often-difficult interplay of memory and futurity. If a difficult future lied ahead, the memory of the past was exposed to all. To think of *pajubá* as a queer archive entails precisely finding these openings to "unlock" a secret, even if one cannot read it.

Final Remarks

Queer scholar Larissa Pelúcio recalls a conversation she had with Cláudia Wonder, a travesti activist. In the late 1990s, Wonder told her that aids had not been an epidemic, but the burning of an archive. The Portuguese expression, "queima de arquivo", is often used to refer to the deliberate act of destroying evidence, often in a court case. Evidence, here, could be a piece of paper, a document, an object, or even a witness – in which case "queima de arquivo" would refer to the murder of a witness. In "destroying the evidence", aids had left a sense of deep emptiness. Perhaps that was "why, at that moment, we had such will to know" (Pelúcio, 2014, p. 15). In this statement, Pelúcio situates the intellectual and affective labour of Queer Theory in the aftermath of an epochal, collective, trauma, in which the feeling of loss fuelled the drive to enquire, to question, and the impossible desire for the wholeness of knowledge. Wonder's resort to the metaphor of the "burnt archive" to speak of queer death is a powerful reminder of the precariousness of queer lives, of the unconventional, non-normative – and, at times, unarchivable – ways in which these lives unfold.

In the present moment, one is perhaps driven by similar anxieties. COVID-19 has again evidenced the precariousness of life, particularly to those affected by the intersectionalities of various kinds. In Bolsonaro's Brazil, the conservative wave has curtailed the political purchase of the human rights agenda in name of an exclusivist, white, elitist, and patriarchal project, affecting minority rights at large, both sexual and religious. Under the Bolsonaro administration, there has been an obvious retreat of feminist and queer politics, while intolerant worldviews gained terrain. Partially as a product of the politicization of Pentecostal evangelism, there has been a renewed attack on both dissident sexualities and Afro-Brazilian religions. As a cultural form that has historically emerged and thrived in the interstices of these worlds, *pajubá* as a queer archive carries with it an important message of resilience, creativity, and solidarity. Let us not let this archive burn.

Notes

1 The entry for *maricas* in the Michaelis Dictionary also includes the archaic definition of a "womanizer" ("an individual who harasses women"), in addition to a contemporary Brazilian slang term by which *maricas* refers to a type of pipe used to smoke marijuana.
2 The language is also called "bajubá" , "Indaca", or "bate-bate", depending on the speaker's preference or location in the country, whereby "bate-bate" is used in the south. While pajubá seems to be the more common variation, this diversity in naming practices itself speaks to the performativity and plasticity of the language. See: Araújo (2018), pp. 44–45 and p. 125; Lima (2017), p. 58.
3 *Travesti* is a form of gender expression found in South America. While the term comes from the verb "*travestir*" (to cross-dress), *travestis* are biological men who socially present as women. See Kulick (1998), pp. 5–6; Vartebedian (2018), p. 3.
4 ENEM (Exame Nacional do Ensino Medio) translates as "National High School Exams" and is taken when an individual is finishing high school. ENEM's scores are considered together with prospective students' marks in the *vestibular*, the specific exam applied by each university in their selecting process. As such, ENEM's scores can be consequential in determining if a student will be accepted or rejected into higher education.
5 The Portuguese word "terreiro" refers to Candomblé's places of worship.
6 Orixá is the Yoruba term to refer to the deities of candomblé.
7 "Boneca" (dolls) is a term commonly used to refer to travestis.
8 "Transvestigênere" is a Portuguese term joining travesti and transgênero (transgender), pointing to an interstitial space between these two identities.

References

3 Uiraras de SP City by Ave Terrena Alves (2018). Directed by Diego Moschkovich [Centro Cultural São Paulo, São Paulo].

Alencastro, L. F. (2018). *The Trade in the Living: The Formation of Brazil in the South Atlantic, Sixteenth to Seventeenth Centuries*. Albany: State University of New York Press.

Araújo, G. C. (2018). *(Re)encontranto o Diálogo de Bonecas: o bajubá em uma perspectiva antropológica*. M.A. Thesis, Universidad Federal de Uberlândia. Available at: https://repositorio.ufu.br/handle/123456789/21850 (Accessed: 1 December 2020).

Barroso, R. R. (2017). *Pajubá: o código linguístico da comunidade LGBT*. M.A. Thesis, Universidade do Estado do Amazonas, Available at: http://repositorioinstitucional.uea.edu.br//handle/riuea/1945 (Accessed: 1 December 2020).

Beniste, J. (2009). *Dicionário Yorubá-Português*. Rio de Janeiro: Bertrand Brasil.

Boellstorff, T. (2005). *The Gay Archipelago: Sexuality and Nation in Indonesia*. Princeton: Princeton University Press.

Boone, J. (2014). *The Homoerotics of Orientalism*. New York: Columbia University Press.

Bucholtz, M. and Hall, K. (2004). "Theorizing Identity in Language and Sexuality Research". *Language and Society*, 33, pp. 469–515.

Butler, J. (1990). *Gender Trouble: Feminism and the Subversion of Identity*. New York: Routledge.

Cage, K. and Evans, M. (2003). *Gayle: The Language of Kings and Queens*. Houghton: Jacana Media.

Camarano, P. A. (2020). *Arquegenealogia Bajubeira: uma análise de práticas de poder e resistência*. M.A. Thesis, Universidade Federal de Goiás. Available at: https://repositorio.bc.ufg.br/tede/handle/tede/10677 (Accessed: 1 December 2020).

Cameron, D. and Kulick, D. (eds.) (2006) *The Language and Sexuality Reader*. London: Routledge.

Capone, S. (2007). "The 'Orisha Religion' between Syncretism and Re-Africanization". In Naro, N. P., Sansi-Roca, R., and Treece, D. H. (eds.). *Cultures of the Lusophone Black Atlantic*. New York: Palgrave Macmillan, pp. 219–232.

Castro, Y. P. de (2005), *Falares Africanos na Bahia*. 2nd edn. Rio de Janeiro: Academia Brasileira de Letras/Topbooks Editora.

Chaib, J. (2020). "Tem que deixar de ser um país de maricas, diz Bolsonaro cobre o combate à Covid-19", *Folha de São Paulo*, 10 November [online]. Available at: https://www1.folha.uol.com.br/equilibrioesaude/2020/11/temos-que-deixar-de-ser-um-pais-de-maricas-diz-bolsonaro-sobre-combate-a-covid-19.shtml (Accessed: 1 December 2020).

Comaroff, J. and Comaroff, John L. (2015). *Theory from the South: Or, How Euro-America is Evolving toward Africa*. New York: Routledge.

Comissão Nacional da Verdade (2014). Relatório Final da CNV, Livro II, Texto 7, "Ditadura e Homossexualidades". Available at: http://www.cnv.gov.br/images/pdf/relatorio/Volume%202%20-%20Texto%207.pdf (Accessed: 1 December 2020)

Connel, R. W. (2000). *The Men and the Boys*. 1st edn. Berkeley: University of California Press.

Cruz-Malavé, A. and Manalansan, M. (2002). "Introduction: Dissident Sexualities/Alternative Globalisms". In Cruz-Malavé, A. and Manalansan, M. (eds). *Queer Globalizations: Citizenship and the Afterlife of Colonialism*. New York: New York University Press.

Duggan, L (2002). "The New Homonormativity: The Sexual Politics of Neoliberalism". In Castronovo, R. and Nelson, D. D. (eds). *Materializing Democracy: Toward a Revitalized Cultural Politics*. Durham, NC: Duke University Press, pp. 175–194.

Dutta, A. and Roy, R. (2014). "Decolonizing Transgender in India: Some Reflections". *TSQ: The Transgender Studies Quarterly*, 1(3), pp. 320–336.

Eler, G. (2018). "O que é o pajubá, a linguagem criada pela comunidade LGBT". *Super Interessante*, 5 November 2018 [online]. Available at: https://super.abril.com.br/cultura/o-que-e-o-pajuba-a-linguagem-criada-pela-comunidade-lgbt/ (Accessed: 1 December 2020).

Farzan, A. N. and Berger, M. (2020). "Bolsonaro Says Brazilians Must Not Be 'sissies' about Coronavirus, as 'all of us are going to die one day'". *The Washington Post*, 11 November [online]. Available at: https://www.washingtonpost.com/world/2020/11/11/bolsonaro-coronavirus-brazil-quotes/ (Accessed: 1 December 2020).

Ferreira, R. (2012). *Cross-Cultural Exchange in the Atlantic World: Angola and Brazil during the era of the slave trade*. Cambridge: University Press.

Florentino, C. de O. (1998). *"Bicha tu tens na barriga, eu sou mulher...": etnografia sobre travestis em Porto Alegre*. M.A. Thesis, Universidade Federal de Santa Catarina. Available at: https://repositorio.ufsc.br/xmlui/handle/123456789/77565 (Accessed: 1 December 2020).

Folha de São Paulo (2018). "Bolsonaro critica questão do Enem sobre gays e promote exames com temas 'úteis'". *Folha de São Paulo*, 5 November 2018 [online]. Available at: https://

www1.folha.uol.com.br/educacao/2018/11/bolsonaro-critica-questao-do-enem-sobre-gays-e-promete-exame-com-temas-uteis.shtml (Accessed: 1 December 2020).

Foucault, M. (1981). *The History of Sexuality, Vol 1: an introduction*. London: Pelican Books.

Freyre, G. (1986). *The Masters and the Slaves: A Study in the Development of Brazilian Civilization*. 2nd edn. Berkeley and Los Angeles: University of California Press.

Fry, P. (1982). *Para Inglês Ver: identidade e política na cultura brasileira*. Rio de Janeiro: Zahar Editor.

Gilroy, P. (1993). *The Black Atlantic: Modernity and Double Consciousness*. Cambridge: Harvard University Press.

Globo (2018). "Veja resolução de questão do Enem que aborda status do pajubá como 'dialeto secreto' dos gays e travestis". *Globo*. 5 November 2018 [online]. Available at: https://g1.globo.com/educacao/enem/2018/noticia/2018/11/05/veja-resolucao-de-questao-do-enem-que-aborda-status-do-pajuba-como-dialeto-secreto-dos-gays-e-travestis.ghtml (Accessed: 1 December 2020).

Green, J. N. (1999). *Além do Carnaval: a homossexualidade masculina no Brasil do século XX*. São Paulo: Editora Unesp.

Hall, K. (1996). "Lexical Subversion in India's Hijra Community". In Bucholtz, M., Liang, A. C., Sutton, L. A., and Hines, C. (eds.). *Gender and Belief Systems: Proceedings of the Third Berkeley Women and Language Conference*. Berkeley: Berkeley Women and Language Group, pp. 279–292.

Hall, K. (1997). "'Go suck your husband's sugarcane!' Hijras and the Use of Sexual Insult". In Livia, A. and Hall, K. (eds.). *Queerly Phrased: Language, Gender and Sexuality*. New York and Oxford: Oxford University Press, pp. 430–460.

Inácio, E. da C. (2018). "Algumas Intersecionalidades e um Texto 'Cuir' para Chamar de '(M)Eu: Retratos da Produção Estética Afro-Lusobrasileira'". *Via Atlântica*, 33, pp. 225–240.

Isfahani-Hammond, A. (2008). *White Negritude: Race, Writing, and Brazilian Cultural Identity*. New York: Palgrave Macmillan.

Jornal do Brasil (1970). "Casa Grande & Senzala Vista dos Bastidores". 2 October 1970 [online]. Available at: http://memoria.bn.br/DocReader/030015_09/17446 (Accessed: 1 December 2020).

Khanna, A. (2007). "Us 'Sexuality Types': A Critical Engagement with the Postcoloniality of Sexuality". In Bose, B. and Bhattacharyya, S. (eds.). *The Phobic and the Erotic: The Politics of Sexuality in Contemporary India*. London: Seagull Books, pp. 159–200.

Kulick, D. (1998). *Travesti: Sex, Gender, and Culture Among Brazilian Transgendered Prostitutes*. Chicago and London: University of Chicago Press.

Leap, W. (2012). "Queer Linguistics, Sexuality, and Discourse Analysis". In Gee, J. P. and Handford, M. (eds). *The Routledge Handbook of Discourse Analysis*. New York: Routledge, pp. 558–71.

Leap, W. and Boellstoff, T. (eds.) (2004). *Speaking in Queer Tongues: Globalization and Gay Language*. Urbana and Chicago: Illinois University Press.

Lewin, E. and Leap, W. L. (2009). "Introduction". In Lewin, E. and Leap, W. L. (eds.). *Out in Public: Reinventing Lesbian/Gay Anthropology in a Globalizing World*. Chichester, West Sussex/Malden, MA: Wiley-Blackwell, pp. 1–24.

Lim, S. L. (2008). "How to be queer in Taiwan: Translation, appropriation and the construction of a queer identity in Taiwan". In Martin, F., Jackson, P. A., McLelland, M., and Yue, A. (eds.). *AsiaPacifiQueer: Rethinking Genders and Sexualities*. Urbana: University of Illinois Press, pp. 235–250.

Lima, C. H. L. (2017). *Linguagens Pajubeyras: Re(ex)sistência cultural e subversão da heteronormatividade*. Salvador: Editora Devires.

Livia, A. and Hall, K. (eds.) (1997). *Queerly Phrased: Language, Gender and Sexuality*. New York and Oxford: Oxford University Press.

López, L. A. (2004). "A Língua de Camões com Iemanjá: forma e funções da linguagem do candomblé". PhD Dissertation, University of Stockholm. Available at: https://www.diva-portal.org/smash/get/diva2:195220/FULLTEXT01.pdf (Accessed: 1 December 2020).

Lugones, M. (2007). "Heterosexualism and the Colonial/Modern Gender System". *Hypatia*, 22(1), pp. 186–209.

Manalansan, M. (2003). *Global Divas: Filipino Gay Men in the Diaspora*. Durham: Duke University Press.

Manalansan, M. (2014). "The 'Stuff' of Archives: Mess, Migration, and Queer Lives". *Radical History Review*, 120(Fall), pp. 94–107.

Massad, J. (2007). *Desiring Arabs*. Chicago: Chicago University Press.

Matory, J. L. (2005). *Black Atlantic Religion: Tradition, Transnationalism, and Matriarchy in the Afro-Brazilian Candomblé*. Princeton and Oxford: Princeton University Press.

McClintock, A. (1995). *Imperial Leather: Race, Gender, and Sexuality in the Colonial Contest*. 1st edn. New York: Routledge.

McLean, H. and Ngcobo, L. (1994). "Abangibhamayo bathi ngimnandi (those who fuck me say I'm tasty). Gay Sexuality in a Reef Township". In Gevisser, M. and Cameron, E. (eds.). *Defiant Desire: Gay and Lesbian Lives in South Africa*. Johannesburg: Ravan Press.

Michaelis Dicionário Brasileiro da Língua Portuguesa (2020) "Maricas". https://michaelis.uol.com.br/moderno-portugues/busca/portugues-brasileiro/maricas/

Miskolci, R. M. (2012). *O desejo da nação: masculinidade e branquitude no Brasil de fins do XIX*. São Paulo: Annablume/FAPESP.

Muñoz, J. E. (1996). "Ephemera as Evidence: Introductory Notes to Queer Acts". *Women & Performance: A Journal of Feminist Theory*, 8(2), pp. 5–16.

Nascimento, E. L. (2003). *The Sorcery of Color: Identity, Race, and Gender in Brazil*. Philadelphia: Temple University Press.

Ndlovu-Gatsheni, S. (2020). *Decolonizaiton, Developement, and Knowledge in Africa: turning over a new leaf*. New York: Routledge.

Pelúcio, L. (2009). *Abjeção e Desejo: uma etnografia travesti sobre o modelo preventivo de aids*. São Paulo: Annablume/Fapesp.

Pelúcio, L. (2012). "Subalterno quem, cara-pálida? Apontamentos às margens sobre pós-colonialismos, feminismos e estudos queer". *Contemporânea: Revista de Sociologia da UFSCar*, 2(2), pp. 395–418.

Pelúcio, L. (2014). "Traduções e torções ou o que se quer dizer quando dizemos queer no Brasil?". *Revista Acadêmica Periódicus*, 1(1), pp. 68–91.

Pereira, P. P. G. (2019). *Queer in the Tropics: Gender and Sexuality in the Global South*. Cham: Springer.

Puar, J. K. (2007). *Terrorist Assemblages: Homonationalism in Queer Times*. Durham: Duke University Press.

Quinalha, r. H. (2017). *Contra a Moral e os Bons Costumes: a política sexual da ditadura brasileira (1964–1988)*. PhD Dissertation, Universidade de São Paulo. Available at: https://teses.usp.br/teses/disponiveis/101/101131/tde-20062017-182552/pt-br.php (Accessed: 1 December 2020).

Radio France Internationale (2020). "Bolsonaro tells Brazil not to deal with pandemic 'like fags'". Radio France Internationale, 11 November 2020 [online]. Available at:

https://www.rfi.fr/en/wires/20201111-bolsonaro-tells-brazil-not-deal-pandemic-fags (Accessed: 1 December 2020).

Rao, R. (2020). *Out of Time: The Queer Politics of Postcoloniality*. Oxford: University Press.

Rudwick, S. and Ntuli, M. (2008). "*IsiNgqumo*: Introducing a Gay Black South African Linguistic Variety". *South African Linguistics and Applied Language Studies*, 26(4), pp. 445–456.

Santos, B. S. (2018). *The End of the Cognitive Empire: The Coming of Age of the Epistemologies of the South*. Durham: Duke University Press.

Santos, B. S. and Meneses, M. P. (2019). *Knowledges Born of Struggle: Constructing the Epistemologies of the Global South*. London and New York: Routledge.

Sedgwick, E. (1990). *Epistemology of the Closet*. Berkeley: University of California Pres.

Silva Pinto, L. M. (1832). *Dicionario da Lingua Brasileira*. Ouro Preto: Typographia de Silva.

Silva, A. de M. (1789). *Dicionario de Lingua Portugueza, vol 2*. Lisboa: Oficina de Simão Thaddeo Ferreira.

Skidmore, T. E. (1993). *Black into White: Race and Nationality in Brazilian Thought*. Durham and London: Duke University Press.

Stoler, A. L. (1995). *Race and the Education of Desire: Foucault's History of Sexuality and the Colonial Order of Things*. 1st edn. Durham and London: Duke University Press.

Stryker, S. (2008). "Transgender History, Homonormativity, and Disciplinarity". *Radical History Review*, 100, pp. 145–157.

Tellis, A. and Bala, S. (2015). *The Global Trajectories of Queerness: Re-thinking Same-Sex Politics in the Global South*. Leiden: Brill Rodopi.

Vartabedian, J. (2018). *Brazilian Travesti Migrations: Gender, Sexualities and Embodiment Experiences*. Cham: Palgrave Macmillan.

20

ARDHANĀRISWARA

Shalinee Kumari and David Szanton

This chapter derives from the conference call for papers that take up a concept from a Southern linguistic universe and explore its potential contributions beyond its own geographical, intellectual, and cultural origins. This raises questions that scholars in both the Global South and Global North now must seriously address: are the critical, analytical, and interpretive concepts that have been developed in Northern scholarship universal, or are they in fact fundamentally local, limited, and culture-bound? And can they be usefully challenged or supplemented by comparable concepts from the South?

Over 200 years ago, Immanuel Kant and Georg Friedrich Hegel repeatedly asserted that analytical, scientific, and philosophical thought derived from the Greeks and that the cultures and civilizations beyond the Euro-Atlantic world had never generated valuable forms of knowledge, theories, or perspectives on human life, social formations, or the workings of the natural world. It is a view still widely held today and recently prompted Dilip Menon's friend, Gopal Guru, a Dalit scholar from India to ask, "can a *dalit* articulate a universal?"

As an anthropologist and an artist, we find it astonishing that anyone today could claim or imagine that none of the hundreds of societies and cultures that have flourished on the globe, no less the great Buddhist, Confucian, Hindu, Islamic, and Andean civilizations, have ever produced distinctive conceptual, intellectual, and aesthetic contributions that might extend beyond their own boundaries. Such an Atlanto-centric hubris almost demands its nemesis. Indeed, the conference and this volume direct us to significant alternative concepts, perspectives, understandings, and possibilities embedded in the languages, literature, art, music, and institutions of Burkina Faso, the Caribbean, China, India, Persia, South Africa, and Uganda, all with direct relevance well beyond their cultural points of origin.

At this point, we propose to add to the texts and musings of the other chapters a distinctive Indian *visual* art form – Mithila Painting – that likewise manifests

DOI: 10.4324/9781003273530-27

significant non-western conceptualizations or framings and enables fresh critical perspectives on four major contemporary Indian, but simultaneously global, phenomena: Capitalism, Patriarchy, Feminism, and Gender Inequality.

Mithila and Mithila Painting

Mithila is an ancient linguistic and culture-historical region of northern Bihar overlapping into southern Nepal with a predominantly Hindu population of some 40 million people today. Located just below the southern range of the Himalayas, most of Mithila consists of a broad, well-watered plain, marked by numerous rivers and natural and dug ponds, in season covered with lotus flowers. Although the once huge Zamindari landed estates have been broken up, Mithila remains both largely agricultural, and highly stratified. Historically, many men of the upper castes, Maithil Brahmins and Kayastha (nominally scribes and accountants), have been well educated and recognized across India as highly literate scholars, writers, poets, religious specialists, government officers, and political leaders. In general, the society is deeply conservative and highly patriarchal.

Domestically, and while this is changing now, as wives, Maithil Brahmin and Kayastha women have for centuries been home-bound – given limited schooling, thus often illiterate, and in *purdah*, meaning limited access to the outside world, to visitors, and to the male relatives of their husbands. In contemporary paintings, married women are often represented as a bird in a cage. In general, however, along with producing and caring for children, meals, and the family's general appearance, married women are deeply committed to, and largely responsible for, their family's numerous annual rituals and spiritual wellbeing, and especially for doing elaborate wall and floor paintings required for the initial "first wedding" (or engagement), and the second (actual) marriage that takes place at the bride's home. In contrast, Maithil Brahmin and Kayastha married men (or grandfathers) have long been the heads of households, decision-makers, and the sources of family income. They also select spouses for their children and negotiate dowries, but only after consulting genealogists to ensure that potential newlyweds have been separated by at least six generations.

Despite the constraints on women's lives, the renowned 14th-century Maithil love poet, Vidyapati, noted that women were painting images of gods and goddesses on the walls of their homes. Popular legend has it that King Janak ordered his subjects to paint their homes to celebrate the wedding of his daughter, Sita, to Ram, the two central figures of the Ramayana. Whether or not this earlier dating for the origins of the painting tradition – perhaps some 3,000 or more years ago – is accurate, Mithila painting is clearly an ancient art form. We know from various texts (Rekha, forthcoming), that the wall painting tradition continued into the 19th century, and it continues today. Most often depicted are the gods Krishna, Shiva, Parvati, Durga, Vishnu, and Ganesh, intended to establish their presence and create auspicious ritual spaces, especially elaborated for marriages.

Here are sections of two wall paintings done for marriages in the 1930s (Figure 20.1).[1]

Brahmin and Kayastha homes in Mithila have traditionally had a dedicated ritual and marriage chamber (*kohbar ghar*) in which at least two essential images are painted or repainted for each engagement or marriage. Here is one photographed in 1940 by W.G. Archer for a marriage that took place in 1937. On the left is a stylized *purain* (lotus pond), representing the bride's beauty. The fish represent desired fecundity. The checkered figure below represents the mat on which the marriage will be consummated on the night of the fourth day of the wedding rituals. On the right, alongside an attendant, is a comparably large and stylized *bans* (bamboo grove) representing the groom's virility and family line. The bans is surrounded by parrots regarded as love birds (Figure 20.2).

Wall paintings for both engagements and marriages often include major Hindu deities intended to provide an auspicious space for the event and the marriage. Here, Parvati stands on the left facing her beloved husband, Shiva, seated on the sacred Mount Kailash. Next comes their son, the elephant-headed Ganesh and his rats (his vehicle or mounts), followed by a partial image of Brahma.

In the late 1960s, however, women's lives, and their paintings, went through a great transformation. During an extended drought that devastated agriculture in north India, Pupul Jayakar, then Head of the All India Handicrafts Board,

FIGURE 20.1 Central images of a *kohbar*, a marriage painting on the wall of a Brahmin bride's home. (Photo, W.G. Archer, BL 379/11) Home of Sambhunath Jha.Village Ujan, Darbhanga, 1937.

FIGURE 20.2 A segment of a wall painting in the home of a Kayastha bride. (Photo, W.G. Archer, 1940 BL 379/3) Home of Ram Krishna Nid, village Samaila, Darbhanga. Painted in 1936, on the occasion of the couple's engagement.

commissioned Bhaskar Kulkarni, an artist from Bombay, to go to Madhubani town and district, a major center of Mithila wall painting, and encourage the women to transfer their paintings from the walls to paper. Jayakar supplied Kulkarni with crates of "Imperial" size paper (22×30 inches) to distribute to the women so they could produce paintings for sale to compensate for the lost family income from agriculture.

A small number of women took up the challenge, but the numbers grew rapidly when Kulkarni exhibited and sold the initial paintings on paper in New Delhi and brought back the profits to the painters. Several women, most prominently Sita Devi and Ganga Devi, who painted in distinctively different styles, turned out to be extraordinarily fine artists. They received numerous public and private commissions and starting in the early 1970s, the government sent them to represent India at cultural fairs in the Soviet Union, Europe, Japan, and the United States. When they returned to their villages in Madhubani with stories of the outside world, many more women began painting and generating family income as well.

In the late 1960s and early 1970s, Indian society still retained a strong Gandhian interest in traditional skills, crafts, and aesthetics. The paintings were popular, the number of painters kept growing, and the repertoire of subjects on paper began to expand. The kohbar and lotus pond, along with images of Shiva and Parvati, Radha and Krishna, or Krishna with his adoring *gopis* (milkmaids), and of Durga, and Vishnu and Lakshmi were the most common. But they were quickly joined by other gods and goddesses, and later by episodes from the Ramayana, and scenes from local tales and village life (Figure 20.3).

Painted in the Brahmin highly colored *bharni* ("filled") style, here is Shiva in his blissful dancing mode atop Nandi, his vehicle bull, with all his traditional attributes: disheveled hair, snakes, tiger skin, trident, drum, crescent moon, and the Ganges flowing from his hair. Although regarded as the ideal couple, Parvati, in this strikingly male-dominant painting, is but the small figure in the lower left (Figure 20.4).

Painted in the *kachni* ("line") style associated with Kayastha painters, here Shiva is in his intense "hot" ascetic mode, seated on nails representing Mount Kailash (compare with Fig. 20.2.) While on the right, Parvati is equally large and is using a fan to cool Shiva, while more comfortably seated on a carpet or bench.

FIGURE 20.3 A dominant Shiva, on his Bull, Nandi, and wife Parvati, in the corner below. A 1974 painting on paper by Bacha Dai Devi. (Photo, Edouard Boubat, 1974)

FIGURE 20.4 Here, Shiva is again seated on Mount Kailash with his now comparably sized wife, Parvati, again in profile, seated alongside on a bench or carpet and using a fan to cool him. A 1974 painting on paper by Ganga Devi. (Photo, Edouard Boubat, 1974)

As suggested by these paintings, Shiva and Parvati have a long history together as major deities of Hinduism, and also represent an important abstraction or concept. Shiva is simultaneously both a creator and destroyer, ascetic, and benevolent. Numerous texts and stories demonstrate these qualities. Parvati, in contrast, is a steadier figure; a powerful mother goddess of love, fertility, bonding, and devotion, who becomes Shiva's consort and wife after years of ascetic devotion to him. In Mithila and much of India, they are regarded as the ideal couple, distinctively different, yet combining the powers and energies of both male and female, often represented abstractly in the lingam and yoni, but also at least since the 5th century AD, in the form of Ardhanāriswara, a single androgynous god, male on the left, and female on the right. As such, Shiva and Parvati represent the ideal married couple and as such have become a standard image in the kohbar on walls and paper as an auspicious model and guide for newlyweds (Figure 20.5).

Compared with the large 1937 Fig. 20.1 kohbar on the wall, this elegant but quite traditional 2005 kohbar on paper, while deeply compressed (to 22×30 inches), is vastly more elaborate. Using a fine pen and ink on paper, instead of a brush on a mud wall, allows for being more detailed and inclusive. The lotus pond now includes not just a fish, but also a turtle, snakes, a crab, and water bugs, while the sun and moon are in the upper left and right corners. The astrological

FIGURE 20.5 Kohbar, by Bhuma Devi, 2005. All the uncredited photographs are by David Szanton.

figures on the left were also absent in the wall paintings but by the 1970s had become common elements of kohbars.

But not only have the materials and technology evolved. The social context was changing as well. Ever since paintings went onto paper for sale in the late 1960s and were for the first time generating income for women, the central lotus pond representing bride had become the dominant figure of the kohbar, while a much-diminished bamboo grove, representing the groom and his family, was regularly squeezed into the upper right corner. In addition, as in Figure 20.4, the comparably sized figures of Shiva and Parvati regularly appeared in the lower left corner. And in this painting, Parvati is holding the cord around Nandi's neck. Also by the 1970s, the kohbars often included, in the lower right corner, a depiction of an actual marriage ritual; the bride, with the groom behind her, is thanking Parvati (represented by a small clay elephant), for finding her a good husband. At least in the symbolism, even if more slowly, in reality, gender roles and expectations were also evolving.

This playful Figure 20.6, a "Fish Kohbar" from 2006, painted just a year later than Figure 20.5, but by a much younger artist, likewise adds to and accentuates these new gender ideals by further emphasis on Parvati's power and equality with Shiva. Not only have the lotus blossoms of the central image, emphasizing the beauty of the bride, become paired fish, emphasizing the idea of fecundity and the desire for children, but the bamboo grove has also become a fecund fish,

FIGURE 20.6 Fish Kohbar, Pinki Kumari, 2006. (Photo, David Szanton)

subtly shifting the emphasis to family and co-parenthood. In addition, Parvati's small clay elephant in Figure 20.5, has become quite substantial and has even replaced Shiva's Nandi, now reduced to a tiny cow.

Linking the idea of Shiva and Parvati as equal presences with equal potency has in the last 20 years led increasing numbers of artists to paint the figure of Ardhanāriswara, its ancient and ultimate expression; with Shiva on the left and Parvati on the right, combined in a single figure (Figures 20.7 and 20.8).

Although Ardhanāriswara does not appear in any of the approximately 170 W.G. Archer photographs of wall paintings from the late 1930s, it became a frequent image when the paintings went onto paper (see Figure 20.7. from 1974). It was used for the logo of the short-lived Mastercraftsmen's Association of Mithila between 1978 and 1981, and since 1980 it has been the logo of the Ethnic Arts Foundation. In recent years, many painters have been drawing on the image of the Ardhanāriswara to convey the relevance and power of the ancient Hindu concept of the complementarity and interdependence of the distinctively different forms of male and female power. In the process, it has given concrete form to the complementarity and interdependence of *difference*, expressed in a single figure that is simultaneously symmetrical, and a-symmetrical.[2] To more fully appreciate the uses of the image and the embedded concept, we turn now to the paintings by the artist and co-author of this chapter, Shalinee Kumari.

FIGURE 20.7 Ardhanāriswara, Sita Devi, 1974. (Photo, Edouard Boubat)

Shalinee Kumari was born in 1986 and grew up as the eldest of four daughters in a small Maithil village near the Nepal border. Her father was employed in the Ministry of Agriculture and her mother was a homemaker. In 2005, recognizing the generalizability in the Ardhanārishwara's capacity to convey the complementarity and interdependence of difference, she produced Figure 20.9, on the positives and negatives of *poonjivaad* – the Hindi term for capitalism.

The central figure is in the form of the Indian Swastika, (the reverse of the Nazi swastika), and an ancient Indian symbol of Prosperity. In Shalinee's painting, it carries the four major elements of Capitalism's enormous productivity; Industrial Production; the Green Revolution (the red and green rice); Globalized commoditization and communication; and Knowledge Creation (the lamp, the book, and beauty of nature are the breaking bomb and the dagger of Ignorance). They are all positive, and are the elements that light up the world below.

FIGURE 20.8 Ardhanāriswara, Godaveri Dutta, 2013. (photo EAF, 2013)

On the right, however, stands a figure to whose hands and feet are attached the negative aspects of Capitalism; guns and rockets, swollen body parts, drugs, alcohol, and tobacco. Note too, that the figure is an Ardhanāriswara (Shalinee's first use of the image), with an overloaded truck on its head, the migraine headache these items cause for both men and women.

Likewise, on the left, a crouching crying woman, is suffering from Capitalism's multiple forms of pollution; automobile exhaust, insecticides and pesticides, noise pollution, and cosmetics that burn women's skin.

The negative products of capitalism on both the right and the left darken the worlds below. They also create toxins that rise to the serpents above who are passing them on to Shiva at the top center, the god who is known, among other things, as the Creator, Preserver, and Destroyer. Here, Shalinee is drawing on the *Samudra Manthan*, a famous story in Hindu mythology in which in order to save the world from the deadly poisons produced by the churning of the primordial Ocean of Milk, Shiva swallows the poisons

FIGURE 20.9 The Positives and Negatives of Capitalism (Poonjivaad) or "Creative Destruction." Shalinee Kumari, 2005.

himself and is only saved by his loving wife, Parvati, gripping him around the neck, preventing the poison from reaching his vulnerable organs, and destroying the world as well!

Shalinee often uses her paintings to ask a question, In this case, it is, "Can Shiva again save the world by swallowing Capitalism's toxins? Or as she put it:

> "Creative Destruction" is about the man-made destructiveness of over development. People must think more about the problems created by what they take to be progress. We are in a danger zone now. Capitalism is driving people to do anything to make more money and have more power. In the process they are creating toxins that are destroying life.
>
> In addition to the central figures, the borders of the painting show humanity's creative hands, a lit lamp, the earth with wings, and the Indian swastika, again, a symbol of prosperity. The positive things of poonjivaara. But along with capitalist development, human life is increasingly threatened with destruction. That is why lord Shiva's triple eyes in the borders are angry; he is worried about human life and suffering.
>
> The fundamental question is: will humans think globally and swallow the toxins they have created, as Shiva did in order to save humanity? Realistically, no. People will never agree to swallow the toxins they have created. Countries everywhere want to develop new means to increase

their power and protect themselves from disasters and terrorists attempting to capture the world.

Yet my heart can't accept such a negative answer. Thus I pray to lord Shiva, please come and swallow the toxins. Shiva lives in my imagination. The countries of the world must join together to be like a Shiva to swallow the toxins. Then a miracle could happen; then the toxins could be swallowed by humans. Then they will be like a Shiva.

★★★

In 2008, Shalinee painted a critique of patriarchy, drawing more explicitly on the Ardhanānriswara, this time to point out the complementarity and interdependence of the internal conflicts that plague women's lives (Figure 20.10).

FIGURE 20.10 Radiant Yet Submissive. Shalinee Kumari, 2009.

Shalinee described it:

> Women are radiant and powerful but face into a dark and difficult world. At the same time, they are submissive to the men in their life represented as naga (serpents) in the painting. Wrapped around their legs, they control women sexually. Hovering over them, men control them socially and politically. And women must constantly make offerings to men.

When I asked her about the serpent on the figure's forehead, she replied "And they have captured our minds!"

In 2009, Shalinee also painted a direct counter to patriarchy and the lingam; a feminist reconfiguration of the Ardhanānriswara – now with Parvati dominant (Figure 20.11).

FIGURE 20.11 Shiva and Parvati – the Divine Couple, or "The Feminist Ardhanāriswara." Shalinee Kumari, 2009.

In recent years, Shalinee and many other artists have been using the concept of the Ardhanārishwara, its a-symmetry yet complementarity, in paintings on other issues. Perhaps, Shalinee's most immediately critical use of the image is a painting she did several years after her marriage, entitled "A Woman's Dharma/ Duties." Once again, it draws on the Ardhanāriswara, but now to critique gender inequality. And once again, it raises an issue and a question (Figure 20.12).

Shalinee described the painting:

> Before marriage girls are responsible to and for their parents: after marriage they become part of and are responsible for their husband's family. The woman's devotional steps around the circle represent her duty, her dharma; the vital roles she must play in her families. Beneath her feet is a lotus, a symbol of purity.
>
> Inside the wheel – facing in opposite directions – are the two sides (ardhnaari), of her familial duties. After leaving her parent's home and facing forward she must devote herself to her husband's family. But facing behind her she must also recognize her continuing responsibility for her own mother and father's family.
>
> However, times are changing now. The circle is bright. Following her dharma, an empowered woman can remove the darkness in her life.

FIGURE 20.12 A Woman's Dharma/Duties, <u>or</u> the Great Unasked and Unanswered Question. Shalinee Kumari, 2016.

On the left, the bride is in a doli traveling to her husband's house from her parent's home. Her footprints (between the two bearers) point towards her husband's house. She must not go back to her parent's home. Yet when she is strong in her devotion to her husband's family, the wheel of her duty and devotion will also point back to her parents. In fact, all around the wheel, her footprints are going in both directions.

Despite these duties, women have no right of succession or inheritance in her husband's family. And while women now have a legal right of inheritance in her parent's family, culturally it is unattainable. Only sons inherit. A daughter would have to take her parents to court to obtain an inheritance from them, a socially impossible act that would totally sacrifice her relationship with her parents. Even a woman's jewelry goes to her daughter(s) in law, and not to her daughter.

Likewise, even though prohibited by law, the dowry system is still at its peak. And most of the increasingly large dowries go to the family of the husband, and not to the daughter getting married. If women had equal rights to inheritance it would undercut the dowry system and maintain more balanced relations between her two families.

I have left the White Circle in the center empty. It is the site of the great unasked, and unanswered, question; After all of a woman's devotion and service to her two families, why can't she be a successor or inheritor in either of her families?

★★★

Shalinee's paintings – and hers are not alone – demonstrate the current relevance, power, and insight of ancient Indian concepts, wisdom, and knowledge regarding the interdependence and complementarity – in effect, the relational construction and mutual constitution – of difference. In a Euro-Atlantic world dominated by Aristotelian opposing concepts; either/or, black or white, true or false, past or present, x and y axes, the paraphernalia of positivism, all pressing toward thinking with binary-bounded units, and mutual differentiation – the Ardhanārishwara provides a compelling alternative that seems much closer to human experience and social reality.

For the purposes of this volume, Shalinee's Mithila paintings using the a-symmetrical yet complementary figure of the Ardhanāriswara provides the "Global North" – with its propensities towards "independent variables," "bounded units", and "either/or conceptions" – with a refreshing and important window into thought from the "Global South." It is a point of entry into another way of thinking, feeling, and understanding the possible. A counter to what the "Global North" presumes and takes for granted, and a useful alternative framework for expressing, defining, and interpreting self, community, the world, and human experience.

Notes

1 Between 1938 and 1940, W.G. Archer, an ICS officer and District Magistrate in the Mithila region of Bihar took at least 170 photographs of wall paintings in 17 Brahmin homes and 11 Kayastha homes in 25 different villages scattered across the region. He had first seen such paintings on the walls of partially destroyed homes following the massive 1934 Bihar earthquake, when he was a Joint Magistrate and Deputy Collector in Madhubani from April 1933 to October 1934. Archer donated to the India Office Library, now part of the British Library in London, 45 3×5 inch prints of those photographs, and approximately 125 one inch square contact prints. All are well documented.

2 Because it is fundamentally a-symmetrical, it is arguably a more subtle, vibrant, complex, and flexible Indian counterpart to the fully symmetrical East Asian image and use of Yin and Yang.

PART VIII

Insurrection

21

AWQĀT/AUKĀT

Francesca Orsini

Why *Aukāt*?

Although its meaning originally was quite different, *aukāt* in Hindi has come to mean status, or rather the *trespassing* of one's "natural" or properly subordinate status, with the promise of retribution or punishment.[1] It is never used in an affirmative utterance ("my/our *aukāt* is") but only in a negative one, typically couched as a threatening question. "*Terī aukāt kyā hai*?" ("What is your status?") really means that you don't have the *aukāt* to behave like this before me. It is, therefore, better translated as "How dare you?", "You count for nothing", "You are overstepping the boundaries of your subordinate condition", "I am warning you".

As an interpellation that suggests that the addressee does *not* have the right to speak or behave in a certain way, *aukāt* takes us directly to moments of confrontation around status. Its momentary utterance is a symptom of wider dynamics and processes over time. As Judith Butler reminds us, the particular moment of the individual utterance "is never merely a single moment … [it] is a condensed historicity: it exceeds itself in past and future directions, an effect of prior and future invocations that constitute and escape the instance of utterance" (1997, 3). While *aukāt* can be used to refer to perceived slurs and status "infractions" in general, its "condensed historicity" relates particularly to Dalits, and the utterance is addressed to them when they are perceived to overstep their position and they need to be put "back" in their place. Which means *whenever* they try to improve their socio-economic conditions, or simply wear better clothes and footwear, get educated, or refuse demeaning social practices or sexual demands imposed upon them. Paradoxically, while *aukāt* as a feminine singular noun meaning "status" hides the original meaning of "times" (m. pl.), it speaks powerfully to changing times.

DOI: 10.4324/9781003273530-29

Aukāt is, therefore, a useful term to grapple with iterative moments of struggle around hierarchy, respect, dignity, and social recognition in contemporary India in which, from one perspective, the hierarchical *status quo* needs to be maintained with the threat of violence, while from the other perspective even modest socio-economic improvements, symbolic affirmations, and claims to dignity and respect can be met with incommensurate retribution, for which a specific term, *narsaṃhār* or collective homicide, has been coined in Hindi. Against the backdrop of state promises of development and contemporary dreams of socio-economic mobility, Dalit education, aspirations, and mobilization are routinely met with enormous backlashes of anger and often violence. The violence that accompanies *aukāt* is, therefore, of a particular, exemplary, kind ("*sabaq sikhānā*" or "teaching a lesson"). Inquiring into the term means inquiring into a whole set of actions and reactions and into the discourse that accompanies such violence. It prompts us to think what terms or expressions are used to the same objective in other dynamics of unequal confrontation (Silva 2017).

Methodologically, *aukāt* gives us a different route into the question of political vocabularies from that of "indigenous categories", or translation and translingual practices under colonization. To put it simplistically, intellectual history in South Asia and beyond has so far been approached in one of two ways. Either it has conceived as a matter of translation (with its implied source-and-target model, in which the original retains a special status) or as translingual practice, as in Lydia Liu's *Translingual Practices* (1995) and, more recently, Chris Bayly's intellectual history of liberalism (2011). Liu reframes source-and-target languages as guest and host languages in order to helpfully lay emphasis on appropriation and on how "guest" concepts begin new lives in the "host" languages. To give one example, the question is not whether the Hindi *loktantra* properly translates or only approximates "democracy", but *how* was "*loktantra*" translated into local political culture, what was its life after it was appropriated? The other approach has been that of *Grundbegriffe*, i.e. the exploration of basic indigenous concepts and their genealogy and shifting meanings; for example, how terms like *nīti* (policy) or *rājya* (rule) or *śūdra* (lower caste, Vajpeyi 2011) have changed over the centuries and across genres and languages (Brunner, Conze, and Koselleck 1972; Hoffmann 2012).

The term *Aukāt* instead takes us to the question of conceptual/political vocabulary from a pragmatic and illocutionary perspective: *when* is it used, *to whom*, and with which *force*? It also takes us away from ideas of caste as a system (Dumont 1980) to a more shifting, yet nonetheless hard, matrix of hierarchical relationships in which the economic and the symbolic are inextricably related. As such, it seems applicable to many other situations of retributive violence, in which movements of self-respect engender excessive violence, forcing us to enquire about the "condensed historicity" of the language that accompanies such violence (Marcus 2002; Reid and Valasik 2020).

Etymology, Meanings, Affines

One of the interesting things about *auqāt* is its remarkable semantic and grammatical journey away from its etymology. *Auqāt* as indexing status (a status that the addressee does not have) is a feminine singular word, whereas etymologically it is the masculine Arabic broken plural (*awqāt*) of *waqt*, meaning "times". Already in Steingass's *Persian–English Dictionary*, *awqāt* is glossed as: "times, seasons, hours (especially for prayers); *circumstances, state, conditions; means, resources, power, ability*" (*awqāt-guzarī* means "stipend, pension", 2000, 121, emphasis added). This seems roughly equivalent to the English "times" in the expression "fallen on hard times," the meaning given in Platt's Urdu–English dictionary as well (Platt, 1974 [1884]: 106). S.W. Fallon's wonderful *Hindustani–English Dictionary* (1879, 177) adds examples to the definition which shed light on the remarkable journey of *awqāt*. It records it as meaning times, employment or occupation of time (*auqāt basarī*, also "livelihood; means of living; source of income") to: 1. State; condition; circumstances ("*Kis ṭarah awqāt basar hotī hai*?", "What are your circumstances?"); 2. Means; appliances; resources …; 3. Ability; strength, power ("*Terī kyā awkāt hai*?"). In the two latter meanings, it is indeed a feminine singular noun. The plural meaning of *awqāt* as "times" remains prevalent in Urdu *ghazal* poetry (https://www.rekhta.org/search/ghazal?q=औक़ात&lang=hi [accessed 22 March 2021]).

The Urdu–Urdu dictionary *Firoz al-lughāt* (1992, 138) glosses *awqāt* as a feminine singular noun with *haiṡiyat* (status, condition, also feminine singular, possibly the reason behind the grammatical shift), but also with *bisāṭ* (<Ar. chess-cloth/board), something spread out on a cloth and, by extension, the extension of one's capacity to feed and entertain guests. *Haiṡiyat* and *bisāṭ* show their affinity to *awqāt* in the phrases "*Uskī kyā haiṡiyat hai?*" or "*Uskī kyā bisāṭ*?" as "What means do they have to [do something]?" – uttered with doubt or disparagement. *Awqāt, haiṡiyat, bisāṭ* – clearly the vocabulary to speak about status is a rich one. How and when did *awqāt* as "times" change into *aukāt* as "status" is unclear, and unfortunately I cannot shed more light on it. Do Hindi speakers know the etymology of *aukāt*? Not necessarily, and why would it matter?

In both direct or indirect utterances ("What is your *aukāt*?", "What is his/their *aukāt*?"), *aukāt* is linked to status, honour or dignity (*izzat*, f.) in a strongly hierarchical context. *Izzat* has a parallel life as a key term for personal, family, and clan honour, particularly to police gender behaviour (Chowdhry 1997; Hossain and Welchman 2005; Kannabiran and Kannabiran 2002). It is uttered to ensure that a certain hierarchy is maintained while claiming different hierarchical positions for oneself and for the other. So while *izzat*, as we shall see, can be and is used routinely in an affirmative fashion as a strong claim to respect, commonality, mutuality, and potential equality *against* a hierarchy that is perceived as demeaning and dehumanizing ("we have our *izzat*, too", "the fight for *izzat* is more important than the one for livelihood"), *aukāt* utterances forcefully deny that claim. The threatened action of physical or symbolic violence is in fact aimed at depriving the addressee of dignity or *izzat* and, to employ a common metaphor, "take [their] water down" (*pānī utārnā*). It is supposed to make the other feel cowed and ashamed (*sharminda*) and bring about public humiliation (*zillat*).

In other words, *aukāt* and its counterpart *izzat* exist at the intersection of discourses and movements for personal and group dignity and social recognition and the reinforcement of hierarchies of caste, gender, and status. Margrit Pernau suggests that political and religious hierarchies shifted in the nineteenth century from a vocabulary of distance vs proximity (to the king or the person of power or to a sacred space or person), to one of high vs low (personal communication 2018). In the 18th and 19th centuries, complaints in texts against rising lower menial orders often employed the term *kāmin* or *kāmin zāt*, literally lesser (Fallon 1879: 946; Hali 1997: 194). They are not part of the old conceptual vocabulary of caste hierarchy (whether to index professional community, *jāti*, or the four-fold system of *varṇas*) and are not directly connected to purity and pollution, although humiliation may indeed consist in inflicting polluting punishments like rape or face-blackening with cow dung.

Within contemporary India's vernacular political lexicon, unlike other terms which we may call affirmative, like *haq* or *adhikār* (right) or indeed *izzat, aukāt* enjoys a penumbral existence. As already mentioned, it is never used in the affirmative ("Our *aukāt* is …") but only as a negative reaction to someone else's self-affirmation or contestation, and it does not appear as part of formal political discourse, whether reported in the press or the news or in speeches, unless as part of a threat. Yet as an utterance is very common. Its meaning is clear to everyone involved, and it often accompanies or is the prelude to violent acts. Perhaps more than *jāti* or caste, it, therefore, helps us understand what appear to be "excessive" acts of real and symbolic violence that have accompanied particularly Dalit mobilization.

Exposing and Narrating *Aukāt*

Although we don't have linguistic corpora for Hindi, the web has become a kind of archive, and a Hindi google search for *aukāt* + *dalit* called up several instances of the use of *aukāt* in the news. On 12 May 2018, A Dalit inspector in Chittaranjan Park, a middle-class locality in Delhi, killed himself:

उनके परिजनों ने द हिंदू को बताया कियहां उनके सीनियर अधिकारी द्वारा भेदभाव किया गया। उनके सीनियर ने कहा कितुम्हारी औक़ात मेरे सामने बैठने की नहीं है।

His relatives told *The Hindu* that he was discriminated against by his senior officer, who told him, "You don't have the *auqāt* to sit in my presence" (https://www.theresistancenews.com/india/dalit-inspector-killed-abuse/ [accessed on 20 October 2018]. See also "The Indian Dalits attacked for wearing the wrong shoes", BBC 19 June 2018, https://www.bbc.co.uk/news/world-asia-india-44517922 [accessed on 8 Feb 2019]).

Within a middle-class locality of India's capital city, the Dalit officer's claim to social recognition and equality through the ordinary act of sitting down, probably repeated over a period of time, ended with a drastic act of self-destruction, exposing what appears to be an incommensurate difference between the ordinary act, the phrase, and its consequences. That the negative utterance appears at all is because it is part of reported speech. Its "condensed historicity" encapsulates the long and troubled history of the relationship between Dalits and the police. In the context of the negative and active role of the police in caste-related crimes, who routinely protect the culprits and harass the Dalit victims, their relatives, and protesters, the remedy is often indicated to be more Dalits in the police (Teltumbde 2008) – but this is what then happens.

My work is with literary texts, which embed terms and utterances within dialogues, characters, and narratives and give us nuances and multiple perspectives. In this chapter, I work through two Hindi texts, one the famous autobiography of the Dalit writer Omprakash Valmiki, *Jūṭhan* (*Joothan,* i.e. Leftovers, 1997, 2003), the other a novel, *Tarpaṇ* (Ancestral Offering 2004), by the respected writer Shivmurti, who to my knowledge is not a Dalit (or at least does not present himself as one) but in this novel writes with great insight about caste conflict in contemporary rural north India.

One of the primary aims of Dalit literature, we know, is to "expose" the persistence of caste discrimination, abuse, and violence against Dalits in contemporary rural *and* urban India, and for this reason, we are more likely to find *aukāt* mentioned here. In *Jūṭhan*, we find two occurrences, both uttered by the middle-caste Tagas (Tyagis) in the village in Western Uttar Pradesh in North India where Valmiki grew up in the 1950s and early 1960s. The first instance occurs in the context of *jūṭhan*, the practice of taking leftover food from the plates of the upper caste. After a wedding feast in the Tyagi household for which Valmiki's parents have worked tirelessly, Valmiki's mother asks for some "clean" leftovers instead of the usual *jūṭhan*:

> *Chauhdrī jī*, now that they've all eaten and left … please give some food on a leaf-plate for my children. They have been waiting for this day, too". Sukhdev Singh [Tyagi] gestured to the baskets full of dirty leafplates and said: "You're already taking a basket full of *jūṭhan* … and now you're asking for food for the children on top of that? *Stay in your aukāt, chūhṛī*! Pick up the basket and clear off.
>
> That day Durga entered my mother's eyes. I had never seen her like that. She scattered the basket there and then. And told Sukhdev Singh, "You pick it up and take it home. Serve it to your guests tomorrow morning…"
>
> Like a shooting arrow, she stood up, grasped my hand and my sister's and left. Sukhdev Singh had been about to raise his hand on my mother but she had confronted him like a tiger. With no fear.
>
> *(1997, 21, emphasis added)*

The second occurrence is a few years later, when Omprakash is about to sit his High School exams, the first Dalit child in the village to do so. He has one day left to prepare for the maths test but another Tyagi comes looking for free labour to plant sugarcane. Omprakash protests feebly but eventually has to go. At lunch time, food is brought. The Dalit free labourers have to sit in the sun and are given only two rotis with a single piece of pickle, "what you would not give even to a beggar". Omprakash refuses to take the food. The Tyagi

> shouted abuse. But I stood my ground. Protest had already began within me. "Hey you son of a *chūhṛā* … come … he's learnt two letters (*do acchar kyā paṛh liyā*) and he's started to think big about himself… *abe*, don't forget your *aukāt* …" [His] words stung my body with a thousand wounds.
>
> *(Valmiki 1997, 72)*

From the furious reactions of Omprakash's parents to these *aukāt* utterances, we understand that their "condensed historicity" already points to of process of change, when traditional practices of subordination and discrimination are being actively challenged, while the Tyagis' "stinging words" show that the upper castes have registered the challenge. The phrases sting Omprakash specifically because they diminish and seek to thwart his aspirations. They get recorded in his autobiography to show not only that the education of Dalit children was bitterly resisted and perceived as a breach of deference, but also that any request, however small or inconsequential for the upper castes, was also perceived as such.

Fast-forward to another UP village in the late 1990s. This is a different historical moment, when Mayawati has already become the first Dalit woman chief minister. The term *aukāt* does not appear directly in Shivmurti's novel *Tarpaṇ* (Ancestral Offering 2004), but haunts the novel in the shape of a whole gamut of expressions, views, feelings, and actions connected to Dalit–upper-caste confrontation. Again, the ground has already shifted. Young Dalit men have left the village to work in factories and cities, while young Dalit women prefer to work in the fields of nearby villages so as to avoid traditional ties of subordination as *halwāh* (ploughman) to the village upper caste. Only one Dalit woman, Lavangi, has accepted to work for the local Brahmin landholder and his wife, the *paṇḍitāin*:

> For the *paṇḍitāin* it was a matter of prestige [*ijjat, izzat*]. Nowadays to keep a *halwāh* has become a matter of greater prestige than tying an elephant to your front door. This is why the *paṇḍitāin* had swallowed her arrogance [lit. "her horns and tail"] and braved the pandit's anger to accept Lavangi's terms. The holding was a field of two *bīghās,* and the master was responsible for the seeds and irrigation. The wages for ploughing and spade work was 6 kg a day. Once a year one pair of dhoti-kurta for her husband and one sari-blouse for her. On feast days a cooked meal for the whole family.

> [Lavangi] will not touch cowdung, manure and fodder, nor will she touch the broom. This will be the Nepali's job. Given the way the times had changed so fast, [the *paṇḍitāin*] had to accept.
>
> *(Shivmurti 2004, 21)*

The novel begins with the pandit's loafer of a son, Chandar, trying to grab Rajmati, a local Dalit girl, in the fields, only to be chased away when the other Dalit women rush to the spot. It then follows the ripple effects of this non- or quasi-action. When the girl's father, Pyare, goes to Chandar's father, pandit Dharmu, to protest, the fact that he does not offer submission (*pāo-lāgī*) grates on Dharmu, who however chooses to keep quiet. Not so his wife the *paṇḍitāin*, who after trying to shift the blame onto the girl cries out against the present times:

> It's not just the rule of the *chamārin*, all the Chamars and Pasis have started pissing on our heads. Such nerve (*itnī himmat*) to come with a stick to tell us off!
>
> *(14)*

To which Pyare retorts:

> You forget, *paṇḍitāin*. We are not the same Chamars who used to listen and bear everything with our ears and tails cast down. We'll make the ant who tried tasting the sugar pay dearly.
>
> *(14)*

The pandit stops the matter from escalating by shutting down his wife. He tells Pyare, conciliatorily: "Big or small, everyone has equal dignity" (*"chhoṭā ho ya baṛā. Ijjat sabkī barābar hai"*, 14). Here, then, we find the recognition of *ijjat* as honour and self-respect as a shared value that needs to be recognized and accepted.

But while Pyare is reluctantly willing to end matters there, the younger Dalits in the village all want to take it further. Dalit men and women debate whether to report the incident at the police thana/station or not (lit. "*do* the police-thana", "*thānā-pulis karnā*", a verb in itself, 15) – some say it will only bring further abuse, humiliation, and expense without any result, some say it is necessary in order to teach Chandar a lesson. Enters Bhaiji, a Dalit activist, who urges Pyare to the report the matter to the police as actual rape. Pyare is reluctant since this is not strictly true, but Bhaiji assures him that the police will do nothing otherwise. This opens an interesting grey space in the novel: Chandar wanted to rape Rajmati and would have done so (in fact, we learn that Rajmati's elder sister was raped and eventually killed herself by jumping into a well); assault is a crime but the police would not prosecute it. Does it mean that the Dalits are morally "wrong"? Or rather that they are willing to "play the game" instead of avoiding confrontation? As Teltumbde points out:

> Dalits have been caught in a "damn if you do, damned if you don't" situation. Damned if they don't protest continuing discrimination and abuse so as to avoid retaliation (since discrimination thrives on its normalisaton and acceptance), and damned if they protest because the retribution is often terrible and far exceeds the violence of the original act.
>
> *(Teltumbde 2008: 176)*

He reminds Pyare of past struggles for better pay:

> That was class struggle (*varga saṅgharṣ*). This is caste struggle (*varṇa saṅgharṣ*). For *ijjat*. The fight for *ijjat* is more important than that for *roṭī*. This is why the *sarkār* has given us a separate law for this struggle. The Harijan Act! It's with this law that we'll put this snake in check.
>
> *(26)*

What Bhaiji is referring to is the relatively new Scheduled Castes and Scheduled Tribes (Prevention of Atrocities) Act of 1989 (or POA Act), which came into effect in January 1990. However, as Teltumbde (2008) shows, the Act neither prevents such atrocities nor helps bring their perpetrators to account. What the novel shows is that skilful manoeuvring can use the Act as part of its strategy.

The first encounter with the "everyday state" to file an F.I.R. (First Information Report) at the nearby police thana is indeed a humiliating and fruitless experience. But soon with Bhaiji's help, Pyare and his son learn how to forge alliances and exert pressure on the police to act. Chandar gets arrested. This comes as a terrible shock to the *paṇḍitāin*, but Pyare is satisfied (lit. "his heart was cooled", 43) and even imagines that Chandar will be taken to the village on a donkey to get their daughter Rajpati to smear blacksoot on his face… As it turns out, Chandar is locked in only for one day. The next day he comes roaring into the Chamar quarter on his motorcycle with a gun slung across his shoulder and a bandana tied around his head (45). The Dalits fear that this time Rajpati will be raped for real and bundle her away to safety.

Yet Bhaiji does not give up, and with the help of the local Muslim Member of the state Legislative Assembly, he manages to initiate a court case. Chandar is arrested again, and again it is a matter of *ijjat*, of prestige and dignity – a currency and a game that everyone understands. The *paṇḍitāin* ("Handcuffs! Handcuffs she has put on him, that *chamārin* … now it's their time to rule in this *kaljug*", the dark age); the policeman who slaps Chandar and rejects the Hindu caste card ("We are neither Hindus nor Muslims, we are policemen", 60) only to accept money to wait a little before taking him away; the Pandit who undertakes elaborate transactions in order to avoid Chandar being taken through the local bazaar in handcuffs; and the Dalits' lawyer who knows that just remanding Chandar in custody and pushing trial dates forward is a symbolic victory. Rajpati's brother celebrates with sweets and a feast, while Dalits from nearby villages help pay the lawyers' fees with a subscription. When, after two months, Chandar is finally released on bail, Bhaiji cries foul play but Rajpati's brother tells him:

> We made him grind the police mill for sixty days. He used to wander with his head high, bellowing like a bull. Now he's got blacksoot on his face. Isn't it extraordinary?
>
> *(93)*

Meanwhile, in jail, Chandar has made new friends and learnt a new style: he wants to be released with great fanfare, just as criminals and jailed politicians do, and he comes home in an open jeep amidst gunshots and slogans of, "Long live Chandar! Chandar *bhaiyā zindābād*" (93–94). His new friends start coming to the village on their roaring motorcycles and stop menacingly before Rajpati's house in the Chamar quarter. Chandar has vowed revenge on Rajpati's brother and on Bhaiji, daring the latter to enter the village again. Finally, when one day Lavangi betrays Bhaiji's whereabouts to Chandar, Chandar goes out hunting Bhaiji with his gun so as to frighten him. Bhaiji scarpers up a tree, but while Chandar circles under the tree like a wolf, Rajpati's brother hits him on the head and finally – urged on by Bhaiji ("Cut the bastard's nose! There won't be another chance. Your name will spread all over", 107) – cuts off Chandar's nose, the ultimate humiliation.

After this scandal, even graver retaliation is feared – the papers announce *narsaṃhār*, a truckful a constables arrive to avert it, and there is general mayhem. But instead of Rajpati's brother, it's her father Pyare who hands himself in to the police. Not so much to save his son but to expiate the sin of generations of Dalits who bore these humiliations in silence. (His eldest daughter, Rajpati's elder sister, was also raped and committed suicide by throwing herself into a well.) He, in fact, *asks* to be taken in handcuffs on foot through the bazaar so that everyone can see. And to the lawyer who tries to convince him to deny the charge, Pyare says: "No *vakīl sāhab*, I have to go jail. I have to expiate by eating jail fare. To expiate my sin, that I bore those people's oppression (*jor-julm*) for so long with my ears and tail cast down". His wife, too, tells the lawyer: "Don't stop him now *vakīl sāhab*. This is his *mukti*. This is his *tarpaṇ*" (116), the ritual water offering to one's ancestors without which they'll find no peace. The fight for self-respect is equated with ritual expiation to Dalit ancestors and with freedom (*mukti*) from the eternal cycle of rebirths, the ultimate religious goal.

Conclusion

Aukāt, to conclude, is the flipside of *izzat*, of dignity and self-respect. *Izzat* invokes a shared mutuality, if not equality ("Big or small, everyone has equal *izzat*"), and challenges the zero-sum mentality of *aukāt*, which thinks that your greater status diminishes mine. But we can see the mentality of *aukāt* at work in many contexts in which historical privilege, whether of white supremacism, patriarchy, or other systems of gender, ethnic, or age-related power inequality, and discrimination, is challenged and responds with extreme retributory violence in an attempt to re-assert control and reinstate what it perceives to be the "natural order" of things. For this reason, *aukāt* usefully directs us to concepts that are used as threats and as challenges, and prompts us to consider the "dense historicity" behind their utterances. *Aukāt* contains a "dense historicity" that works both at an individual and a collective level, as Valmiki's autobiography showed: the promising Dalit boy who is swotting for his exams must be "shown his place", and both he, his family and caste fellows understand that it is not just individual retribution but an attempt to push back change for all of them. Here, the novel *Tarpaṇ* fudges things a bit by setting up the confrontation between Dalits and a lumpenized Brahmin. As scholars like Anand Teltumbde and K. Srinivasalu have pointed out, the majority of "excessive" retributive violence against Dalits in recent decades has not been at the hands of the upper castes but of low-middling castes ("Other Backward Castes" or OBCs in official parlance). The point to take away is that, as in the novel itself, what is at stake is not so much the "ritual hierarchy" of the caste system (Dumont 1980) but the reproduction of socio-economic and symbolic subordination. On the Dalits' side, too, the economic and the symbolic are inextricably tied together – do Dalits choose to work outside the village because of better wages or because even hard manual work outside the village comes with *izzat*?

A further point that Shivmurti's novel reveals is that the state is inevitably part of this game – to learn how to "play the game", to exert influence and counter-influence, to "do the state" as one "does" the thana-police, is crucial. Whereas earlier there was no way to expiate *brahmandokh*, the terrible sin of killing a Brahmin, now, Chandar's uncle says, there is *chamardokh*, "and nothing cuts through the law of *chamardokh*" (95).

Finally, *aukāt* signals confrontation, and this is why, as we well know from the news, the stakes are extremely high, a matter of life and death. But whereas earlier it was only the high castes who spoke of *aukāt*, now Dalits, too, also use the term with similar illocutionary force. After a recent incident (7 May 2017) in which Thakurs entered a Dalit *basti* in North-Western Uttar Pradesh armed with naked swords, killing one, wounding many others, and setting fire to houses, a Dalit boy said in an interview:

> "Most people had gone out to reap wheat. Had they fought face to face they'd found out their *aukāt*". While Sandeep was speaking his eyes show clearly his pain and anger.
>
> *(Kaif 2017)*

The fact that it is now Dalit youth who utter the work *aukāt* as a threat, that subject and indirect object – *who* and *to whom* – have changed, signals a new "condensed historicity" of struggle. Those using *aukāt* may or may not know that it originally meant "times", but they are making a point about times changing anyway.

Note

1 I would like to dedicate this chapter to Prof Anand Teltumbde, one of India's most brilliant intellectuals, and professor at the Goa Institute of Management, who was arrested by the Pune police on 2 February 2019 in relation to the 2018 clashes between the middle-caste Marathas and Dalits at the 200th-anniversary celebration of the Bhima Koregaon battle of 1818; several activists were arrested and charged of being Naxalites. Despite a stay order of the Supreme Court of India, the police refused to release Prof Teltumbde.

Bibliography

Bayly, Christopher A. 2011. *Recovering liberties: Indian thought in the age of liberalism and empire*. Cambridge: Cambridge University Press.

Brunner, Otto, Werner Conze, and Reiner Koselleck, eds. 1972. *Geschichtliche Grundbegriffe: Historisches Lexikon zur politisch-sozialen Sprache Deutschland*, vols. 1–9. Stuttgart: Klett-Cotta.

Butler, Judith. 1997. *Excitable speech: A politics of the performative*. London & New York: Routledge.

Chowdhry, Prem. 1997. "Enforcing cultural codes: Gender and violence in northern India." *Economic and Political Weekly* 32.19 (May 10–16): 1019–1028.

"Dalit inspector killed." https://www.theresistancenews.com/india/dalit-inspector-killed-abuse. Accessed 20 October 2018.

Dumont, Louis. 1980. *Homo hierarchicus: The caste system and its implications*. Chicago: University of Chicago Press.

Fallon, S.W. 1879. *A new Hindustani-English dictionary*. Benares: Benares Light Press & London: Trübner & Co.

Firozuddin, Maulvi. 1992. *Firoz al-lughāt. Niū i al-lu*. Saharanpur: Zakariya Book Depot.

Hali, Altaf Husain. 1997. *Hali's Musaddas: The flow and ebb of Islam*. Translated, and with a critical introduction by Christopher Shackle and Javed Majeed. Delhi: Oxford University Press.

Hoffmann, Stefan-Ludwig et al. 2012. "Introduction: 'Geschichtliche Grundbegriffe' reloaded? 'Writing the Conceptual History of the Twentieth Century.'" *Contributions to the History of Concepts* 7.2: 79–86. JSTOR, www.jstor.org/stable/24573111. Accessed 10 February 2019.

Hossain, Sara and Lynn Welchman, eds. 2005. *Honour: Crimes, paradigms and violence against women*. London: Zed Press.

Kaif, Aas Mohamad. "Sahāranpur jātīy saxample.com?id=book"/24573111"h Century.'led-abu." (Caste struggle in Saharnpur: what do local Dalit youths think?). http://twocircles.net/2017may08/409113.html. Accessed 10 February 2019.

Kannabiran, Kalpana and Vasantha Kannabiran. 2002. *De-eroticizing assault: Essays on modesty, honour and power*. Bombay: Popular Prakashan.

Liu, Lydia. 1995. *Translingual practice: Literature, national culture, and translated modernity – China, 1900–1937*. Stanford, Cal.: Stanford University Press.

Marcus, Sharon. 2002. "Fighting Bodies, Fighting Words: A Theory and Politics of Rape Prevention." In *Gender struggles: Practical approaches to contemporary feminism*, Edited by Constance L. Mui and Julien S. Murphy. Oxford: Bowman & Littlefield, pp. 166–185.

"Nankānā sāhab gurudvārā hamle par bhane"ited"– China, ." 2020. *Jansattā*, 4 January. https://www.jansatta.com/national/kumar-vishwas-angry-nankana-sahib-gurdwara-attack-says-time-come-show-pakistan-status-jsp/1274727/. Accessed 22 March 2021.

Platts, John. 1974 [1884]. *A dictionary of Urdū, Classical Hindī, and English.* Oxford: Oxford University Press.

Reid, Shannon E. and Matthew Valasik, eds. 2020. *Alt-Right gangs: A Hazy shade of White.* Berkeley: University of California Press.

Shivmurti. 2004. *Tarpaṇ.* New Delhi: Rajkamal Prakashan.

Silva, Daniel, ed. 2017. *Language and violence: Pragmatic perspectives.* Amsterdam/Philadelphia: John Betjemans.

Steingass, F. 2000. *A comprehensive Persian-English dictionary.* Reprint. Lahore: Sang-e-Meel Publications.

Teltumbde, Anand. 2008. *Khairlanji: A strange and bitter crop.* New Delhi: Navayana.

"The Indian Dalits attacked for wearing the wrong shoes." *BBC News.* 19 June 2018. Available at: https://www.bbc.co.uk/news/world-asia-india-44517922. Accessed 8 February 2019.

Vajpeyi, Ananya. 2011. *The Sudra in history: From scripture to segregation.* Centre for the Study of Developing Societies. Available at: https://works.bepress.com/ananya_vajpeyi/53/. Accessed 10 February 2019.

Valmiki, Omprakash. 1997. *Jūṭhan.* New Delhi: Rajkamal Prakashan.

Valmiki, Omprakash. 2003. *Joothan: A Dalit's life.* Translated by Arun Prabha Mukherjee. Kolkata: Samya.

INDEX

Jesus & ~~Coffee~~ Counsel

The Perfect Cocktail – Prayer, Counseling and Sometimes Medication.

By

Queen E. Lacey

Author of Sexually Driven

Published by Hemingway Publisher
Printed in United States of America

Dedication

To all those that didn't judge me but
wanted the best for me.
Thank you so very much!

About the Author

Author Queen Esther Lacey began her early years in the chilly region of White Plains, New York, prior to relocating to sunny Arizona in December 2001, where she now enjoys hot summers in the new land of promise. Of the fruit of her womb yields one son and one daughter who has yielded her two grandchildren. Battling through childhood depression, Queen Esther wrote through her plight after becoming inspired by a teacher who noted the gift of writing and gifted her with a book by author Langston Hughes. Throughout her journey of life, writing was always a part of what Queen Esther considers her "private life" until becoming the published author of her first work in 2009: "It's Not About Religion, God Wants a Relationship. God's Love is Unconditional," a thoughtful depiction of personal experiences and inspirations written in poetic form. Queen Esther has since authored and published eight books to date. Queen Esther is one who deeply cares for the hurting and is passionate about using her gift of writing to reach multitudes of women and minister healing and encouragement to all who are seeking to find hope in whatever situation they find themselves.

PEbyQueen@yahoo.com

Table of Contents

Introduction

My last publication was titled Injured and Scarred but Not Broken. The main thing I was trying to say with that was I had been through a lot of things in life, but it didn't leave me damaged.

When my mother passed away, it uncovered my fear of dying to an overwhelming level, but because of the last title, I couldn't share my struggle because I felt like that would make me a liar and that I'm not damaged or broken.

Yes, I'm saved, so I knew I could not take my life and not escape hell's fire. Yet still, I feared every day that one day the darkness would overtake me.

Was I a liar? Was I broken? Was I damaged goods? Maybe not broken, but not completely whole. We take medication for everything that ails us, so why is there such a stigma connected to something to balance the chemicals in the brain? Despite the stigma, today, I reached out for help. Am I still saved? Yes! I think about the scripture in Jerimiah 18. The vessel being marred but still in the hands of the potter (God's hand).

Having faith in a situation is good. However, faith without works is dead. Works can come in the form of medication and/or counseling. You can consult experts and doctors to gain knowledge about mental illness, I just want to share my testimony of how Jesus & Counsel (and sometimes medication) can be a winning combination.

BE ENCOURAGED EVERY DAY!!!

-Queen Esther Lacey

Chapter One

The Doctor's Diagnosis for Queen

Mental Illness:

Variants or mental disorders or, less commonly, mental diseases are any of a broad range of medical conditions (such as major depression, schizophrenia, obsessive-compulsive disorder, or panic disorder) that are marked primarily by sufficient disorganization of personality, mind, or emotions to impair normal psychological functioning and cause marked distress or disability and that are typically associated with a disruption in normal thinking, feeling, mood, behavior, interpersonal interactions, or daily functioning.

With the doctor diagnosing mental illness, it was felt group therapy and medication would be the answer to the question of what is going on with this child. My group therapy was about 4 or 5 children. We would meet at the hospital in what felt like a classroom. If I remember correctly, sometimes, we would sit in a circle and go around the room and talk about things. At the end of the session, we would have a snack. The therapy came more in-depth as I got older. I was seeing the therapist one on one in their office. Hospitalize three times because of depression and not wanting to live.

As I got older, more and more labels were added.

- Bipolar (Manic Depression)
- PTSD
- Social Anxiety Disorder
- ADD
- Basic Health Issues:
- High blood pressure
- Enlarged Heart
- Diabetic
- Thyroid
- High Cholesterol
- Kidney Disease

- Anemic
- Arthritis (Needing Knee Replacement)

*Note – I mention trigger throughout the pages – It means what sets me off and what causes me to explode or withdraw.

As a little black girl that was having a hard time dealing with life. Acting out and just misbehaving. The school system wants to label it as slow or special ED. Somehow I was seen by a therapist, and it was determined I had a chemical imbalance in my brain and would need group therapy and medication. I guess when you are a child, it is better to handle it as a group, and as I got older, it was through individual sessions.

Some think if you are depressed, you can just turn and be happy. But when there is a chemical imbalance, it takes medication to level that individual out. I don't know if medicating was easier, but I know I went through several dosages of different medications until they got it right. Sometimes it takes hospitalization as it did with me. I'll talk about that later.

Chapter Two

Queen and Bipolar (Manic Depression)

Bipolar Disorder (Manic Depression):

A mental illness in which a person experiences periods of strong excitement and happiness followed by periods of sadness and depression.

Court Experience:

The first time I must have been about 19 or 20, and CPS (Child Protective Services) took me to court. Apparently, someone reported me, stating I wasn't a good parent. There was a young representative that came to see me at my place of business and asked me a bunch of questions. I don't like answering those questions. She said you are young and don't want to be a parent. I shut down. I showed up to court and was so upset because the judge was beginning the same with the questions in a very degrading way. He would spell it out like I was stupid when he said do you understand?

That triggered my shutdown. Looking back now, maybe if I had been able to answer differently, I might not have lost custody. Once I go into depressed mode, I am not able to pull myself out.

Another time I was planning to move to AZ, one of my children said they wanted to come back home, and I told the father I needed the birth certificate to get the child enrolled in school. The next thing I knew, I was back in court. The agent for the child was asking me questions that triggered me. I went into a deep depression and couldn't shake it. The judge said the child was to be removed from the home immediately. I was in a state of shock. So, I didn't have custody of my children from elementary school. I am still trying to have a healthy relationship with them. It's not easy because I feel like I must watch what I say not to upset them. Do I have to pay the price for being a horrible mother for the rest of my life?

One day I would love to hear my children say they love me and celebrate me on birthdays, Mother's Day, and holidays. To meet up and go on trips would be awesome. But they live such different lives. I can't blame them; I just hope and dream.

Hospital Experience:

There were several times my actions landed me a shared room in the local hospital mental health ward. There was such a dark cloud over my life. I always used to write, not realizing it was a gift because my writing was so dark and depressing. I was just getting my feelings out.

I would go to a session with my doctor, and the doctor would feel I was a danger to myself and/or others.

There were times when I would cut myself. There were times I would save up my medication and plan to take it at once to end it all. There was a time I took the wrong drug that was laced with something that was detrimental to me.

I remember I found myself on a bridge during one of my night walks (I would walk the streets at night when I couldn't sleep). I was standing there thinking about jumping. Now, I'm afraid of bridges, and I was there like frozen. It must have been the Lord or just a coincidence that someone came by and ministered to me not to proceed.

Outside of the time with drugs, I would go through a therapy session, and they would suggest I be hospitalized. Right from the start, it was a humble experience. All my life, I have looked at it in a negative way. However, now, I can see how people were looking out for my safety. I have been hospitalized three times. It was like a prison to me. You are body searched and must change into simple clothes so that you can't hurt yourself. And you are watched around the clock. Yes, a prison.

When I ate, I had to sit at the nursing station for a length of time so that my food would digest long enough that I wouldn't bring it up. It was almost at the point that I was doing it so much I could will myself to throw up. I didn't have to stick my fingers down my throat.

It was explained having an eating disorder was a way of wanting to harm oneself as well. Having your freedom taken from you is never fun. I was always being watched. But again, it was for my safety. While in the hospital, I was put on SSI, so when I left the hospital, I didn't return to work and was treated as an outpatient.

Relationship Experience:

I can't really explain, but my thoughts about love were so warped. There would be days that I would feel so good I couldn't sit still. I didn't understand all my triggers. Then after I performed acts of giving my body to any random person, I would hit the very lows of depression.

The only way I can explain to you my struggle with sex is to share different episodes or adventures. I'll leave it up to you how you want to describe it. Just to give you a little understanding, sex is not a pleasurable loving experience for me; each experience brought a darker hate for it and for myself. In my mind, I wanted to be loved and feel like I was worth something, but more and more, I realized I was only good for one thing in life, and no one was going to love me.

As a child, we would go over different family members' homes, and sometimes I was left alone with cousins who would touch me in ways no child should be touched: both male and female. I never thought about it before, but they must have been touched too to know what to do. So, I learned from an early age this is something I was put on this earth for. I didn't share with my parents, but I would act out in different ways. I remember as early as kindergarten attacking the teacher.

During the times of my extreme highs, I believe that is where my addiction formed. Sex, to me, was not a form of showing someone you love them; it was a form of torment. I was tormenting myself as well as others out of control. I write about the life of suffering from this torment in my book "Sexually Driven". Any relationship I entered, I would destroy before they could leave me. I wanted to be loved in my heart, but in my mind, I could not receive that. No one was off limits. Talk about girl code or friend code. I think that is the area I beat myself up the most, thinking I'll never be clean or holy enough deserving of a love of my own and walking the streets at night to 1-900 lines. Just one torment after another. My self-esteem was so low, and I devalued myself. My relationship with people was like a revolving door, and sometimes there were financial transactions.

I didn't even know how to have a relationship in a general atmosphere and surroundings of basic family members. There weren't many hugs, and I love you. You knew you were loved (I guess), but it wasn't shown like "normal" family gatherings. When I am in Hobby Lobby and see signs of the gathering place, it seems so strange to me.

Also, I didn't feel worthy of a healthy and loving of loving relationship. I would push everyone away and would have outbursts. I was throwing dishes, punching walls. Driving dangerously with my partner in the car, threatening to end our lives, and other times attacking with knives. Now this is going to sound crazy, and my trigger was someone trying to show me love. I even had a partner that would go to therapy with me, trying to understand me to be a help to me. However, my outbursts of violence were too much for one to endow. Being promiscuous proceeded as I grew.

One night I was hanging out at the club and met Mr Apple. We spent the night talking and laughing, and nothing out of the ordinary. He offered me a ride home, and I accepted. We pulled over to the side of the road and just talked. Somehow the conversation went to what things we would do that we never did before. Then I asked him, what if I asked him for money? Would he give it to me? He said yes. I asked him for $100, and he gave it to me like it wasn't a problem. That was so interesting and powerful to me at the same time. After hanging out with him, I ran into the house and put the money in the dresser drawer under my clothes. A few days after that, I would look at the money, not believing how easy it was.

I went out to the club again and met Mr Berry, and we sat at the bar all night just talking about different things. Then the conversation subject was sex. I explained I had no desire for sex, which wasn't satisfying. He said he could make me feel excited and could satisfy my needs. I agreed to allow him to try and succeed at this task. We drove to another city and pulled into the parking lot of a motel. It was my first time doing something like this, and I wasn't afraid but a little shame, not wanting anyone to see me there. He went into the front office, came back out, and drove us around to the back where our room was located. He began to perform his acts of sex with me, and as always, there was nothing on my part. I was a basic lay-there type of person that the individual could do whatever they wanted to do. Then I would shower.

He brought me back to the club thinking he showed me, but no, he just made my belief even stronger. There is nothing to sex, and I hate it. I hate myself for allowing someone to touch me.

A lot of times, when I get depressed, I would move furniture around in my place, or I would go for a walk. One day I was walking down the street and ran into Mr Cherry working at a car dealership. He stopped me and struck up a conversation. I invited him over the next day for lunch. I offered to serve him a sandwich or something. He showed up the next day. I made him the sandwich, but we ended up having sex. Of course, he got what he wanted, but I just took my shower and moved on.

Another evening on another walk, I met Mr. Danish. He was a repeat offender. I would hook up with him a few times. One night we were at a public complex; it was late at night, so it didn't matter. The first time I was exploring in the automobile. Then there was a knock on the window by the police. I was so afraid I was going to jail. It made the experience crazier. Then we took it inside.

Interestingly enough, if I did meet someone wanting a real boyfriend/girlfriend relationship, I didn't want to have sex with them. I wanted more. Once I gave myself to someone, I didn't like them anymore. Men are very interesting. They feel they can make you feel all kinds of wonderful. They can have you climaxing over and over. Foreplay and orally, but nothing worked for me. I didn't recognize the pattern right away. I would want to watch porn more and more on my own, and I wanted more self-gratification. I had to self-gratify myself more than once each day, or I truly thought I would die.

I began to look at men as objects to use and didn't have any feelings for them. I was getting high being with the next victim and branching out to females as well. Single or married, spouses of people I knew or partners of people I knew. Bills are paid, flowers are sent to the office, and money is left on the nightstand. It even got to the point where I thought I might star in one of the porn movies or become a prostitute. Just heartless and not caring. One day on one of my walks, I met Mr. Edible. We started talking. He said he was the CEO of a company that was up the street. It was a

24-hour operation, but overnight it was mostly him. One night he called me to come to hang out with him. We talked, and then he started to massage my shoulders and then started caressing my whole body. I just allowed him to explore all areas. Right there in the front lobby, he expressed his feelings that flowed through my flesh. Then I just went to the ladies' room and washed all evidence away as routine as the last and the next.

I learned about phone sex and began calling the 1-900 numbers. Then I became a friend of one of the callers and found out it was a job. I thought, okay, I could do this to make a living because I was on the phone all night anyway. I could make up things to say to keep someone on the line. The trick was you keep them on for a certain amount of time, and then it would cut off so they could call back. Each time they call back, they could be charging more money over and over. I became so detached from reality.

I can give you stories of meeting Mr A to Mr Z, but I think you understand now. The more I hated myself, the more destructive I became. To me, getting AIDS would be a way of my life ending and still going to heaven because I didn't take my life. That's how crazy my thoughts became. I was so disgusted with myself, and I never felt clean. I would shower over and over. To this day, I just don't feel clean enough. I refuse to give myself to anyone. I feel like this is my punishment for never being able to find true love because I don't know how to be intimate with anyone.

Financial Experience:

I learned about payday loans. It's a place you go and apply for a loan, and based on your ability to pay back from your paycheck, they would front you the money. It really isn't based on your ability to pay back because you get into this vicious cycle of being unable to pay. I would get several of them. As soon as they gave me the money, it felt so good. I would automatically think about where I am going to spend the money. There were different people in my life that no matter what, they could help me spend.

These spending binges would satisfy me on a level I can't even explain. However, when payday came, I never would have any money because the payday loan companies collected out of my check before I even got my check. I have lost ownership of cars because they might have been signed over for collateral. I would have to close bank accounts because they had access to them. I have even filed for bankruptcy because I would become overwhelmed. I would tell myself I just needed a fresh start, and everything would be okay.

Unfortunately, if you don't take care of the root of your problems, they will cause a cycle of the same patterns over and over. Yes, that is how my life has been, one horrible cycle.

Chapter Three

Queen and Social Anxiety Disorder

Social Anxiety Disorder:

Anxiety is characterized by persistent and exaggerated fear of social situations (such as meeting strangers, dating, or public speaking) in which embarrassment or a negative judgment by others may occur and that causes significant distress, often resulting in an avoidance of such situations and impairment of normal social or occupational activities. I knew I suffered from anxiety in general.

I would go into a panic, my blood pressure would raise to stroke level, and I would have trouble breathing. The ambulance was often called while at work when I had an attack. I think the ladies I work with don't mind because they always talk about how good-looking the firemen are. Yes, they are, lol. I was given meds to calm me down. I didn't relate that to mental illness. However, there was another anxiety I was experiencing.

I just thought I was shy and afraid to be around people in large crowds. I would be assigned to speak in front of a group, and just before it was time for me to come before the people, my heart would start racing, and I would get lightheaded, thinking I would faint. My therapist told me I was suffering from a social anxiety disorder. I never knew what that was.

Sometimes the panic attacks would come from a memory of something that seemed like it was happening right then. I was then diagnosed as having Post Traumatic Stress Disorder (PTSD).

Chapter Four

Queen and PTSD

Post-traumatic stress disorder: PTSD

A psychological reaction that occurs after experiencing a highly stressful event (such as wartime combat, physical violence, or a natural disaster) outside the range of normal human experience and that is usually characterized by depression, anxiety, flashbacks, recurrent nightmares, and avoidance of reminders of the event.

If you said, PTSD, the first thing that came to my mind is someone that is suffering after being in the military. However, I have learned it is related to having experienced some trauma.

Now I could go out to the clubs and socialize with friends after a few drinks. I felt like a whole different person. However, when sober, I just thought I was shy and afraid to be around others.

My mind was always thinking people really didn't want me around and didn't really like me.

But when there were assignments at work or church or whatever, I would get anxiety that would have my heart racing. It never failed, I'm on the schedule to read a poem or something, and I would just freak out. I remember being part of a prison ministry and being asked to do a read and to share with a group of ladies. When it came to the time I was to speak, my breathing became harder to do. I began to cry, and I became so afraid. My desire is to share with young ladies to encourage them. Maybe it's called public speaking, but it seems like a task that will end my life if I continue pursuing it. Recently, I have been invited to participate in a Toast Master group. It is to help you with public speaking. I have tried it twice before, but I didn't follow through like anything else. Maybe this time, I will.

I also wonder if it was because, as a child, being molested or, as an adult, being manipulated by men in authority. Or the most traumatic thing in my life was the night I went out with my friend to the club, and we were having a good time, and then I ran into Mr Evil. I had been dating someone and met him through that boyfriend. He came into the club and was talking to me and then asked if I would go for a walk with him. I thought nothing of it, and he knew my man. At least he was the man in my mind and heart. So, we went for a walk. Then he said he had to pick up a package for a friend and asked if I would mind coming with him. So, we stopped by his apartment. I was just sitting there, and he went into another room to get the package. He returned to where I was, not with the package but with a gun. He began to ask me different questions about sex, and I did not want to answer. He told me to take my clothes off. I refused and started to struggle with him. I began to yell, and he hit me over and over with the gun. Then he put the gun down, and I thought I could get free, and he had a knife in his hand. He began to rape me, and I thought that night I was going to die. When he finished, he told me I had to come back each week, or he would kill me. I was walking home, and the police drove by. I guess he could see I was all beat up and disoriented. He pulled around, got out, and started asking me if I needed help. I agreed to go with him to the station. I think I was in shock. When we got to the station, they got a female officer and asked me questions and the person's description. I did the best I could, and then one of the officers came back with a picture and asked if it was the person. I freaked out; yes, it was the person.

I had to go to court, and I had to go to counseling. I never completed the counseling. I thought if I just buried it, I would be fine. However, I could be walking uptown just to go shopping, and if I thought I saw that person, my heart would start racing, and I would be so scared. To this day, I have that fear in the back of my mind that I will be found and killed.

Chapter Five

Queen and ADD

Attention Deficit Disorder (ADD):

A Developmental disorder that is marked especially by persistent symptoms of inattention (such as distractibility, forgetfulness, or disorganization) or by symptoms of hyperactivity and impulsivity (such as fidgeting, speaking out of turn, or restlessness) or by symptoms of all three and that is not caused by any serious underlying physical or mental disorder.

Now I heard of ADHD, and I thought it was something children suffered from. I didn't know it was something adults suffer from. I would always want to study or start something. There was no problem setting it up. That is just it, and I was always starting. Always setting up. But would never follow through. I'll be honest: I believe the school system pushed me through. I didn't really apply myself. I wish I had done better. I love learning. I love studying the bible. I desire to go back to school to better myself. I feel like I have a second-grader reading level. It is the one thing that shames me. When I'm asked to read aloud if we are in a group, I find out what I will have to read and read it upfront to ensure I know all the words. It is a very exhausting thing to do. I feel like a big liar—an imposter. Also, the other thing is whenever I am in a conversation with someone, and I try so hard to let them get out what they want to say without cutting them off. It never happens, I will cut them off over and over.

Okay, a light bulb just went off. Maybe that is why it's hard to do group settings because I want to cut everyone off in their talking. It isn't easy for real.

No matter how much I try to have some type of order, I just can't focus, and I would just sit and stare into space, wasting away many hours.

I keep experiencing three recurring dreams. I don't know what the connection to dreams is:

- Running and falling off a mountain
- Driving or riding and crashing
- In a house and looking for a secret room

Chapter Six

Queen and Being Saved

In my opinion (my opinion and experience alone), I say this next thing. The church wasn't support of someone dealing with mental illness. If you dealt with anything outside of what was considered living the holy life, you were sinning.

At the age of 9 in Arkansas, I received the Holy Spirit. My cousins and I were jumping around, and it hit me for real. They brought me to the car, and I was still under. I tried to live to save but experienced many unsaved life experiences. However, every time I went to church, some preacher called me out for prayer and spoke different things over me. Expressing how anointed and gifted I am. To this day, I have just felt I aborted everything because I didn't understand my part of the responsibility when someone speaks over your life. So, my goal now is to research everything and pray that God makes things clear to me so that I may walk in the plans of the Lord for my life.

Words are spoken over and into my life:

Prophet to the Nations and Seer:

I put these two together, believing they intertwine. I have dreams and see things as if I were watching a movie. The things I see seem to give me a warning. There have been times when I have given others words of encouragement through a dream or thoughts that impressed me.

Intercessor:

Praying on behalf of others. There are times I feel others' pain. I can be around them, and I go into a cry of sadness that I cannot explain. I believe that is mixed with a little discernment as well. Feeling someone else's pain. Because of a lack of knowledge, I was afraid to walk in this area. I thought I had to be perfect to be used. I felt if things were going on with me, I couldn't pray for others, fearing my issue would spill over to them. Maybe that is why the Lord says His people perish for the lack of knowledge, and in all, thy getting gets understanding.

I am hoping the Toast Master's classes that I spoke about in chapter four really help. This way, I will be able to pray in a corporate prayer setting and not fear.

Healing and Encourager:

I put these two together because I believe they intertwine.

Permission to lay hands on others and pray for them. Also, the gift of writing is to encourage others. I feel that is a form of healing emotionally.

As I am creating this book, I know of a pastor who has completed his life coaching course in mental health. That is so encouraging because the more people educate themselves in mental health, the more individuals can get support. Just someone's understanding is priceless! The one thing that is so upsetting is telling someone who deals with depression just to be happy.

I would like to share a poem about how I used to feel. Maybe it is where you or someone you know is at. Be encouraged that things can change for you as well. My daily prayer now is depression is not my portion and the joy of the Lord is my strength. So, I will declare God's word over my life, and if I need it, I will take medication.

∞∞∞

As I sat with a drink in one hand and a bunch of pills in the other,

The plan to end my life didn't work; I'm still here to face another.

Lord, I know I fall short in loving you,

I walk around knowing your word but acting like it's not true.

Help the areas where there is unbelief,

For I realize it is of my privileges that I live beneath.

It's not like I haven't been down this destructive road before

It's like I want to just give up and not be saved anymore

I can't seem to break the strongholds to just give into the flesh,

Instead of praying and waiting on Heaven's best.

Since I have breath in my body, there is still time to turn this thing around.

You will not hear on the news that it is my body they have found.

I will reach out to others to do whatever I can

I realize this is spiritual warfare, and when I've done all I can do, I'll still stand.

I'll make that dinner for two and instead of saving some for tomorrow

I'll take half and go share it with someone who is lonely in their sorrow

Instead of turning on that TV, I'll read your word, and I'll pray

Yes, Lord, I know there is purpose for my life; thank you for another day

∞∞∞

Chapter Seven

Queen Seeking Help

On March 3, 2023, I received a text from Walmart that my medication was ready. I still have mixed feelings. I'm ready to get my mind stable, and I know I will feel better. As I shared with the doctor, I know it will make me feel better, but then I start thinking I can do it on my own, and I think about how much it is costing, and I stop taking them. Now that we have a new health plan at work, it really will cost me. Our new insurance does not work in our favor. I heard someone say everything is going up but the paycheck, lol there is some truth in that.

Let me say this. Not everyone needs medication. With me, it helps me to bring my thoughts in and focus and drown out the thoughts that my life will end. It balances the chemicals in my brain. I'm able to have discussions and not be all over the place. One would say, well, that seems like a no-brainer to just be on the meds. That would be easy to say if there wasn't such a stigma to being in therapy and the ignorance of the Christian community.

But then there might be some that ask the question. "If I go on medication, will I be on medication forever?" I have written this book to give my testimony. Not to say, what I share is what will happen for everyone. I share my testimony to give someone hope that they may experience things as I do. I can say no to that for myself. Through therapy and true spiritual guidance, I have learned how to manage my mood swings. I have learned when I am going through stressful moments, I must slow down and give great thought to my surroundings and what is real and what is in my head. I will also say it is important who you surround yourself with. People mean no harm. Sometimes they can alter how you feel. Be around upbeat people. Not someone that will feed depression.

Don't always be alone at home. Get out of the house. Maybe go to a park and take a walk. Sometimes that might be easier said than done. Push, press, and don't give up. I started doing things I was afraid to do. Trust me, and I have a list. I believe one day, I shall be able to do what I believe I am here on earth to do. I will take all that I write about and speak about it before lots of women to encourage them in person. To put a face behind the pen!

I have learned that I must speak up and share what is on my mind. I can get so lost in my thoughts. I used to think I was a realistic person speaking the truth when I, in fact, was a negative person not speaking about life situations. Does medication help me stay levelheaded? Yes. However, having the help of a psychologist and a life coach has helped me work through what my thoughts tell me. One day in the week, I would see the psychiatrist that would follow up with me and monitor my medication. Then another day throughout the week, I would see the psychologist that would follow up, but we would discuss better ways to handle situations. All sessions were not good for me because always I wouldn't say I like answering questions repeatedly, but when I leave the session, I would think back on what was said and end up writing a poem. I truly believe more than ever that God gave me that to help me to de-stress. As well as to encourage others.

Today's doctor's appointment (general wellness check) went a little differently. I had been feeling drained and just not feeling connected to different things going on. Every time I go to the doctor, they give me a form to fill in that has a list of questions regarding my mental status. I never filled it out, but for some reason, I filled it out today. After I met with the doctor, someone from behavioral health came in the room and asked if I wouldn't mind speaking with someone because my numbers were too high on the form I filled out. I said sure. Then we went to another room. As soon as I sat down, I felt myself getting ready to go into that dark place where I withdrew. I said you want me to speak to someone so I don't kill myself when I leave here. To save yourselves. Then the counselor came on. I hate answering questions over and over about how I feel and such things like that. But today was different, and I was able to talk with her. In the end, she asked about introducing me to something else. She spoke with the associate that brought me into the room, stating that there are concerns around death, but it's not suicidal. For the first time, someone listened. Because of my faith, I would not kill myself, but I do have a FEAR of dying. It's overwhelming that I believe I won't be able to prevent it. My anxiety builds, and I think I'm going to die. Or even worse, I will pass out and be buried alive. I had been having dizzy spells as well.

So, the new process they want to try with me is called EMDR (Eye Movement Desensitization Reprocessing). It has something to do with your eye patterns and knowing I still may have negative thoughts, but I will be able to channel the negative thoughts, and I won't get and/or be stuck.

Once I get my finances together and better insurance, I may investigate. Working smarter, not harder, mind frame. If there is a better way of doing things, without such a struggle, of course, why not give it a try?

I would like to share a poem about how I used to feel. Be encouraged again. It's always the darkest before dawn. It will get better. One day at a time. Process is key!

∞∞∞

My desire to live is almost non-existence.

But what can I do about it, for to take my own life would be a sin?

But if depression is a sickness not in my control.

Then maybe God would not hold me responsible and forgive me, and Heaven would still be my home.

I've learned to block my feelings away deep inside

Would it be true to say my life is one big lie?

In all my thoughts, I can't think of one thing good; my past hunts me day and night.

I've even thought maybe a makeover would make things right.

A makeover for the ugliness I wear on the outside and on the in

There's no one to love me; why doesn't God answer that one prayer for all of this to end

People I call my friends sometimes they hurt me, and they don't even know they do

Because I don't tell them because I want to protect them from hurting too

I wasn't a good daughter, mother, nor a good wife

Why, God, why did you give me life?

So many people I know are dying each day.

It seems like I'm being punished I want to go too, and He says no, you must stay.

I don't know my purpose in life; I don't know what's ahead.

I just know each day; I wish I were dead.

I've been abused in so many ways, to tell you; I wouldn't know where to begin.

I wish I could be a virgin again, free from sexual sin.

I wanted to be loved and held, so I believed all the lies the men would say

Girl, you know I love you; I'm never going away.

I can't give you one reason to explain why I feel the way I do, nor to explain why it would justify wanting to die.

I just know there is a pain inside that won't go away nor ease up, and all I can do is cry.

They say if I talk to someone and take the meds, I will be able to see

That there are brighter days ahead for me

Should I really lay it all out there and trust some-one with my deepest thoughts and desires?

Would it really make a difference, or would they just nod their head, pretend to care just because they were hired?

∞∞∞

Chapter Eight

Queen's Passion to Encourage

On February 26, 2023, I gave a testimony on how I had been suffering from the torment of suicidal thoughts. After praying, my pastor received a word from the Lord, and I was inspired to write this poem. Maybe you will be encouraged by it. Know that anything the devil comes to you with, he has to get permission. He only has permission to test you and does not have the authority to kill you. Do not give him more power than he has. Through the gift of the Holy Spirit, you have authority. Rebuke fear and anything else that keeps you in bondage and/or torments you. I pray for peace and joy into and over your life!

∞∞∞

You may have permission to test me,

But you don't have authority to kill me.

I shall live and not die;

Devil, you can't torment me anymore because everything you say is a lie.

I shall sleep at night with sweet rest,

Because now I know I have passed the test.

So now I shall walk in the authority given to me,

No longer walking in fear and defeat.

No longer walking in depression with my head hung down,

Devil I serve you notice to get thee behind me now.

I am encouraged even the more

To walk in purpose and declare the works of the Lord.

∞∞∞

OTHER WORKS BY THE AUTHOR

IT'S NOT ABOUT RELIGION, GOD WANTS A RELATIONSHIP

Subtitle – God's Love is Unconditional

FROM MY HEART TO YOURS

Subtitle- Nothing Shall Separate You From God's Love

SEARCHING FOR REAL LOVE?

Subtitle – It Won't be Found in Someone Else's Bed

YOUNG HEARTS NEED LOVE TOO

Subtitle – Bringing Awareness to Adults/Parents of Some Struggles of the Youth

FROM THIS DAY FORWARD

Subtitle – Letting the hurts of the past die so you can live in the blessings of today

SEXUALLY DRIVEN

Subtitle – One Church Girl's Struggle with Sexual Addiction and a Desire to Be Loved

SEXUALLY DRIVEN II

Subtitle – Returning to My First Love I

INJURED AND SCARRED BUT NOT BROKEN

Subtitle - Sharing Questions That Lead to My Wholeness

Workbook

Milton Keynes UK
Ingram Content Group UK Ltd.
UKHW022353221123
433027UK00004B/89